FIELDING'S

Australia

1 9 9 3

FIELDING'S ALPINE EUROPE 1993
FIELDING'S AUSTRALIA 1993
FIELDING'S BENELUX 1993
FIELDING'S BERMUDA AND THE BAHAMAS 1993
FIELDING'S BRAZIL 1993
FIELDING'S BRITAIN 1993
FIELDING'S BUDGET EUROPE 1993
FIELDING'S CARIBBEAN 1993
FIELDING'S EUROPE 1993
FIELDING'S FRANCE 1993
FIELDING'S HAWAII 1993
FIELDING'S ITALY 1993
FIELDING'S MEXICO 1993
FIELDING'S NEW ZEALAND 1993
FIELDING'S PEOPLE'S REPUBLIC OF CHINA 1993
FIELDING'S SCANDINAVIA 1993
FIELDING'S SELECTIVE SHOPPING GUIDE TO EUROPE 1993

FIELDING'S THE GREAT SIGHTS OF EUROPE
FIELDING'S WORLDWIDE CRUISES 6th revised edition
FIELDING'S ALASKA AND THE YUKON
FIELDING'S BUDGET ASIA Southeast Asia and the Far East
FIELDING'S CALIFORNIA
FIELDING'S FAMILY VACATIONS USA
FIELDING'S FAR EAST 2nd revised edition
FIELDING'S HAVENS AND HIDEAWAYS USA
FIELDING'S LEWIS AND CLARK TRAIL
FIELDING'S LITERARY AFRICA
FIELDING'S SPANISH TRAILS IN THE SOUTHWEST
FIELDING'S TRAVELER'S MEDICAL COMPANION

FIELDING'S Australia

1 9 9 3

by
ZEKE
and
JOAN **WIGGLESWORTH**

FIELDING TRAVEL BOOKS

℅ WILLIAM MORROW & COMPANY, INC.
1350 Avenue of the Americas, New York, N.Y. 10019

Recognizing the importance of what has been written, it is the policy of William Morrow and Company, Inc., and its imprints and affiliates to have the books printed on acid-free paper, and we exert our best efforts to that end.

ISBN: 0-688-10583-1

Printed in the United States of America
Second Edition
1 2 3 4 5 6 7 8 9 10

Text design by Marsha Cohen/Parallelogram

All maps by Mark Stein Studios

For Jim and Peggy then; for J.B. and Thelma now.

CONTENTS

MAPS

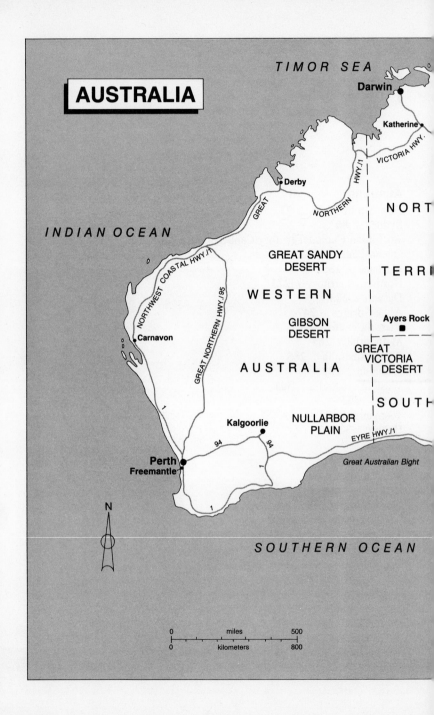

FIELDING'S

Australia

1 9 9 3

AUTHORS' FOREWORD

A couple of years ago, Paul Hogan was asked during an interview on the ABC (Australian Broadcasting Commission) why he created the immensely popular and immensely successful movie, *Crocodile Dundee*. In addition to trying to make a buck, he said, he did it because Australia has no heroes these days and he wanted to create one. Like anyone else pondering such a task, Hogan drew on what he knew—the Aussie mystique—but he shook a little dust off it, took a look around at the 20th century, and came up with Mick Dundee, an Australian hero unlike any before him, yet one *so* Australian you'd recognize him anywhere.

Time was, to the outside world, that Australians were guys in strange hats pinned up on one side, guys who with that wonderfully peculiar Aussie accent made terrific soldiers and great beer drinkers, guys (sexists) who loved chasing their "sheilas," guys on horses herding millions of sheep across vast deserts, guys who met everybody on an equal social footing be they king or commoner, guys with an independent and often outrageously down-to-earth approach to life.

How successful Hogan was in creating a modern Australian hero is best left to historians. But from this side of the Big Pond, we have to say that he builded better than he knew. On purpose, perhaps, or even without knowing it, Crocodile Dundee ended up being a pretty good example of what Australia is all about.

Few Australians actually live like Dundee, out in the bush, hunting crocs on the sly, but the attitudes Hogan gave his alter ego are plainly 20th-century Australian. The self-reliant spirit is there, as is the amazing ability Australians have of shedding social inhibitions. Recall Dundee in Manhattan: After a day, everybody living in a mile-wide radius is calling him "Mick," and he ends up charming the socks off the whole city. In real life, the same thing happens. Within 10 minutes of hitting Heaven, Australians would be on a first-name basis with God. If they're ever awed by anybody, we haven't seen it happen yet.

There are other revelations in the movie. Dundee, in spite of his very real ability to cope with the world, has self-deprecating humor, making it pretty obvious that to cast a male shadow in Australia, you don't necessarily have to be a sexist, bigoted drunk. He solves problems in a typical pragmatic Australian fashion (realize, of course, that because he is a movie hero, the solutions are sometimes larger than life), and he always assumes that other people are as honest as he is—until proven otherwise. There are also signs that Dundee, like a lot of Australians, is groping with the country's identity. The great scene where he takes on a rowdy group of city slickers out on a drunken midnight kangaroo hunt mocks the image of the fierce Aussie backwoodsman, and the scene where he attends an Aboriginal ceremony—as a member of the tribe—is also significant because it shows modern Australians are publicly admitting—at long last—that there just might be something worthwhile in the lives and philosophies of their native peoples.

You can't help liking Crocodile Dundee, partly because he is Paul Hogan (known to almost everyone in Oz as "Hoages") and the performing Paul Hogan is a totally likeable person, but also because Dundee is everything we Americans like to see in our Australians. Americans like to think we're very much like the Aussies: honest, hard-working, independent, resourceful, frontier-minded—and we see in their lives a mirror of our own. And it's true, our two cultures share many things. It is only one of the reasons why an increasing number of Americans are heading Down Under for a look. What they will find is not a whole continent of Crocodile Dundees, any more than an Aussie visitor here would find the streets full of John Waynes.

What visitors to Australia *will* find are 16 million people living on one of the most peculiar and fascinating continents of the world, and 16 million people struggling to meet the 21st century, as are we all. And as they drive through the Outback, or see the sunrise on the Coral Sea, or shop the stores of beautiful Sydney, perceptive travelers will also discover that like any great myth, there are big threads of truth in the saga of Crocodile Dundee.

A personal note:

We think it necessary, for you to judge this work in its approach and authenticity, to know a bit about us. Travel books, like any other form of journalism, carry within them the biases of their creators. Could there be, for instance, any more completely prejudiced view of the pitfalls of 19th-century Continental life than the often nasty (and almost always accurate) views of the father of American travel writers, Samuel Clemens, in *The Innocents Abroad?* We, too, are biased, because over the years and over the miles as we wandered around the world, we developed habits and patterns of enjoyment and methods of criticism that we apply to our travels, our selection of accommodations, our fancies in food, and our methods of conveyance. There is nothing wrong with this, certainly, as long as the predilections are made plain.

So, first, we must tell you that we are in love with Australia, its people, its animals, its magnificent wastelands, its gum trees, its mountains, lakes, rain forests, and reefs. At the same time, there are things in Australia we find less than lovable, including the current state of the Aboriginals there, as well as persistent wisps of latent sexism, racism, colonialism, and what seems sometimes to be an almost casual governmental disregard for the natural resources of the continent. The Australians are not alone in this, of course, but then, this book is about Australia, not other nations. We have tried to take the Land Down Under as it comes, warts and all, and have found it, on balance, to be a society that ranks high as one of the world's most honest, most friendly, and most successful.

Second, we should tell you that we are Americans, which carries with it hordes of prejudices concerning clean toilets, potable water supplies, and legal rights; but more, we are also Californians—not by birth, but by necessary choice, given climate, employment opportunities, and natural splendors. This means that we have certain outlooks often found only on the West Coast, including a decided snobbery when it comes to any wines not produced in Napa, Mendocino or Sonoma counties, a love of sun and surf, and an irresitable urge to devour fresh artichokes and eat tons of fresh garlic. (There is no such thing as too much garlic.)

Before California, we lived in the Midwest, a most excellent place to raise children and cattle, but also a place of inclement winters and buggy summers. We have fond memories of driving across Nebraska at night on Interstate 80, the darkened way mileposted by hog farms so pungent and vile they streaked the windshields, but we also have fond memories of Minnesota evenings when the temperature on the thermometer hung on the tree out behind the house hit $-40°$. From the Midwest we get a love of quiet farmland and small, well-organized cities, of fresh air and low housing prices, of snow and fireplaces, of bass fishing in farm ponds and of long portages through the Canada–U.S. wilderness carrying 70-pound canoes and losing a quart of blood a day to the mosquitoes and black flies.

The female half of this effort hails originally from the nation's capital, bringing with her the somewhat disgusting ability to devour a half-bushel of Chesapeake Bay crabs without pausing for air, but also bringing memories of Maryland forests and insect-thrumming ponds, animals and birds, clean air—and water singularly lacking in heavy metals. Given a choice between paying the rent and sending the monthly take off to Greenpeace, there is to her mind little choice. Only by force of will (and threats of divorce) is she stopped from flying to Japan and singlehandedly taking on the whaling fleets. At present, her favorite animal in the world is a moth-eaten but immensely cuddly Benjie-dog— and a half-dozen obnoxious wallabies living in a rain forest in Tasmania.

As for her partner in this affair, a Coloradoan by birth, he retains an almost religious regard for straight arrows—in some circles, a confession of regard for the works of John Wayne and Clint Eastwood might be met with scorn—still, he admits it freely, claiming that the Colorado blood in his veins makes him heir to all the rules and regulations that make up The Code of the West. (Always tip your hat to a lady, never rob a bank at night, don't draw first, and never, ever kiss your horse with your eyes closed.) This love of Western mythology explains in part why he feels comfortable in Australia—the mythical credo of the American west lives Down Under with a vengeance, and the rules are basically the same. If you don't like songs about outlaws and truck drivers, and think that country-western music is only for red-necks from Tennessee, stay out of Australia.

We have both spent a lot of time wandering around the Great Out-back of the United States, the western deserts, which is fine basic train-ing for anybody pondering a visit to anyplace in Australia more than a day's drive in from the coasts. We like isolation and wilderness, and camped out more than our share back when the kids were small and even a Motel 6 was a budgetary impossibility. But we also have ex-plored cities, from New York to Casablanca, and Oslo to Teheran, and we have real fondness for paved streets and room service and flush toilets. You can only spend so much time stuck in a tent in the rain or a dingy hotel in the boonies before sanity disappears and it becomes imperative that bodies be placed in a first-class shower or tub, and throats be laced by a very expensive aperetif—served up neat, thank you, no ice. We are not reluctant to sup with strangers when necessity or instant friendship arises, and have been known to take bus tours and actually enjoy them. We have learned to be patient and flexible; to be other is to court the wrath of the Travel Gods.

But given a choice, we would be strangled by no timetables, hemmed in by no itinerary. Trains have their place—so do buses and guided tours. But for our tastes, the only way to travel is by personal vehicle, be it car or camper van—we are too lazy for bikes and too conventional for motorcycles. Monetary and time restraints often make such modes of independent travel impossible, of course, but whenever possible, we are on the road, enjoying the freedom of being able to stop where and when we want, of taking any back route that comes along, of making our days as long or as short as we choose. We think this is important in Europe or Asia or Africa, but almost a necessity in Australia if you are going to even get a glimmmer of what this huge continent-nation is all about. We fully realize that this approach is not for everybody, and in truth, is often simply unfeasible. There are those who backpack, and those who like tours, and those who prefer to train it or bus it or thumb it. We find no fault with these approaches, and indeed, have always tried to take disparate appetites into account. Like a close and often addled relative once put it: "If you can't go first class, go anyway."

If there is one message we want you to get from this book, it is that no matter how you get there, where you stay, or how you decide to get around, Australia is necessary for your education, for your sense of humor, and for your own good. It is a fascinating continent and its reality is immensely larger than just a Never-Never Land stuck off someplace in the South Pacific with strange animals and guys in big hats who talk with a funny accent.

What's an Aussie? That's a heavy question. We have some definite ideas and we have tried to make them plain. Don't worry about the Aussies being offended if we just go ahead and tell you what is right or wrong with their country, because they've never been reluctant to tell us what's wrong with ours. That's probably the most precious similarity we share with them: the gut-deep belief that unless you have the right to complain about your country—and anything else, for that matter— you aren't a free society. (We must be honest and say, however, that of all the democratic peoples, the Aussies are among the loudest complainers. They can deny it all they want, and they will. Loudly.)

Who are these people who live up to their ears in kangaroos and koalas and have sheep grazing from hell to breakfast? Who are these people who live on a great big island out in the middle of nowhere but somehow keep producing great movies and super-star rock groups? Who are these men and women who have so captured our imagination and admiration? Who are these people who claim, without so much as a blush, that they single-handedly won World War II?

Who are these Aussies? Well, hang around, and we'll try to show you.

Finally, we'd like to thank the Australian Tourism Commission offices in Los Angeles and Sydney, as well as all the great people who helped us out at the various state and regional public relations offices in Australia and California. Qantas was gracious in providing occasional air transportation, and various Australian state offices helped with transportation, some housing, information, and logistics. We want you to know that when such help was offered—and accepted—it was offered with no strings, no final veto power on the opinions or observations contained in this book. They lent a hand now and then, and we accepted the help now and then. We have tried, throughout this project, to remember that the final word is up to those who will read what we have written. We are sure that if we have erred, either in fact or perception, we will shortly hear about it. And, we would have it no other way.

HISTORY

Of course Australia is destined for greatness—its people have been chosen by the finest judges in England.

—Old Aussie adage

For the peoples of Asia, the most profound change brought on by the upheavals of World War II was the disappearance of European colonial powers, most especially the dissolution of the British Empire. One of the nations most affected by the end of the Raj was Australia. The 150-year-old umbilical cord connecting Mother England to Australia was quickly and efficiently cut shortly after noon on Dec. 10, 1941 off the coast of Malaya by a force of Japanese Navy bombers and torpedo planes.

For most of its history, Anglo-Saxon Australia had clearly understood that should anything ugly or untoward arise to ripple the calm Caucasian waters of Southeast Asia, the mighty Royal Navy, operating from impregnable bases at Singapore and Hong Kong, would take care of matters in short order. This manifesto of the British Empire was noisily ignored by the Japanese, who sank two capital ships of the Royal Navy that December day off Malaya, including the pride of the entire fleet, the 35,000-ton battleship Prince of Wales. It was a profound surprise for the British, comfortable in their Etonian belief that the Japanese—small, near-sighted and racially deficient—were no match for European technology and breeding. Winston Churchill later wrote: "In all the war I never received a more direct shock. As I turned over in bed the full horror of the news sank in upon me. Over all this vast expanse of waters, Japan was supreme, and we everywhere were weak and naked."

If he felt naked, you can imagine how the Australians reacted. Soon after the Prince of Wales and the battle cruiser Repulse were sunk, Singapore fell. This, added to other Japanese advances—Hong Kong, Burma, the Philippines, Pearl Harbor—put an end to the British empire in Southeast Asia. Within months, Japanese armies were in the Solomon Islands, the Dutch East Indies and New Guinea, and Australian cities—notably Darwin in the Northern Territory—were being bombed by Japanese aircraft. It seemed that nothing could stop them from taking Australia. The British had their hands full in Europe and North Africa, and the United States Pacific fleet, it was believed, had died at Pearl Harbor. The notion that Great Britain was not immortal was to have a profound effect on the Land Down Under. As they stood on the shores of the Coral Sea and watched the skies above the Torres Strait and waited for invasion, "everywhere weak and naked," the Australians abruptly entered the 20th century and began the final mental and emotional metamorphosis that made them what they are today.

The Japanese attack also served to increase the ties between the United States and Australia, ties which dated back to the early years of the Island Continent's settlement by white Europeans. Taking a realistic look around him in 1942, Australian Prime Minister John J. Curtin saw clearly the end of an era.

"Without any inhibitions of any kind," he said, "I make it quite clear that Australia looks to America (for help) free of any pangs as to our traditional links or kinship with the United Kingdom." As it turned out, the aims of the United States in the Pacific melded nicely with the protection of Australia, and the end of World War II saw the continuation and expansion of friendly relationships between the two former crown colonies.

To appreciate why the humiliation of Great Britain at the hands of the Japanese was such a rip in the national fabric of white Australia, you must understand the immense psychological bonds that have traditionally tied the two nations together. England, in its long and powerful reign, gave birth to many children. Australia was the bastard baby, born on the wrong side of the blanket, and more than any of the other children, has been the one who tried to please its parent most, to prove its place in the family, to somehow erase the shame of its birth. The English have, for the most part, treated Australia with a fair amount of disdain, as if it were a rather vulgar brat from the wrong side of the tracks who really shouldn't be let into any club frequented by gentlemen. (This never stopped Great Britain from using Australian troops whenever the Empire was at risk, however.) The result of all this has been a love-hate relationship between the two countries that has lasted to the present day. The story of Australia is an improbable saga in many ways, because few other nations can claim to have started so low and risen so high in such a short time.

To 16th- and 17th-century European explorers and cartographers, busily filling in the gaps of their knowledge of the mostly unknown world, there was a need for balance. As they plotted the coasts of continents, planted their flags on isolated islands, and happily confiscated the lands of less-advanced peoples, it seemed that things were a bit top-heavy. Here were Europe and the New World, Cathay and the East Indies, all more or less north of, or close to, the equator. South American went far below the equator to partially make things harmonious, but given that the earth was a sphere, did it not make sense that some-where, far to the southeast, there should be another continental land mass positioned to make everything nicely symmetrical?

The mythical land came to be called "terra australis incognita," the unknown southern land. Australia had already been nibbled at, and was thought to be just a piece of New Guinea, so the search for the missing land mass continued well into the 18th century.

The credit for the first thorough investigations of any part of Aus-tralia falls to the Dutch, who had, by the beginning of the 17th century, taken firm hold of Indonesia. Ships sailing southeast from Batavia—modern Jakarta—chanced upon the west and north coasts of Australia. Throughout the 1600s, Dutch traders and explorers flushed out the maps of western, northern and southern Australia.

In 1688, the English pirate ship *Cygnet* made landfall on the north-western coast. The occasion was historic in two ways. First, William Dampier, one of the crew, became the first recorded Englishman to stand on Australian soil. Second, his account of the Australian natives set the tone for three centuries of racial bias:

> *The inhabitants of this country are the miserablest people in the world . . . setting aside their humane shape, they differ little from brutes. They are tall, strait-bodied, and thin, with long limbs. They have great heads, round foreheads, and great brows. Their eyelids are always half-closed, to keep the flies out of their eyes . . . They are long-visaged, and of a very unpleasing aspect; having no one graceful feature in their faces.*

In the summer of 1769, there was to be a transit of the planet Venus—Venus would pass between the earth and the sun—which was an astronomical event of major importance. The Royal Navy, at that time not occupied with any major wars, decided to send a spare ship off to take a look. It was the *Endeavor,* a sloop and former coal ship of 34 tons, under the command of Capt. James Cook, without doubt one of history's most successful and adventerous explorers. While he was at it, the Admiralty said, he was to attempt to determine, once and for all, if the mythical great southern land mass existed. He was ordered to go as far south as 40 degrees latitude, then sweep west until he either found the missing continent or reached New Zealand, abandoned by the Dutch after Abel Tasman's discovery. Sweep he did, failing to find anything, arriving in New Zealand in October 1769. With his usual careful attention to detail, he spent six months charting almost 2500 miles of Kiwi coastline.

The *Endeavor,* about 100 feet long, carried a crew of 94. In addi-tion to Cook, there were several scientists, including an astronomer and two botanists—Joseph Banks, a fellow of the Royal Society, and Daniel

Carl Solander, a brilliant pupil of the great Swedish botanist, Carolus Linnaeus.

Cook left New Zealand on March 31, 1770. He tried to retrace Tasman's tracks, but gales and heavy seas forced him farther north than expected and he missed Tasmania completely. At about 6 a.m. Friday, April 19, 1770, he had his first glimpse of Australia, generally believed to be a rocky promontory in Victoria.

The account of Cook's exploration of what is now the coast of New South Wales and Queensland is an almost unbelievable adventure. Cook chose to stay fairly close to the shore, usually no more than 10 or 15 miles out, sounding depths and drawing charts as he went. A modern map of Australia's east coast is full of place names he gave to capes and bays and mountains as he passed.

On April 28, he sailed into a bay, "tollerably well shelter'd from all winds," and anchored two miles offshore.

Cook spent about a week exploring the bay, gathering food and fresh water and trying to make friendly contact with the Australians, who were having none of it. He first named the place Sting-Ray Harbour because of the large number of rays he and the crew supped on, but later in the voyage changed the name to Botany Bay to honor the accomplishments of his two young botanists. Cook wrote at one point:

We made an excursion into the country which we found diversified with wood, lawns and marshes. The woods are free from underwood of every kind, and the trees are at such a distance from one another that the whole country, or at least a great part of it, might be cultivated without being obliged to cut down a single tree. We found the soil everywhere, except in the marshes, to be a light white sand, and produceth a quantity of good grass.

A few days later, he made the log entry that was to convince England that something might be made of this backwater continent:

. . . We landed and travel'd some distance inland. We found the face of the country much the same as I have described, but the land much richer, for instead of sand I found in many places a deep black soil, which we thought was capable of producing any kind of grain. At present it produceth, besides timber, as fine meadow as ever was seen; however, we found it not all like this, some few places were very rocky, but this I believe to be uncommon.

Having had his fill of Botany Bay, Cook sailed again, soon passing, 15 miles to the north, the entrance to a bay he called Port Jackson. He was in a hurry and made no effort to explore it. That would have to wait for 18 more years and another English sea captain. A glance at a map of Australia will show you that in the south, near Botany Bay, there is nothing to the east but open water for a thousand miles. But as you go north, the Great Barrier Reef starts coming into shore. It's shaped like a large funnel, with the mouth to the south and the ever-narrowing neck to the north. It was into this funnel that the unsuspecting Cook sailed. He had no charts; indeed the reef's very existence was unknown to European navies in those days. There is some evidence to suggest, however, that the French explorer Louis Antoine de Bougainville came upon the reef a year or so before Cook, at a point about 125 miles east of present Cooktown in 1768.

As he began to encounter shoal water near modern Heron Island and the other islands of the Capricorn group, Cook, ever the careful captain, often had small boats go ahead of the *Endeavor* sounding the depth. He still had no inkling what he was getting into. In early June, he made his way through a group of large islands northeast of Mackay and christened the route the Whitsunday Passage. A few days later, he was about 120 kilometers north of modern-day Cairns, skirting shoals in all direction and coming to the conclusion that there were probably a lot of places in the world easier to take a sailing ship than this. Around 11:00 at night under a clear, moonlit sky, he met the reef.

"Before 10 o'clock we had 20 and 21 fathoms (of water beneath the keel) . . . until a few minutes before 11 when we had 17, and before the man at the lead could heave another cast, the ship struck and stuck fast." It was not immediately clear what damage, if any, the ship had sustained, and Cook did what he could to get the *Endeavor* off the reef, sending boats out to pull (no effect), then dropping an anchor off the starboard side in an effort to kedge it off the coral. He even tossed several tons of stuff overboard trying to lighten the ship: "Guns, iron and stone ballast, casks, hoop staves, oil jarrs, decay'd stores, etc," which divers have been trying ever since to find. Nothing worked.

Ponder the situation facing Cook and crew: They're several thousand miles from the nearest European port, stuck on a reef in the middle of nowhere with food and water supplies ashore very iffy propositions. If the *Endeavor* sinks, he and the crew are marooned in a strange land with a bunch of natives who have, up to this point, been less than receptive to the idea of European intrusions. Nobody knows where he is, and given how much trouble he has had meandering through the shoals and reefs, rescue is unlikely.

The next day, he managed to float the ship off the coral, but it was leaking badly. Some four days later, the *Endeavor* hove into a bay where a river flowed into the sea (now called the Endeavor River) and began repairs. The spot is the site of modern Cooktown. Here he made the discovery that no fictional adventure would dare to create: the reef itself had saved the ship. Cook wrote:

It appeared very extraordinary, that she made no more water than she did. A large piece of coral rock was sticking in one hole, and several pieces of the (patching material), small stones, etc. had made their way in, and lodged between the timbers, which stopped the water from forcing its way in in great quantities.

Cook and company, having gotten the *Endeavor* back into reasonable repair, began the exasperating task of finding a way out of their trap. Every direction they tried, they ran into shoals and reefs. Finally, in the middle of August, he came to an island with high hills. He climbed and saw what he thought was the outer reef, and thus, perhaps a passage to the open ocean. He named it Lizard Island, today site of one of the poshest resorts along the Barrier Reef. The *Endeavor* made its way out, and by August 22, had sailed north past the tip of the Cape York Peninsula, proving that it was not connected to New Guinea. On a small island, called Possession Island, Cook raised the British colors and claimed the entire east coast of Australia for England, naming it New Wales.

One of the major social concerns the English faced in the 18th and 19th centuries was what to do with their criminals. In the early 1700s, the English banishment laws were amended to allow minor offenders to be sent to the American colonies for seven years, major offenders for 14. This cozy relationship lasted for the better part of 80 years, with England getting rid of some of its undesirables, the colonies getting captive labor. The happy partnership ended abruptly in 1776 when the upstart Americans told George III to take a hike.

The successful resistance of the Yankees during the War of Independence caused the English a spot of bother, don't you know. English jails were on the brink of bursting, so much so that as an interim measure, until they could figure out a solution, (or win the war in America, which they were clearly losing) prisoners were kept in old, rotting, incredibly filthy ships in southern English ports—the so-called "hulk system." In 1786, the transportation of felons to the far-away shores of New Wales was approved by Prime Minister William Pitt. The plan was announced by Thomas Townshend, the Vicount Sydney, the home and colonial secretary. (Yes, that Sydney). All that was needed now was somebody brave enough (or dumb enough) to go set up the new colony.

As heroes go, Capt. Arthur Phillip was reportedly about as dull as they come. He had been a good enough captain, as his 30-year service record starting in the late 1750s proved, but he seemed to be no Horatio Hornblower, just an average English naval officer competant enough to get the job done. One contemporary portrait shows a middle-aged man in cocked hat, with a prunish mouth, cow-brown eyes and a big nose—not the sort of guy you'd want to go buckle your swash with. Still, he was given orders that would make even the brave Capt. Hornblower blanch: sail from England in charge of a convoy of diddly little ships containing about 1500 felons, guards, administrators, officers, and sailors, navigate his way down the South Atlantic through some of the worst seas in the world, cross vast stretches of the South Pacific, then proclaim himself governor of a colony that would jolly well become self-sufficient after two years—or else.

The true worth of this apparently colorless captain was soon revealed. If it had not been for his single-minded, stubborn efficiency, the first voyage (and, indeed, the colony itself) would have almost certainly ended in disaster. You name it—it went wrong.

Chandlers tried to stiff him, the brains behind planning the colony tried to give him too much of one thing, not enough of another, the convicts came in trickles rather than all at once (causing housing and guard problems), there was a strike by merchant seamen on some of the transports, and there was an outbreak of typhus. Somehow, Phillip got it all sorted out, and by early May, 1787, he was ready to go.

In all, Phillip had 11 ships. Two—including his flagship, the *Sirius*—were regular British Navy; the rest were private craft hired for the trip. The ships, of course, were inadequate for the job, being too small for the number of people they carried. The largest was a 114-foot transport that carried 195 male convicts plus crew, guards and officers. The smallest, *HMS Supply*, the other navy ship, was 70 feet long and carried 50 people in all. On May 13, Phillip set sail from Portsmouth with his colonists: around 750 convicts (568 male, 191 female), 250 or so Marines, 20 officials, 210 Royal Navy seamen, 230 or so merchant seamen and 13 children, belonging to both convicts and guards. (The exact number of people on the first voyage is unclear; because of bad record keeping, a variety of figures exist from a variety of sources.) The convicts ranged in age from over 80 (a woman) to under 10 (a boy).

The First Fleet, as it is called, is to Australians what the *Mayflower* is to Americans. And the myths are about the same, too. Every third Anglo-American would like to claim at least one relative on the *Mayflower*. Same thing in Australia, where they call it having "a ball and chain in the family." The actual number of present-day Aussies who can lay claim to an ancestor with the First Fleet is tiny.

The trip took 252 days. From Portsmouth, the fleet sailed to Tenerife, then down the South Atlantic to Rio de Janiero. Turning east, it sailed to the Cape of Good Hope, then due east again, 6500 miles without sight of land to Australia. The successful voyage was a miracle, beset as it was with terrible weather, bad food, overcrowding, poorly outfitted ships, disease, and unsuccessful attempts at mutiny. Still, Phillip made it to Botany Bay on Jan. 20, 1788.

Armed as he was with only Cook's logs, Phillip expected a lot more than he found when he dropped anchor in Botany Bay. He took one look around at what was supposed to be a fertile continent and got so disgusted (and probably just a tad apprehensive) that he didn't even stay long enough to take possession of the new colony or declare himself governor. The black soil of Cook's description was missing, the bay itself was a poor anchorage, too open to the sea, the water supply was almost non-existent, and in general, things looked fairly grim. But Phillip was, as we have noted, a stubborn man, so he gathered a troop of Marines and decided to explore about 15 miles farther north and take a look at Port Jackson, the bay Cook had noted in passing in 1770 but failed to explore. And what they found was one of the finest anchorages in the world, big enough, Phillip later wrote joyfully to the Admiralty, to stash "a thousand sail of the line." It also turned out to be one of the most beautiful bodies of water in the world, the place we now call Sydney Harbour. Despite the fact that for many years nobody even lived around Botany Bay, the name stuck in England and elsewhere and became synonymous with transportation and banishment.

Phillip ordered his 11 ships out of Botany Bay and into the new anchorage, and about 7 p.m., Jan. 26, 1788, the First Fleet entered the bay. He formally took possession of New South Wales (as all eastern Australia was now called) on Feb. 7, 1788.

From all reports, you would think that everyone in Australia had at least one great-great-grandfather or great-great-grandmother who was transported to Australia by the bloody English. In fact, only between 150,000 and 170,000 men, women, and children were sent to Australia by English courts during the 80 years that transportation was in effect. Only about 25,000 of those transported were women, which had a long-lasting influence on the male-dominated society of Australia for many years afterward.

A main part of the Aussie prisoner myth holds that most of those transported were just innocent victims of harsh and unfair English law, sent to the ends of the earth either for a minor crime they probably didn't commit or for political reasons, torn from the bosom of their poor-but-honest parents, fated to be the tool of a psychopathic prison guard whose major joy in life was lashing poor unfortunates with a cat-o'-nine-tails. To be sure, there were cases like that, but the vast majority of the felons sent to Australia were guilty as hell. But it cannot be denied that Australia's penal beginnings have colored its people and contributed to their attitudes up to the present day.

We are not trying to suggest that those transported to Australia found a bed of roses, especially those sent to Norfolk Island and to the Port Arthur prison in Tasmania (then called Van Dieman's Land) where brutal excesses were common. But many of the convicts who served time in Australia worked off their sentences and became upright citizens of the new colony. However, it is also true that there was enough wrong with the treatment of prisoners in New South Wales for a hue and cry to begin for its abolition almost the minute it started. The movement to get rid of transportation got especially noisy in the 1830s and 1840s, but it was not until 1868 that the last boatload of convicts was dropped off in Western Australia. Transportation to New South Wales ended in 1840, and to Van Dieman's Land in 1852, but the settlers of parched and wild Western Australia claimed they needed convicts to make the colony a success.

When the time came to end transportation, it was not just do-gooders, prison reformers, and humanists who made the biggest noises about abolition. There were also those Australians who considered themselves to be upstanding citizens of the Empire and who wanted to get as far away from their convict history as possible. As good little Victorians, they shared that wonderfully enlightened philosophy about criminals—out of sight, out of mind. They wanted nothing to do with the criminal classes, and it seemed highly unfair to them that England was still treating Australia as a refuse dump. Somewhere along the line, using the blinders of prosperity and their new-found sense of propriety, they conveniently forgot the past. Like a case of leprosy in the family, the convict era was something never spoken about in public, especially if one's grandfather had been a charter member of the club.

It was not until the latter part of this century that Australian historians began looking at the convict days with any degree of professional detachment. One of the first and best was Manning Clark's *A History of Australia* series, which not only addressed the various myths of Australian history, but also dealt honestly for the first time with the two-century destruction of black Australian society. Another book, one that has probably laid more phantoms to rest than any other, is the exquisitely researched and written chronicle of the first days of Australia called *The Fatal Shore,* by Australian journalist Robert Hughes.

Despite Hughes and other historians, the convict myth persists. This is to be expected, because it's just too good a story to do away with. If Americans can have their Chisholm Trail, and the English their King Arthur and Robin Hood, then surely Australia can keep its ball and chain.

By the end of the second decade of the new century, the colony was getting crowded, but movement inland was blocked by the Blue Mountains, a part of the Great Dividing Range that runs along the entire east coast of Australia. Many early settlers thought the mountains were inpenetrable. Like pioneer Americans facing the Appalachians, the Australians needed a Cumberland Gap through the mountains. It was found in 1813 by William Charles Wentworth, a journalist and major figure in early Australia. You can get a good idea of the difficulty of that journey by taking a modern train from Sydney to the resort towns in the Blue Mountains—the deep valleys and high ridges are thick with vegetation, and even today, it would be impossible to hack your way through many areas. Two years later, using convict labor, Governor

Lachlan Macquarie pushed a path through on the Wentworth route—which he named the Western Road—which connected Sydney with Bathurst, 130 miles away. It was rough and dangerous, but it opened up the vast grazing areas of western New South Wales to the settlers.

Early settlers believed that a vast lake would be found in the center of the country, or at the very least huge areas of rich grazing or wheat lands would lie far beyond the Great Dividing Range. Adding to the speculation was the tantalizing fact that all of Australia's great southern rivers—the Murray, the Darling, the Lachlan, the Murrumbidgee—flowed from the Great Dividing Range west into the interior. One of the first attempts to follow the rivers to the great inland lake was led by Charles Sturt, who took a party through the Murray River system of New South Wales and South Australia in 1830. (The river system, rather than flowing into an inland sea, empties into the ocean in South Australia.)

The most famous exploration of the furnace-like interior was the fatal expedition of Robert O'Hara Burke and W. J. Wills in 1860. In August, Burke and Wills, accompanied by a 30-camel train and the dozen or so other members of the party, set off from Melbourne. They made it to the Gulf of Carpentaria in February 1861 and immediately started back. On the delayed return trip, Burke, Wills, and John King, a member of the party, stumbled into their supply camp, only to find it deserted. The depot party, assuming the worst because Burke and Wills were two months overdue, had left only seven hours before. Burke and Wills died, and only King, who was nursed by Aboriginals, lived to tell the tale.

The most famous animal in Australia is probably the kangaroo, followed closely by the duck-bill platypus. But there is another animal that has played such an enormous role in Australian history that it should probably be placed on the national coat of arms rather than the interesting but basically useless emu: the sheep.

It was sheep that made Australia a prosperous colony, and it is sheep that have made Australia a prosperous independent nation. The statistics are fairly impressive: the country has about 170 million sheep; something like two billion pounds of wool are shorn every year; the wool business employs about 300,000 people, and export earnings total well above U.S. $3.5 billion a year. Fully a third of the world's entire output of wool is produced in Australia.

After World War II, there was a huge boom in wool prices, caused by world-wide shortages, that climaxed in 1969 when there were 180 million sheep in Australia. A huge bust followed, and in less than 10 years, the total flock was down to 130 million. In the midst of the decine, the Australian Wool Corporation was established to set and maintain wool prices. With price stabilization, the number of sheep has climbed to its current total of around 170 million head.

At present, there are about 100,000 sheep farms and stations in

Australia, and wool accounts for between 12 and 15 percent of the nation's total export earnings (it's the number one export) and has shown steady rises the last decade. Between 1985 and 1988, for example, wool export revenues doubled. The two largest customers are Japan and China. Australia is also the second-largest exporter (after New Zealand) of mutton and lamb in the world, something on the order of 300,000 tons a year.

While the cow has not received as much publicity as the sheep in the agricultural affairs of Australia, it is also a major industry: Australia is the world's biggest exporter of beef and veal, almost 630,000 tons a year. With that many cows around, you can't escape the fact that Australia had to evolve its own brand of cowboy.

In Australia, they call them drovers or stockmen, and they herd bullocks instead of cows and they use stock whips instead of lariats, but aside from that, Pard, they're just like the guys who hang out around Calgary or Miles City. Cowboys, y'all, cowboys. They look alike, they ride alike, they all have holes in their boots and cowpies on their Levis and they all think drinking beer and riding in rodeos is better than free air. Would you believe that country-western is the most popular music in Australia? Would you further believe that the most famous country-western singer in Australia is named Slim Dusty? (There was also a very popular Kiwi C&W artist in Australia, now dead, named Tex Morton.) You have to love the way they talk down there, too. Cows don't stampede in Australia, they rush. As in: "Struth, the bloody bullocks rushed and it was fair dinkum feeding time at the zoo, my bloody oath," and other such cowboy-type talk. There is a fair amount of lore surrounding the Aussie stockman, and much of it is quite reminiscent of your basic North American cowboy. One of the all-time great cattle drive movies (which usually comes on at 3 a.m., it's that popular) is a little Aussie classic called "The Overlanders," starring an instantly recognizable but virtually unknown actor named Chips Rafferty. The drill is this: Darwin is being bombed by the Japanese, invasion looks imminent, and rather than shoot all the cattle to keep them out of the enemy's hands, Chips says he'll drive the mob all the way from Wyndham in Western Australia to the Queensland coast. Wonderful stuff: bad weather, stampedes (excuse us, rushes), crocodile-infested river crossings, clouds of dust, terror, anxiety, wisps of western widsom in the air. Yahoo, yippee, etc. Chips was in many Hollywood movies, usually playing an Australian coastwatcher. He had a perfect Aussie face and a great accent and looked a lot like Paul Hogan's uncle.

While we're talking about Western Lore and such, you can also tell we're the Aussie's kissing cousins by taking a quick look at their road signs. Holes in them, people, bullet holes. Buckshot, rifle and pistol holes, a sure sign that the frontier mentality (dangerous as it might be) still lives. We had an English schoolteacher friend visit us here in the States once, and we took him on a tour of the Four Corners area out in northern Arizona just to show him some frontier-type vistas. While we were about it, we showed him a cowboy or two, some cows, a rattlesnake and, just so he'd know that Out West men are men, we showed him some bullet-holed signs. He was aghast, neighbors. "That's appalling," he said, very proper and very English. Sure, but then he's never tried it, either. (Besides which, things are so close together in England, you shoot a road sign, you'd probably hit the vicar, the vicar's wife and the vicar's wife's pet dachsund. Only in big, really big, countries is it safe to have bullet holes in road signs.)

That's one thing Americans, Canadians, and Australians share that the English simply cannot understand: wide open spaces. (Actually, this inability to understand just how big we really are is true for almost everybody in Europe and many people in Asia.) If anything, the Aussies have an even more advanced sense of frontier freedom than we do because not only are they completely surrounded by water, most of their wide-open spaces are butt-busting, almost unlivable deserts. Plus on a land mass almost exactly the size of the continental United States, they have a population of only 16 million. That's elbow room, folks. But before you go to thinking that every Aussie wears spurs and carries a stock whip, just remember that the bulk of the population lives in urban areas.

This lack of tight borders has allowed the citizens of all three countries to think big, act big, brag big. It has colored their approach to life and their approach to other smaller (and thus more insignificant) nations. This has led the other, smaller nations to think that we think we're better than they are. Which we do.

The enormity of the country confused even many Australian prisoners, who being only human, managed to escape from prisons (they were called "bolters"). While a lot of them died in the bush or were recaptured, some managed to last a long time by becoming bandits. Yet a fair number of them, being fresh off the streets of London and thus unaccustomed to practicing open-country geography, assumed they could reach China if they took off into the bush. They did not find China; what they often found was a bunch of very upset local black citizens who had by this point in history decided that the only good convict was a dead convict and took appropriate measures.

Australia had become a frontier nation, what with remittance men and gold strikes and drifters and gamblers and fallen doves and drovers, and you can't have a real-live frontier unless a bunch of the populace has been seduced by the dark side, so the escaped convicts were joined in their evil ways by men and women who figured hold-ups were more cost-effective than farming. In Australia, the guys in black hats are called bushrangers, and the stories and sagas about them are as popular—and mostly as inaccurate—as the stories about Billy the Kid or Jesse James.

Some of the bushrangers were true bad guys, murdering and pillaging; others were minor folk heroes, hidden or protected by local farmers, generally applauded by the citizenry who were also a bit tired of government interference. (Does this all sound familiar, buckaroos?) The idea of bold banditry being honest work took deep root very early in the Australian subconscious—if you were a prisoner of His Majesty, the one thing in the world you didn't like was cops, and if you were an escaped prisoner turned bushranger, you *really* didn't like cops. Only a small number of Australians, convicts or not, actually became bad guys, but like Butch Cassidy, it made for an interesting role model. This is why in many folk songs dealing with Aussie brigands, you find outlaws living the free, glorious life of excitement—and the police are almost always the thugs.

There were some guys around whose style just naturally made them popular. There was, for instance, the Gilbert gang, composed of Ben Hall, John Gilbert, and Frank Gardiner, who were quite adept at such spicy activities as robbing 60 people at one time—in between shooting a lawman now and then. One rainy day in 1863, having nothing much else to do, they wandered into Canowindra, west of Bathurst and beyond the Blue Mountains in New South Wales, and kidnapped the whole damned town. They tossed the local constable into jail and threw a three-day party for the Canowindrans, who were more than happy to share the free booze and fiddle music that ensued.

The most famous bushranger of all was Ned Kelly. When they're on the prod, the Aussies like to get us cornered in a pub and remind us that Jesse James only robbed two trains and five banks, whereas Mr. Kelly and his bonny band followed the example of the Gilbert mob and captured whole towns. (We are willing to allow them to quote these statistics for Jesse and Frank; it's too much trouble to look them all up. Besides, they wouldn't accept any contrary figures even if they were printed in blood).

Ned was of Irish stock, as the saga goes, and being Irish, knew at birth that the English administration of Australia was out to get him. Along with his comrades, he hid out in the mountains of Victoria for a while. Then, hearing that the gendarmes were coming by train to snuff them, he and his brother and two gang members kidnapped all the citizens of Glenrowan, Victoria, held them in a hotel pub, and tore up the tracks to stop the cops. The police just stopped the train outside of town, walked in bold as brass and started blasting away. Ned, a designing chap, had the foresight to make himself up a suit of armor for just such an occasion.

The Kelly gang and the coppers went on discharging their firearms at each other for some hours when, apparently tiring of the fun, Ned put on the armor and attempted to escape. He was wounded and the cops torched the hotel and the other three members of the gang died in the flames rather than surrender. Four months later, Ned was sentenced to hang on the gallows at the Old Melbourne Gaol, which he did on November 11, 1880. The fable has Ned's mother coming to the big house and telling him to "die like a Kelly," and also reporting that his last words on the gallows were: "Such is life."

Another reason why Canadians and Americans think like Australians is because we had a gold rush or two, all three of us. The first one was in California in 1848–49, followed immediately by one in New South Wales and Victoria in 1851, then in Queensland starting in 1867, then the last big strikes in Australia at Kalgoorlie in Western Australia in 1892–93, followed by the Yukon strikes at the turn of the century. Gold booms cause instant immigration, but more importantly, they perpetuate that old belief that any slob who works hard has a shot at fame and fortune. This is a bedrock philosophy in all three societies. The fact that only a handful of guys ever made it big in the gold fields doesn't matter. It's the thought that counts.

When James Marshall found gold on the American River in California in January of 1848, John Sutter, who was in charge around those parts, tried desperately to keep it quiet, knowing full well what would happen if the word got out. Nearby, however, lurked storekeeper Sam Brannan who, hearing of the strike, immediately set off for civilization. Prospectors would need supplies, you see, and he just happened to own a store near the gold field . . . well, anyway, being a mouthy, capitalistic American, he blabbed to anyone who would listen and started the great Sierra gold rush, for which the citizens of San Francisco remain thankful, they think. Just to prove something or other, when gold was first discovered in 1841 in New South Wales by the Rev. W. B. Clarke, the news was immediately quashed by the then-governor, Sir George Gipps. Gipps, cleverly remembering that he was surrounded by hordes of felons and former felons, told the reverend to cool it: "Put it away, Mr. Clarke," he cried, "or we shall all have our throats cut." Amazingly, Mr. Clarke did just that and gold was forgotten until Edward Hargraves, a veteran of the 1848–49 California rush found the magic metal in a tributary of the Macquarie River near Bathurst in 1851. Within two months, other strikes had been made in Victoria and gold madness was upon the land.

By 1860, the population of the country was around a million, a 10-year increase of 600,000, many drawn by gold fever. Included in that number, by some estimates, were 20,000 Americans. When the Yankees came, they were welcomed openly, as is seen in this Melbourne newspaper editorial:

From which side soever we look on the American people, from the literary, mechanical, or the commercial, we must acknowledge that there is a freshness and vigour connected with the intelligence they develop. Our American brethren are among our most energetic and enterprising citizens.

That trend has continued: the Australian government estimates that 80,000 Americans have migrated to Australia since the end of World War II.

The gold fields of the 1850s also produced one of Australia's most famous exclamations of personal freedom, the so-called Eureka Stockade incident. As usual, it was the cops who got the blame for starting it all, this time in the goldfields in the Eureka Valley at Ballarat near Melbourne. Some bright public servant ordained that gold miners should pay a monthly license fee, whether they struck gold or not. To collect the tax, the government sent in the police, many of whom were ex-convicts from Tasmania. The result was inevitable. On Nov. 29, the miners, figuring enough was damned well enough, formed the Ballarat Reform League and burned their mining licenses. The government sent in reinforcements, the miners built a stockade and vowed to fight for their rights. And they raised the now-famous Eureka flag: the Southern Cross minus the English Union Jack, the first overt sign that maybe Australians were spiritually emerging as a separate nation from old Mother England. In the ensuing fight at dawn on Dec. 3, 300 government troops stormed the 150 or so miners behind the stockade, and within 15 minutes, 24 miners and six soldiers were killed. As a result, the government backed down, and within a year had done away with mining licenses.

In addition to boosting the population of the country, the early Australian gold strikes also hastened the end of transportation. The system was already being attacked in Australia and England, and the gold rush pretty much ended forever the idea that Australia was the Siberia of the South Seas. It was hard to threaten an English felon with prison Down Under when half the male population of England was already on its way to the gold fields.

Until the end of World War II, it seems to us outsiders, the Australians were well and truly trying to out-English the English. The early robber barons and wealthy sheep squatters showed it by setting up lordly English-style estates every bit as ostentatious as those Back Home (or at least as ostentatious as the rugged frontier of the Outback would allow.) English history was taught in Aussie schools. Things English were things good, and the bumpkin colony out in the southern thules knew it. For most of the 19th century, like Americans in the 18th century, many Australians felt themselves simply to be Englishmen living overseas. And in no other way did the Australians try to prove their worth to beloved and haughty England than by fighting on the world-wide battlefields of the Empire.

New South Wales sent troops to join the imperial armies in the Sudan in 1885, and all the colonies combined to send 16,500 troops to the Boer War in 1899. Aussies have a terrible habit of calling each other by their first names—even officers—which simply is not done in Her Majesty's Forces. It didn't take long for Australian soldiers to get a reputation as great fighting men—and hopelessly rowdy characters who actually believed all men were created equal, officers or not.

World War I came along, for reasons few people down under really understood or cared about, and the Aussies were right there. Australian prime minister William Morris Hughes, the "Little Digger," promised to support England to Australia's last penny. During the Great War, Aussie forces totaled about 416,000, or about half of all men of military age in 1914; of these, about 330,000 served overseas and incurred 226,000 casualties, including 60,000 killed—an astounding figure of 68.5 percent, and the highest Allied casualty rate of the war. This from a population of less than five million. The first Australian troops were sent to Egypt for training. Joined with troops from New Zealand, they were known as ANZACs, and their first major participation in the war was in the spring of 1915 on the Turkish coast at a place called Gallipoli. The ANZAC troops, plus French, British, and other imperial forces, were pinned to their landing areas from April 25, 1915 (now celebrated as Anzac Day) to December 20 when they finally withdrew. The ill-advised invasion was the brainchild of the First Lord of the Admiralty, Winston Churchill. The Allied losses were bad at Gallipoli: 78,000 wounded, 35,000 dead. Of the dead, 8587 were ANZACs.

The Australians showed their loyalty to the Empire true enough, but many in the country wondered out loud if it had really been necessary to participate in a silly European war so far from their shores. But 20 years later, they were involved in another war, this one a whole lot closer to home.

Closer to home actually meant Broome, a tiny pearl-fishing town in Western Australia, and Darwin, in the Northern Territory, both of which were bombed in February 1942 by Japanese aircraft. The Aussies, because of their relation with England, had been at war since 1939 after the Munich agreement failed and Hitler attacked Poland. Most of the first Australian forces sent to help the Empire went to the Near East, where they rapidly turned into the Desert Rats of North Africa.

By the time of Pearl Harbor, most of Australia's troops were far from home—four Australia divisions were either in the Near East or guarding Empire outposts in Singapore and Malaya. (When Singapore fell, 15,000 of the 130,000 captured troops were Australian.) The remaining Aussie troops back home, about 34,000 men, were incorporated into a combined command called ABDA (Australian, British, Dutch, American) and were about the only troops left to protect the Solomon Islands, the Dutch East Indies, and Australia. Faced with a Japanese invasion, the Australian government decided to bring troops home from the Near East, a move that incensed the British—how dare the Aussies try to protect their own country when the Empire was at risk—but the Australian held fast and brought the Desert Rats home to fight in some of the dirtiest battles of the war defending their own shores.

Just as they had in World War I, the Australians soon gained a reputation for being some of the toughest soldiers in the world. Their valor in North Africa now legend, they became among the best jungle warfare troops in the whole war, fighting in the incredibly harsh and often brutal conditions of the Pacific islands. Throughout the South Pacific, Aussies fought the Japanese—or helped win the war in other ways. One group of Royal Australian Navy forces, known as coastwatchers, hid on Japanese-held islands and spied on enemy ships and airplane movements; one even rescued future president John Kennedy from capture. At sea, the Australian Navy played a crucial role in operations throughout the Pacific, particularly during the Battle of the Coral Sea in May 1942 when Japanese expansion was, for the first time, turned back.

As in World War I, the cost of Australian participation in war was high. About a million Australian men served in the Second World War, and half of those were either killed or wounded. Of those taken prisoner by the Japanese, more than 8000 died, a bitter statistic not forgotten in Australia.

With the end of World War II came the end of Churchill's hope of saving the British Empire. Asia was never to be the same, and the largest predominantly Caucasian country in Asia—Australia—changed with it. The biggest change after 1941 was the fact that for a time Australia had a new parent: the United States. Remember wartime Prime Minister John J. Curtin: "Australia looks to America free of any pangs as to our traditional links or kinship with the United Kingdom."

After the war, the Aussies, ever ready to prove themselves, paid back the debt they thought they owed. Korea came, and again, Diggers went off fight and die to help their protectors in a far-away land. And 20 years later, they went to Vietnam, partly for a friendship and partly, like the Americans, because it was the only war they had. But it was becoming apparent that Australians were growing increasingly less and less eager to fight other people's wars, a sign, perhaps, they had finally started to become something other than England's willing bastard baby or America's naive cousin.

In the 50 years since the sun went down on the British Empire, Australia has changed greatly. It would be false to say that the United States has replaced England as the mother figure. The government of Australia sent troops to Vietnam, true, but the end result was the same as in the United States: the people did not approve and the policy was abandoned. It also dawned on many Australians that the peoples of Asia were wondering why Australia—an Asian nation—was even involved in what was widely viewed in the Pacific Rim as an exercise in military imperialism. The United States and Australia remain friendly, of course, and the Aussies are probably the strongest ally we have anywhere in the Pacific, including our major trading partner, the Japanese, or our former great hope, the Philippines. The Aussies like us and respect us, but after Vietnam, they no longer necessarily support every policy we advance. Perhaps even more importantly, Australia is coming to grips with its location. It has forged strong ties with its Asian neighbors in trade, commerce and mutual cooperation, even with the once-hated Japanese. It has changed its immigration policies to allow Asians to immigrate, it has looked less and less toward the all-Caucasian Commonwealth and more toward its geographic brothers. It is a nation truly struggling to find itself.

And the struggle always seems to come into clear focus whenever the queen arrives in Australia. On a trip to open Parliament in early 1992, her appearance was boycotted by several legislators who said "Australians should be politically mature enough to have their own head of state and flag." And it got worse. At one point, the new prime minister, Paul Keating, being Australian, showed his friendship to the queen by putting his arms around her shoulder. This is a large no-no in royal circles (one never, ever touches Her Majesty), and the British press went insane. "Boring Boors Down Under," said one headline, with a story that said, in part, "It's a question of manners—something, apparently, that some Australians know little about." And just to add a finishing touch, the prime minister's wife, Annita, refused to curtsy to the queen, a habit we Yanks got into some years back. It all proved that the love-hate relationship continues, and the traditional snobbery of the English toward the Aussies is alive and well.

And still and all, despite their warts and their problems, the Australians are basically among the nicest people on earth. They are our cousins, black and white, and their future and their conflicts are, in many ways, the same we face in the United States.

THE LAND DOWN UNDER

ABORIGINALS ....

If you were one of the million-plus people jammed together around the shores of Sydney Harbour on Jan. 26, 1988 to celebrate the 200th anniversary of the arrival of Europeans in Australia, you probably will never forget the incredible spectacle of hundreds of boats, from dinghies to tall ships, bobbing in the water to honor the memory of the First Fleet. You'll probably also remember the arrival of the Prince and Princess of Wales (she wore green), and the fireworks that went off high in the air, spraying the harbor with Aussie flags. But unless you knew where to look—and why—you probably missed the little puffs of orange smoke rising now and then from the water near a spit of land on Farm Cove known as Mrs. Macquarie's Point.

The orange wisps were from smoke cannisters dropped into the water from canoes by Aboriginal Australians protesting the celebration. They saw no reason for rejoicing, because to them, the arrival 200 years before of the first white Europeans to settle in Australia was the beginning of a two-century-long nightmare. To them, it was not a settlement; rather, it was an invasion.

Wisps of orange smoke quickly lost in the breeze, largely ignored in the massive and boisterous birthday party the Aussies threw themselves that day in January. That was about all that ever came of the bicentennial Aboriginal protest; wisps of smoke. There was a protest march, to be sure, the largest protest march ever staged by Australian Aboriginals, and there were speeches duly attended by reporters from around the world asking the right questions (at the wrong time), but when it was all over, it was just wisps of orange smoke. This more or less sums up the present state of affairs for those often called "the First Australians."

The 200-year destruction of the Aboriginal world and its systems of religion and ethics is a stain on Australia's history, one which no end of rationalization will change. Despite many protests to the contrary, and despite the general policy after World War II to increase

24

immigration from Asia, there is an underlying bed of racism in Australia that has not yet allowed the nation to completely come to terms with its past, its present—or its future. This is particularly true with regard to white Australian attitudes toward black Australians. The surprise is not that today's black Australians live as they do—but that they are alive at all.

It's yet one more experience Canadians and Americans share with their Aussie cousins, this dispossession of native groups who stood in the way of frontier expansion. The white Europeans who settled the three colonies lied, stole, murdered, and cheated the natives of their lands, and destroyed ancient ways of living with little or no flickers of conscience, content in their beliefs that manifest destiny ordained that lesser peoples must be pushed aside. By lesser peoples, they meant any peoples who were non-Caucasian and untutored in the superior force of European technology. There were Americans and Canadians and Australians who thought, even at the time, that what was happening to the native peoples was not right, but the end result in all three cases proved that theirs were voices in the minority.

And it's not just black native Australians who have run into the wall of racism. Indeed, one of the first tasks faced when the country became a federated, independent nation in 1901 was the codification of a set of rules and laws that came to be called the "White Australia Policy," which set the tone for the Australian government toward its own natives as well as its Asian neighbors for the next 80 years. Australia for Australians was the national watchword, and what that meant was Australia for Anglo-Irish Australians.

The experiences of the Australian Aboriginals have been no better and no worse than the native peoples in North America. The experiences have been Australian, of course, meaning that what happened to the First Australians probably could not have happened just the way it did anywhere else in the world.

Anthropologists and archaeologists are not precisely sure when the first humans arrived in Australia, with guesses ranging to as far back as 150,000 years. It is generally agreed that the waves of immigration that took place began in Southeast Asia and the Indian subcontinent and coincided with the world's ice ages. As the polar ice caps grew, the level of the oceans dropped, and ancient peoples were able to island-hop their way from Asia to Australia. It is now believed that the present Aboriginals descended from a group that arrived on the Australian mainland between 30,000 and 40,000 years ago, when the oceans were about 500 feet lower than today. This period is about the same time that humans crossed the land bridge from Asia into North America.

In the centuries since that last ice age, the oceans rose to create the Torres Strait, disconnecting Australia from New Guinea, and also rose to cut the land tie with Tasmania. The continent became an isolated island and the climate started to change, turning drier and hotter. The humans on this land changed as it changed, adapting to new environments, new shortages of food, new challenges.

The isolation, coupled with the environment, kept the human population low. It is estimated that in 1788, when the Europeans arrived, there were only about 300,000 Aboriginals on the whole continent, most of them living along the eastern and southern coasts, and in Tasmania. Even by Stone Age standards, they were a primitive people, living a precarious life as hunter-gatherers. They were often unclothed, and knew nothing of elaborate shelters such as the kind made by North American Plains Indians. They simply took pieces of tree bark, put them on the ground to act as windbreaks, and curled up. They had, of course, never seen a horse. Even with so few numbers, they were diverse, with perhaps 300 languages and between 500 and 1000 tribes. They seemed always to be at war with each other, and deaths from combat were common.

During his exploration of the east coast of the continent, Capt. James Cook tried many times to make contact with the Aboriginals, and he took many notes on their character. Cook wrote:

> *"From what I have said of the natives of New Holland, they may appear to be some of the most wretched people upon Earth; but in reality they are far more happier than we Europeans, being wholly unacquainted not only with the superfluous, but with the necessary conveniences so much sought after in Europe; they are happy in not knowing the use of them. They live in a tranquility which is not disturbed by the inequality of condition. The earth and sea of their own accord furnishes them with all things necessary for life. They covet not magnificent houses, household stuff, etc; they live in a warm and fine climate and enjoy every wholesome air, so that they have very little need of clothing . . . in short, they seem'd to set no value upon anything we gave them, nor would they ever part with anything of their own . . . This, in my opinion, argues that they think themselves provided with all the necessarys of life.*

(In some histories of Australia, up to the middle of this century, the Cook quote stopped after the description of the Aboriginals as "the most wretched people on Earth.")

They had no written language. Instead they had an oral tradition, a complex and massive body of knowledge handed from generation to generation for thousands of years. Their creation myths begin in an era in the distant past called the Dreamtime. Before the Dreamtime, the universe was void, and without form. Then came mythical creatures who created the land and the people, rocks and rivers and deserts and mountains and flowers. The people—the Aboriginals—were given the responsibility of guarding the land. They did not own the land, the land owned them.

It can be argued that it took a while for the guardianship to get straightened out. The Aboriginals brought wild dogs with them—the dingos—which have been particularly hard over the millennia on native animals. And they brought with them the ability to hunt by fire. Aboriginal hunters, carrying firesticks, set whole forests on fire to scare out kangaroos and possums and other food, thinking nothing about the slaughter of the other animals and plants in the process.

But millennia passed—the fire-human thing has been going on for so long, that by now the bushlands of Australia must be torched once in a while to make them viable. There are species of plants that will not seed until they have been through a fire. Modern Australian land management recognizes the need for a good blaze periodically. Generally, though, like other primitive peoples with a low level of technology, these first settlers were good to their land, killing and eating only what they could carry, destroying very little.

The Aboriginals were realists, living much like wolves and other hunting species who are dependent on fluctuating food supplies. There were times to have children, and there were times when children were a danger to the tribe. They practiced abortion and infanticide, and included in their elaborate rituals were taboos designed to prevent close-relationship marriages. The concept of ownership of anything—a rock, the ocean, a piece of land—was completely alien. It was not an alien concept, of course, to the Europeans who began coming to Australia after 1788.

There had been minimal contact between Europeans and the Aboriginals for centuries before the First Fleet arrived, not always friendly and never with any understanding. The Europeans looked at the Aboriginals as complete savages. And by European standards, they were right. The native Australians had no concept of sanitation; when a camp got to be too gamy to be lived in, they simply moved on. They went around naked, they poured fish oil on themselves to fend off mosquitoes, they had no knowledge of firearms or anything else modern, they could neither read nor write, they used only the crudest of tools, and all in all they seemed to be just as the pirate William Dampier has described them in 1688, "the miserablest people in the world."

It doesn't take a genius to figure out that the Australian people were just a disaster waiting to happen. It was a miracle that a land mass the size of Australia had been sitting around for as long as it had without being tied up in a ribbon and given to a king by some explorer type looking for gold and glory. But eventually, it was claimed and handed over, to no less a light than good King George III. It was the Aboriginals' bad luck to be on the other end of the English convict trail, because if you look back at it all, the "miserablest people in the world" were probably the poor slobs coming Down Under in chains.

It is impossible to expect any group of humans (English or no) who have been brought up in an ignorant and prejudiced social system such as existed in 18th-century England to behave in any other manner than the settlers of Australia did. The convicts were, as we have described, at the bottom of the English social ladder and not prepared to treat anyone with any degree of compassion, having had none themselves—especially when the other guys were black and primitive. Partly, perhaps, it can be explained by the fact that history shows us that it is in the nature of the underdog to always try to find another underdog under him.

But it was not just the convicts, it was also the free folks of "quality" who came to Australia who saw the Aboriginals as just more pests to be disposed of, much the same way American pioneers felt about the Sioux and the Apache.

To be sure, it was official crown policy to treat the Aboriginals with respect. They were not to be attacked or molested, and each royal governor was given specific instructions to deal harshly with settlers who violated these policies. But then, London was a long, long way away, and as things started going from bad to worse between blacks and whites, it was difficult to tell a fellow English settler that he had to go to jail just for shooting a black native who was killing his sheep.

In one respect, Mother England and her white Australian children were a bit more pragmatic than the Americans. Our ancestors signed treaties with our native peoples that were to last as long as waters ran and grasses grew and the sky was blue, which in some cases was less than a decade. The English just decided to declare Australia "terra nullius," meaning that, from the preposterous English point of view, the land was unoccupied and therefore such niceties as treaties with the Aboriginals were unnecessary because there was no one to sign treaties with.

In addition to outright violence, the Aboriginals also fell easy prey to European diseases, one of the little side benefits of the colonial system that had occurred all over the world, from Hawaii to India. Thousands of Aboriginals died of smallpox and venereal diseases. The process of destruction was, for the most part, slow, urged on mainly by the ever-expanding need of the white Australians for more wheat acreage and sheep and cattle grazing areas. The fact that the sheep and the cattle were threatening the Aboriginals' food supply was of no great moment.

One of the greatest single examples of the destruction of the Aboriginals took place during an 80-year period in Tasmania. It is estimated that in 1788 there were about 4000 Aboriginals in Tasmania. That figure was reduced to a handful by 1870. The near-century process was often cruel beyond comprehension.

In 1828, the governor of Tasmania, George Arthur, ordered all the Aboriginals in the colony to vacate "settled lands," or those lands being farmed by the white settlers. Two years later, apparently because the 2000 Aboriginals left in Tasmania were vacating a tad too slowly, Arthur organized what came to be called the "Black Line." Every white male in Tasmania, 2200 freeman, troops and convicts, created a human chain across the island with the intention of driving the Aboriginals, like tigers in an Indian hunt, onto the Tasman Peninsula, a southeastern spit of land with a very narrow connection to the main island.

The line carried with it 300 pairs of handcuffs, 30,000 rounds of ammunition, and 1000 muskets. It took the men seven weeks to make the sweep, and in the end, they caught two men and a small boy—the rest had simply melted away. It was further proof that the ignorant savages the white settlers were facing were not quite that ignorant. The white Australians had learned quickly that the Aboriginals could be crafty guerilla fighters when they wanted, and in some cases, the whites got the hell knocked out of them. The settlers retaliated by hunting the Aboriginals or putting out sacks of poisoned flour for them to find.

Eventually, the remaining Aboriginals in Tasmania were led away by an English evangelist named George Robinson. Robinson, accompanied by other Aboriginals, visited every tribe in Tasmania, promising the people a haven where whites could not bother them. The haven was an island in the Bass Strait, where the Aboriginals were given Bibles, Christian names, and a healthy dose of English morality. In the end, the island became a prison and they simply died away. The last Tasmanian Aboriginal—named Trucanini, a woman who had helped Robinson in his work—died in 1876.

There were many incidents all over Australia as the white majority pacified the land, and the number of whites and blacks killed in the process is a matter of speculation, much as it is in the history of the American West. One particularly barbaric incident took place in 1838 in New South Wales at a place called Myall Creek. A group of Aboriginals had been rustling cattle and stampeding them, so a party of 12 men took chase. About 60 kilometers away, they came on a small band of blacks, later proven not to be the culprits. They rounded up almost 30 unarmed men, women, and children, roped them together, then killed them with rifles and cutlasses. The bodies were chopped and burned. Seven of the vigilante group—all either convicts or ex-convicts—were convicted of murder and hanged; four went free. The 12th man testified against them. A similar incident took place in the Northern Territory in 1927, but in that case, no witnesses could be found to testify.

There have been no comparable incidents such as these reported in post-war Australia, but the life of many Aboriginals is often dire, indeed. It is estimated that about ⅔ of them now live in urban environments. They are caught in the same terrible dilemma that faces Indians in the United States and Canada: how to live in two worlds at once. For many, it has become a struggle with alcohol and poverty. In the sandy stretches of the Todd River near Alice Springs in the Northern Territory, you see small enclaves of wretchedly poor Aboriginals, often drunk, mostly ill, living off the dole. The Alice Springs group is by no means an isolated case. Few Aboriginals anywhere in Australia return to the old ways of hunting and gathering the vast stretches of the Outback, and many studies claim that many Aboriginals are living in less than Third World conditions. They have diseases, such as tuberculosis, trachoma, leprosy, and respiratory infections. They are often illiterate, they have a high infant mortality rate, their life expectancy is far lower than their white opposites, and although they comprise only about one percent of the population, they account for 30 percent of the prison population.

There have been some advances. In 1967, the voters of Australia decided to give the power to deal with major Aboriginal problems to the federal government. Vast stretches of land have been deeded back to the Aboriginals—even Ayers Rock, Australia's most famous land mass, has been given back. In 1980, the Aboriginal Development Commission was formed. It is a federal authority empowered to acquire land for Aboriginal groups and provide money for such things as housing and business ventures. The land policies have not really solved anything, however, although innovative ADC programs have seen Aboriginal groups become ranchers and the owners of businesses.

To many Aboriginals—who seem to get a little more militant but no more potent every year—the land policy is not enough. They say the entire continent is theirs because they were invaded. (A 1963 lands case involving mining leases on traditional Aboriginal lands was decided for the state because it was ruled that, as a conquered people, the Aboriginals had no rights to the land. This legal view is changing.) With the acquisition of the lands have come decisions to close the deeded-back lands to all but the blacks, a policy that has upset many white Australians—whites can even be fined for trespassing on Aboriginal lands. "It's bloody stupid," a fellow camper told us around a fire in the Northern Territory. "See, the black Australian can go anywhere he wants to in this country because he's a citizen. But white Australians can't go onto tribal land. Is that fair?"

There are a few signs that the Aboriginals are trying to stabilize their life. One of the problems in recent years was a reluctance on the part of young black males to undertake the training and endure the rituals necessary to become a true member of an Aboriginal tribe—much of which is learning the ancient codes of ethics and tribal beliefs that have been handed down for the last 30,000 years. Guides at Kakadu National Park now report, however, that some groups of young males, apparently realizing that their traditional ways might have value, are undergoing the training. If this happens, the lessons and myths of the Dreamtime have a chance of survival.

And to be sure, there have been Aboriginals who have made the leap into white Australian society, including tennis star Evonne Goolagong; Neville Bonner, a member of parliament; Kath Walker, a famous poet, and Albert Namatjira, who won great fame as a landscape artist but died of alcoholism. They are the definite minority.

The reality is that even with the advances of the last 20 years, the Aboriginals are nowhere close to sharing the benefits of modern, prosperous white Australia. One of the most damning situations facing the nation today is the tragic record of Aboriginals who have died while in jail or in police custody. The numbers appeared to be so outrageous that a special commission was created in 1987 to study the situation. Western Australia had the highest death rate. The deaths were almost always suicides, and preliminary commission findings showed that Aboriginal prisoners—many with alcohol problems—tended to have mental problems and went into deep despair when faced with jail. The commission also said that police often ignored these mental problems. In one case, a prisoner had an epileptic fit and died after being hog-tied by officers.

The commission—formally called the Royal Commission into Black Deaths in Custody—issued its final report in early 1992, and the picture was grim. Among its findings was the fact that in the five years it had studied the problem, Aboriginal jailings increased 25 percent overall, but jumped 80 percent in New South Wales, 75 percent in Victoria and 24 percent in Western Australia. The study, significantly, said the increase in Aboriginals going to jail was not the result of more crimes being committed, but rather an increase "in government policies advocating jail as a punishment . . . it is important to analyze and question the effects of government policy which has promoted the use of imprisonment and which has adversely impacted on Aboriginal people." In the end, the commission decided that Aboriginals did not, in fact, die in prison at a greater rate than non-Aboriginals, but said Aboriginals were 30 times more likely to be in jail in the first place. The commission specifically recommended that jail terms for minor offenses such as drunkeness be done away with to reduce the number of Aboriginals in jail, but found that many states, especially Western Australia, were taking "retrograde steps" by passing legislation which actually increased Aboriginal jail sentences.

But the commisson was also hearing about lots of things taking place outside of jail. There was evidence of whites-only bars, of white people being threatened because they were friendly to blacks, blacks being locked in punishment cells naked without blankets—a very depressing list. Some Australians saw the commission inquiry as a very healthy thing. Helen Corbett, of Perth's Committee to Defend Black Rights, told *Time* magazine: "It's a big school lesson for the non-Aboriginal community of Australia on Australian history, and Aboriginal people are giving the lesson."

As for white Australia, the problem simply remains. Many believe the situation is hopeless because in the 200 years of English Australian occupation, the Aboriginals have not learned the lessons they ought: to get jobs, to buy houses and tend gardens, to join the lawn bowling league, to go into the Outback only on camping trips. Others try to begin programs to teach Aboriginal history and ethics in schools as part of an Australian history that once only began in 1788. And some would not object to having the whole issue simply go away.

Former Prime Minister Malcolm Fraser said, "We should not be guilty for our sins of 200 years ago. If that were so, there would not be a nation on earth that would not be guilty. When the English came from England, they behaved brutally. They were Englishmen. Not me, I'm Australian."

The condition and treatment of minority groups in Australia has now become a topic of international discussion. Sydney has put in a bid for the 2000 Olympics, and the Australian Olympic Committee is quite aware of the country's less-than-perfect racial record.

John Coates, president of the Australian committee, told reporters in Sydney in 1991 that the city had two large hurdles to overcome: the feeling that Australia is simply too far away and too expensive to have the Olympics, and "we have to accept that there is a perception that the old 'whites only' policies persist. We must accept that some of the world's sports officials come to Australia and do not see many black/colored people competing and they wonder why. Sydney's benefits are obvious—but we do have to work hard to show that this perception is not accurate."

The decision on Sydney's bid for the games will be known in October 1993 when the International Olympic Committee announces its choice at a meeting in Monaco.

GEOLOGY ....

Australia, like the other continents of the earth, traces its ancestry back to a point millions of years ago when the proto-continent called Pangaea started breaking up into two smaller land masses, Gondwana and Laurasia, from which finally evolved today's seven continents.

Australia was part of Gondwana, a name given to the ancient land mass by a Swiss geologist. Around 130 million years ago, Gondwana itself started splitting apart, and around 65 million years ago, Australia and Antarctica separated. Tasmania and New Guinea were part of Australia during times of low sea levels—Sahul was the name given to the low-water land mass that included Australia and New Guinea during the Ice Age. When the last ice age ended and sea levels rose, New Guinea and Tasmania were cut off again. Although Australia was never covered by one of the polar ice formations, glaciation took place because of the extremely cold temperatures.

Geologically, Australia is considered the oldest continent. Here you can find rocks containing crystals formed 4.3 billion years ago—part of the earth's very first crust. Before the Permian Period and its widespread glaciation, Australia had already gone through most of the uplifting and shifts that were responsible for creating its alpine ranges. The continent had been flooded by seas and subjected to tidal forces and the effects of glaciation, rifting, fracturing, volcanic eruptions, and finally, erosion. In fact, while the rest of the continents were changing and forming into what we know today, Australia was already in decline, its landscapes flattening out, its climate drying up.

The Western Plateau was once an island in the middle of a flooded Australia. It spreads across almost half the continent, taking in the Kimberley and Hamersley Ranges, the Great Sandy Desert, the Gibson Desert and the Great Victoria Desert. Though it was flooded many times, it was always the essential core of the continent.

Fossils of some of earth's oldest creatures have been found on the plateau—3.5-billion-year-old stromatolites, layered rocks resembling cabbage heads that are produced by the activity of photosynthetic organisms. (These fossils are also found in southern Africa, along the shores of Lake Superior and in the Grand Canyon.)

In Shark Bay, on the northwest coast of Australia, are some modern cousins of those ancient life-forms: the blue-green pillars of the Hamelin Pool are living stromatolites. The pillars, standing on the sunlit shallow seafloor, give us some idea of what the scenery was like 2000 million years ago.

In Bitter Springs, in the Northern Territory, remains of green algae dated at about a billion years have been found. Green algae are recognized as one of the first living organisms that contained genetic material. Just recently, the oldest known fossil of a flowering plant found anywhere in the world was discovered in southwestern Australia. When first studied, it was thought to be a fern, but examination under a microscope revealed it to be a flowering angiosperm with fruit around its seed. It is only one inch tall, but it is 120 million years old and may be the ancestor of all the world's seed-bearing plants.

ANIMALS..

Marsupials and Monotremes

The first time you see a platypus, kangaroo, or frilled lizard, you figure the animals in Australia were designed by a committee headed by Dr. Suess. When descriptions of some of Australia's more peculiar life forms reached Britain after colonization began, they were simply not believed. Later, when specimens were taken back to England, they were written off as more evidence that things were totally screwy in His Britannic Majesty's colony Down Under—after all, harummph, what could you expect from a country that was, well, upside down?

The marsupials and monotremes of the Island Continent prove beyond a doubt that Mother Nature does have a sense of humor. When Australia drifted off by itself after the breakup of the ancient proto-continents, it took most of the world's supply of marsupials with it. Today, 13 of the 16 known families of marsupials are found in Australia. There are more than 180 species around the country, which have filled in almost every niche held in other parts of the world by placental animals. By a process called convergence evolution, many of the marsupials closely resemble their placental counterparts.

Not content with planting most of the world's marsupials in Australia, nature also decided to bestow monotremes on the continent, the only place in the world they are found. There are only two species: duck-bill platypuses and echidnas.

The term monotreme means the animals have only one passage for both waste and reproduction. Both species are egg layers but suckle their young and seem to be a link between reptiles and mammals. Monotremes have eye and bone structures similar to reptiles, and their young even have tooth-like structures resembling egg teeth when they are born. But they also have milk, are warm-blooded, and have fur.

Both species of monotremes in Australia have filled a placental niche. The platypus is Australia's freshwater otter, and the echidna is Australia's hedgehog or porcupine.

Platypuses are shy aquatic feeders, normally under two feet long with fine, thick fur. When underwater, their eyes and ears are covered by flaps of skin and they find food using their very sensitive bills. They can eat their weight in grubs, worms and shrimp every day. Like muskrats and beavers, platypuses are diggers, living in extensive and winding burrows hollowed in riverbanks. They are normally solitary animals, coming together only for mating, which is done in the water. Because they are aquatic animals, evolution decided not to give them a pouch. Instead, the mother builds an elaborate burrow where she lays her eggs, then uses body heat to incubate them. In about two weeks, the eggs hatch and the babies begin suckling. The young might stay in the nesting chamber for as long as four months before they are allowed to hunt in the river or lake bottom with their mother. Like so many other things in Australia, platypuses are deceiving. The male, while normally a docile creature, does have poisonous spurs on his hind feet.

Echidnas, about the size of a large house cat, have short quills, about two to three inches long. They are equipped with powerful digging claws, a long, tubelike snout and a sticky tongue. They feed on ants and termites, and are nomadic land-dwellers tolerant of temperature extremes, and thus much more common than platypuses. Because they are constantly on the move foraging for food, they have adapted a marsupial-like method of reproduction. After about two weeks of gestation, the mother finds a temporary burrow to lay her eggs. In the meantime, she develops a temporary pouch where the eggs are placed after they are laid. She continues to move around while the eggs are incubated in the pouch for about 10 days. When the young are born with the aid of an egg tooth, they are about a half-inch long and feed from milk oozed from the mother's mammary glands. They stay in the pouch until they develop spines, then live in a temporary nest for about three months. They are able to live at least 50 years.

The results of convergence evolution in Australia will often astound you. The critters Down Under almost always remind you of something back home (the kangaroo is a definite exception.) Where you look for a chipmunk or squirrel, you find the sugar glider. If you look for a small primate in a rain forest, you find a brush-tailed possum or a cuscus. There are marsupial moles, marsupial rats, marsupial mice. There are wombats, which are similar to the capybaras of South America and look like guinea pigs on steroids. There was also the Tasmanian wolf (thylacine) now believed to be extinct, and the spotted-tailed quoll, the present marsupial answer to a wild cat.

Marsupial comes from the Latin word, marsupium, meaning pouch, or purse. Marsupials are mammals, but differ from mammals in the way they reproduce. Depending on the species, the gestation period for a marsupial is from about a week to around 40 days. The young are born tiny and undeveloped, and by some unknown process—instinct, gravity, smell—must migrate from the birth canal to their mother's pouch to find the milk source. If they become disoriented and lose their way, they die. If everything goes well, the babies will be attached to their mother's teats within three minutes or so, and it is in the pouch, permanently attached to the teats like an umbilical cord, that final development takes place.

The most successful of Australia's marsupials are vegetarians, and they are also among the most famous—koalas and kangaroos are both herbivores. But there are also carniverous marsupials, the most famous of which is the Tasmanian devil. The devils, although wary of humans, are formidable scavengers and have jaws with chewing pressure equal to a shark. There are also marsupials that will eat anything, and include bandicoots and the many species of tree-dwellers that like insects and small reptiles as much as fruit and nectar.

Probably our favorite animals in Australia are the Bennett's wallabies we met near Cradle Mountain National Park in Tasmania. Bennett's are about three feet tall with black velvety noses and hands. The ones we fed were gentle, which is good because wallabies and kangaroos have hindclaws that can tear you open. The park wallabies are fed vegetable pellets because bread and candy can kill them. You won't find it hard to feed animals in Australia. There are animal reserves all over the country where people are allowed to cuddle a koala or feed and pet the wallabies in controlled environments. However, we have heard of instances when kangaroos got upset because the food ran out and they started kicking tourists around, so be watchful.

There are 17 families of kangaroos, divided into 52 species and a multitude of sub-species. They range in size from nine inches tall to more than five feet—not counting tail. Kangaroo is normally used to describe the three largest species: reds, grays and the mountain kangaroo, also known as a wallaroo. The other, smaller species are known as wallabies and the smallest of the lot are called pademelons. Since the arrival of Europeans in Australia, four species of kangaroos have been exterminated and 10 other species are on the verge of extinction.

The largest of the roos is the red, so named because the male aquires a bright red chest during mating season. Reds can run 60 miles an hour for short periods, can weigh as much as 160 pounds, and can jump six feet standing still and 30 feet from a running start. Gray kangaroos are almost as large as the reds, but have black-tipped tails; the reds have pale tips. Wallaroos have black hands and feet and live in hilly locales. They can withstand heat and drought better than the other kangaroos.

Young kangaroos are still connected to the umbilical cord when they start the climb to the pouch. After about five months, when it weighs four to eight pounds, the young roo—called a joey—leaves the pouch for short periods. Eventually, Mama kicks the kid out and he or she joins the herd. Kangaroos often mate just after birth, so there is a continuing supply of small roos, but during drought periods, the fertilized eggs will remain dormant until the rains come.

As the climatic conditions in Australia changed over the eons, so did the feeding habits of kangaroos. They were once forest tree-dwellers, but dwindling food supplies forced them onto the vast grasslands of the continent. They learned to eat and digest the tough grasses of the new climate, developing a new set of choppers to handle the job. Kangaroos normally go through four sets of cheek teeth in their lifetime, and roos that live beyond their normal 15 to 20 years face starvation because the supply of grinding teeth has run out.

The battle between pastoral animals and kangaroos has been going on since the first cows and sheep were introduced into Australia. Kangaroos, being native animals, are able to eat grasses sheep and cattle cannot, but they also compete with farm animals for pasture fodder. Ranchers get upset because roos are hard to contain. The fences they put up all around Australia to keep out dingos and rabbits are no match for a big roo that can jump over—or through—them.

The kangaroo is on the Australian coat of arms, and it seems a bit perplexing to realize that they routinely shoot one of their national symbols, make dog food and steaks out of it, turn its paws into ashtrays and tan its hide for leather. Not that shooting national symbols is a new thing to the world. The American bison was virtually wiped out but we still managed to put it on a nickel, anyway. If the Australians are, as they claim, smarter than we are, maybe they'll take better care of the kangaroo. Without kangaroos, why would anybody want to go see Australia, anyway?

Now, we've all seen those top-secret Space Shuttle and military rocket launches where the astronauts go up and stash high-tech satellites in orbit, right? And you probably figured they were put up there to spy on the Russkies or maybe Iraq, right? Naw. They're in orbit to count kangaroo poo.

We kid you not, some U.S. military satellites are being used to monitor the droppings of kangaroos and other Outback animals in an effort to decide who's responsible for all the environmental damage to Australia's grasslands. Environmental groups blame the millions of sheep wandering around, and farmers blame the kangaroo. (Both sides also blame wild goats, which are a very serious—and populous—threat). The satellites, in conjunction with researchers using small receivers on the ground, monitor the amount and type of droppings to determine population densities and to create computer maps and maybe settle part of the sheep-versus-kangaroo argument once and for all. It's a rotten job, but somebody has to do it.

This brings us to that most photogenic of all Aussies, the koala. Its scientific name means "pouched bear," and the word koala is Aboriginal for "drink-not," which is inaccurate because they do. Also, you have to know right up front that the koala is probably the world's best example of a successful PR campaign. Thanks in part to Qantas airline ads, plus their cute little bods, everybody thinks koalas are slow-moving, sweet little animals just ready for adoption.

Pshaw. Most Aussies will tell you that koalas are stinky, spaced out, mean-tempered little beasts. They spend their lives half-swacked on eucalyptus oil and come mating season, the males get very uptight— and mean. An Aussie farmer told us about a randy koala that disembowled a cat and a dog because they got in its way. They have evil-looking claws and are ready to use them to protect their harems, usually two or three fair damsel koalas.

Anyway, the koala has been cashiered. Qantas hired a new advertising agency in late 1991, and the grumpy koala, who became internationally famous by hanging from a tree and saying "I Hate Qantas" because it was bringing noisy people to Australia, was dumped for a new ad campaign. The thrust of the new ads is on service, safety and friendly staff. The koala may get a bit part now and then.

One of the most popular places to see a koala up close is at the Lone Pine Sanctuary outside Brisbane. The sanctuary charges five bucks to have your photo taken with a koala, and this will prove several things to you: First, Aussies are capitalists. Second, koalas have big claws. Third, koalas stink.

Note to Canadians: Not to worry. We were assured by the koala keepers that the little fellas only go toity on Japanese and American tourists. They figure about every 1,000th tourist gets his or her chemise dampened. We were 998 and 999.

Koalas were hunted almost to extinction for their cute, cuddly little pelts, and are now protected by the federal government. Koalas reproduce slowly—maybe once every other year—and are in constant danger from fires because the eucalyptus trees they live in literally explode in bush fires. There are more than 30 species of eucalypts in Australia, and the koalas will feed on about 20 of them. Their favorite is the sugar eucalyptus. They have highly refined livers that filter out the bacterial cultures and poisons in their food supplies. Koalas must eat about 20 pounds of foliage a day, which is digested with the aid of an appendix four times the length of their bodies.

At least one group of folks still think the critters are worthwhile. In early 1991, a group of Japanese and Australian women in Tokyo set up a fund to plant blue-gum eucalyptus trees in Australia to replace those cut down in koala habitats. The leader of the group, a Japanese ballet instructor, said since Japanese companies were the ones cutting down most of the trees, it was only right that a Japanese fund be set up to help the koalas. The goal is to plant a forest of 2,800 trees in the next 10 years. The trees will be planted in Cowra, about 200 miles west of Sydney.

The Tasmanian devil, made famous in Bugs Bunny cartoons, is the largest known carnivorous marsupial in Australia. There are people who claim to have seen the extinct Tasmanian wolf from time to time, but until and if one is definitely spotted, the devil is the meat-eating champ. Once found all over Australia, they are now found only on the island of Tasmania. Some researchers speculate that the introduction of the dingo by migrating Aboriginals caused too much competition for the devils on the mainland and they died out. Dingos never made it to Tasmania.

The devil's body shape is much like a badger with a bear-like head. They grow about two to three feet long, and are solitary animals, although they will congregate to share in a large chunk of carrion. The cartoon image of the devil was not far wrong—they will eat damned near anything. When presented with a half-carcass of a road-kill kangaroo, they start at the end of the tail and go forward, no thought about tender parts at all. Their incredible jaw pressure allows them to feast on bones, gristle, whatever.

Devils become sexually mature around two years old, and females never give birth to more than four babies—she has only four teats. The little devils stay in the pouch for about three months, and then move to a burrow, usually a tree trunk or an old wombat burrow. The young are dependent on the mother for at least five months.

One of the most common groups of marsupials in Australia are phalangers, called possums by the Aussies. Possums form a large group of species, all tree-dwellers, whose second and third back digits have fused, creating a sort of two-pronged fork. They have apposable big toes and some species have prehensile tails. In size, they range from the dormouse possum at eight inches long to the four-foot-long, 15-pound cuscus. Among the many species are the gliders (four types), striped possums, ringtails, brawny brush-tails and the tiny honey possum, which feeds on nectar. Almost all are nocturnal. Hard to spot in the wild, many species are found in zoos all over the country. A cousin to the tree possums is the bandicoot, which also has the fused back digits, which are used for digging rather than hanging onto branches.

There are native mammals in Australia as well, but only a few species, mostly rats or bats. The best known of these is the flying fox, a large fruit bat with a wing span of up to about five feet. They are nocturnal, but do not use sonar to find food. They can range as far as 30 miles or more foraging for food.

Probably the most famous Australian mammal is the dingo, generally believed to have been brought to the continent by the Aboriginals. They are adaptable, sometimes hunting in loose packs for large prey such as kangaroos, sometimes feeding on insects and road kills as solitary hunters. They also prey on domestic livestock and are well and truly hated by ranchers. In addition to putting out poison meat for them, ranchers over the years built a fence to keep them out—the fence was 3000 kilometers long. Dingos can howl but not bark, and are nocturnal hunters.

Birds

The other animal that graces the Australian coat of arms with the kangaroo is the emu, Australia's answer to the ostrich and the rhea. There is only one species of emu left in Australia, and it can reach five feet tall and weigh 120 pounds. Emus are not well liked by ranchers, who see them as competitors for fodder, and who are not reluctant to crush their eggs when they are found, put out poison food, or shoot them. As recently as 1964, Western Australia had a bounty on them, and the folks in South Australia, taking a page out of the dingo book, built a 500-kilometer-long fence to keep the big birds out of sheep pastures.

Emus are pretty stupid. It's hard to tell the sexes apart; females are *slightly* larger. About ten eggs are laid at a time, and the incubation and hatching is left to the males. They seem to be fairly unaggressive, and will eat out of your hand. They are popular zoo animals.

Another of Australia's flightless birds is the cassowary, which can also hit five feet. You find them in the rain forests of Northern Queensland and New Guinea. They have distinctive heads, with a helmet of bone and bright purple, blue and yellow skin, and a red wattle. Males are again left in charge of hatching and raising the kids.

Australia also has three species of mound-building birds: the mallee fowl, the brush turkey, and the scrub fowl. The birds spend 11 months a year preparing a nest, laying eggs, and maintaining the nest. The females help dig the basic nest and lay down a compost layer. After the eggs are laid, they are covered up and the heat of the compost incubates the eggs. The males are in charge of opening and closing the nest hole to regulate the temperature, and when the chicks have hatched, they must dig themselves out. After the kids make it to the world, the parents take a month off, then start the whole thing all over again.

Birds in Australia are just like the marsupials. You look at them and they sure seem familiar, but there's always something just a little out of whack. Swans? Sure, but they're black. Pelicans, all right, but with pink bills, gray feet, and black and white feathers. A bird that is the spitting image of a red-winged blackbird, except the wing markings are white. The list goes on and on, making the 750-odd species of Australian birds a bird-watcher's dream come true.

Australia's best-known bird is probably the kookaburra, the laughing bird. There are two types of kooks in Australia; one makes the famous insane laugh; the other, while more colorful, is mostly silent. The birds, giant kingfishers, are sometimes very pesty around campfires, and a treeful of them can wake you from a very sound sleep.

If you come from North America, where parrots and parakeets are in cages and cockatoos are in zoos, Australia will drive you crazy. How about a whole tree filled with parakeets or parrots, or the sky white with cockatoos? The cockatoos, as a matter of fact, are noisy, obnoxious, and the bane of campers all over the country. In Australia, they're called galahs, which is also an uncomplimentary word for somebody who has a big mouth.

Many of the most colorful of the country's birds are found north of the Tropic of Capricorn. Here you find the dazzling little bee-eaters, finches, flycatchers, bowerbirds, and ducks—something like 117 species. A favorite birding area is Kakadu National Park, whose flood plains and waterways are major nesting areas for such birds as the Australian storks, magpie geese, herons, fish eagles, and sacred ibis. Australia's major aerial predator is the wedge-tailed eagle, which has been trapped and killed in large numbers because ranchers mistakenly assumed it was preying on livestock. The hawks are mostly carrion eaters and have been instrumental in keeping the rabbit population under control. Rabbits, one of the more destructive pests introduced into the country, at one time were as bad as locusts.

The Australian bustard, a large, slow-flying bird, is endangered because the early settlers found it was quite tasty. Although it's now against the law to shoot them, they are still hunted. The prize for best hustle in the forest goes to the various species of bowerbirds. The males create elaborate bowers to entice lady friends. The bowers are decorated with anything colorful that can be found, and the birds are notorious camp robbers. Some species are so precise about the whole thing that if an article is put into the bower and doesn't suit his color scheme, he'll remove it. Once the lady has come calling, if she does, the bower is abandoned. This is the ultimate in bachelor pads, built with only one thing in mind.

The prize for best overall performance, however, has to go to the male lyrebird, which woos the lasses with magnificent silvery tail feathers, aided by a courtship dance—plus a courtship structure along the lines of a bower. All the while that's going on, he is mimicking every bird call in the forest.

Reptiles, Amphibians, Fish, and Snakes

Just when you thought it was safe to go into the desert . . . meet the perentie goanna, a little number that lives near Ayers Rock and can grow to eight feet. The Australian goannas—a corruption of the word iguana—are monitors, one of 500 species of lizards found in Australia. About 200 of them live in arid areas, feeding on termites. The termites, called white ants in Australia, survive by eating the hardy and widespread spinifex plants.

The most spectacular of the reptilian beasties is the frilled lizard, so named because when disturbed, it stands up on its skinny hind legs, opens parasol-like fans of skin along its throat, and runs like hell. Australia has several species of skinks, both legged and legless varieties, and there are also several species of geckos.

Australia has two species of crocodiles, the saltwater and the freshwater. The saltwater, or esturine crocodiles, live in fresh and saltwater coastal waters and grow to huge lengths. They are highly dangerous. The freshwater variety is *supposedly* no danger to humans.

There are no true toads native to Australia, but one of the ones that came calling is now a major problem. The cane toad was introduced from Hawaii in 1935 in an effort to control beetles eating the cane. The toads are not ground dwellers, however, and didn't bother eating the beetles. Before they knew what was happening, Queensland farmers had a useless—and dangerous—toad on their hands. The toads are large enough to eat small mammals and reptiles, and they also have poison glands behind each eye powerful enough to kill a dog. The Queenslanders are fighting back; one method being tried is broadcasting recordings of male cane toads in an effort to lure the females into traps.

Snakes? Yes, indeed, Australia has snakes, and the general rule is, if you see a snake, it's probably poisonous. There are no true vipers, but there are 70 species of elapids, or front-fanged snakes. It's not clear how these snakes got to Australia, because they are comparatively recent arrivals in the snake world. The two deadliest snakes are the taipan and the tiger snake, found in Northern Queensland and the Northern Territory. Another one to watch out for is quaintly called the death adder. Others to avoid are the Australian copperhead, brown snake, and the red-bellied black snake.

As long as we have your attention, you might as well know about two very nasty spiders that can cause major harm to humans: the red-back (black widow genus) and the funnel web. The red-back is mostly a desert spider found under old pieces of debris. The funnel web, according to popular lore, is found under toilet seats and only in the Sydney area. And let us not forget the bird-eating spider, about the size of a mouse and fond of noshing on frogs and rodents.

Australia has some of the most beautiful moths and butterflies in the world. The largest and most spectacular are the Cairns birdwing butterfly and the brilliant blue Ulysses. The female birdwing is huge, eight inches from wingtop to wingtop. Once she has mated, she can produce eggs for life, a fact often overlooked by the smaller but more colorful male who keeps trying to get another date. Both the birdwing and the Ulysses are found in rain forests in Queensland and some close-in islands. The largest moth in Australia, and one of the largest in the world, is the Hercules moth. The females have a wingspan of more than eight inches. The poor ladies have a sad story. They are born without mouths, so after they mate and lay eggs they starve to death.

The very worst insects in the whole country, as far as most people are concerned, are bush flies. They don't bite, but they get in your eyes, up your nose, down your blouse, and up your shorts, and have created what is widely known as the "Australian wave," a constant back-and-forth flutter of the hand to keep the damned flies away from your face. They are, by the way, just one of 6300 species of flies in the country. Bush flies, as far as we know, are impervious to anything short of an atomic bomb. Even Rid, the very powerful repellent sold in Queensland, doesn't affect them.

Water Creatures

Finally, because it is surrounded by water, Australia is the home of thousands of aquatic animals and plants, from world-class marlin to plankton that have drifted in from Antarctica and are in turn eaten by right whales who come to eat and mate. Just to whet your appetite:

Fur seals along the coast of South Australia and Western Australia. Dugongs in submarine meadoes on the east coast. Something like 2500 species of fish in the waters surrounding the continent. Sea horses off South Australia. The very poisonous and small blue-ringed octopus in the Barrier Reef, along with deadly cone shells. Crown of thorns starfish, which can strip a reef bare of coral in months. Hard corals. Soft corals. Three-foot-wide clams. Sharks. Salmon. The incredible edible barramundi. Prawns, oysters, crayfish. All you need is a marine guide and some drawn butter.

FLORA....................................

If you wonder what sort of tree you're looking at in Australia, the chances are it's a eucalypt—95 percent of the continent's 700 varieties of trees are eucalypts. Familiar to most people in the San Francisco Bay area (some freeways are lined with them), eucalyptus trees were first brought to California from Australia in 1856, and are used as wind-breaks and ornamental timber because of their rapid growth. (Actually, we planted them so visiting Aussies would have a little reminder of home.) There are whole generations of Californians who think they're native to the state. In the fall of 1991, many residents of Oakland learned first hand what a lot of Australians had known for a long time—eucalyptus trees literally explode in a fire. The terrible blaze that hit the Oakland hills was partially fueled by large stands of blue-gum eucalyptus trees, which cover many neighborhoods all over the state. The city of Oakland is thinking about banning the planting of any more eucalyptus trees, but getting rid of the ones that are left will be difficult. The trees are tenacious—if you don't pull the stumps and all the roots completely out, full-size trees will grow back within 10 years. In Australia, the various varieties of eucalypts that shed their bark are usually called gum trees. Aussie eucalypts can range in size from small shurbs maybe 1.5 meters high to giants that rise more than 200 feet into the air.

Australian plants are just like Down Under animals—they all look familiar, but somehow, there's always something just a little bit wrong with them. Just to add to the confusion, the Aussie names for some plants vary from state to state. We made the mistake (several times) of asking the locals the name of a plant—it was like taking a poll. Also, forget Latin names. Why use dull nomenclature when you can deal with such things as "she-oaks" and "cathedral figs?" Anyway, from the rain forests of Eastern Australia and Tasmania to the hardy and often grotesque plants that inhabit the wastes of Central and Western Australia, the continent has wonderfully diverse plant life.

The forests of Northern Queensland are full of hiking trails and campgrounds, and here you find such dandy floral creations as the giant moss, which can have individual plants 20 inches in diameter. Australian rain forests are also home to some very beautiful orchids, many species of which can be shipped back to the United States if you want to grow them. You also find palms and some 30 species of mangroves. The mangrove roots often grow above ground because there is no oxygen in the swampy soil, and can be as tall as a man. In the Queensland highlands is red cedar that was highly valued in Victorian England— tons of the stuff were shipped off to build Old Bailey, the London courtroom complex. The Aboriginals made wide use of native plants. One, the Leichhardt tree, supplied them with bark for canoes, poisons for fish, pain killers, and dyes.

There are 16 species of fig trees in Australia, the most interesting being the strangler figs. In the Atherton Tablelands near Cairns are two superb examples of the strangler, the cathedral fig and an even more dramatic example, the curtain fig. (See Atherton Tablelands.)

Nut cases will be interested to note that another native Australian plant has also been introduced into the United States besides eucalyptus trees: macadamia nuts. Rarely seen in their natural state any more in Australia, the nut trees have proven to be a boon to the Hawaiian economy—if the residents of the Big Island can keep the lava off their farms.

Also, Australia being Australia, something has to be nasty, and in this case it's stinging shrubs, which have very painful stingers that can cause swelling, shock, and breathing difficulty. Sometimes the symptoms last for months. The plants usually grow in cleared areas—such as beside well-used trails. If you wear shorts while hiking in a rain forest, don't touch anything.

The rain forests all over the country are noted for huge ferns, but in Tasmania the tiny backyard ferns we're used to in North America have run amok. One species, called the man fern, is very ancient, with fossil records going back 300 million years.

Even in the vast arid center of Australia, all it takes is a little water and suddenly you have flora as far as you can see. Look for Sturt's desert pea, the state flower of the Northern Territory; rose dock, an imported variety of hops that turns the desert floor near Ayers Rock a crimson in the spring; the yellow-stalked flowers of the mulga trees; the blues of the wild potato bush; the bitter melons, whose seeds are so loved by cockatoos. In vast and arid Western Australia alone, there are more than 7000 varieties of wildflowers.

Australia also has varieties of some of the oldest plant species in the world. In a tiny gorge in the Northern Territory, for example, is a grove of cycad and cabbage palms. This type of plant (they have exposed seeds, much like pine cones) first appeared on earth about 350 million years ago. A close relative, the macrozamia cycads, is found in Western Australia. It's fascinating to note that one of the ways these cycads survive such a harsh environment is with a little help from an even older species: blue-green algae live on their roots and help provide nourishment.

Throughout the arid regions of the country you find spinifex, which from a distance looks like sagebrush. There are blackboy trees that resemble the strange Joshua trees of southeastern California. And up in the mountains of Victoria and New South Wales, you find alpine flowers. In national parks not far from Sydney, you can find snow-gums (sub-alpine) and forests of Antarctic beeches. Near Melbourne are some remaining groves of the native mallee trees, a form of scrub eucalyptus that was a real pain to early farmers trying to clear the land.

The islands off the eastern coast, both coral and continental, have rain forests where you can find octopus bushes (they have long flowering arms) and dwarf poinsettias. Magnetic Island, off Townsville, has pine trees, banyans, she-oaks and the orange and scarlet blooms of the poincianas.

The country is also filled with food plants, from the banana and pineapple groves of Queensland to the grapes of Western Australia and the apple orchards of Tasmania.

There are so many plants in Australia *only* found in Australia that you could spend your whole vacation Down Under tracking them down. Because so many of the plants are alien to the Western Hemisphere, we strongly urge you get a guide book when you get to Australia, even if it's very basic. This will stop you from going mad when you wander across some strange Aussie fern that looks like something from the other side of the looking glass. One of the best sources of such books can be found at the various national park headquarters around the country. Park flora guides, usually priced below A$5, have the added advantage of concentrating on the plants in the immediate area.

MAINTAIN AN EVEN STRINE ....

Yes, most Australians do have a peculiar accent. And, like North Americans, the width and complexity of that accent varies from city to city and state to state. Some Aussies speak English like the English; others are almost impossible for the North American ear to understand. Many New Zealanders feel it's a mortal sin if you confuse them with the Aussies; same for Australians similarly mistaken for Kiwis. We can't detect many differences between the two—but don't feel bad, because most Australians and New Zealanders can't tell Canadians and Americans apart either, eh.

Some observers like to make a big deal out of Australian slanguage—affectionately called ''Strine'' (from ''Aus-strine,'' the way they say ''Australian'')—and make it sound like you're about to enter some sort of linguistic haunted house. But rest assured you will not, in most cases, need an interpreter. The Aussies will tell you, of course, that it's we who have the accent. Being polite and peaceful, we never bother telling them that when the first of Mel Gibson's Road Warrior flicks *(Mad Max)* was shown on American network TV, the whole thing was dubbed by American actors so us poor Yanks wouldn't have to contend with all that garble. In truth, and this sounds peculiar to Americans and Canadians who speak old-fashioned Midwest North American, it's probably going to be the Aussies who have trouble understanding you, not the other way around.

The scene is a general store in the Queensland Outback. Our hero, discovering he has failed to pack a towel, asks the matronly lady for help. ''Need a towel,'' he says. Blank look. ''You know,'' slowly, like he's talking to somebody in Hungary, ''a tow-el?'' Further blank look. So he tries charades, pulling an imaginary towel to and fro over his back. ''Oh,'' she says, finally understanding, ''you're wanting a tawl.''

If you really get into it, Aussies slang is fascinating. The linguists will have you believe it's a combination of Irish and English cockney slang, added to and enhanced over the years by Aboriginal words and the peculiar lifestyle forced by the rigors of the Australian landscape. Whatever, it's a rich and bubbly stew. The only basic rule we know of is that if you give the Aussies a good, workable noun, they'll immediately put ''ie'' on the end of it. A truck driver is a ''truckie.'' Morning sustenance is ''brekkie.'' Your swimsuit is a ''cossie,'' as in costume, and of course Hogan always puts that shrimp on the ''barbie.'' That's also why they call themselves ''Aussies'' (make sure you pronounce that ''Ozzies''), and why that state south of the Bass Strait is called ''Tassie,'' pronounced ''Tazzie.'' A secondary diminutive form is to add an ''o'' to a noun, as in ''going troppo'' for somebody who's gone nuts in the tropics, "arvo," afternoon, or a favorite in these quarters, "journo" for a member of the press.

There's only one way to describe the way a true Aussie speaks, and that's like an Australian. Take the expression: "Rise up, lides." A plea for insurrection? Nope, those are the things you shave with. This is another major Aussie trait: A's are like I's, which is why that most famous of all Aussie words, "mate," comes out sounding like "mite." You'll also find that the Australians, being an earthy lot, tend to have a fair number of earthy expressions wandering around. Like describing a tall, arrogant person as "a thin streak of pelican shit." Or like leaving in a hurry, "off like a bride's nightie," or extremely morose, as in "happy as a bastard on Father's Day." One of our particular favorites is the "technicolor yawn," which is what you do when you've had too much to drink. Bastard, by the way, is the universal Aussie word, used generally as a term of endearment, but also used to show derision, as in "pommie bastard," the standard description for any Englishman. "Bloody" comes in a close second, being the universal adjective as in "my bloody oath," a common expression.

There are a few things you should know, just for self-preservation. For example, if some clot wearing an Outback hat asks you, as a gesture of Aussie-American harmony, to "shout the bar," tell him to get lost. When it's your shout, it's your turn to buy a round for your pals. If you shout the bar, you just bought one for the whole bloody pub, you poor bloody bastard.

A couple of phrases are all it takes to be a dinky-die (real, authentic) Aussie:

No worries—Everything's dandy, thanks.
She'll be right—The Aussie equivalent of "don't worry, be happy."
Dinkum, fair dinkum—honest, genuine.
Too right—Absolutely.
You're right, she's right—No worries.
Galah—noisy clod, named after bird of the same name.
Seppo, septic—American, from septic tank. We're not sure how this one got here, but apparently it came about because of the influence of cockney rhyming slang, and tank rhymed with Yank, not because the Aussies hold us in, uh, low regard.

The thing to do, if you're really crazy about Strine, is to find a good travel bookstore someplace that has an Aussie dictionary. Or wait until you get Down Under and find a little gem called *The Dinkum Aussie Dictionary,* by somebody called Crooked Mick of the Speewa, which has a nummy assortment of Australianisms with which to wow the crowd. (Child & Associates Publishers.)

Finally, if you really want to get in good with the blokes Down Under, learn The Song. For most of its history, white Australia managed to get along without an official national anthem, being content to let *Waltzing Matilda* do the job. But apparently some folks thought it was a bit demeaning to have a national tune based on a bum who steals a sheep, then commits suicide when the cops show up, so they picked up a new anthem, *Advance Australia Fair.* The new number is pretty uninspired, and sounds like most of the national anthems in the world: very pompous and sort of English. But at heart the true Aussie national hymn remains *Waltzing Matilda,* a tune that is almost universally associated with Australia.

So here goes:

Once a jolly swagman camped by a billabong,
under the shade of a coolabah tree.
And he sang as he watched and waited 'till his billy boiled,
"Who'll come a-waltzing Matilda with me?"

(The chorus throughout always repeats the last two lines of the previous stanza, so:)

Waltzing Matilda, waltzing Matilda,
You'll come a-waltzing Matilda with me;
And he sang as he watched and waited 'till his billy boiled,
"Who'll come a-waltzing Matilda with me?"

(A swagman, or "swaggie," was a hobo, so called for his swag, the tied-up bag or roll of personal belongings he carried around. A billabong is a pool of water that remains in a dry creek bed after the rainy season ends. A coolabah tree is a species of gum, or eucalyptus. A billy is a tin can or pot used to boil water for tea. "Waltzing Matilda" itself has many definitions inside the song; here it means to wander around with your pack, or matilda.)

Down came a jumbuck to drink at that billabong,
Up jumped the swagman and grabbed him with glee;
And he sang as he stowed that jumbuck in his tucker bag,
"You'll come a-waltzing Matilda with me."

(Jumbuck is a lamb or young sheep. Tucker bag is a bag where the swaggie kept his food, or tucker. Waltzing Matilda here means the swaggie plans to nosh on the sheep.)

Up rode the squatter, mounted on his thoroughbred;
Down came the troopers, one, two, three.
"Where's that jolly jumbuck you've got in your tucker bag,
"You'll come a-waltzing Matilda with me."

(Squatter was a wealthy rancher or farmer, troopers were probably the local cops. Here waltzing Matilda means they're going to incarcerate the poor swaggie.)

Up jumped the swagman, and sprang into the billabong;
"You'll never catch me alive," says he.
His ghost can be heard as you pass by the billabong,
"You'll come a-waltzing Matilda with me."

The normal way to sing *Matilda* is loudly, with great feeling. The last chorus, about the swaggy's ghost, is often sung softly. Aussies will do Matilda at the drop of a hat, so memorize the words and join in. It's a lot easier to sing than the *Star-Spangled Banner* and has a lot more teeth than *Oh, Canada.*

DRIVING ·····································

It was somewhere between Hughenden and Cloncurry, in north-central Queensland, no houses and no people for a million miles, when we decided to pull off the bitumen and take a break. That's what they call pavement in Australia, bitumen, pronounced "bitch-oo-min." So we pulled off and parked under the shade of a big gum tree. That's when we discovered that there's more to driving in Australia than just being on the wrong side of the road.

See, you can't trust Aussies because they're outrageous kidders and love nothing more in the world than to slip one past some poor Yank tourist. So when we rented the pop-top VW camper, back in Townsville, the guys in the pub gave us all sorts of horse hockey about giant, man-eating kangaroos in the Outback, and 300-pound koalas, and herds of deadly snakes and, of course, bulldust.

"Struth, mate," one of the worst fibbers told us, "there's places out there where they've lost whole trains in the dust. It's 30 feet deep and looks like solid rock, fair dinkum." Well, we did our research, and we knew there were no giant carnivorous roos in Queensland any more, let alone 300-pound koalas. So we just ignored all the stuff about treacherous pools of bulldust.

Bad mistake, very bad mistake.

It was nice and cool in the shade of the old gum tree after we pulled off and parked, and we had a cold beer and a hot sandwich and enjoyed the crows and the breeze. And when we started to back out, we knew we were well and truly in deep yoghurt. Or in this case, deep dust.

Bulldust may not come in 30-foot-deep pools, but there's enough of it around to get novice Outback drivers in all sorts of trouble. Bulldust is fine, very fine dust, almost like baby powder, and you can't get traction in it at all. It sits in the sun and gets a crust on it and looks just like solid ground. Eventually, some tourist pulls off the highway onto what looks like hard dirt and buries his or her car or camper up to the axles. It's not only Canadians, Germans and Americans who end up mired, either, because a fair number of slickers from Sydney and Canberra have met the same fate. And without 4-wheel drive, bulldust can ruin an otherwise perfect day. (With some fancy back-and-forthing, rocking and popping the clutch, we finally managed to get out of the foot-deep dust and back on the main road. Not having 4-wheel drive, we were very lucky).

We raise the spectre of bulldust not to dissuade you from driving in Australia; indeed, it ends up being one of the little challenges of driving Down Under that makes a trip just that more memorable.

At the same time, bulldust and the other hazards of driving in Australia are not to be taken too lightly. Our little set-to with the dust was not serious—the biggest threat we faced was mortification if anybody ever found out. But there are some roads, in some places, where only a damned fool (or a damned fool with a good guide) should go.

We have driven all over Australia, from the Kansas-flat stretches of cattle and sheep country in Queensland to the forests of Tasmania to the red-coated stretches of the Stuart Highway from Darwin to Ayer's Rock. And seeing that we highly recommend that anybody serious about seeing Australia rent a car or camper and take off, it's only fair that we try to fill you in on some of the subtler forms of disaster you can run into tooling around Down Under. In addition to good old bulldust, try these:

THE BASIC PROBLEM—This is, of course, the fact that we drive on the right and the Aussies drive on the left. Depending on your coordination and reaction times and common sense, this can be a very large deal, indeed, or no big thing. The most common mistake North Americans and continental European drivers make is looking the wrong way at the wrong time, usually at cross streets. The basic rule is the same that you see painted at every pedestrian crosswalk in London (where they lose an American at least once a day): LOOK RIGHT. This tendency to look the wrong way cuts both ways, of course. No less a light than Winston Churchill was hospitalized in 1931 after being knocked on his poopdeck by a New York City taxicab while he was trying to walk across Fifth Avenue. (He forgot to look left.) A sense of direction is particularly important in Australia when approaching that devilish English invention, the roundabout. We'd call it a traffic circle. Just remember to look right, because anybody coming that direction has the right of way. Once on the roundabout, remember, clockwise, go clockwise. Once on the circle, you supposedly have the right of way, but we observe the California Freeway Right-of-Way Rule: if they want it, let 'em have it.

You'll also notice that if you've rented a camper or car with a manual transmission, you have to shift left-handed (the foot controls are the same). This is no problem, and allows you to get a driver's tan on your right arm for once in your life. The bottom line is probably this: if you're a good driver in the New York or Ottawa, with a little thought and concentration, you'll be a good driver in Australia.

THE ROADS—Around major population centers and between major cities along the coasts, Aussie highways are every bit as good as North American ones, though perhaps just a tad narrower. They are well marked (make sure you're up on your international traffic signs) and well maintained. It's once you've gone past the Great Dividing Range (or in the case of Western Australia and the Northern Territory, when you get out of sight of the coast) that things get a little more challenging.

Outback roads tend to be either narrow and paved or wide and unpaved. The paved stretches, in addition to being narrow, sometimes have bad edges with jagged pavement and one-foot drops to the shoulders. And the drier the country, the more bulldust you find on the shoulders. Sometimes even pulling off two or three feet will bury your axles. Road conditions seem to be at their least maintained in rural Queensland, as any body in the state will tell you, blaming the potholes on politicians and other lowlifes.

The dirt roads are often in better shape than the pavement, particularly if a grader has been through recently. Note well, however, that nobody in the world makes washboard dirt roads like the Australians. There are some dirt roads so badly washboarded that you can lose tooth fillings from the shaking. The Aussie solution to this problem is to drive as fast as possible. This, they say, means the tires are only hitting the tops on the washboards and this reduces the shakes. We tried that once and immediately stopped before we either blew a tire or broke an axle.

The recognized rule on Outback dirt roads is to slow down when meeting another vehicle. This is so that you don't throw gravel or rocks through each other's windshields. This is a nice theory, like everybody yielding to right-hand traffic, but we estimate about half the cars we've met on dirt roads passed us doing Mach 4 (to avoid the washboarding, no doubt). You should also know that some rental companies will not insure the car or camper once it's on dirt roads. We raise this because even doing casual driving in Australia in the country can end you up on dirt roads. Unless you're in the middle of the great deserts, you should have no problems on dirt, aside from breathing dust and getting the stuffings rattled out of you. If uncertain, ask a local. Maybe he'll tell you the truth.

BUMP IN THE NIGHT—Once out of the cities, sometimes just by the time you get into the burbs, you start seeing cars and trucks with what look like aluminum roll bars attached to the front bumpers. These are called bullbars, and they have one function in life: to stop kangaroos and other creatures of the night from going through the engine when you hit them at 80 miles an hour.

Most Aussies who live in rural areas have bullbars on their vehicles, despite strong evidence to suggest that if you hit a large roo, all the bars do is slide the beast up past the engine and through the windshield. "Oh, yay," says an Aussie friend of ours, "that's usually the way tourists see their first kangaroo—coming through the windscreen." He was not joking. You'll also see a fair number of vehicles with screen mesh over the windshields. This is supposed to stop rocks from hitting the glass (and has little or no effect on incoming marsupials). From all this, you probably think your basic Australian car looks like a Sherman tank. Not true. An armored personnel carrier, maybe.

You can get some idea of how sturdy your average Australian kangaroo is built from a tragic incident related by World War II historian Martin Caidin. A fully loaded American B-17 heavy bomber, weighing in the neighborhood of 40 or 50 tons, was taking off from an Australian airfield when a kangaroo hopped in front of the heavily loaded plane. One of the B-17s tires hit the 'roo and the aircraft flipped onto its back and exploded, killing the crew.

Once out of the city lights and into the country, you should beware at all times of critters on the highway, especially at night. Back in the States and Canada, driving on country roads, you might see a rabbit or an armadillo once in a while (or now and then a moose or deer if you're in God's country—and as anybody from Alberta who's ever hit a moose will tell you, it ain't pretty.) In Australia, kangaroos love to park in the middle of the road or else jump in front of you, and there are any number of collisions involving emus, sheep and cattle. It's a jungle out there.

Probably the worst place for this is the Northern Territory. Fenced land in the Territory is infrequent, so the beasts wander around at will. The Stuart Highway is lined with carcasses. Most of the damage to animals in the Territory is not from cars. Nossir, it's mostly caused by that peculiarly Australian threat to life, limb, tourists and stray animals: the road train.

Road trains are big, humping trucks, driven by insane Mad Max types who believe that all highways in the country are one-way—their way—and that anyone or anything that gets in their way has no right to live on this planet now or at any time in the future. The trains are really semi-trailer rigs, except higher and longer. Typically three units hooked together, these little wonders can reach 50 meters in total length, headlights to back bumper—that's half a football field, folks, and if you meet one on a narrow Outback stretch of bitumen, you have one of two choices, and we almost always head for the sidelines. The truckies (that's what they call the drivers) are so lost in their distant and powerful world, they never even see you disappearing into those 30-foot-deep pools of bulldust.

So we were renting a camper in Darwin, ready to head for Alice Springs, and the guy says: "Don't drive at night, under any circumstances, now or forever." Hawso, we figured, loose water buffaloes and kangaroos, sliding up over the bullbars into our laps, right? "No," he says, "roadtrains. They drive right down the middle of the bloody road 100 miles an hour and won't move over for anybody. It's worth your bloody life to drive in the territory at night." The funny thing is, you get those guys out of their half-football-field-long rigs, and they're among the nicest Aussies in the country. They do tell outrageous lies about bulldust, though.

SIGNS OF THE TIMES—Most Aussie road signs are straightforward, but there are some worth noting. They don't yield, they "Give Way," and when you come to a detour, the signs say "Sidetrack." That's where we get our expression for being sidetracked—country roads are called tracks, even some that are wide and in good shape. One of our favorites is a "jump-up," meaning a road that goes up onto a plateau or over a hill. Once you get into cow or sheep country, you'll probably see a sign now and then saying "Grid." That means cattle guard. Or maybe you'll see a sign: "Gladstone T/O 5km." That's the Gladstone turn-off. Driving here and there will give you proof positive that not all English is American. Take the sign that says "Refuse Tip." Should you now ignore folks who try to give you a gratuity for services rendered? No, it means you're approaching a garbage dump. And nothing stirs local pride more than being able to hang a sign out on the track that proclaims "Aussieberg—1992 Tidy Town Recipient," The Australian equivalent of the All-American City awards.

RULES OF THE ROAD—Wearing seatbelts in Australia is mandatory—get stopped, and you could earn a fine. The Australians are also serious about drinking and driving, and they pay no heed to the nationality of the driver. The legal level is .05 percent, which you can hit with a couple of rounds in a pub. The normal speed limit in cities and built-up areas is 60 kph and 100 to 110 kph on freeways and highways. (This rule does not apply to Sydney bus drivers, who go no less than 60 miles an hour in any situation and are a greater hazard to life than atomic bombs.)

CAR RENTALS—Americans and Canadians can rent cars or campers (the Aussies call them caravans) with a valid driver's license as long as they're 21—some companies have restrictions for drivers under 25 or over 60.

The major rental agencies in Australia are familar to North American drivers: Hertz, Avis, Budget and Thrifty. In addition, there are many other local agencies, which often have cut rates. One of the largest in the Northern Territory, for example, is our old fave, the Cheapa Rent-a-Car Co., with small cars going for as little as A$18 a day plus kilometerage. Most rental contracts give you unlimited kilometerage and are on a per-day or per-week basis. North American insurance is not valid in Australia, and all contracts carry mandatory third-party insurance. A few things to know:

• The normal way to rent a car is by credit card, even if you intend to pay the bill in cash later. If you don't want to use a card, most companies require that you pay the total estimated costs of the car for the rental period plus a A$100 deposit. If you spend less than the estimate, you get a refund when you turn the car back in. Rental agencies also require you return the vehicle filled with gasoline. One-way rentals must be arranged in advance and there is often a drop-off charge.

• Gasoline (called "petrol" Down There) varies widely in price, with city pumps running around A80 cents a liter. In the boonies, it can go for more. This means gas prices of around US$3 a gallon. Compact, manual transmission cars get about 30 miles to the gallon. Gas stations are common on major coastal highways and in cities, but tend to get scarce in rural areas. We stopped at a place in the Northern Territory and were told the pumps were out of gas; fortunately we had enough to get to the next town. The major gasoline companies are BP, Shell, Caltex, AMPOL, Mobile and Amoco. Many gas stations will take Visa or MasterCharge cards, bless them.

• Rates vary from company to company and depend on the rental period, but for cost estimating purposes, figure a small car goes for about A$50 a day; a compact, A$55; a medium, A$60 and a large, A$75. Most car companies in Australia offer fly/drive packages. Also, good deals are sometimes offered through the various state travel offices.

Information on current packages and rates is available from a travel agent or by contacting these companies:

Avis, (800) 331–1084 USA; Budget, (800) 472–3325 USA and Canada; Hertz, (800) 654–3001 USA or (800) 268–1311 Canada; Dollar, (800) 800–4000; National, (800) 227–3876 USA and Canada; Thrifty, (800) 367–2277 USA and Canada.

CARAVAN RENTALS—Of all the ways to see Australia, this is probably the best all-around combination. A camper—called a caravan in Australia—lets you go where you want, when you want, and you're carrying your hotel with you. While not everybody's cup of tea, a caravan vacation is a great way to see the country and meet the natives. We guarantee, within five minutes of pulling in, you'll be on first-name basis with the Aussies parked on either side.

Caravaning is one of the favorite Aussie ways to take a vacation, and the extensive system of caravan parks all over the country proves it. The basic parks have water, electricity and facilities (showers, toilets, a laundry) and can range in size from a mom-and-pop outfit to enormous parks such as the one at Ayers Rock, which can accommodate hundreds of rigs. A night, including electricity, averages around A$10. Most larger parks also have on-site caravans that can be rented for a night or week and come equipped with bedding, kitchen equipment, and other necessities of life. These units normally rent for between A$15 and A$40 a night for two persons.

How good your mileage is in a caravan depends on where you're driving—and how fast. In the flatlands of the Northern Territory, for example, driving a small, cab-over self-contained camper, we got between 17 and 22 miles per gallon. In Tasmania, hilly and curvy, it dropped as low as 10 or 11.

The rental cost of caravans, as with cars, varies from company to company depending on size and rental period. Some Aussie nomenclature: a campervan is usually a pop-top, and a motorhome is closer to the North American view of an RV. They range in size from cozy to huge, even some with inside plumbing. Approximate costs are about A$760 a week for a campervan, A$1000 for a small motorhome. Some companies offer unlimited kilometerage, others add a per-kilometer charge of around A15 cents after the first 1000 kilometers. Most RVs, regardless of size, come with pots, pans, dishes, propane, refrigerators, color TVs, radios with tape decks, and more and more, microwave ovens, which are the camper's saviour. In some instances, there will be a charge of about A$20 for blankets, linens, and some kitchen equipment. In spite of the number of caravan parks, it is sometimes essential to make reservations, particularly at high-volume places such as Kakadu National Park and Ayers Rock. Caravans, like cars, are sometimes in short supply, especially around Christmas and school holidays, so advance bookings are a good idea.

In addition, most major caravan agencies have fly/drive packages available, and state tourist agencies often have special rental packages. *Information on the major rental companies is available from a travel agent or by contacting these agencies:*

Budget, (800) 472–3325 USA and Canada; Thrifty, (800) 367–2277 USA and Canada; Horizon Holidays, (818) 990–8431; Newman's, (800) 421–3326 USA; Guthreys, (800) 234–2254 USA or (800) 321–2145 Canada.

FOUR-WHEEL DRIVE—If you're thinking about a four-wheel drive, you're probably thinking about an excursion into the incredibly rugged desert and mountain country of Australia. This means you're either crazy or an old Jeep hand. Unless you've had a fair amount of experience driving around southern Utah or the California desert, we strongly recommend you avoid the true Aussie wilderness by yourself. It's moot anyway, because Aussie four-wheel drive agencies are very picky about who they let rent their vehicles. In addition to Hertz and Avis, another company that has four-wheel-drive vehicles available is Brits Rentals, Adventure Centre, 5540 College Ave., Oakland, Calif. 94618, (800) 228–8747 (California), or (800) 227–8747, USA.

Prices for four-wheelers will depend on where you are and how big a vehicle you're renting. As an example, we rented a small Suzuki to go to Cape Tribulation north of the Daintree River in north Queensland. The road wasn't that bad, but because it was dirt, washboarded and subject to flooding, we couldn't take a regular rental car. The rate was about A$90 a day, with a free 200-kilometer-a-day allowance. But we had to give them a A$1000 security deposit, which usually has to be on a credit card. You're responsible for any damage to the vehicle, including dings, dents, broken windows or undercarriage problems. This is a pretty standard contract you'll run into around the country. And, like normal rentals, you have to bring the 4-wheelers back full of gas.

This is not to say that you shouldn't try it. But if you do, play it smart. Even old Aussie desert rats tend to travel in convoys, and there are a number of four-wheel-drive clubs in the country who welcome strangers along on trips—state automobile clubs have details. The alternative is to take a guided trip with people who know what they're doing—you still get to see the incredible beauty and isolation of the Outback, but without the terror of breaking an axle all by yourself 5000 miles from the nearest mechanic. Many operators run safaris where you bring your own vehicle, and they provide routes, mechanical help, and planning.

One idea is to contact Mount Seaview Resort and Safaris, which offers a number of four-wheel-drive tours in air-conditioned, eight-seat-vehicles. The itineraries include Tasmania and a trip from Adelaide to the Alice via Coober Pedy. With hotels and food, the trips ranges from US$300 to US$1295. For information about the company, contact So-Pac, 7080 Hollywood Blvd., Suite 201, Hollywood, Calif. 90028; tel. (800) 551–2012.

A few other agencies that do trips include AAT King's, Australian Pacific Tours, Centralian, Desert-Trek Australia and Trekabout Expeditions. The Australian Tourism Commission has further information about four-wheel-drive vacations.

SOS—The Australian equivalents of the AAA and CAA can be a big help for visiting drivers, offering map service, accommodations guides, national park information and brochures. The Aussies have reciprocal agreements with us, so take along your automobile club card.

Addresses:
New South Wales: National Roads and Motorists' Association (NRMA). 151 Clarence Street, Sydney NSW 2000, (02) 260–9222; Queensland: Royal Automobile Club of Queensland (RACQ), 300 St.

Paul's Terrace, Brisbane, QLD 4006, (07) 253–2444; Australian Capital Territory, National Roads and Motorists' Association (NRMA), 92 Northbourne Avenue, Canberra City, ACT 2601, (06) 243–8900; Victoria, Royal Automobile Club of Victoria (RACV), 550 Princess Highway, Noble Park, VIC 3174, (03) 790–2211; South Australia, Royal Automobile Association of South Australia (RAA), 41 Hindmarsh Square, Adelaide, SA 5000, (08) 223–4555; Western Australia, Royal Automobile Club of Western Australia (RAC), 228 Adelaide Terrace, Perth WA 6000, (09) 421–4444; Northern Territory, Automobile Association of the Northern Territory (AANT), 79–81 Smith Street, Darwin NT 0800, (089) 81–3837, and Tasmania, the Royal Automobile Club of Tasmania (RACT), corner Patrick and Murray Streets, Hobart TAS 7001, (002) 38–2200.

FOOD ....

The Lucky Country is aptly named when it comes to its abundance and variety of food. The Australians, despite many reports to the contrary, do eat other things besides ants, goannas, greasy mutton, and stale pumpkin scones. They are blessed with many exotic fruits, more than 2500 species of edible fish, the best lamb in the world, lean beef, and, thanks in part to the immigration rules that were changed after World War II, almost any sort of ethnic food you want.

Maybe because of the exotic food sources in the country, traditional Australian dishes generally tend to be more innovative and spicier than the usually dull colonial English fare they are based on. Still, there will not be many surprises for North American palates, which are already familiar with a number of diverse culinary styles. But the surprises, when they do come, are often strange, indeed. The first that always comes to mind is Vegemite, a dark-brown, gooey, salty vegetable yeast extract that Aussies use in much the same way we use peanut butter. They put the stuff on toast, over crackers, and in sandwiches, and start eating the junk when they're toddlers—we opine that Vegemite is one of the few things the folks Down Under have that they can keep all to themselves. Yecccch.

Another example of an acquired taste must be the use of beets on hamburgers. You must be vigilant when ordering "the works" on your burger, because in addition to the beets (they call them beetroot and they're not pickled), they love to stick in shredded carrots, which while healthful, are a definite surprise for North American hamburger aficionados.

Also, you must use care when ordering the type of bread you want your burger wrapped in. Make sure you ask if it comes on a "roll" (hard) or a "bun" (soft). If it comes in a roll, get out your knife and fork, because the roll is so hard, all the meat slides out when you chomp. We thought it was very strange to see Australians eating hamburgers with a knife and fork—but now we know why.

For the most part, you will recognize everything served up on your plate, but recognizing it on the menu can be a problem. It is easier than tackling a German, French, or Italian menu, but still, it helps to learn your way around Aussie food nomenclature. A few clues to help you with the fare d'jour:

When you see crayfish on the menu, do not order six dozen, as you might in New Orleans. Being huge fans of Lake Pontchartrain crawfish (or crayfish or crawdads), we were delighted to see crayfish offered on a menu, assuming they had discovered the little devils in Australia, and accordingly, we ordered a couple of pounds. You can imagine the surprise when instead of a few dozen small crustacea, they wheeled in a spiny sea lobster weighing about a kilo. But it was no loss—Aussie "crayfish" have sweet, firm meat and you'll have trouble eating just one. The best ones come from along the eastern shore of Tasmania, or from the cool waters of the Bass Strait, which separates mainland Australia from Tasmania, or from the waters off Western Australia. We recommend stopping at a fish market and picking up a pre-cooked, chilled crawfish. Add a bottle of Hunter Valley wine, some local cheese and bread, and a quiet beach—well, you get the idea. Crays, as they're called, are also known in some places as Southern rock lobsters.

Queensland's mud crabs are very popular around Brisbane, but probably not as big a favorite as Morton Bay bugs. Before you reach for the Raid, realize that the bug is really a small crustacean, sort of a cross between a lobster and a crayfish. In restaurants around Brisbane, you can get bugs in almost any style you want, from curried to just plain with drawn butter. Outside Queensland, Morton Bay bugs are sometimes called yabbies. And remember what Australians call prawns, we call shrimp—they only bait their hooks with shrimp. When ordering fish, we always find out what the local catch of the day is—with 2500 species to pick from, it's essential to find out which came from nearby waters. Some Australian species we can recommend are the John Dory, trumpeteer, barramundi, coral trout, redfish, gemfish, and sole.

The Australians have a strange name for chickens: they call them *chooks*. Where the name comes from, nobody seems to know, but you'll see it here and there, as in signs offering *fish and chooks*. Chicken is just becoming an alternative to red meat in Australia. A standard we always found on the menu was *Maryland chicken,* which is chook covered in breadcrumbs and then fried. (One of us grew up in Maryland and never heard of such a thing—maybe the Aussies decided that Maryland was close enough to the Confederacy to substitute for Southern-fried chicken.) Anyway, one of the more delicious ways to have your chook and eat it too is to try broasted (grilled on a spit) chicken, which can be found in fast-food places.

If your steak or salad comes with *capsicums,* it means you'll be eating green or red bell peppers. On a salad, you might get *avos,* or avocados; *pines,* or pineapples, or *paw-paws,* which are papayas. Queenslanders are fond of using pines and bananas as well as other fine fruits in everything. Do not be surprised if you find tropical fruit stuck into a steak. Also a horrid thing might happen if you order a Queensland pizza with all the trimmings—it'll come with pineapple.

In Australia, *scones* are the equivalent of our biscuits, but their biscuits are like English biscuits, meaning a cookie. Scones are often served with clotted cream as part of Devonshire teas. Adding to the confusion, you should know that a *water biscuit* is a cracker, and an *Anzac biscuit* is a popular cookie. They are a chewy, oatmeal concoction made with brown sugar. *Damper* is a campfire bread and can usually be found in cafes and restaurants in touristy areas. Hot, with lots of fresh butter, damper makes a good breakfast or complement to an afternoon tea. Often, damper is cooked with fruits added, such as raisins. For a real treat, try an Australian pancake, which is thin like a crepe, then rolled and filled with sugar and fruit. With whipped cream on the side, they are heavenly, and much less filling than Yankee flapjacks.

If it's a *brekkie* menu you are reading, you'll probably run across *snags.* Snags are sausages, and can be either fat and short (probably pork) or long and thin like hot dogs. Snags are not as spicy as North American sausage, and are made with bread filling—if you've ever had English or Scottish bangers, you'll know the taste. Pretty bland.

If you like your first meal of the day on the largish side, try an Australian *mixed grill,* a hearty dish of broiled meats, usually lamb chops, steak, and snags, along with broiled tomatoes and maybe some mushrooms. For lunch, it would include chips—french fries.

Our next breakfast offering is *toad in the hole,* a dish that can also be served for lunch or dinner. The toad in question has no warts: it's comprised of sausages cooked in an egg batter. If your server asks you if you want Vogel toast with breakfast, say yes—it's a tasty multi-grain bread. As for crisp bacon, forget it. Aussie bacon is very lean, like Canadian bacon only more so, and you can grill it all day without crisping it up.

Now we come to desserts, foremost of which are the two that Australians are proud to call their own: the pavlova and peach melba. *Pavlova,* named after the famous Russian ballerina, Anna Pavlova, is a baked meringue filled with whipped cream mixed with fresh fruit. Done properly, it's nummy; done badly, or stale, it can be like eating a used truck tire. *Peach melba* is named after Dame Nellie Melba, a beloved

Aussie soprano who supposedly had more affairs than Errol Flynn, which is saying something. You can find this dessert in many American restaurants, but if you've never had one, it's a piece of sponge cake placed in a glass dish or parfait glass, then topped with a peach half, sprinkled with sherry, and covered with whipped cream and pureed rasberries or strawberries. Both desserts are exceedingly sweet.

For an afternoon snack, you might find a *Lord Lamington's* on the menu (he was the Queensland governor at the turn of the century). Again, a sponge cake, this time cut in squares, dipped in chocolate icing, then sprinkled with coconut. (How's your cholesteral these days?) Another popular type of dessert is a *slice,* which as far as we can tell, is baked pastry sliced into strips and filled with cream custard, then iced. If you want a real cup of tea, find a tea room. You will know you're in the real thing when they bring a small tea strainer along with your pot of tea. Sorry to say, too many places simply bring a pot of hot water and a bag. The Empire, remember, has faded away.

As in England, a big Australian lunch favorite is fish and chips. The fish is usually whiting, although shark is also popular. If you're looking for ketchup for your chips (they call it *tomato sauce*), you might have a hard time; instead, they allow you to douse them in vinegar— which, as anyone knows, is the only way to eat french fries anyway. The chips, by the way, will probably not be crisp. The Aussies like them soggy (it brings out the flavor, they claim) and the chips are usually wrapped in with the fish. While we think this is a top take-out food, the Aussie favorite seems to be meat pies. The mass-produced ones we tried were not impressive; homemade ones are supposed to be better. There are many variations on the meat pie, such as sausage rolls, chicken and pork pies, and egg and bacon pies (very much like a quiche). You can buy pies almost everywhere from sporting matches to supermarket freezers, corner stores to pubs. Pies, by the way, are supposed to be eaten with tomato sauce. Ketchup, that is.

Thanks to Paul Hogan, most Americans know what a *barbie* is. In many places all over the country, you'll find pubs or restaurants that will sell you fresh meat or seafood and also have a barbie on the premises so you can cook things the way you like them. Everyone seems to enjoy the informal atmosphere, and the pubs also do a bang-up business. Barbie parties, by the way, are the single most popular way to entertain in Australia. They think, you see, that they invented the barbecue, and we haven't had the courage to tell them the truth.

A word that kept popping up at lunch counters had us mystified for a long time—*jaffles.* These turned out to be grilled—not broiled—sandwiches that come with a variety of fillings such as cheese, ham, baked beans, and even spaghetti. And of course, unless you're quick, beetroot and carrots. Potted meats (a poor man's pate) are popular as a sandwich spread when they run out of Vegemite (or the smell drives them out of the house). Be advised—in Australia, the sandwiches are thin, and the bread is almost always spread with butter.

If you see a sign that says *Milk Bar,* you've found the neighborhood corner store. You can buy milk, of course, as well as ice cream bars and maybe a milk shake. But you can also buy newspapers as well as small cooking items such as soup, soft drinks, and snacks. Never ask for a "soda" because they'll think you're after unsweetened carbonated water. If your palate hasn't been destroyed by too many pavlovas, ask for a *lolly,* or candy. And if you want some potato chips, ask for *crisps*—if you order chips, they'll probably stick in some fish. One staple of the small corner store are *cordials,* and we don't mean the alcoholic kind you find in bartenders' books. Cordials are made of sweet, non-carbonated concentrates of various fruits, usually mixed with water to make hot-weather drinks. Lemon squash cordial is mixed with soda water and is an acceptable ladies' drink in pubs.

If you come from someplace that has a Chinatown, and the folks who live there are mostly from Canton, Aussie Chinese food might throw you a curve. What they call dim sum in Canton and San Francisco is called dim sim in Sydney and Melbourne. We thought it was a misspelling, but dim sim is the Mandarin version of the same stuff—which in Australia is quite good.

Have you ever heard of a Singapore food hall? We have second-rate ones in some of our malls in the States, and usually call them ethnic food stands or specialty food shops. In some Australian cities, we only found them operating at lunch time. But in Brisbane, for example, they are open for dinner. The food hall solves the problem of satisfying a bunch of appetites at one time without moving the car. There are usually a half-dozen or more different ethnic foods to choose from, as well as the regular fish and chips and meat pie places. Italian, Chinese, Greek, Lebanese, Malaysian, even German fare is offered. In most food halls, there is also a central bar where you can get wine or beer. The drill is simple: pick out your food, pay for it (usually at a central cash register), and find a table someplace in the hall. In some fancy food halls, you put a number on your table, go pick out the food and pay for it, and the staff brings it to the table. There are usually dessert places around, as well. Some halls even have piano players or other forms of live entertainment, and the prices are almost always reasonable.

THE ESSENTIAL AUSTRALIA

WHEN TO GO • Australia, being south of the Equator, is all backwards. (They insist it's the other way around. But then, they also say we drive on the wrong side of the road.) Anyway, after 200 years, they're used to having Christmas when there's July-like weather outside and chilling out when it really is July. For example, Sydney in July averages between 8° and 16° Celsius (46°–60°F); in January, it's between 17° and 25° (62°–77°F). Alice Springs, in the geographic center, averages between 4° and 19° in July (40°–66°F), but between 22° and 37° in January (72°–98°F). (Darwin is always easy to figure: It varies between hot and steamy and hotter and steamier.)

At first blush, this would seem like a dandy arrangement for North American tourists. When we're freezing to death up here, all you have to do is hop down to Oz and it's summer. Or if you're a skiier and want to spend the whole year on the slopes, when the melts start at Squaw Valley in May, it's just beginning to get frosty in the Snowy Mountains. Only problem is, the airlines and hotels on both continents know all about the temperature differences, so the most expensive time to go to Australia is in the North American winter. The best times to go, as a balance between climate and cost, are in the shoulder periods, basically North American spring and fall. North American summer is okay for a trip to Australia, too, as long as you stay north in Queensland, or go to Western Australia or the Northern Territory. Also, the kids down Under get their summer off (our winter) and reservations start becoming necessary, especially around Christmas. There are also school holidays in May and in August-September.

GETTING THERE • Any way you cut it, getting to Australia is a long haul, one of the reasons many otherwise eager explorers have given it a pass. From San Francisco, for example, it's at least 15 hours to Australia, and if you're coming from the East Coast, add another five or six hours—if you're lucky and get a good connection. From Vancouver, the total trip time to Sydney is almost 17 hours, counting a layover in

Honolulu. Even in a spacious 747, it's a long, hot, grueling trip down through the South Pacific.

It's also a fairly expensive trip, although the expansion of airline service in the last few years has helped keep things competitive. From the West Coast, during high season (November–March) an APEX economy fare is around US$2000, although we've seen specials with prices just about half that—and lower. A variety of U.S., Canadian and international carriers have regular service from North America to Australia. They include Continental Airlines, American Airlines, Canadian Airlines International, Qantas (the Australian national carrier), Northwest Airlines, United Airlines, and Air New Zealand.

Note that a number of flights from the West Coast arrive in Australia at Cairns or Brisbane in Queensland. There is a Los Angeles-Sydney non-stop; the rest all haul in at Honolulu for a layover, usually about an hour. The normal flying time is five hours from the West Coast to Honolulu, then nine hours to Cairns; Honolulu-Sydney is about 10 hours.

FORMALITIES • Australia has some of the toughest—by that we mean thorough—customs and immigrations procedures in the world. Getting through Aussie passport control is not a rapid process. Anyone entering the country (aside from New Zealanders) must have a visa and a current passport plus proof of return airfare. Getting a visa in Canada or the United States is usually easy, and they're free. Visas for tourists are usually issued for 12 months and are good for multiple entries. In most visa-issuing agencies, you can get the paperwork done the same day if you go in person; you can also have it done by mail.

Visas can be issued by the following offices in the United States:

Australian Embassy, 1601 Massachusetts Avenue N.W., Washington, D.C. 20036–2273, (202) 797–3222, 10 a.m.–3 p.m.; Australian Consulate General, 636 Fifth Ave., New York, N.Y. 10111, (212) 245–4000, 9 a.m.–2 p.m.; Australian Consulate General, 611 N. Larchmont Blvd., Los Angeles, Calif. 90004, (213) 469–4300, 9 a.m.–3:30 p.m.; Australian Consulate General, 1990 Post Oak Blvd., Suite 800, Houston, Texas 77056–9998, (713) 629–9140/9138, 10 a.m.–noon and 1 p.m.–3 p.m.; Australian Consulate General, 321 N. Clark Street, Suite 2930 Quaker Tower, Chicago, Ill. 60610, (312) 645–9444, 11 a.m.–1 p.m., 2 p.m.–3 p.m.; Australian Consulate General, 1 Bush St., San Francisco, Calif. 94104–4413, (415) 362–6160, 10 a.m.–4 p.m., and the Australian Consulate General, 1000 Bishop St., Penthouse Suite, Honolulu, Hawaii 96813, (808) 524–5050, 8 a.m.–4 p.m.

In Canada: Australian High Commission, 50 O'Conner Street, Suite 710, Ottawa, Ontario K1P 5M9, (613) 236–0841, 9 a.m.–noon and 2 p.m.–4 p.m.; Australian Consulate General, Suite 314, 175 Bloor Street

East, Toronto, Ontario ONT M4W 3R8, (416) 323–1155, 10 a.m.–1 p.m., and the Australian Consulate General, P.O. Box 12519 Oceanic Plaza, Suite 800, 1066 W. Hastings St., Vancouver, British Columbia V6E 3X1, (604) 684–1177, 8:30 a.m.–noon.

Don't forget to get a visa or just assume you can get one at the airport in Australia. The airline personnel of the carrier you're riding to Australia won't even let you on the plane without it. If you've purchased an APEX ticket and prepaid a tour or hotel and car costs, you're out the money, depending on the mercy of the airlines and other services, which often is non-existent. Don't laugh; it's not unheard of for a passenger to show up at San Francisco or Los Angeles International airports without a visa, and it's not a pretty scene.

Your passport must be current enough that it not be due to expire while you are in Australia; the authorities there recommend it expire at least three months after you leave Australia.

Australia is an island, and as such, has been spared many of the problem diseases found in other parts of the world—they want to keep it that way.

They are very careful about allowing you to bring in fresh or packaged food, vegetables, seeds, animals or animal products (especially any internationally recognized endangered species) or birds—they are so careful, even the packaged nuts you get aboard the inbound aircraft are verboten. We once took in a jar of American instant coffee and declared it. We were told that technically it was illegal, but the customs officer let it go. Others might not.

If you're over 18, you can bring in, duty-free, 200 cigarettes or 250 grams of tobacco products, one liter of alcoholic products, and goods up to the value of A$400 carried in personal luggage. The country is rabies free, and if you plan to take a pet along, the quarantine process takes five months. There is an A$10 departure tax per person for all persons over 12 years of age leaving Australia.

EMBASSIES AND CONSULATES • If your passport is stolen or lost, it must be replaced before you can leave Australia. U.S. authorities are very good about replacing passports, providing you follow the correct procedures.

First, embassies do not issue passports, consulates do. There are consulates in most major Australian cities. Then, you must be able to prove you're an American citizen. This can be done with proper identification, such as a birth certificate. If you've lost everything, your traveling companion can swear to your citizenship—as long as he or she is carrying a U.S. passport. You'll also have to file a police report about the theft or loss, and supply two passport-sized photographs. The charge for issuing a replacement passport is the same as getting a new one: $65. In an emergency situation (your flight leaves the same day) the consular service can issue a passport in a matter of hours. In Australia, the U.S. embassy (and consulate) is located at State Circle and Perth Avenue in Canberra (Yarralumla), (06) 270–5000. The Canadian Embassy is on Commonwealth Avenue, Yarralumla 273–3844.

Consulates are listed in telephone Yellow Pages under "consulates and legations." The U.S. consulate in Sydney is at the T&G Towers, Park and Elizabeth Streets, tel. 264–7044; the Canadian consulate is in the AMP Building, 50 Bridge Street, tel. 231–6522. In Melbourne, the U.S. consulate is at 24 Albert Road, tel. 699–2244; the Canadian at No. 1 Collins Street, tel. 654–1433.

MEDICINE • Vaccinations are not required if you're flying directly to Australia from the United States or Canada. Health certificates are not required unless you're entering the country from an area where there has been an outbreak of yellow fever, smallpox, cholera, or typhoid 14 days prior to your arrival.

The Australians become very displeased by people carrying unauthorized controlled substances. If you are carrying medications, declare them. You're allowed to take in a four-week supply of personal medicines. It is wise to take a prescription with you, not only to show customs, but in case you need a refill. After an Australian physician has signed your prescription, you can get it filled at a pharmacy (called a "chemist" in Australia).

MONEY, WEIGHTS AND MEASURES • Australia is yet another country that uses the dollar as its currency. The Aussies used to have the pound, with all its English holdovers (sovereigns, ha'pennies, tuppence) but got smart in 1963 and went metric. There was a little flap about what the name of the new money would be (was it a sign of weakness to adopt Yank names?) but in the end they finally settled on dollars and cents. Banknotes come in $5, $10, $20, $50 and $100 bills. Coins are 5, 10, 20, and 50 cents, plus $1 and $2. The $2 coin was first issued in 1988, and like the U.S. Susan B. Anthony $1 coin, immediately caused a flap—for the same reason. The problem is the Aussie $2 coin is almost the same size as the old 2-cent piece, and the amount of bitching rising from irritated Australians is enormous. It's a very pretty coin, however, gold-colored and the only coin not to have an animal on its obverse; instead, it features an Aboriginal man. H.R.H. the Queen is on the face of all Australian coins.

At this writing, the Aussie dollar was worth between 70 and 75 U.S. cents. The Yankee buck has been sliding against foreign currencies since 1985; the Aussie dollar was only 68 U.S. cents back then.

Aussie weights and measures are officially metric, although you'll find many folks still hanging in with the old English measures. An Aussie friend of ours was measuring a length of board for a project and reckoned it was "two meters and about a quarter-inch." And in some parts of the country, they still figure beer in ounces and vow to never give in. Canadians, who have already gone metric, will supposedly have no problems. For Americans, mostly all you need to know is that gasoline comes in liters, distances are posted in kilometers, temperatures are in Celsius and things are weighed in kilograms.

It's not that tough. If you're in a rental car, the speedometer is in kilometers, so if the limit is 60, just drive 60 and forget miles. (If you absolutely have to know, multiply the number of kilometers by .62 and you'll get the miles.) For temperatures, just remember water freezes at 0°, 20° is mild, 30° is damned hot and if it's 40°, you're probably in the desert country of the Northern Territory and should be headed for a cold pub. A kilogram is about 2.2 pounds. If you forget all this, don't worry, just ask somebody. After all, they've only been at this metric business for about 20 years.

ELECTRICITY • Aussie current is 240–250 volts, 50 hertz. Just to be difficult, the usual European two-round-prong plug is not used. Instead, they use a three-pronged flat plug that looks like a smaller version of the plugs Americans use on electric clothes driers. Norelco's international travel kits have a plug that will work in Australia (two, rather than three prongs, but okay) and converter plugs can be found in some department stores and camping outlets in Australia. The Norelco kit is a good idea, anyway, because it contains a 50-watt and 1600-watt transformer in case you're carrying appliances that won't convert to 220. If you're going upscale, forget all the electricity differences, because most high-grade hotels in the country have 110-volt outlets in the bathrooms, or if not, loaner transformers that will do the job. (Many of the 110-outlets will not safely handle hair dryers and other high-wattage appliances, however.)

TIME • Australia is the other side of the International Date Line from North America, so it's always ahead of us. The country has three time zones: Eastern Standard, Central Standard and Western Standard. That's the easy part; from there it gets a little complicated, especially when either the U.S. or Australia goes on Daylight Savings Time.

Eastern Standard (Queensland, New South Wales, Victoria, Tasmania) is 18 hours ahead of San Francisco—when it's 4:00 p.m. in San Francisco, it's 10 a.m. the next day, in Sydney. One way to make it a little easier is just forget the 18-hour bit and figure that Sydney is six hours behind San Francisco, but a day ahead. Make sense? If it's 10 a.m. Monday in Sydney, then it's six hours later in San Francisco, or 4 p.m., but a day earlier, or Sunday. The easy way around the whole thing is to buy a watch with room for two time zones.

Central Standard (South Australia and the Northern Territory) is 17½ hours ahead of San Francisco and Western Standard (Western Australia) is 16 hours ahead.

Going to Australia, the 18-hour difference fries your brain. Coming back, because of the quirks of jet travel, you arrive on the West Coast the same day at almost the same time you left Australia. This also fries your brain, but after you tell your body that no time has passed, everything will be all right.

HOURS • Most banks are open from 9:30 a.m.–4 p.m. Monday–Thursday and until 5 p.m. Fridays, and are closed on holidays and weekends. Airports in major cities have bank outlets for currency exchanges. Post offices are open 9 a.m.–5 p.m. weekdays, closed on weekends. Most retail outlets are open from 9 to 5:30 weekdays. Many stores in the big cities stay open late at least one night a week.

PHONES • Most hotels and many motels have direct-dial international and domestic capability, and it's also very easy to make international collect calls from pay phones. Local calls are 30 cents. Emergencies (police, fire, accident) can be reported by dialing 000, no coin required. If you do much calling in Australia, you'll soon run into the Aussie habit of doubling and tripling numbers when they talk. For instance, an American would read this phone number—544–1117—as "five-four-four, one-one-one-seven." But the Aussies would say "five-double four, triple one-seven," which, when spoken rapidly and with an Australian accent, can be most confusing. They also double and triple street addresses.

For local calls, red public phones are found all over in stores, malls and pubs. For in-country long distance, you need one of the gray-green STD (Subscriber Trunk Dialing) phones. Like European phones, you can feed a number of coins into the phone and as you talk, the coins drop. When you run out of coins, the conversation is ended unless you keep pumping them in. The same system is used for ISD (International Subscriber Dialing) calls. If you want to direct dial and not call collect, just have a handful of 50 cent pieces on hand. To call the United States or Canada, dial 0011 for overseas, then 1, then the area code and number. Public ISD phones are becoming more common, but if you can't find one, check the general post offices or airports. On both ISD and STD phones, when you start to run out of coins, a red light will start blinking to remind you to feed in some more. The country has also started using plastic phone cards which work in special phones. The cards can be bought in many stores.

If you want to call Australia from North America, dial 011 (the international access code), then 61 (the Aussie code), then the city code, then the number. The major city codes in Australia are: Canberra, 06; Sydney 02; Melbourne, 03. If you're in the city calling a local number, drop the city code.

Calling home: Find an STD phone, dial 0011, then 1 then the U.S. area code and number. Ma Bell has made it even easier, though, with a service we've used all over the world: USADirect. From any phone in Australia, dial 0014–881–011 and you'll be connected to an AT&T operator, who can dial the stateside number you want. Either call collect or use your AT&T credit card. That way you avoid local hotel phone charges and don't have to remember a bunch of international numbers. For information about USADirect, call (800) 874–4000, extension 359.

GETTING AROUND • Airlines—In 1989 and the first months of 1990, most of the pilots who flew for domestic airlines were on strike, hampering internal transportation. Major tourist areas, such as Queensland, suffered large losses and getting around the wide spaces of the country was sometimes very difficult. The pilots have been replaced, and according to Australian tourist authorities, things are back to normal. Internal airfares in Australia tend to be expensive, but there are breaks for foreign tourists, who are eligible for discounts on flights around the country. There are three main domestic airlines: **Ansett Airlines of Australia, Australian Airlines,** and **East-West Airlines.**

East-West has several types of **air passes** for international passengers, depending on your destination. One pass, for example, allows you to fly as far south as Hobart or as far west as Ayers Rock on an unlimited, 14-day basis for around A$600. East-West flies mostly in New South Wales, with connections to Queensland, Victoria, Tasmania, Western Australia, and the Northern Territory. It also has flights to Norfolk Island. Passes can be purchased before leaving North America. *Information and bookings:* **East-West Airlines,** (800) 366–1300 USA and Canada.

Australian and Ansett offer the **"Go Australia Airpass,"** which allows a 30-percent savings on regular economy fares. Both airlines fly to all major and most minor cities in Australia. Passes can be purchased before or after arrival in the country and are available to passengers flying on APEX or promotional fares only. *Information:* **Ansett Airlines of Australia,** 9841 Airport Blvd., Suite 418, Los Angeles, Calif. 90045; (213) 642–7487, or U.S.A. and Canada, (800) 366–1300 **Australian Airlines,** 510 W. 6th St. Suite 312, Los Angeles, Calif. 90014; U.S.A., (800) 922–5122, Canada, (800) 448–9400.

In addition, there are a number of smaller, regional air services, including such carriers as **Air New South Wales, Kendell Airlines, Sunstate Airlines, Lloyd Aviation** and **Air Queensland.**

Internal flights in Australia are closely regulated as regards carry-on luggage. The limit is one piece, and they mean it. We once had to spend an extra day in Brisbane to pick up a carry-on bag because the flight crew confiscated it as we boarded the plane in Alice Springs. The airlines will not guarantee that carry-on luggage so confiscated will make the next flight—and in this case, it didn't.

Smoking is not allowed on domestic flights, but is allowed if a flight inside the country is a continuation of an international flight.

BUSES—These are called *coaches* in Australia, and offer substantial savings over air travel. Buses are, of course, a lot slower and Australia is a big country, so it's a trade-off. The major coach operators with national connections include **Greyhound, Deluxe, Pioneer Express** and **Bus Australia.** In Tasmania, service is supplied by **Redline Coaches,** which is used by Greyhound, Pioneer Express and Deluxe in their pass networks.

All the Australian bus companies have **passes** or packages which provide a relatively inexpensive way to let you see the country and not have to worry about driving. Depending on the carrier, these passes range from a week to three months; some even include accommodations. There are daily express routes between major cities, some of which are long hauls. Adelaide to Perth, for example, is 36 hours. Most of the buses are new, air conditioned and toilet-equipped. Some even have TV systems.

The passes include:

Greyhound Aussie Explorer, which is good for a year. The pass comes in six types, depending on what part of the country you're interested in. For example, the **Best of the East** pass allows a circuit from Sydney, up the coast to Townsville, over to Alice Springs and down to Adelaide and Melbourne, back to Sydney, for about A$480 for an adult, A$380 for a senior citizen, student or child. The most inclusive of the passes is **the Ultimate All-Aussie Holiday,** which allows a year of travel anywhere in Australia for A$870 per adult, A$700 for others. Greyhound also has a regular bus pass, which starts at around A$200 per adult for a week, increasing in a number of increments to about A$1300 per adult for a 120-day pass. A variation on this, called the **Great Bus Pass,** includes accommodations. A 21-day pass, allowing 17 nights in a **Flag Inn,** for example, goes for about A$1100. Greyhound passes must be purchased prior to arrival in Australia. *Information and bookings in the United States:* **Greyhound International,** (800) 828–1985, or write Greyhound International, 735 Market St. Suite 1100, San Francisco, Calif. 94103. In Canada, Goway Travel Ltd., 2300 Yonge St., Suite 2001, Box 2331, Toronto, Ontario MP4 1E4.

The **Pioneer Express Aussiepass** comes in 21-day, 30-day and 90-day versions. The basic 21-day pass, for example, costs around A$470. The next step up is the Super Aussiepass, an extension to the basic ticket, which offers unlimited travel and some accommodations in four price ranges. The Yellow Pass (budget accommodation), is about A$380 per person double; Green (slightly better), A$450 per person double; Blue (moderate), A$530 per person double, and Red (premier), A$592 per person double. Note that the accommodations passes are in addition to the basic Aussiepass, and do not include meals. *Information and bookings:* **Greyhound International,** (800) 828–1985; Canada, Overland Australia, (800) 331–6360 or (617) 460–0734.

Among deals offered by **Deluxe Coachlines** is the **Koala Pass,** which allows unlimited travel, from a 7-day pass around A$220, to a 90-day pass for around A$1300. If you're not in a rush, there's the **Space Pass,** which allows unlimited travel on a space available basis for about 30 percent less than the Koala Pass. The **Aussie Wanderer** allows you 12 months to make a one-way trip around the country on one of four itineraries; the all-Australia trip costs about A$850. The trip can be taken over a period of 12 months if desired. *Information:* **ATS/ Sprint,** (800) 423–2880 USA, (800) 232–2121 California, or write ATS Tour Pacific, 1101 E. Broadway, Suite 201, Glendale, Calif. 91205.

TRAINS—It was, as a very English friend of ours is wont to say when faced with similar vistas, "about 400 miles of bugger all." Since before dawn, the train had been on the Nullarbor Plain, and the reports were accurate, there ain't no trees. About noon, the train stopped at some wide spot, and we piled out of the air conditioning and into the blast furnace of southwestern Australia just to stretch our legs and get off the train, which it seemed like we had lived on for a month. It was Cook, maybe, or Loongana or maybe Naretha. Someplace, at any rate, out in the middle of nowhere. We didn't get five feet before the bush flies attacked, and we were just nasty enough to be glad we didn't live in this godforsaken little town. There are ways and ways of seeing the Aussie Outback, neighbors, but driving through the Nullarbor at high noon is not one of your better choices. The only way to do this vast sea of emptiness is aboard one of the last great train trips left on earth: the Indian-Pacific from Sydney to Perth. You get some idea what you're dealing with by noting a stretch of tracks, between Watson and Ooldea, that runs absolutely straight for almost 300 miles, the longest piece of straight track in the world.

The **Sydney-Perth** train gets the name because it goes all the way from the Indian Ocean at Perth to the Pacific at Sydney. It runs three times a week and takes three days to make the trip. To supplement the Indian-Pacific service, another train, the **Trans-Australian,** runs between Perth and Adelaide twice a week each way. It takes 37 hours to make the trip. Whichever you take, you cross the Nullarbor, which, if you're a train freak, is like climbing a major-league mountain. The Indian-Pacific has a long run: 4348 kilometers, or about 2700 miles, almost all of it through raw desert and bush.

The cross-continent trains are popular with Australians as well as tourists, but not as popular at the more famous Ghan, the train that runs from Adelaide to Alice Springs. The Ghan runs along the pioneer route up through the Red Centre, and is named after the Afghan camel drivers who carried supplies and equipment up and down the route before the rail line was completed. It's Australia's pride and joy, and popular enough that some periods have to be booked a year in advance. There are several other tourist-type routes in the country, including the Queenslander, which runs from Cairns to Brisbane, and the Overland, which links Melbourne and Sydney.

All these trains have sleepers and, using rail passes, you can go all over the country in comfort and not break the bank too badly. Some for instances:

The Ghan • The train that opened the Outback was an adventure right from the beginning. There was no air conditioning, so the windows were kept up. It helped a little, but now and then the wind would kick up and spew clouds of red sand into the cars (which was periodically shoveled back outside). Flash floods washed out tracks, white ants (termites) ate the cross ties, and on one famous trip, the chef ran out of food and fed his passengers by shooting wild goats. The schedule was somewhat loose—it took anywhere from three days to a month to get to Alice Springs. The tracks between Port Augusta (Adelaide) and the Alice were begun in 1879, and the last stretch linking Alice Springs was completed in 1929.

The Ghan was recently done over, a process that took almost three years and cost A$2.5 million. Major work was done on the first-class bar cars and first-class sleepers. The economy coaches still need work; there are no economy sleepers on the Ghan. The first-class bars and the new first-class restaurant are the showpieces of the train. The Oasis Bar, done in a jungly motif, is almost as long as two regular cars. The upholstery is supposed to match the designs of the camel blankets the Afghan drivers used. It's airy and quite pleasant; it's the smoking bar. The non-smoker is the equally attractive but smaller Dreamtime Lounge, done in desert motif with Aboriginal overtones. The Stuart Restaurant is reddish Art Deco in flair, with etched glass half-dividers between booths. Going north, you get two meals, dinner and breakfast; coming south, three meals. The menu has such offerings as Liechardt's Lust (chicken schnitzel with potatoes pariesenne), grilled snapper in hollandaise sauce, and peaches with rum and creme. It's pretty good bush tucker. There is no meal service for economy passengers; there is a buffet/bar car for their use.

The train's twin sleepers are not huge; basically two bunk beds with fold-down washbasin and toilet, all of which fold up in the daytime to give a decent-sized compartment. Single first-class sleepers are even smaller. It takes about 22 hours to make the 1559-kilometer haul from Adelaide to the Alice. The train leaves Adelaide Thursday at 2 p.m. throughout the year; from April–October, there is also a train at 2 p.m.

Monday. The trains arrive in Alice Springs at 11:10 a.m. the next day. Note, however, that the Ghan is legendary for not running on time. Southbound, the train leaves at 5:10 p.m. Fridays all year; from April–October, there is also a Tuesday train. Both arrive in Adelaide around 4:30 p.m. the next day. Economy one-way fares are about A$150; sleepers are about A$400 per person, which includes meals. The Ghan also has motor-rail service. The one-way fee to carry a compact car is about A$200; larger cars up to A$500.

The Indian-Pacific • It took a long time to connect the two oceans. Tracks started in 1912 and Sydney was finally connected to the line in 1982. By far the most fascinating part of the trip is the Nullarbor, so if you're not keen on spending three days on a train, you could opt for the shorter Trans-Australian service from Adelaide to Perth. The basic amenities are the same on both trains. Sleepers include a deluxe compartment (Indian-Pacific only) with three-quarter bed and lounge chairs; first class twinettes with shower and toilet; family units (Indian-Pacific only) basically two interconnecting twinettes; first class roomette (single passenger, with showers and toilet down the hall); economy twinette (very small, toilets and showers down the hall). Coach cars have reclining seats, and washrooms and toilets are at the end of each car. Coach passengers can get food and refreshments in the cafeteria club car, but must take meals in their own coaches. There is a lounge car and dining car for sleeper passengers. Fares for first and second class sleepers include meals.

The Indian-Pacific leaves Perth at 9 p.m. Sunday, Tuesday and Thursday. It arrives in Sydney about 6:30 p.m. three days later. The return trip leaves Sydney Monday, Thursday and Saturday at 1:30 p.m., arriving in Perth at 7 a.m. three days later. The Trans-Australian leaves Perth at 9 p.m. Saturday and arrives in Adelaide at 1:30 p.m. two days later. The return leaves Adelaide Wednesday at 5 p.m., arriving at 7 a.m. two days later.

First class sleepers on the Indian-Pacific are about A$850 per person; economy class sleepers are about A$650; economy coaches are about A$250. Railcar service is available; Sydney-Perth about A$500; Adelaide-Perth about A$300.

First class sleepers on the Trans-Australian are A$560 per person; economy class sleepers are A$425, and economy coach seats are A$170.

The Queenslander • Here's the sugarcane express, a long, mostly boring trip down the coast from Cairns to Brisbane. The cars are new and well appointed, but a little smaller than normal: the train is narrow gauge. It takes about 32 hours to travel the 1680 kilometers between cities, and the overwhelming memory is of miles and miles of sugar cane and pineapple plantations. It is far better, however, than driving the same stretch. The new train has roomettes and twinnettes as well as coach seating. The roomettes come with a toilet, sink and small hanging closet. The twinettes are spacious, and are arranged like a European train with outside corridor. They have a sink and mirror, no toilets. There are showers and toilets at the end of the sleeper cars. There are no economy sleepers available. The first-class lounge is airy and very nice. The restaurant car is fairly small and the meals, while good, are not on a par with the Ghan. The Queenslander leaves Cairns at 8:15 a.m. Tuesday, arriving in Brisbane at 4:25 p.m. Wednesday; it leaves Brisbane at 9:10 a.m. Sunday, arriving in Cairns at 5:20 p.m. Monday. The first class fare, including meals and beds, is A$350 per person; economy coaches are A$215. Railcar service from city to city is about A$210.

Railways of Australia has a couple of passes to ease the cost if you plan to do a lot of rail travel. The Austrailpass is available for periods of 14 up to 90 days. The 14-day, first class pass is A$700; the 90-day first class pass is A$1700; 14-day economy passes are A$425; 90-days A$1100. You can buy one week extensions on both sets of passes.

The Kangaroo Road n' Rail passes, good for both rail and bus service, are issued for 14, 21 and 28 days. The 14-day first class pass is A$850; 21-day, A$1000, and the 28-day, A$1225. Economy passes are 14-day, A$550; 21-day, A$950, and 28-day, A$950.

These passes are for seats only. To get a sleeper and meals, you must pay additional costs. A first-class sleeper on the Ghan, plus meals, would run about A$100 extra; a first class sleeper and meals on the Indian-Pacific, add an extra $45 a night for the bed and A$100 for meals for the trip; economy sleeper on the Indian-Pacific, add A$30 a night, plus the A$100 for meals.

Trains are better booked in advance, especially in holiday periods. For booking information about train service and passes in Australia, contact ATS/Tour Pacific, 100 N. First St., Burbank, Calif. 91502; tel. (800) 423–2880; (800) 232–2121 California only, or (818) 841–1030. In Canada, contact Goway Travel Ltd., 2300 Yonge St., Suite 2001, Box 2331, Toronto, Ontario M4P 1E4; tel. (416) 322–1034. In Vancouver. (604) 687–4004.

Once in Australia, information on train travel is available from the **Rail Travel Centre of New South Wales,** Transport House, 11–31 York Street, Sydney 2000; tel. 29–7614, or **Railways of Australia,** which represents the five state-owned rail systems in the country, at 85 Queen Street, Melbourne, Victoria 3000; tel. (03) 608–0811.

INFORMATION—A good first glance at Australia is provided by the *Destination Australia Book,* printed annually and available free by contacting the **Australian Tourist Commission,** 2121 Avenue of the Stars, Suite 1200, Los Angeles 90067; (800) 445–4400. In Canada, the ATC office is at 3080 Yonge St., Toronto M4N 3N1; (416) 487–2126. Lots of valuable stuff and also contains visa application forms.

Information can be also obtained from agencies representing the individual Australian states. These include:

Tourism Commission of New South Wales, 2121 Avenue of the Stars, No. 450, Los Angeles 90067; (213) 552–9566.

Victorian Tourism Commission, 2121 Avenue of the Stars, #1270, Los Angeles, CA 90067; (213)553–6352; or 3080 Yonge St., #5052, Toronto, Ontario M4N 3N1, (416) 487–1151.

Queensland Tourist & Travel Commission, 611 N. Larchmont Blvd., Los Angeles 90004; (213) 465–8418. In Canada, 2 Bloor St. West, No. 1730, Toronto, Ontario M4W 3E2; (416) 922–2305.

Tourism South Australia, 2121 Avenue of the Stars, #1210, Los Angeles 90067; (213) 552–2821.

Tasmanian Department of Tourism, 2121 Avenue of the Stars, #1280, Los Angeles 90067; (213) 552–3010.

Western Australian Tourism Commission, 2121 Avenue of the Stars, #1210, Los Angeles 90067; (213) 557–1987.

Northern Territory Tourist Commission, 2121 Avenue of the Stars, #1210, Los Angeles 90067; (213) 277–7877, (800) 468–8222.

Once in Australia, you will find individual state tourist offices in most major cities. These offices are excellent at providing information about tours, airfares, and hotels, and can make reservations. Often, individual states will have special deals available that no one in North America has heard about yet; always worth a check, if for nothing more than brochures.

HOLIDAYS—In addition to the various national holidays, all the Australian states have a slug of days off throughout the year specifically designed to thwart tourists trying to find rooms or cash traveler's checks. Before making reservations Down Under, thus, always check with either the **Australian Tourist Commission** or the Aussie state office you're planning to visit.

Major nationwide holidays include New Year's Day, Good Friday, Easter Saturday, Easter Monday, Anzac Day (April 25), Christmas Day, and Boxing Day (Dec. 26). School holidays get very complicated, because each state schedules them at a different time. Generally, the kids get off from late June or early July through the middle of July; then from the middle of September through the middle of October, and from the middle of December through late January or February.

NEW SOUTH WALES

New South Wales, and especially Sydney, is the spiritual heart of Australia. Other cities and other states will proclaim their importance in the scheme of things Australian, to be sure, and there is a lot of the same sort of territorial rivalry you have between Texans and folks from Massachusetts, or between the farmers of Saskatchewan and the striped ties of Ottawa. But, at the bottom, Australians know Sydney is the core of the country.

As we have noted, Capt. Arthur Phillip and the first shipload of convicts from Merry Old England sailed into Sydney Harbour on Jan. 26, 1788, to begin the history of white Australia. Indeed, for most of its early history, mainland colonial Australia was known as New South Wales. The place where Phillip and his scruffy wards landed—Sydney Cove—remains today the heart of the city. The Rocks, the sandstone formations above the cove where the first halting steps at creating a city took place, still show signs of its colonial past, and a number of classic buildings from the transportation era still stand around the city.

Almost a third of Australia's 16 million people live in New South Wales, 3.5 million of them in Sydney. Once you get away from the harbor, you soon discover that metropolitan Sydney is huge—670 square miles, containing seven cities and four counties. New South Wales is large enough—about 300,000 square miles—and goes all the way from the ocean to the Outback. In fact, the dusty regions of the Outback comprise a full two-thirds of the state. Canberra and the Australian Capital Territory are completely surrounded by the state, stuck down about 180 miles southwest of Sydney. Sixty percent of the nation's coal comes from the Hunter Valley, Illawarra, and the Blue Mountains, and the zinc, lead, and silver deposits near Broken Hill gave start to the country's biggest conglomerate, BHP—the Big Australian. The state also is the nation's major wheat producer and has a third of the country's sheep.

The Hunter Valley northeast of Sydney produces great wines. The Snowy Mountains are where many Aussies go to ski. The state offers caves to explore, houseboating, deep-sea fishing—take your pick; a vacation here allows you to see all the things Australia is famous for, from kangaroos to the Opera House to tons of sunny beaches to the cool green escapes of the Blue Mountains.

The Essential New South Wales

INFORMATION • For information about the State, contact the **Tourism Commission of New South Wales,** 2121 Avenue of the Stars, No. 450, Los Angeles, Calif. 90067; tel. (213) 552–9566. In Sydney, contact the **Travel Centre of New South Wales,** 19 Castlereagh St.; tel. 231–4444, or the **New South Wales Tourist Commission,** 140 Phillip St.; phone 231–7100.

GETTING THERE • Sydney's international airport is served by all major international carriers, including those that fly from North America. Other major cities in the state are served either by **Ansett** or **Australian Airlines,** the two largest domestic airlines, or by East-West and Air New South Wales. Service to any other state in Australia, including such popular tourist spots as Ayers Rock and the Great Barrier Reef, is available from Sydney. *Information:* **Australian Airlines,** 693–3333; **Ansett airlines,** 268–1111.

Many of the major settlements along the east coast as well, and inland areas, are served by rail and bus companies. Several well-known rail routes, such as the Indian-Pacific, start in Sydney. General information about **train travel** in the state is available from the NSW tourism commission or the **State Rail Authority,** 11 York St.; tel. 29–7614.

Bus service, unless you're heading for a major destination such as Melbourne or Canberra, can be slow. **The Sydney Coach Terminal** is at the corner of Riley and Oxford sts. The major bus companies are **Pioneer** 268–1331; **Greyhound** 268–1414, and **Deluxe** 212–4888. A one-way ticket from Sydney to Melbourne is about A$50; to Brisbane about the same.

If you're **driving,** road and accommodations information is available from the **National Roads and Motorists Association,** 151 Clarence St., Sydney 2000; tel. 260–9222.

CLIMATE • New South Wales is far enough south of the equator to get nippy in places during the winter, but generally, the climate is warm. The Snowy Mountains get snow, and the northern beaches are mostly sunny. Temperatures in Sydney will average around 70° to 80° Nov.–Mar., and around 45° to 60° in the winter. It can rain a lot any time of year.

TIME • New South Wales is on Eastern Standard Time, meaning it's 18 hours ahead of San Francisco. The state observes daylight savings time from October–March; clocks go ahead one hour.

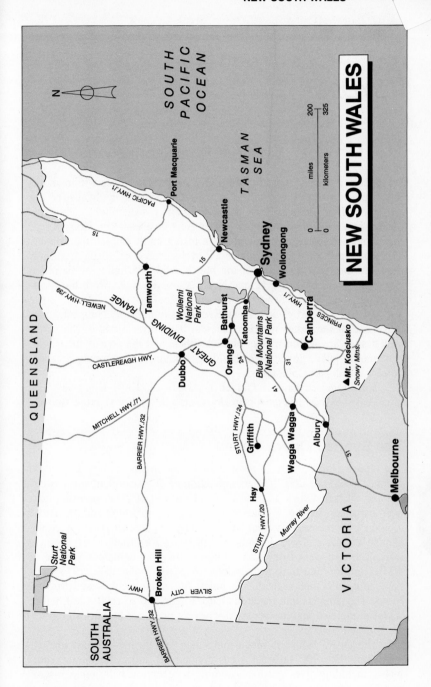

SYDNEY

THE HARBOUR AREA ....

It probably comes as outright treason for anyone who lives within shouting distance of San Francisco to suggest that Sydney might just be the most beautiful harbor city in the world, but it's definitely a thought. Sydney is always compared to the other great lovelies—Rio, Hong Kong, San Francisco, Vancouver—and it's a losing battle to pick the winner. The water part of Sydney—named Port Jackson by Captain Cook—is probably the most beautiful of the bunch, with 180 miles of shoreline and many picturesque coves and bays. It's seven miles from the headlands and the Tasman Sea to downtown Sydney.

The central part of downtown Sydney is remarkably compact, making it one of the better walking cities in the world. Some of the major tourist sites are within blocks of each other, and the area is filled with restaurants, pubs, government buildings, boutiques, shopping arcades, hotels, and department stores.

San Francisco has the Golden Gate Bridge, Hong Kong has Victoria Peak—Sydney has the Opera House and the Sydney Harbour Bridge.

The Sydney Opera House

The **Opera House** is one of those edifices that seems to allow no middle ground. Some see it as the personification of the Australian spirit, soaring and vibrant. Others think it looks like a nest of giant mollusks mating—barnacles, maybe. Whatever, it is a striking structure, and the harbor wouldn't be the same without it. Designed in the 1950s by a young Danish architect, Joern Utzon, its billowing form supposedly depicts sails. The cost went from A$7 million to the final completion figure of A$102 million and took a ridiculous 16 years to complete (1973). Utzon, apparently not keen on the noisy Australian politics and Mickey Mouse shenanigans that made his baby so late and so costly, left before it was completed and has reportedly never gone back to Australia to see the finished product.

The Opera House is much more than one theater—it has, in fact, something like 900 separate areas contained under the mating mollusks, including five rehearsal studios, a reception hall, three restaurants, a library, six theater bars, 60 dressing rooms, a bar/canteen for the artists, administrative offices and large foyer/lounge areas. In addition to the Opera Theatre, there is also the 2700-seat Concert Hall, a vast hall done in beige.

The best way to see the Opera House is on a conducted tour. General tours, which go through the main performing halls and other public areas, are available from 9–4 seven days a week. The one-hour tours cost about A$7. On Sundays, there are also backstage tours, 90-minute treks that show you the behind-the-scenes areas and explain the workings of the theater areas. These tours, which also run between 9 a.m. and 4 p.m., are about A$10; kids under 12 not allowed. Tours might be curtailed or canceled if theater activities are scheduled. To book a tour, call 250–7250.

The box office is open from 9 a.m.–8:30 p.m. Monday–Saturday. Note that tickets for most performances go on sale six weeks before. You can also do telephone bookings (there's a A$4 charge), and you can charge them to a credit card. For phone bookings, call 250–7777. For Mail bookings, write to Box Office Manager, Sydney Opera House, P.O. Box R239, Royal Exchange, NSW 2000.

The two major restaurant are **The Bennelong,** an ala carte, upscale eatery popular for pre-theater dinners, and the Forecourt. The Bennelong is also open for lunch. Open Monday–Saturday, hours vary. Expensive. Phone 250–7578.

The very popular Forecourt is a brasserie-style restaurant that specializes in seafood and char-grilled meats. Hours are 9 a.m.–midnight, Monday–Saturday, and 11:30 a.m.–8 p.m. Sundays. Moderate to expensive. Phone 250–7300. Reservations for both restaurants are advisable.

There is also the Cafe Mozart, which offers light meals before and after performances, and the Harbour, which is outside and is open for lunch Monday–Saturday, and dinner from 5 p.m. It also has take-away food.

For disabled-information, call 250–7178 or 7185 from 9:30 a.m.–4 p.m. weekdays.

If you'd like to pre-book a package before leaving North America, contact **ATS/Sprint,** 1101 E. Broadway, Glendale, Calif. 91205; (800) 423–2880 USA and (800) 232–2121 California. The packages, called **An Evening at the Opera House,** can be booked 12 months in advance, but are not available on Sundays or public holidays. The festivities start around 4:45 p.m. with the tour, followed by dinner, then the performance. The cost of the package depends on what you will see and what time of year you're in town, but generally expect a tab of between A$70 and A$130 per person. A tour and dinner without the performance is around A$50 a head. **Qantas** also has an Opera House booking service for its passengers.

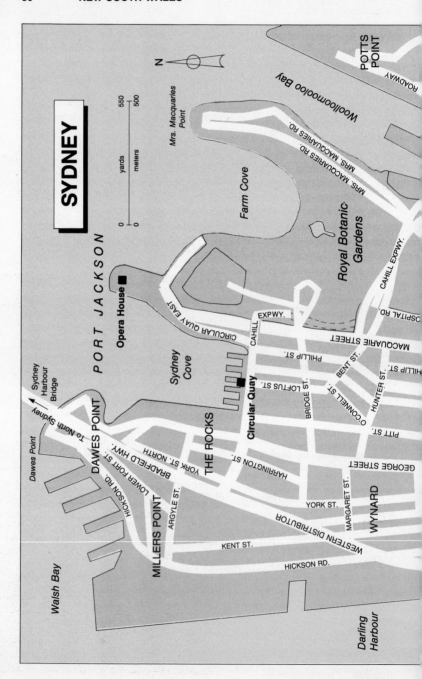

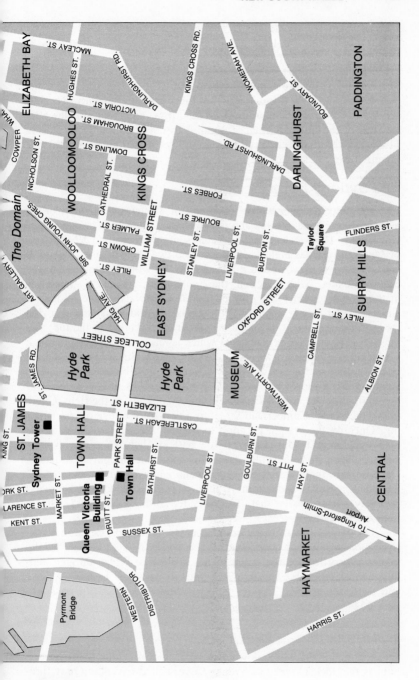

You can get to the Opera House from anywhere in the city by taking a bus, train, or ferry to Circular Quay. It's also a stop (No. 2) on the Sydney 111 Explorer Bus.

Don't try to drive to the Opera House—there's no parking nearby. The best bet is to take a special Opera House bus. Park your car at the public ramp at **The Domain** (on Sir John Young Crescent). The bus service runs Monday–Saturday from 5:30 p.m. until five minutes after the start of the last performance; the last trip back to The Domain is at 11:45 p.m. Matinee bus service on Saturdays runs from noon until five minutes after the start of the last matinee.

The Sydney Harbour Bridge

The **Harbour Bridge,** which spans one of the narrowest inlets in the harbor, was opened in 1932 and is one of the largest arch bridges in the world. It is 1650 feet across, contains somewhere around 52,000 tons of steel, and carries eight traffic lanes and two railroad lines. (It is, of course, always crowded and a tunnel is in the works to help out.) The bridge is called, with affection, the *Coathanger*. You get a great view of the harbor and city from the pedestrian crosswalk on the bridge, or an even better idea is to climb to the top of the bridge's southeast pylon for a 360-degree view of the entire harbor area. To get to the top, you have to first get to the bridge deck, which is reached by walking through **The Rocks.** The easiest way is to walk up Argyle Street from the Orient Hotel (corner of George and Argyle Streets). Just before you come to **Argyle Cut,** a tunnel hacked through the old rocks with convict labor beginning in 1843, you'll see a set of stairs going off to the right. Climb these, then cross Cumberland Street to a two-story bridge access building. Once on the bridge, go north to the pylon entrance. Climbing the 200 or so steps to the top takes you past art displays on the interior walls of the pylon and video programs about the bridge construction. Once on top, there are toilets, and a panoramic, if windy, view of the city. The pylon is open from 10 a.m.–5 p.m. daily to mid-February; Saturday–Tuesday after that. The entry fee to the pylon is A$1. Information 218-6451.

On the north end of the bridge, across the harbor, is **Luna Park,** Sydney's largest amusement park. The park can also be reached by taking a ferry from Circular Quay. It's open from Friday through Sunday; admission charge for unlimited rides for kids 4–7 is A$6.50; for 8 and over, about A$11. Parents get in (no rides) for A$3; *Information: 922-6644.*

The Quay

The anchor for the whole downtown area, as well as the transportation hub, is the dockside area of Sydney Cove, called **Circular Quay** (pronounced "key"). It has always been the major port facility for the city, and recently a new cruise ship docking area was added. Behind the quay, toward downtown, are a number of fast-food joints, newspaper and film kiosks, and usually a fair number of street musicians. The quay also has a major downtown railroad station and is the location for ticket offices for the city's extensive system of commuter ferries as well as for the boats that take tours of the harbor.

The ferries, operated by the State Transit Authority, run from the Quay to various locations around the harbor. The ferry docks are numbered 2 through 5. Among the ferries are ones to Manly, the resort area across the harbor north of the city, which leaves from Dock 3 (or hydrofoil service, from Dock 2); the Taronga Zoo, from Dock 2; Darling Harbour, from Dock 5, and Neutral Bay and Mosman, from Dock 4. The price of the ferries depends on your destination and whether its a regular service or high-speed. The hydrofoil to Manly takes 15 minutes, and costs about A$5 one-way; the regular ferry takes 35 minutes and costs about A$3.50.

State Transit also operates some sight-seeing trips around the harbor. Among these are:

Harbour History Cruise • Daily at 10 a.m. Takes in major historic spots, from Shark island to the east all the way past Darling Harbour to the Paramatta River. The cruise is 2½ hours long. The fare is A$10.

Harbour Sights Cruise • This takes you to some very fancy houses sitting all over the harbour, plus a run out to the headlands where ocean swells rock the boat as they roll into the harbor. Great views looking back at the city. It's also a 2½-hour trip, also A$10. It leaves at 1 p.m. weekdays, 1:30 p.m. weekends.

Harbour Lights • An evening cruise with the Opera House, the Rocks and downtown Sydney all lit up. Very nice trip. It costs A$8, and leaves at 8 p.m. Monday–Saturday.

For information about ferry trips and costs, call 954–4422; or, there are timetables and information at the various docks along the Quay.

In addition, several private companies run tours and food cruises around the harbor. One of the best deals is the **Sydney Harbour Explorer** operated by Captain Cook Cruises. The Explorer lets you cruise around the harbor, but also lets you get off at various spots, see the sights, then hop the next available boat to continue your tour. The boats stop at the Opera House, Watson's Bay (on South Head at the harbor entrance), Taronga Zoo, Darling Harbour and Circular Quay. The boats leave from Dock 6, the private ferry wharf. The boats stop at the various locations about every two hours. The fare is about A$20. Captain

Cook Cruises also has coffee cruises and dinner cruises. Information available at the dock or by calling 251–5007.

If you're around Darling Harbour, **Matilda Cruises** has several catamarans that do harbor cruises. The tours are for two hours, departing at 11:30 a.m. and 1:30 and 3:30 p.m. Like the Explorer, you can get on and off at other locations (Circular Quay and the zoo). The fare is about A$25. Information is available at the Aquarium Wharf in Darling Harbour, or by calling 264–7377.

For those more sail-minded, there are two cruises aboard the sailing catamaran **Tafua,** which offers luncheon and dining trips. The boat is equipped with a good wine list and very good food. The three-hour luncheon trip is A$30, leaving at 12:30 p.m. The three-hour dinner cruise leaves at 7 p.m. and is A$50. Information 262–3595.

A good bet for booking a wide variety of harbor cruises, from budget tours to glamorous candlelit dinner cruises, is to try Molly's Booking Service at Dock 2 at Circular Quay. For example, you could book a trip on the **Sydney Showboat,** a paddle-wheeler that has a dinner and hour-long cabaret show, for about A$70 per person. Or an hour-and-a-half budget harbor tour goes for A$15. Molly's is open seven days. Phone 247–5151.

The Rocks

One of the most touristed areas in the center of the city, but one that manages to cope anyway, is **The Rocks.** In its infancy, the area, which lies at the base of the Harbour Bridge above the waters of Sydney Cove across from Circular Quay, was safe for neither man nor sheep. All the things that would later evolve into late 20th-century quaint—tiny alleys, stone walls, pubs, shanghai gangs, houses of ill repute (they were called ''harpies' dens'')—made The Rocks famous the world around with sailors looking for rum and romance beneath the Southern Cross. The jolly tars have been replaced by lubbers from Maine and Kansas, but a lot of the old spirit pervades the area. Restoration projects have helped preserve the historic buildings, although many were intentionally destroyed in 1900, when bubonic plague broke out in the city, and later, when more fell to make way for the Harbour Bridge. Preservation began in the early 1970s.

The main drag through The Rocks is George Street, named after Good King George III, lined with shops, pubs and many old historic buildings. You can explore the area by yourself or take one of the daily walking tours. In any event, your first stop should be at **The Rocks Visitors Centre** at 104 George St., down the block on the right from the Orient Hotel. The center, housed in what was once the Coroner's Court, is open 8:30–5:30 weekdays, and from 9–5 weekends and holidays. There's an audio-visual program about the area, plus information about shops, restaurants and other attractions. *Information: 247–4972.*

Next door to the center is Sydney's oldest building, **Cadman's Cottage,** which dates from 1816. It is believed to have been built under the direction of the convict architect, Francis Greenway. Across George Street are the **Unwin Stores** (1844), and next to them, the **Orient Hotel** (1843). Across Argyle Street from the Orient is The Rocks police station, an old Victorian building. If you go up Argyle Street, you come to the **Argyle Centre,** four old restored warehouses, the earliest dating from 1826. The buildings, clustered around a cobblestoned interior courtyard, are now filled with speciality shops and restaurants.

Continuing on Argyle through Argyle Cut, you come to one of the city's oldest neighborhoods. To your left going up the hill is Observatory Park, the highest point in town. On this site in 1796 was built the fledgling colony's first windmill, used to grind flour. In 1858, the **Sydney Observatory** was built. Today, the facility has a regular program of exhibitions, films, lectures and night viewing. Daytime visiting hours are 2–5 p.m. weekdays; 10 a.m.–5 p.m. weekends; free admission. The evening programs are open all year (closed Wednesday). The programs include a short walk, a tour of the building and telescope viewing. Admission is A\$3. *Information: 241–2478.*

On up the hill to the right is **Holy Trinity Church,** also called the Garrison Church because it was used by the military in colonial days. The church, dating from 1848, is lovely inside. Nearby is Argyle Place, the oldest village green in Sydney, flanked on one side by cottages dating back to the 1830s. A couple of very nice old pubs are in the area, the **Lord Nelson Hotel** (1834), and the **Hero of Waterloo** (1844). We like the Hero of Waterloo because of the service but also its tawdry history. At one time, there was a trapdoor next to the bar, used to shanghai unsuspecting sailors. There's a room down below with manacles still on the wall. Ask the publican, he might give you a tour. The Hero claims to have the oldest liquor license in Sydney, and must also have one of the oldest pub bands in the city. The band members, all in their 80s, are former vaudevillians who play on weekends. They are a hoot and quite good—say howdy to Naomi. The pub, if you care, has American beers. (For all we know, the trapdoor is still there.) The Hero is down Lower Fort Street from Argyle Place; the Lord Nelson is at the end of Argyle Street.

The pubs along George Street are local hangouts, but they will let polite tourists in. A couple of favorites are the **Fortune of War** (which also claims the oldest liquor license in town), 137 George, and the **Ox on the Rocks,** 155 George St. Both have good pub food. Go up one flight in the Fortune of War, and you find a door into **Nurses Walk,** site of the Australia's first hospital (1788). Here, a noted Aussie artist has opened a gallery (his originals ain't cheap). The Ox has a good restaurant on the second floor where you can get seafood, including Morton Bay bugs.

Some other places to catch a bite are the **Lowenbrau European Restaurant** on Argyle Street, with outside seating or booths in a nicely dark bar; the **Argyle Woolshed** in the Argyle Centre, which has an excellent buffet lunch, and the **Orient Hotel,** which is getting a little seedy but does a good lunch and dinner business. It has live jazz weekends from 3–8:30 p.m. and live music Monday–Saturday from 10 p.m.– 3 a.m. It gets a bit noisy.

If you haven't been to Australia before, you might try the **Jolly Swagman Show,** a dinner performance with sheep shearing, raw Aussie humor, some didgeridoo music and, a new wrinkle, some scantily clad showgirls. It's funny the first time. The show is given seven nights; the tab is about A$60 a person, including the meal. The show can be booked at the Argyle Centre ticket office. Information 247–7782.

A couple of new attractions in The Rocks are **The Earth Exhange** and the very good **Story of Sydney.** The Earth Exchange, 18 Hickson Rd, is a blend of simulated earthquakes, volcanoes, sulphur vents and other geologic activity, plus a look at an underground mine and a collection of valuable minerals. It's open 10–5 daily; about A$10. The Story of Sydney is a multi-dimensional trip through the history of the city. You'll see convicts and Aboriginals, refugees and brigands. The city rises, the city burns down. It's pretty good theater. There is also a book store and terrace cafe. It's located at 100 George St., next to the Visitors Centre. Hours are 9–5 daily; admission A$10.

Also worth a look are:

Geological and Mining Museum • 36 George St. Gold, gemstones, mining and geology exhibits. Hours 9:30–4 weekdays, 1–4 Saturday, 11–4 Sunday and holidays. About A$7. *Phone 251–2422.*

Australian Wine Centre • 17 Circular Key West, one street over from George Street on the harbor. A chance to taste some of the 450 Australian wines on hand. Wines can be shipped home. Hours are 10 a.m.–7 p.m. Monday–Saturday; 10–5, Sundays. Phone 27–2755.

The Rocks Walking Tours, • owned by Captain Cooks Cruises, can be booked at 39 Argyle St, between George and Playfair streets. The tours, which are about A$10 per person, take about an hour and a quarter. You can leave from the tour office, or be picked up at the visitors center. Weekdays, tours leave at 10:30 and 11:30 a.m., and 12:30, 1:30 and 2:30 p.m. On weekends, they leave at 10:30, 12:30 and 2:30. *Information 247–6678.*

In addition to the visitors center, information, as well as tour bookings around Sydney and the rest of the country, are available at Tourist

Newsfront, 22 Playfair St. The agency is open seven days. Very friendly folks. *Phone 247–7197 or 241–2637.*

Darling Harbour

Often, when cities get all lathered up for a world's fair or a major celebration, some good is actually accomplished. Two recent examples are the dreary and dilapidated dockside areas that were cleared and improved in Brisbane for the 1988 World's Fair and in Vancouver for a similar party in 1986.

New South Wales decided, as its major contribution to the bicentennial, to take Darling Harbour apart and put it back together. Once a prosperous cargo area to the west of Circular Quay, Darling Harbour decayed into an ugly area of ratty buildings. The ambitious, US$1.5 billion development—named after Sir Ralph Darling, the colonial governor from 1825 to 1831—includes the **National Aquarium,** the **Australian National Maritime Museum,** the **Powerhouse** (a huge science-technology museum), a seven-story **convention center,** a **Chinese garden** (designed and built by architects from Guangdong Province), the huge **Sydney Exhibition Centre** (25,000 square yards of column-free space), several parking garages and the **Harbourside** (a marketplace area to house 200 retail outlets, terrace cafes, and restaurants). Also included is the **Darling Harbour Park,** which creates a large green space along the harbor edge. It is adjacent to **Darling Walk,** a major entertainment center. The first phases of the development, including the Chinese Garden, were completed in time for the 1988 bicentennial.

There were misgivings about the project at first, some people feeling that it was conceived on a bit too grand a scale to be workable, and there were also murmurs about the monorail system that was installed to take passengers from downtown Sydney to Darling Harbour. But all seems well now, and the area is one of the most popular in the city, not only for shopping, but for eating and taking in a show. One advantage here is that stores and some attractions stay open later than most of the other places in Sydney.

Among the reasons to go to Darling Harbour:

The Sydney Aquarium • As we have reminded you from time to time in this book, entering the oceans and rivers of Australia is also entering the food chain. Here, you get a chance to see all the nasties up close without having them take you to dinner—crocodiles, sharks, a reproduction of the Great Barrier Reef right before your eyes. For the price—under A$15—it's one of the best aquariums around. It's open 9:30 a.m.–9 p.m. seven days a week. The aquarium is located on the harbor off King Street. If you're walking, there's a stairway down from King. If you're on the monorail, get off at the Harbourside station and walk back across Pyrmont Bridge to the aquarium. The sandstone bridge, by the way, is another Sydney landmark, and is supposedly the oldest electrically operated swing bridge in the world (1899). *Aquarium information: 262–2300.*

Powerhouse Museum • A close cousin to the air and space museum at the Smithsonian in Washington, D.C. The emphasis is on technology, and you can see everything from steam engines to replicas of the Space Shuttle. The city claims it's the number one tourist attraction in the state. Maybe. Anyway, it's free, and open daily from 10–5. *Information 217–0111; hotline number for current displays information, 11–600.*

National Maritime Museum • A special place for those of us who cheered the Aussies on to victory when they took the America's Cup away from us Yanks. In the museum, in all its glory, is Australia II, the boat that did the deed. Also on hand is the only known remnant of the Endeavor, the ship Capt. James Cook sailed to explore Australia in 1770 (the same one that hit the reef). After his first voyage, the Endeavor was sent off to the Falkland Islands, then turned into a whaler, and eventually what was left of it ended up in a museum in Newport, Rhode Island. Because of the importance of Cook to Australian history, the Newport museum graciously gave the chunk of ship—a piece of the sternpost—to the Maritime Museum. It's like having a piece of the Mayflower on view.

The museum displays fill in the period between Endeavor and Australia II—ships, Aboriginal canoes, explorers, naval history. In all, a very interesting collection. Open daily. Admission about A$10. To get to the museum, take the monorail to the Harbourside depot. Information 552–7777.

Chinese Garden • The gardens are a maze of winding paths, small fish-filled ponds, waterfalls and Chinese-decor buildings. It's awash with trees and plants, everything from flowering apricots to camellias to guava to weeping willows to bamboo. The site is about 10,000 square yards in area, and contains a teahouse and store. It costs A$2 to enter; a cup of coffee and a custard cake will run you A$4. The gardens are open 9:30–sunset weekdays, 9 to sunset weekends. *Information 281–6863.*

Harbourside • This shopping center is split into two pavilions. The north pavilion tends to have the up-scale stores; the south has a lot of souvenir places, but also contains a food hall on the second floor for snacking up while you're shopping. Outside, the area is crawling with buskers—street entertainers—as well as bands playing everything from Sousa to calypso. A couple of fun eateries are **Arnold's Diner** (right out of Happy Days) and the **Craig Brewery.** The Craig specializes in Aussie barbecue. Great for lunch from noon on, seven days. At night, there's Bobby McGees nightclub with dancing and dining until the wee hours. Take the monorail to the Habourside depot.

Another brew pub worth a shot is the **Pumphouse,** housed in an historic old building on Pier Street at the south edge of the harbor development. It has a wide variety of beer and a really good blackboard menu. And it stays open: 11 a.m.–midnight Monday–Saturday; noon–10 p.m. Sunday.

The Monorail • The new monorail, completed in 1988, runs in a circuit from the Centrepoint Sydney Tower, down Pitt Street to Liverpool, down Harbour Street past Chinatown and the Sydney Entertainment Centre, down the west edge of Darling Harbour to Pyrmont Bridge, then back to the city center. It costs A\$2 to make one circuit. There are depots at City Centre (near the tower); Park Plaza (near the Town Hall and the Queen Victoria Building); World Square (big new office development at Pitt and Liverpool); Haymarket (Entertainment Centre); Convention (at the new Convention Centre, with a 3500-seat auditorium and 25,000 square yards of column-free display space), and at Harbourside.

Turnstiles in the depots will take either tokens or \$2 coins. The tokens can be purchased on the spot from vending machines that take paper money. Kiosks in the depots have souvenirs and film. Operating hours 7:30 a.m.–9 p.m. Monday–Thursday; 7:30 a.m.–11 p.m. Friday–Saturday; 8:30 a.m.–8 p.m. Sunday. *Information: 552–2288.*

If you're driving, the Darling Harbour complex has four large parking ramps with spaces for about 6000 cars. They are on the west side of the harbor. *Information on parking and other Harbourside activities 281–3999.*

The best deal in town is the Darling Harbour Super Ticket. For about A\$30 per person, you get a cruise on one of the Matilda catamarans; a free sightseeing ride on the monorail; admission to the aquarium and Chinese Gardens; a 10 percent-off voucher for any participating store at Harbourside, and a free lunch or dinner at the Craig Brewery. Tickets are available from Darling Harbour information kiosks, Matilda Cruises or the aquarium. *Information 262–2300 or 264–7377.*

OTHER SYDNEY SIGHTS ....

Royal Botanic Gardens

Behind the Opera House and to the east of Circular Quay are the city's largest gardens, where the convicts planted their first vegetable gardens.

It has been a botanic garden and park since 1816. There are more than 400 varieties of plants from around the world in the park, which is free and open from 8 a.m. to sunset.

Included among attractions are the National Herbarium, with an information desk open from 9–5 weekdays; a visitors center and shop (open 9–5 daily), and the new **Sydney Tropical Centre,** with enclosed specimens of tropical plants, open from 10–4. There is a A$5 charge to enter the tropical center buildings; phone 231–8104. Free guided tours of the main gardens are available at 10 a.m. Wednesday and Friday and 1 p.m. Sunday, starting at the visitors center. *Information 231–8111 or 8125.*

Located within the confines of the park are **Government House** (not open to the public) and the **Conservatorium of Music,** designed by the famous convict-architect Francis Greenway in 1817 as the colonial horse stables. Lunchtime concerts are held periodically. Phone 230–1263. At the harbor end of the park is **Farm Cove,** which got its name because of the early attempts at horticulture; the shores are now lined with shaded walkways.

Near the herbarium, on the east side of the park, is **Mrs. Macquarie's Road,** honoring the wife of Lachlan Macquarie, the most important of the early 19th-century colonial governors. At the end of the road is **Mrs. Macquarie's Chair,** a seat cut into a rock outcropping where legend has it that Herself sat, watching to make sure Hubby was hard at work.

Three blocks west of the park on Bridge Street (across from the conservatorium) is **Macquarie Place,** a tiny triangular park containing an obelisk from 1818 designed by the Francis Greenway. At one time, all distances in the colony were measured from the stone. Also in the park is an anchor from *Sirius,* the flagship of the First Fleet, which was later sunk off Norfolk Island.

The Domain

South of the botanical gardens is another large green space. **The Domain.** On Sundays, the park is alive with soap box orators who are met with enthusiasm by hecklers and supporters as well. In the center of The Domain is the **Art Gallery of New South Wales,** which houses an impressive collection of Australian art, including Aboriginal works, plus a selection of European pieces from Renaissance through 20th Century. The gallery is open from 10 a.m. to 5 p.m. Mon.–Sat., noon to 5 p.m. on Sun. Admission is free to the permanent exhibitions; a fee might be charged for special shows. *General information, 225–1700; exhibition information, 225–1790.* At the south end of The Domain is a parking ramp, strategically located for downtown area visitors.

Hyde Park

The park is split into two parts by Park Street. On the north side is the **Archibald Fountain,** commemorating the French-Australian alliance in World War I, featuring a statue of Apollo. To the northeast, between Hyde Park and The Domain, is **St. Mary's Cathedral,** a gothic Revival Catholic church begun in 1831, opened in 1928—and still not finished. The interior is quite nice, and it's open for a look.

In the southern half of the park is the art deco **Anzac monument** honoring soldiers who served in World War I. To the east of the south section of the park is the **Australian Museum,** the nation's largest natural history museum, with an Aboriginal section, a re-created New Guinea village, and examples of all the odd critters Down Under, including a dandy diorama on the Great Barrier Reef. The museum, located at the corner of William and College sts., is free and open from 10 a.m.–5 p.m. daily. *Information: 339–8111.* There is a gift shop attached to the museum with Australiana and a lot of dinosaur stuff; all credit cards accepted.

Macquarie Street

The good governor was Sydney's first major mover and shaker, starting an energetic building program that changed the settlement from a rude colonial outpost into a city—and in the process, naming almost everything after himself. Sydney, up to his arrival in 1810, had grown haphazardly, a village of tiny, twisty streets, such as still can be seen in The Rocks. He envisioned a city with wide streets, parks and public areas, and much of what he built still stands.

Soon after he arrived, he laid out Macquarie Street himself, deciding that the major colonial buildings should be located along the east side, and the west should be the site of homes for the landed gentry. Several of the colonial buildings still standing along the road were designed by Francis Greenway.

Greenway was sentenced to death in England for fraud, but the sentence was commuted to 14 years transportation to Australia. He made the acquaintance of Governor Macquarie who knew talent when he saw it and named Greenway acting government architect.

In addition to the **Conservatorium of Music** in the Royal Botanic Gardens, Greenway also designed the **Hyde Park Barracks** (1819), located just northeast of Hyde Park. The story goes that the governor was so pleased with the barracks, which housed convicts, that he granted Greenway a full pardon. The barracks is now a museum, with displays of Australian history from colonial days to the 1950s. Admission is free; hours are Wed.–Mon. 10 a.m.–5 p.m.; Tues. noon–5 p.m. *Informa-*

tion: 217–0111. If you hunger, the **Barracks Square Cafe** has lunches and teas.

The other Greenway building in the area is **St. James Church** (1819), the oldest church in town, located in Queens Square just off Macquarie next to the northwest corner of Hyde Park. He also designed **St. Matthew's Church,** now standing in the Sydney suburb of Windsor. It's the oldest Anglican church in the country, built in 1817.

Two other colonial buildings that still stand along Macquarie Street are part of what was once the first permanent hospital in the colony—the **Rum Hospital.** Built between 1811 and 1816, it got its name because Macquarie (finding the public coffers lacking) paid off the contractors by giving them a virtual monopoly in the rum trade, which in those days was a major force in New South Wales.

One wing of the former hospital houses the **Old Mint,** now the site of a free museum dedicated to the nation's decorative arts. It's open 10 a.m.–5 p.m. Mon.–Sun.; Wed. noon–5 p.m. *Information, 217–0111.* Another wing of the old hospital now serves as **Parliament House.** It was first used by the state legislature in 1829. When Parliament is sitting, visitors are admitted to the public gallery after 9:30 p.m. Daily tours are available. *Information from the sergeant-at arms, 230–2111.* Next to Parliament House is the **Sydney Hospital,** a Victorian heap opened in 1879 to replace the old hospital.

Other buildings of interest along the street include the **State Library** of New South Wales, which maintains the early records of the colony and holds periodic displays, open 9 a.m.–9 p.m. Mon.–Fri. 9–5 Saturday, and 11–5 Sunday, 230–1414; and the **Royal Australian College of Surgeons,** (145 Macquarie), housed in one of the last verandahed Georgian townhouses in the city.

Martin Place

All cities should have at least one fine pedestrian area amidst all the glass and concrete, and **Martin Place** fits the bill to a tee in Sydney. It cuts from George to Macquarie sts. in the heart of downtown. It's lined with shops and food outlets, and also has a bandshell where noontime concerts are a favorite with the urban bees who work in the area. Between George and Pitt sts. is the huge **General Post Office,** an impressive hulk of a building built in what is fondly called Venetian Renaissance style. It's a good place to pick up postcard stamps or mail stuff back home. Near the post office is a cenotaph honoring Australia's war dead, defaced with Aboriginal slogans during the Bicentennial, now clean again.

Sydney Tower

The city dads decided you couldn't have a major-league metropolis without a tall tower (look at Seattle, Calgary, or Minneapolis), so they flung the

900-foot-high **Sydney Tower** into the heavens at the corner of Pitt and Market streets (it's also known as Centrepoint Tower). Up on top there is an observation deck where, on a non-smoggy day, you can see the Blue Mountains 60 miles away. *Information and hours, 229–7444.* There are also two revolving eateries; one a la carte, one cafeteria-style, for both of which reservations are recommended; 233–3722. The a la carte restaurant is closed Sun. (See the Restaurant section.) To get to the ticket outlet to catch the elevator that whips you to the top, you have to take escalators up four floors from the street level, passing through **Centrepoint Arcade,** full of 200-odd shops and fast-food emporia and one of the better places in town to grab a quick bite. The ride up to the observation desk costs about A$5. Being Australian, the tower also has to serve a sporting purpose, and every June a bunch of crazies stage a race to the top—up the 1500 or so stairs. This is just another excuse to have a beer when it's over, of course.

Chinatown

Small by San Francisco or New York City standards, the Sydney **Chinatown** area is nonetheless a center of fine food, markets, and culture, well worth a stop if you like your diversions in the Asian manner. It's located about four long blocks up George St. from the Town Hall, essentially between Hay and Harbour sts. Dixon St., which cuts through the heart of Chinatown, is closed to vehicles and has Chinese arches at either end. Across Harbour St. is the **Sydney Entertainment Centre,** where visiting rock groups and other entertainers of note hold forth.

The centerpoint of the Chinatown area is the Sussex Centre, located between Sussex and Dixon streets. It has more than 30 speciality shops, an Asian food hall, and the huge 500-seat **Yumsing Seafood Restaurant.** The center is open seven days from 10 a.m.–9 p.m. The area can be reached by taking the monorail to the Entertainment Centre station.

Kings Cross

If a city has to have a 900-foot-high tower in order to compete with other famous urban spots, it follows that it must also have a certain amount of sleaze. Enter **Kings Cross,** Sydney's answer to Market Street in San Francisco or Soho in London, located southeast of The Domain just north of William Street. But Kings Cross is Aussie sleaze, meaning it's not very serious, and amid the neon-lit strip joints, sex shops, and nightclubs, are some good eateries and even a reputable shop or two. The future of The Cross looks gloomy—if you're into porn. It's being slowly but surely yuppified as The Loo—the Woolloomooloo district of town to the north—starts to expand. The Cross is probably safe enough to walk around in at night unless you're by yourself. If you like to wander around seedy areas of big cities at night, Kings Cross should keep you occupied. It ain't Kowloon, however.

Among the bouncier places in the Cross area are these:

Bourbon and Beefsteak • *24 Darlinghurst Road* • Open 24 hours, a favorite place for late-evening and/or early morning revelers. Constant music, good food. Moderate. *Phone 358–1114.*

Hard Rock Cafe • *121 Crown St., Darlinghurst* • The Aussie member of the international Rock Cafe group. Yankee food, rock n' roll, crowds, noise, confusion. Open noon-midnight seven days. Budget to moderate. *Phone 331–1116.*

Kardomah Cafe • *22 Bayswater Rd* • One of the more popular and populous places in the Cross. Live music and dancing seven nights a week; good place to catch some top Aussie rock bands. *Phone 358–5228.*

Springfield's • *15 Springfield Ave* • Another rock house, also dealing in popular and wannabe Australian bands. Open seven nights until late. *Phone 358–1785.*

The Cauldron • *207 Darlinghurst Rd., Darlinghurst* • Old and new, more stylish than some of the other places. Dancing to oldies as well as the latest screams. Open 7:30 p.m.–3 a.m. *Phone 331–1523.*

Porky's • *77 Darlinghurst Rd* • If skin's your thing, they show a lot of it at this joint. It's open from 10 a.m.–2 a.m. seven days and has a licensed bar. You can't miss it—look for the big red neon sign and the piggy next to it. *Phone 357–1180.*

There's a bureau de change next to the library at the corner of Darlinghurst and Macleay streets, open 8 a.m.–midnight seven days. And there's an information kiosk at the library itself. Walk a few blocks down Macleay to Potts Point and you'll find a post office. The shopping around the Cross is mixed, from souvenirs to garden hose and sex paraphernalia. One major shopping area is the **Kingsgate Shopping Centre,** underneath the Hyatt Kingsgate Hotel between Kings Cross and Bayswater roads. It also has a money exchange and a post office. For dining in the Cross, see the restaurant section.

Paddington

Southeast of the center city is this recovered Skid Row area, whose steep hills and twisted streets are now classed as one of the most desirable parts of the urban scene. Formerly crime-ridden, it now holds, as one observer noted, "large dogs and well-spoken children." Paddington's old Victorian terrace houses, once eyesores, have been lovingly restored a la New Orleans (they drip with iron filigree work), and the whole district is filled with ethnic restaurants, bistros, art dealers, antique shops, and bookstores, the end result being very chi-chi. The heart of the area is **Oxford Street,** also reputed to be the gay center of Sydney. A speciality of the shops along Oxford is **clothes,** offered by some of the country's leading designers. One of the best times to visit Paddo, as the area is called, is on Saturdays when the **Paddington Village Church Bazaar** fair is held at the Uniting Church, 395 Oxford St. Crowded, punky, food available, 8 a.m.–4 p.m. *Information: 331–2646.*

One of the major draws in Paddo is the **Victoria Barracks,** a massive sandstone building erected between 1841 and 1848. Starting at 10 a.m. Tues., you can watch the changing of the colonial-uniformed guards in front of what is considered to be the finest Georgian edifice in the city. It was used as a barracks and later as a school for artillery and cavalry troops. After the changing of the guards, there is a guided tour where you can check out the military museum and the manicured grounds. *Bookings essential: 339–3543.*

Also near Paddington is **Centennial Park,** opened in 1888 to celebrate the centennial. It's a little worn around the edges these days, but kids like to fly kites there, and there are bikes for rent. It also has a horse track and plenty of ponds and places for a picnic.

Glebe and Balmain

These are a couple of the newest toney parts of the Sydney scene, small communities west of the city across from Darling Harbour. Glebe's main drag, **Glebe Point Road,** is lined with some of the best **ethnic restaurants** in the city, mostly found in little mom-and-pop sized places. Glebe has a large student population, thanks to its proximity to **University of Sydney.**

For its part, Balmain seeks to out-Bohemia its cross-town rival, Paddington. The lots are postage-stamp sized, the houses of stone, the populace heavily leavened with writers, publishers, and other superior-type humans. Some very nice little pubs are around, as well as a coffeehouse or two.

Beaches

Australians love the sun, as their very high rate of skin cancer attests, and take every opportunity to hit the beaches. The coast east of Sydney is lined with good beaches, with something for all tastes from nude bathing to surfing. The official beach season, when regular lifeguards are posted, begins in October and runs through March. It's pretty stupid to swim when and where guards are not around, because most of the beaches have dangerous riptides. The waters around Sydney also have sharks, and routine patrols are on the water and in the air to warn swimmers. Shark attacks in the area are extremely rare, however.

One of the treats at many Australian beaches is a chance to watch the lifeguard squads practicing. The squads take their activity very seriously and go through their drills in precise military fashion, marching in step and perfecting the techniques used in life saving. Squad members are easily recognizable: they wear funny-looking caps—but don't tell them that. Lifeguarding is almost a national sport, as evidenced by the annual **National Surf Life Saving championships** held in March. In addition, there are frequent competitions among the squads. Information about these free events is available from the **New South Wales Surf Life Saving Association,** 663–4298.

The two most popular beaches in the Sydney area are **Bondi,** pronounced "Bond-eye," and **Manly.** Bondi is patrolled all year, and in the height of the Aussie summer, is up to the gills in oil-glistened bodies soaking up rays. Nearby are fast food places, dressing rooms, and hotels. The area around Bondi is, quite frankly, a bit worn at the edges, but the sand is fine and the water is cool. Getting to the beach is easy: catch a 380 bus from downtown or take a Bondi Beach train from the Quay and catch a beach bus at Bondi Junction.

Manly is a beach community northeast of Sydney across the harbor, also a bit creaky at the joints, abundant with fish and chips outlets and surfers. Like Bondi, the beach at Manly is patrolled all year. It's an interesting walking-around area, particularly on weekends when droves of city dwellers hop the ferry for a day of sand and snacks (something like 7 million people a year visit Manly.) You can get to Manly by slow ferryboat or fast hydrofoil from Circular Quay.

The Manly beachfront has a stand of very nice Norfolk Pines, and there are some fast food places dotted here and there. On the Sydney Harbor side is the Manly Oceanarium, built onto the ocean floor, which houses the requisite number of sharks, poisonous fish and colorful sea creatures. A moving walkway takes you through a transparent tunnel so the beasts are all around you. Also on hand are some Australian and New Zealand fur seals. The facility is open from 10 a.m.–5 p.m. daily. Admission about A$15. The Manly Tourist Information Office is located on South Steyne on the beach side of town. A good place to eat is **Faulty Bowers** (you must forgive them), an oceanside restaurant with large portions and good views. It's located on Marine Parade—from the ferry dock, go down Corso Street to the beach and hang a left. It's open for breakfast 8–10:30 a.m. on weekends; noon–3:30 p.m. daily for lunch. BYO. Reservations advised. *Phone 977–5451.*

You'll notice a bit of sprucing up when you arrive on the ferry—

the old 1940-era Manly Wharves have been restored and stuffed full of 85 specialty shops, four waterfront restaurants, a food hall and a small amusement park. The wharf is open from 9 a.m.–9 p.m. daily. *Information: 976–2555.*

Beaches near Sydney are designated either as northern or southern, depending on which side of the harbor entrance they are located. The southern beaches are easier to reach by public transport than those north of Manly. On the **south side,** in addition to Bondi, favorite beaches include

• **Coogee**—Look for the Coogee Bay Hotel and beer gardens. To get to the beach take Coogee Buses No. 373 or 374.

• **Cronulla**—Sydney's longest (two miles), quiet and calm. Take the Cronulla train.

• **Tamarama**—Near Bondi, a lot quieter, but with often dangerous riptides. Take the Bondi bus and walk south. Close by is **Bronte Beach,** wider and more open than Tamarama. Walking distance from Bondi.

Northern beaches in addition to Manly include:

• **Long Reef**—Adjacent to the Long Reef Golf Club; can be quite dangerous. Nearby is **Dee Why Beach,** good surfing, two miles of sand.

• **Harbord**—Between Manly and Dee Why, favorite for body surfing, shops close by. To the north of Harbord is **Curl Curl,** another mile-long beach.

Most of the near-Sydney north-side beaches can be reached by bus; check with the Urban Transit Authority, 954–9422.

Zoos

Coming to Sydney, but unable to head for the Outback—and thus in danger of missing the wonders of Aussie wildlife? Not to worry, because you still have the chance to cuddle a koala or check out the kangaroos without even getting your feet dusty.

The prettiest and most convenient of the city's animal facilities is the **Taronga Zoo,** a short ferry ride across the harbor from Circular Quay with great views of the city. The zoo has more than 4000 animals, including one of the best collections of Australian fauna in the country. One of the highlights is a seal pool, where there are free shows daily. You can also visit nocturnal critters, lions, some of Australia's more lethal snakes, and a childrens' zoo. There is a zoo train that circles the facility every half hour, and wheelchairs and baby strollers are available. The zoo is open all week, 9 a.m.–5 p.m.

The easiest way to get to the zoo is to buy a zoo pass at Dock 2 at Circular Quay. The pass, about A$15, give you round-trip ferry service, a pass on the bus that goes up the hill from the ferry dock to the zoo and zoo admission. Feeding time for the koalas is 3 p.m.; throughout the day there are talks at various locations by zoo staff. *Information: 969–2777.*

Koala Park, about 15 miles west of downtown, is the oldest private koala sanctuary in the state, and features breeding koalas and their wee families. There are also kangaroos, wombats, emus, and other native animals. Here's your chance to feed or pose with a koala or a kangaroo. Admission: about A$10 adults; open 9 a.m.–5 p.m. daily. *Information:* Koala Park, 84 Castle Hills Road, West Pennant Hills; tel. 484–3141. Another small sanctuary is **Waratah Park Animal Reserve,** about 30 miles north of downtown, where there are koalas and kangaroos to pet, as well as dingos, wild fowl, and foxes to examine. Admission, about A$7 adults, A$4 children; open 10 a.m.–5 p.m. daily. *Information:* Waratah Park, Namba Road, Duffy's Forest; tel. 450–2377.

The Arts Scene

Australia has a remarkable amount of activity in the arts, given its small population, from movies to rock music, ballet to bush music, and you can take a large taste of what's current on the Australian scene at places all over the Sydney area.

A sampling of what's available:

• **Classical music**—Many events are held in the Concert Hall at the **Sydney Opera House** or the **Sydney Town Hall.** Among the series to watch for are concerts and recitals presented throughout the year by the **Australian Broadcasting Commission.** Regular performances are made by the **Sydney Symphony Orchestra** in its subscription Recital Series. *Information* on ABC activities is available by calling the ABC concert department, 339–0211 or the Opera House box office.

The leading chamber music group is **Musica Viva,** which has subscription series each year at the Opera House and in the Seymour Centre in Chippendale. *Information* on chamber concerts is available by contacting 29–8165.

Other classical performances by various groups are held at the **Conservatorium of Music** in the Royal Botanic Gardens; regular concerts are scheduled by students, as well as the conservatorium's own symphony orchestra. *Information: 230–1263.* Other student players can be heard at the **University of Sydney's Music Department,** which also offers a series of professional concerts; performances are held in the Great Hall of the university. *Information: 692–2923.*

Another popular group is the **Sydney Philharmonia Choir,** which performs with the Sydney Symphony as well as presenting its own series of programs during the year. There are actually two choirs, one for large works and one for a cappella pieces. Many of the performances are at the Opera House.

The local newspapers' music sections on Thursday or Friday carry information on what's playing around town; in all cases, reservations are probably necessary.

● **Opera**— Many of the offerings are heavily booked by subscription, but some tickets are usually available. In January, the opera company gives an outdoor performance in The Domain. Information is available from the Opera House Box Office; performances can be pre-booked before leaving North America (see above under Opera House.)

● **Dance**—The **Australian Ballet** performs in all of the country's major cities, and has two seasons: Mar.–May and Nov.–Dec., with frequent appearances at the Opera House. *Information: 357–1133 or the Opera House box office.*

The **Sydney Dance Company** performs modern dance as well as classical ballet works, also in the Opera House. *Information: 358–4600 or the box office.* For a real treat, try the Aboriginal works performed by the **Aboriginal and Islander Dance Theatre.** *Information: 660–2581.*

● **Theater**—An evening of farce or tragedy is almost always available around Sydney, where more than 200 plays are presented every year. Tickets can be purchased by calling the individual theater box offices, or by contacting the Mitchell's BASS agency at 266–4800. Also, the Sydney Convention and Visitors' Bureau operates Halftix, through which you can buy half-priced tickets to theaters, Opera House performances, and offerings at the Sydney Entertainment Centre. Tickets are available only on the day of the performance; the Halftix outlet is at the convention bureau's kiosk on Martin St. between Castlereagh and Elizabeth sts. Hours are Mon.–Sat., noon–6 p.m.; phone 235–1437.

A few theaters:

The Footbridge Theatre, located at the edge of the University of Sydney campus in Glebe, concentrating on light fare and musicals; ticket price around A$25. *Information: 692–9955.*

Her Majesty's Theatre, 107 Quay St. downtown, a favorite for staging touring Broadway and London offerings, but also dramas and one-person performances; tickets around A$30. *Information: 212–3411.*

Ensemble Theatre, 78 McDougall St., Milson's Point, Sydney's oldest professional theater company, light drama, comedic works; tickets about A$15–A$20. *Information: 929–8877.*

Sydney Opera House Drama Theatre, where the Sydney Theatre Company holds forth, comedy, drama and musicals, often Australian works; tickets A$20–A$30. *Information: the Opera House box office.* The Sydney Theatre Company also performs at the Wharf Theatre at Pier 4, Walsh Bay, offering experimental and abstract works. *Information: 250–1700.*

Seymour Centre, at Sydney University, three theaters in all, offering a variety including Aussie works. *Information: 692–3511.*

Theatre Royal, one of the city's major sites for big-stage musicals and plays, seating around 1000, MLC Centre on King's Street downtown. *Information: 231–6111.*

Have a Go, Sports

All the major forms of football Down Under can be found here and there in Sydney—**Rugby Union** (amateur), **Rugby League** (pro), **European football** (soccer) and **Aussie Rules Football** (madness). Matches are played during the Aussie winter. Papers carry times and locations of major matches.

The **Sydney Cricket Ground** is where the city hosts international matches during the season (Oct.–Mar.). Also held at the grounds are **Sheffield Shield** matches, which feature games between the Australian states. Ticket prices run between A$15–A$30 for sheltered stands; around A$10 for open seating.

For golfers, there are around 40 public courses in the Sydney area, with greens fees running about A$10 for 18 holes. Among courses are the **Bondi Golf Links; New South Wales Golf Club,** 661–4455; **Castle Cove Country Club,** 406–5444; the **Moore Park Golf Course,** 663–3960, and the **Northbridge Golf Club.**

Tennis buffs also will find hundreds of public courts around the city, with court costs running A$5–A$10. Some close-in courts are **Rushcutter's Bay Tennis Centre,** 357–1675; **Trumper Park Tennis Courts; Moore Park Tennis Centre,** 662–7005, and **Cooper Park Tennis Courts,** 389–9259.

The Essential Sydney

INFORMATION • Maps, brochures, and general information about the city and its environs are available from the **Travel Centre of New South Wales,** located at 19 Castlereagh St. downtown. Open 9:30 a.m.–5 p.m. Mon.–Fri.; tel. 231–4444.

The **Sydney Convention and Visitors' Bureau** operates a kiosk on the Martin Place pedestrian mall between Castlereagh and Elizabeth sts. It has theater tickets as well as information. Hours are 9 a.m.–5 p.m. Mon.–Fri.; tel. 235–2424.

A quick source for visitors is the **Tourist Information Service,** a telephone line with advisors who are up to date on what's happening around town and also have tips on tours, restaurants, boat hires, galleries, and most any activity you'd want to try in Sydney. It's staffed from 8 a.m.–6 p.m. all week; tel. 669–5111.

If you're in The Rocks area, check with **Tourist Newsfront,** an agency that has brochures and information and can book tours and vacations anywhere in Australia. It's near the Argyle Centre, at Suite 3,

Penrhyn House, 22 Playfair St. Hours are 9 a.m.–5 p.m. all week; tel. 247–7197.

There is also a **general information office** at the Sydney Town Hall, corner of George and Druitt Streets, which has theater bills and bus schedules. Hours are 9 a.m.–5 p.m. Mon.–Fri.; tel. 265–9007.

GETTING AROUND • **Public transportation** is efficient and widespread in the Sydney metropolitan area. The international airport is about six miles from downtown, and is served by large yellow airporter buses (number 300) that run to Circular Quay and Kings Cross. The fare is A$4. Phone 369–8333. A private company, **Kingsford Smith Transport,** picks up and drops off passengers at a number of hotels along the way. The one-way fare is about A$4; tel. 667–3221 or 667–0663. The company also has stretch limos for about A$35 one-way.

Once in town, several services are available to get you around. One bus, the 777, is free and runs in a loop through the city center— just hop on and ride. Another free bus, the 666, runs from the Art Gallery of New South Wales in The Domain along George and Macquarie streets to the Wynard Station near the Holiday Inn.

Most of the major tourist attractions in the city are on the route of the **Sydney Explorer,** which has 22 strategic stops. A one-day ticket costs about A$12 and can be purchased on board. With ticket in hand, you can get on and off at will. Special bus stop signs tell you where to pick up the buses. Included among the stops are The Rocks, the Town Hall, Kings Cross, Chinatown, and the Central Railway Station. The Explorer buses run every 17 minutes from 9:30 a.m.–5 p.m., all week except Christmas Day. The Explorer is one of the best ways to orient yourself to the city. Tickets and information can be obtained ahead of time at the Travel Centre of New South Wales; tel. 231–4444.

Even better is the three-day *Sydney Pass,* which for A$35 lets you travel on the **Sydney Explorer** bus, the **Airport Express,** the morning harbour history cruise, and the afternoon **Harbour Lights** cruise, allows unlimited travel on the city ferry system (including the hydrofoil to Manly) and unlimited travel on city buses. All you do is hop on, show your pass, and away you go. You can buy the pass at the international airport information office, from Ansett or Australian airlines sales agents at the airport or at the NSW Travel Centre at Spring and Pitt sts. A tremendous deal.

Another good deal is the *Cityhopper,* a pass that allows you unlimited one-day travel on the city's train system anytime after 9 a.m. and all day Saturday and Sunday. The train system does a big circle around town, from Kings Cross to St. James (next to Hyde Park) to Town Hall to Circular Quay and around again. The price is about A$2.50, another great deal. *Information 954–4422.*

An invaluable source of information on all buses, trains, and ferries in the Sydney area is **Metro Trips,** which operates a telephone service from 7 a.m.–10 p.m. all week; tel. 954–4422.

Taxis are plentiful (except when, as in all modern cities, it's raining). Meters start at about A$1 and then it's around 80 cents a kilometer. A trip in from the airport will run around A$15. Major cab companies are **Taxis Combined Services,** 332–8888; **ABC Taxis,** 922–2233; and **RSL Cabs,** 699–0144.

For information about rail trips from Sydney to other spots in the state or the rest of the country, contact the **Rail Travel Centre of New South Wales,** Transport House, 11–31 York St., Sydney 2000; or **Railways of Australia,** which represents the five state-owned rail systems in the country, at 85 Queen St., Melbourne, Victoria 3000; tel. (03) 608–0811.

Where do you want to go in and around Sydney? Ask and ye shall receive. There are tours for just about everything. Some examples:

Australian Pacific Tours will take you on an all-day trip that includes a stop at the Featherdale Wildlife Park outside Sydney (home of the Qantas koala), a cruise on a Captain Cook luncheon cruise, a tour of all the major Sydney sights including a stop at Bondi Beach, and finishing up with a ride on the monorail and a tour of Darling Harbour. The cost (meals not included) is about A$70 per person, which includes free hotel pick up. Or for about the same money, you can do the north beaches, The Rocks, Sydney sights, Bondi and Darling Harbour. Or try a tour of the Opera House, Darling Harbour, Sydney sights and Bondi. A wide range of other options are available, including trips to the Hawkesbury River with a cruise and visit to Old Sydney or a day tour of the Blue Mountains. For the racier, there's a night tour of the city with dinner and admission to a strip club in Kings Cross for about A$90. To book tours or for information, stop at a Sydney travel agency or call 252–2988, 24 hours a day. Similar tours are offered by **Great Sights South Pacific;** see a travel agent or call 241–2294. If your time is limited in Australia and you're not driving, one of these tours might be a good idea.

The city's international and domestic **airports** are officially called **Kingsford Smith,** named for Australia's greatest early aviation pioneer. They are also lumped under the name of **Mascot Airport,** named for the suburb where they are located. The international airport is fully equipped with bars, restaurants, shops, and travelers' information. From the domestic airport, you can catch flights to all locations in the country. Flight information is available from individual airlines.

CLIMATE • Reversed, remember. Summer here is winter there. In the warm months (Dec.–Feb.), average high temperatures are normally around 70°–75°. Fall, (Mar.–May), highs are around 60–70°. Winter, (June–

Aug.), highs around 50°–60° degrees. Spring (Sept.–Nov.), highs around 60°–70° degrees. Fall and winter tend to be rainy.

BANKS • There is a **Westpac Bank** bureau de change on the ground floor at Kingsford Smith International Airport that stays open until the last flight has arrived at night and opens at 6 a.m. Major banks will cash foreign travelers' cheques (mostly for a fee). Banks are normally open 9:30 a.m.–4 p.m. Mon.–Thurs., 9:30 a.m.–5p.m. Fridays. Some change bureaus are open longer.

POST OFFICES • The main **post office** in Sydney is located on Martin Place between Pitt and George Streets. You can buy stamps or make international telephone calls 24 hours a day, seven days a week. Normal hours are 8:15 a.m.–5:30 p.m. Monday–Friday; 8:15–noon Saturday. *Information: 230–7122, or 230–7593.* A postcard to the United States or Canada is about A50 cents; a letter goes for around A90 cents.

SHOPPING • Stores in Sydney are generally open from 9 a.m. to 5:30 p.m. Mon.–Friday; until 9 p.m. Thurs., Sat. 9 a.m.–4 p.m.

As befits a city of its size, Sydney has a store for every interest and every pocketbook. There are intimate boutiques, huge department stores, open markets, and duty-free shops. The places that don't take major credit cards are rare; there are a few, however, that won't take American Express cards. With Visa or MasterCharge you won't have any problems. (Even some taxi drivers will take Visa.)

Most visitors would like a chance to pick up a piece of Australiana, and there are a number of stores specializing in Aussie works—and there's also a fair amount of junk floating around. The moral is that if the price is cheap, the goods probably are, too. Aboriginal art is coming into its own, meaning the prices are going up. Even in the Outback, Aboriginal art is not inexpensive anymore. In Sydney, check the **Aboriginal Artists' Gallery** at the corner of Market and Clarence sts., where native artists sell works on consignment. In The Rocks, try the **Aboriginal Arts Centre Dreamtime Gallery** in the Argyle Centre; there is also a branch in Paddington. *Information: 27–1380.*

The major shopping centers in the downtown area are:

Centrepoint (site of the tower), jewelry, upscale fashions, about 200 shops, corner of Market and Pitt sts. *Information: 231–6222.*

MLC Centre, corner of King and Castlereagh sts., next to Martin Place. Leather goods, lots of fast food places. Open to 5 p.m. Sat. *Information: 231–6411.*

Strand Arcade, a Victorian (1833) shopping complex, George St. between King and Market sts. Lovingly restored with wrought iron and one of the nicest places in town to browse. Some of the city's top clothing designers hang their wares here.

Shopping Size Chart							
Ladies							
USA	4	6	8	10	12	14	16
Australia	8	10	12	14	16	18	
MEN Shirts							
USA	14	14½	15	15½	16	16½	17 (in)
Australia	36	37	38	39	40	41	42 (cm)
MEN Sweater/T-Shirts							
USA, Australia		S		M		L	XL
MEN Suits/Coats							
USA	36		38		40	42	44
Australia	46		48		50	52	54

Argyle Centre, the main shopping arcade in The Rocks, 18 Argyle St. Knicks and knacks, glass, porcelain, lots of souvenirs. *Information: 241–1853.*

Queen Victoria Building, probably the most picturesque shopping area in Sydney—and one of the best in the world, for that matter. The QVB, as it's called, is a small miracle unto itself. It was built in 1893 to celebrate the diamond jubilee of Queen Victoria, and was designed to be a market place. Things didn't work out, and for years the old heap was boarded up and became a major downtown eyesore. The city dads decided to tear it down in the 1950s, but saner heads prevailed, thank God. The building, purchased and restored by a Malaysian company, is a wonder, complete with some of the nicest Victorian frippery you'll ever see. One of its most striking features is the central dome, which rises 200 feet from the ground floor. The QVB contains about 200 stores, from Chinese restaurants to Aboriginal art dealers.

The QVB is centrally located, occupying a whole city block on George St. across from the Hilton and near the Town Hall. Fast food available 24 hours. *Information: 264–1955.*

Major department stores in downtown Sydney include:

David Jones (two locations, at the corner of Market and Elizabeth sts. and the corner of Market and Castlereagh sts.) is most often compared to London's Harrods; the Elizabeth St. store specializes in women's clothing. There are branch stores in Bankstown, Bondi Junction, Paramatta, Brookvale and Campbelltown. *Information: 265–5544.*

Grace Brothers (436 George St.) is not as prestigious as David Jones, but still up to its cavern-sized floors with goods; friendly staff. There are branches all over the Sydney metro area. The downtown store has entrances on George, Pitt and Market sts. *Information: 238–9111.*

Woolworths (corner of George and Park sts.) is just what you'd expect. Good place to replace stuff lost or broken on the trip. *Information: 232–4633.*

Duty-free shops are available to tourists who have proof they are tourists. Officially, you're supposed to show them a return air ticket, but flashing a passport usually works as well. Some of the prices are about what you'd pay back home, but they do have tons of souvenirs of the stuffed-kangaroo variety and the normal booze-perfume-electronics-camera counters you'd expect. Among the stores are:

Downtown Duty Free (84 Pitt St.) is one of the biggest, with a wide selection of Australian opals; camera equipment. *Information: 232–2566.* Another outlet at 20 Hunter St., tel. 233–3166.

Sterling Nicholas Duty Free, 105 Pitt St. *Information: 33–3251.*

Orbit Duty Free, 74 Pitt St. *Information: 233–8399.* And at 276 Pitt St. *Information: 267–2159.*

Sydney Airport Duty Free, in the departures section of the international facility. *Information, 667–4153.*

ACCOMMODATIONS......................

One of the best views of Sydney Harbour is also one of the most expensive: looking out the windows of one of the pie-shaped corner rooms high atop the Regent of Sydney. The Opera House on your right, the Sydney Harbour Bridge to your left, the wide expanse of the harbor on both sides and far, far below, The Rocks. It might be one of the best A$400-a-night vistas on the planet.

But if you like your feet closer to the ground—and your rooms a tad less expensive, there's another hotel near the Regent that fits the bill: the Russell Hotel in the heart of The Rocks, a small hotel built in 1887 that oozes class and goes for A$300 a night less than its much fancier and taller neighbor.

These are our two favorite hotels in Sydney. The Regent is, well, the Regent, meaning five-star all the way, and the Russell is, well, the Russell, proving you can have quality and service and still share the bathroom with your neighbors. The two hotels show the variety of hotels available in the downtown area. But realize, like most major metropolitan areas around the world, hotel space in Sydney is generally expensive. It's hard to find a decent moderately-priced place anywhere near the city center.

The Rocks
Regent of Sydney ● *199 George St.; tel. 238–0000* ● City view rooms start at A$280; harbour views from A$385; the Regent Suite is A$2000. Large rooms with kings or big twins, mini-bars, three restaurants, two bars, health club, pool, parking. Great location on the edge of The Rocks.

Old Sydney Park Royal • *55 George St.; tel. 252–0524* • Doubles from A$265. Located in the heart of The Rocks down the street from the visitors center. A special delight is the plant-shrouded, 8-story atrium; art-bedecked lobby, rooftop pool garden with a tremendous view of the area. A popular spot for noshing and sipping is the Playfair bar/brasserie.

Park Hyatt Sydney • *7 Hickson Rd.; tel. 241–1234* • Standard doubles from A$385; harbour view with balcony, A$435; suites from A$600. The city's newest waterfront hotel, built in a curve on a small bay right under the Sydney Harbour Bridge. The decor is all marble and air, with some great views of the Opera House. The view from the rooftop pool and spa ain't too shabby, either. Most rooms have balconies and views of the harbor, Opera House or the city. Health center, two restaurants, one bar. Butler service on every floor. Not as nice, we think, as the Regent, but a very good location, indeed.

The Russell Hotel • *143A George St.; tel. 241–3543* • Shared facilities from A$100–130; doubles with baths are A$150–170; apartments and suites A$200–220. Built in 1887, the rooms in this narrow but cozy hotel are all different, all furnished with antiques. There are 13 rooms with shared facilities, seven doubles with private bath, plus the apartments and suites. It's about as centrally located as you can get in The Rocks, with views from a rooftop garden. A full continental breakfast is included in the room rates; have it in your room or in the small restaurant downstairs.

Harbour Rocks Hotel • *34–52 Harrington St.; tel. 251–8944* • Rooms with shared facilities, A$100; rooms with private baths, A$160; Located one block up from George Street, the hotel is housed in what was once a wool store and workers' cottages. It has had extensive renovations and, like the Russell, has a range of facilities from shared baths to a luxurious penthouse (about A$300 a night). Handicapped facilities. Our first love will always be the Russell, but the Harbour Rocks is close behind.

The Stafford • *75 Harrington St.; tel. 251–6711* • Doubles A$160; one-bedroom apartments A$275. Another restoration project, this one involving seven old terrace houses dating from the 1870s and 1890s. The 60 or so units have kitchens, TV and daily maid service. There is a guest laundry, pool, sauna, spa, and mini-gym. Good location, very good price considering.

The Mercantile • *25 George St.; tel. 247–3570* • Doubles A$95. This B&B hotel, built in 1914, has a stash of valuable Art Nouveau tiles, and was recently refurbished. It's probably the best deal in the area. It has a bridal suite (A$105 a night) and an Irish pub. The 14 standard rooms have shared baths, tea and coffee-making equipment, fridges, TVs. There is a guest laundry.

Downtown Area

Hilton International Sydney • *259 Pitt St.; tel. 266–0610* • Doubles from A$330; suites from about A$500. Probably the best central downtown location, right across the street from the Queen Victoria Building, meaning next to major bus stops and close to shopping and government buildings. On site is the famous Marble Bar, a restored Victorian saloon open at odd hours but worth a stop. Pool, spa, sauna, secretarial services. It has several weekend packages which combine dining with reduced room rates. The hotel is close to two monorail stations.

Hotel Intercontinental Sydney • *117 Macquarie St.; tel. 230–0200* • Doubles from A$285–385. The real way to get into the hotel is off Philip Street a block west of Macquarie. The hotel is close to the Botanic Gardens, within walking distance of both Circular Quay and the Opera House and has some good harbor views. Valet parking, two restaurants, three bars, pool, spa, sauna, health club, business services.

Sheraton Wentworth Sydney • *61–101 Philip St.; tel. 230–0700* • Doubles A$280–385; suites from A$420. In the heart of the downtown business district, close to Martin Place and a couple of blocks from the Quay. Five restaurants, four bars, business services. Nice leathery lobby, small shopping arcade, parking available.

Holiday Inn Menzies Sydney • *14 Carrington St.; tel. 299–1000* • Doubles A$250–280; suites from A$300. Situated on Wynyard Park near the Wynyard railway station and close to a Sydney Explorer Bus stop. Four licensed restaurants and four bars. Pool, three saunas, spa. Valet parking. Baby-sitting available; physician on call. Weekend packages offer substantial savings on rooms and some include tickets to area attractions. The Executive Club floor offers concierge service with complimentary breakfast and evening cocktails and a private lounge. Rooms on the floor go for about A$300.

Wynyard Travelodge • *7 York St.; tel. 299–3000* • Doubles A$150–225. Also close to the Wynyard railway station. Small, conventional hotel with restaurant and bar, tea and coffee making facilities, pool.

The Southern Cross • *Corner of Elizabeth and Goulburn Sts.; tel. 282–0987* • Doubles from A$275. Family rooms (two-room suites) from A$400–500. Near the Central railway station a couple of blocks from Hyde Park. Handicapped accessible. Licensed restaurant, piano bar, rooftop swimming pool, baby-sitting, valet parking, courtesy transport.

Hyde Park Plaza • *38 College St.; tel. 331–6933* • Doubles A$185–220; suites A$200–400. At the corner of Oxford and College streets at the southwest corner of Hyde Park, close to the YWCA and near a Sydney Explorer Bus stop. Pool, sauna, spa, cooking facilities, mini-bars.

Greetings Oxford Koala • *Corner Oxford and Pelican sts., Darlinghurst; tel. 269–0645* • Doubles A$140; suites from A$180. Close to an Ansett Airlines office and a city bus terminal, about a block from Hyde Park. Some rooms with cooking facilities, TV, tea and coffee facilities, guest laundry, pool.

Grand Hotel • *30 Hunter St.; tel. 232–3755* • Doubles from A$100. B&B located near the Royal Botanic Gardens, close to Parliament House. Rooms have TV and coffee/tea facilities. No parking available.

Kings Cross Area

Hotel Nikko Sydney • *81 Macleay St., Potts Point; tel. 368–3000* • Doubles from A$275; suites from A$365. Up the street from Kings Cross, and one of the newest in the city. The Japanese-owned hotel is strong on service, and the decor is pastels and washes—sterile by some tastes, soothing to others. Good views of the harbor from the opposite side of the Opera House. Two executive floors with private bar service and business amenities. Sunday brunch includes clowns for the kids.

Sebel Town House of Sydney • *23 Elizabeth Bay Rd., Elizabeth Bay; tel. 358–3244* • Doubles A$260–340. Here's one of the most elegant small hotels in town, as befits its membership in the Leading Hotels of the World organization. Located near King's Cross with views of Rushcutters and Elizabeth bays. The large rooms have dressing rooms and balconies. Health club, pool, sauna, parking. Several specials are available for any-day arrival, including one that offers harbor view, full English breakfast and dinner with a bottle of Australian wine and use of the health club facilities for about $A300.

Gazebo • *2 Elizabeth Bay Rd., Elizabeth Bay; tel. 358–1999* • Near Kings Cross, with some balcony rooms offering great views of the harbor. The rooms are pastelish and airy; the suites large and well-appointed. The glass-enclosed pool overlooks the harbor, as does the bar, which is great for night-time views of the area. The hotel, built in a salt-shaker style, has handicapped facilities, baby-sitting, medical facilities, complimentary parking, mini-bars, restaurant/cocktail bar and a cafe. A good bet.

Top of the Town • *227 Victoria St., Kings Cross; tel. 369–0911* • Doubles A$160–200. The rooftop pool overlooks Sydney Harbour and the Kings Cross area, as do some of the balcony rooms. Deluxe rooms have private spas, and the hotel was renovated in 1989. Free parking, guest laundry, bus stop at the front door or 200 yards away is the Kings Cross train station. Holiday season specials offer substantial reductions. Restaurant/bar.

Out of Town

Sydney Airport Hilton International • *20 Levey St., Arncliffe; tel. 597–0122* • Doubles from A$225; suites from A$400. Located in the suburbs near Botany Bay and the international airport off Highway 1 southwest of the city. Tennis courts, pool, close to golf course. Two restaurants, disco/supper club, business services.

Manly Pacific Park Royal • *55 North Steyne, Manly; tel. 977–7666* • Doubles A$160–185. On the beach in the North Shore resort of Manly, not far from the ferry dock. Rooftop pool with views of the beach area, health center, sauna, spa, business facilities. It also houses **Gilbert's,** a good seafood restaurant specializing in such goodies as goose liver with abalone, Hawkesbury River crayfish and medallions of buffalo fillet. It has a very good luncheon buffet. Expensive.

Serviced Apartments

Sydney, like other major Australian cities, has a group of serviced apartments which usually offer good prices, especially for folks wanting to hang around town for a week or so. Basically what you get is a furnished apartment with hotel-style services. The units offer some of the best locations and prices in the city. Among the ones worth looking at are:

York Apartments • *5 York St.; tel. 210–5000* • Located about half-way between Darling Harbour and downtown Sydney. It has 130 apartments, from studio units to a penthouse. There is room service, restaurant/bar, pool with spa and sauna. Laundry services, handicapped access, free parking. All units have balconies. Daily rates are doubles A$190–230.

Metro Inn Apartments Darling Harbor • *132 Sussex; tel. 290–9200* • Daily room rates A$140; weekly, A$850–950. Corner of King and Sussex, very close to Pyrmont Bridge, which leads into Darling Harbour. Views of the harbor as well as the Sydney Harbour Bridge. Apartments will accommodate two to four persons; TV, phones, laundry, parking garage.

Downtown Serviced Apartments • *336 Sussex St.; tel. 261–4333* • Daily room rate A$140–160. Close to the Chinese Garden area of Darling Harbour and close to Chinatown. Two-bedroom units for three to five persons. Laundries, pool, communal spa, tennis court, parking.

Park Apartments • *16 Oxford St.; tel. 331–7728* • Daily double rate from A$240–260. At the southwest corner of Hyde Park near the Hyde Park Plaza Hotel. Room service, sauna, laundry, pool, communal spa, handicapped access.

Hostels

The city has a fair number of hostel and budget-priced accommodations, from YHA facilities to small hotels. Realize that some of these are pretty basic and some are downright grungy. One central place to look for an el-cheapo room or hostel is in the Kings Cross area. The city information centers have reams of material on backpackers facilities in Sydney and the metropolitan area. A few suggestions:

Wattle House Newton (formerly the Billabong Hostel) • *11 Egan St., Newtown; tel. 550–3236* • About A$15 per person. In the burbs between the airport and downtown, one of the nicer facilities with pool, kitchen, parking, near the bus and train station, free pickup from the airport, TV lounge.

Forest Lodge YHA • *28 Ross St., Forest Lodge; tel. 692–0747* • A$15 per person. Off Parramatta Road across from the University of Sydney, a very nice area. Housed in a restored Victorian mansion. Close to downtown bus routes.

Original Backpackers • *162 Victoria St., Kings Cross; tel. 356–3232* • A$15 per person. Another old Victorian, located in the heart of the Cross, close to the train station.

Beachside Backpackers • *186 Arden St.; tel. 315–7888* • From A$10. Some doubles available. In Coogee Beach south of South Head, one of the better tanning spots on the Pacific side of the city. Easy to get a food fix, as well—it's above a McDonald's. Nearby bus station (10 minutes to city). Free daily bus to the city, airport and to the bus depot. Free weekly barbecues, adventure trips, in-house video, free airport pickup.

Harbourside Hotel • *41 Cremorne Rd., Cremorne Point; tel. 953–7977* • A$10 and up. Price includes breakfast and linens. Most rooms are doubles. Located on the north shore across from downtown Sydney. TV lounge, courtesy pickup service. Great views.

YWCA of Sydney • *5–11 Wentworth Ave.; tel. 264–2451* • Dorms from A$15 per person; doubles A$70. Close to Hyde Park. Cafeteria, coin laundry, TV lounge, non-smoking facility.

RV Parks

The closest caravan park to downtown Sydney is in the northern suburb of North Ryde: the Lane Cover River Van Village, 11 kilometers from town. It's one of the Big Four group; phone (02) 805–0500. It's close to bus and train services, and sits in about 20 acres of bushland in a national park. In addition to RV spots, there are tourist cabins for about $A50 double and on-site caravans for about $A40. Features a pool, a store, canoe hire, fishing, barbecue facilities, laundry services, and kitchens. Getting to town is pretty straightforward and you get a chance to ride a train across the Sydney Harbour Bridge.

RESTAURANTS......................................

One of the things that makes Sydney such a popular international tourist town is the wealth of restaurants and wide variety of cuisine available—another way the city compares well with San Francisco. Not surprisingly, given its location, many of the better places in Sydney specialize in seafood, but there are also some really fine Aussie-style places serving up lamb, vension, buffalo and other national specialities. And there are, of course, scores of ethnic restaurants. Some of the best dining we've found around town has been in hotels. But you explore and discover your own favorites. Some of ours:

The Rocks

No. 7 at the Park • *7 Hickson Rd.; 241–1234* • In the Park Hyatt Sydney Hotel on the harbor below the Sydney Harbour Bridge. If you like stunning night views, accompanied with stunning food, this outdoor harborside terrace restaurant should do the trick. The food is described as "contemporary Sydney cuisine," which in this case means an Asian flare, but not excluding Italian and South American influences. The Australian wine list is excellent. Lunch noon–3 seven days; dinner 7–11 p.m. seven days. *Expensive.*

The Kables • *199 George St.; 238–0000.* • In the Regent of Sydney. Tasmanian lobster with caviar butter sauce? Grilled venison medallions with boneless quail? You get the picture. This always-winning-awards restaurant is one of the priciest in town, but if you're looking for outstanding service, quality and decor, this must be the place. Open for lunch and dinner. *Very expensive.*

Waterfront Restaurant • *27 Circular Quay West; 247–3666* • On the waterfront, the theme of the outside dining area of this eatery is sailing ships, from the overhead sails to wooden masts. Not far away, fishing boats unload fresh catches for the restaurant, which is in a contest of sorts with Sydney's most famous seafood place, Doyle's—try them both and you decide. The Waterfront has three floors of indoor dining space, which, depending on your tolerance for nautical decorations, is maybe a bit gaudy but doesn't get in the way of the chow. Open for lunch and dinner seven days. *Expensive.*

The Waterfront is one of three restaurants owned by the same man; the other one in The Rocks is the **Italian Village,** which also has three floors of dining. The ground floor is supposed to look like an Italian village, complete with lampposts, a fountain and antiques, all imported from the Old Country. Fine views of the harbor from the restaurant. Open for lunch and dinner seven nights. *Moderate to expensive.*

Cafe Sorrento • *13 Playfair St.; 247–9328* • Casual, Mediterranean decor, inside or outside dining, nestled inside three old terrace houses. Try the grilled king prawns with lotsa garlic and peppers, or the grilled snapper and really good Greek salads. Lunch and dinner Monday–Friday; Saturday, dinner only from 5 p.m. *Moderate.*

Lowenbrau European Brasserie • *18 Argyle St.; 247–7785* • German, Swiss, Italian and American food, either in the enclosed glass outside area or inside. Casual, full of tourists. You don't have to eat to go in; there's also snacks or just bar service. Live oom-pah band Friday and Saturday nights. The last time we stopped in, our waiter was an American college student. Open early to late seven days. *Moderate.*

Fish at the Rocks • *29 Kent St.; 252–4614* • Near the Lord Nelson in the Argyle Place area. Small and intimate, where the chef comes to the table and grills your seafood selection on the spot. Among the choices: calamari, barrimundi, barbecued scallops with herb mayonnaise, good salads and real filtered coffee. Lunch Monday–Friday; dinner from 5:30–9 p.m. Tuesday–Saturday. *Moderate.*

Imperial Peking Harbourside • *15 Circular Key West; 247–7073 or 223–1128* • In the same complex as the Waterfront Restaurant. The Peking serves traditional Chinese food in traditional Chinese decor—but being close to the waterfront, you should expect seafood. And the Imperial has four tanks of live seafood on hand for the famished—would you believe live abalones? Try the lobster in ginger and shallot sauce. Or pick from prawns, mussels, scallops, squid and eel. Extensive wine list. Lunch noon–3 p.m. seven days; dinner 6–11 p.m. Sunday–Thursday, 6 p.m.–midnight Friday and Saturday. *Moderate to expensive.*

Doyle's at the Quay • *Overseas Passenger Terminal, Circular Quay; 252–3400* • This is the younger brother of the original and more famous Doyle's over at Watson's Bay on South Head. The Doyle family has been serving seafood for five generations—the Watson Bay restaurant has been in business for more than a century. The Circular Quay restaurant is nowhere near as sexy as the one across the harbor, but the food is still Doyle's, meaning platters of steamed shellfish, grilled John Dory, crabs and the famous Sydney rock oysters. Both restaurants are licensed; both are open seven days for lunch and dinner, and neither one takes reservations. To get to the Watson Bay restaurant, call Doyle's Water Taxi at 252–3400. The taxis leave from the private ferry dock (Number 6) at the Quay starting at 11 a.m. and run until late at night. It's about A$6 for a round trip. *Expensive.*

Downtown

The Treasury • *117 Macquarie St. in the Intercontinental Hotel; 230–0200* • Formal dining in an elegant Victorian-style dining room, complete with pianist and stately service. A speciality is the fixed menu, eight-course lunch for those who wish to take the afternoon off, with such goodies as oysters in sherry, clear quail soup and scallop salad. For dinner, you might try medallions of venison or maybe a lobster. The wine list matches the decor—up to and including a bottle of Chateau Lafite-Rothschild 1900. Reservations recommended. Lunch noon–2:30 Monday–Friday; dinner 7–10:30 p.m. Monday–Saturday. *Very expensive.*

Garden Court • *61 Philip St.; 230–0700* • In the Sheraton Wentworth Hotel. Another elegant formal dining room, with international cuisine—beluga caviar, salmon, pheasant and venison. It has a dance floor for after-dining exercise. Breakfast 7–9:30 a.m. Monday–Friday; lunch noon–2:30 Monday–Friday; dinner 6:15 p.m.–midnight Monday–Saturday. *Expensive.*

Papillon • *71 York St.; 262–2624* • French cuisine using Australian seafood and fresh game. The restaurant is housed in an National Trust building, complete with high ceilings and a century-old cedar entrance. Especially noted for its desserts. Menu changes with the seasons. Reservations recommended. Lunch noon–2:30 p.m. Monday–Friday; dinner 6–10 p.m. Tuesday–Friday. *Expensive.*

Diethenes Greek Restaurant • *336 Pitt St.; 267–8956 or 264–3476* • Very Greek with the usual items on the menu: taramosalata, moussaka, octopus, Greek-style lamb, Greek salads and some Greek wines. Ohpa. Reservations advised. Lunch and dinner Monday–Saturday. *Moderate.*

Sydney Tower Restaurants • *Corner of Pitt and Market sts.; 233–3722* • There are two revolving restaurants high above the city in the Sydney (or Centrepoint) Tower. The Level 1 Restaurant is a formal restaurant, with ala carte international menu and full service. Level 2 is cafeteria-style. Neither one is especially economical—in fact, both restaurants come precious close to being more than they're worth, but they are very popular with tourists. You're paying for the view, remember. Reservations are required at both.

Level 1 offers appetizers such as wild buffalo from the Northern Territory, scallops and prawns au vent, Sydney rock oysters and escargot. Main courses include rack of lamb, chicken cordon bleu and Queensland prawns. Counting appetizer, main course and dessert, look for the bill to be about A$60 per person without drinks. There's a A$20 per person minimum and on Saturdays, a 10 percent surcharge—for the increased labor costs, it says.

Level 2 offers fixed-price menus, normally a three-course offering of appetizer, main course, dessert and coffee, tea or soft drink. The main courses include a lot of roasts, but there is also seafood, Asian fare and steaks. The three-course dinner menu is between A$30 and A$40, wine, beer or liquor not included. There is also a surcharge Saturday, Sunday and holidays (those increased labor costs again).

Level 1 is open for lunch from 11 a.m.–3:30 p.m. Monday–Friday; dinner 5–11:45 p.m. Monday–Saturday. Closed Sunday.

Level 2 is open for lunch 11–3:30 Tuesday–Sunday; dinner 5–11:45 p.m. Closed Monday. Special rates for early dinner before 6 p.m.

Claudine's • *Two locations:* The Strand Arcade, *412 George St., second floor, 233–3473; and* Claudine's on Macquarie, *151–153 Macquarie St.; 241–1749* • The Strand facility overlooks the Victorian splendor of the arcade; the table decor is nothing special, but the food and view are fine. Specials include Snowy Mountain rainbow trout and hot and cold seafood platters; racks of lamb, thoroughly decadent desserts. More of the same at the Macquarie Street location. Hours at both are the same: lunch from noon Monday–Friday; dinner from 5:30 p.m. Monday–Friday. Reservations for Macquarie. *Moderate to expensive.*

Nikko's • *503 Kent St.; 261–8181* • Down the street from St. Andrew's Cathedral. Japanese in many forms—sushi, teppan barbecue, traditional. Private tatami rooms. Lunch noon–3 p.m.; dinner 6–11 p.m. seven days. *Moderate to expensive.*

Nearby is another Japanese restaurant, the **Suntory,** with a wide range of food styles available: sushi, tempura, sukiyaki, teppan. *It's at 529 Kent; 267–2900.* Lunch noon–2 p.m.; dinner 6:30–10 p.m. Closed Sundays. *Moderate to expensive.*

Forbes • *155 Forbes St, Woolloomooloo; 357–3652* • Licensed and BYO. Award winner for being one of the best value restaurants in the city—like three courses for around A$15. Italian food in courtyard or indoors. The antipasto buffet changes daily, and the rich Italian desserts are famous. Lunch noon–3 p.m. Monday–Friday; dinner from 6 p.m. seven days. *Budget to moderate.*

Harry's Cafe de Wheels • *1 Cowper Wharf Rd., Woolloomooloo; no phones* • Are you ready for gourmet Australian meat pies? Hot dogs and pasties, coffee to wash it down. This always busy pie cart is a favorite with late-night Sydneysiders. Open 7 a.m.–3 a.m. *Budget.*

First Floor Restaurant • *252 Sussex St.; 261–8408* • Actually on the second floor above St. Elmo's Bar with views of the harbor. International cuisine; such goodies as king prawns with roasted garlic and pine nuts, Cajun blackened fish and brandied fig ice cream. *Moderate.*

Darling Harbour

Jordan's Seafood Restaurant • *197 Harbourside; 281–3711* • Inside or outside dining with a fine view of the harbor and the Sydney skyline. Live jazz goes along with Darwin mud crabs, Sydney rock oysters, barrimundi, prawns and the fresh catch of the day. Open for lunch and dinner seven days. *Moderate to expensive.*

Kings Cross

Watermelon Restaurant and Bar • *15 Kellet Way; 357–3824* • Late night favorite with European flare and almost California-style food: poppy and pecan bread, mango puree with lime hollandaise sauce and a dandy little number called "Death by Chocolate." Open courtyard or inside dining—go for a snack or a full meal. Open 6 p.m. until late seven days. *Budget to moderate.*

Bombay Indian • *33 Elizabeth Bay Rd.; 358–3946* • Licensed and BYO. Mughlai and tandoori cuisine from the north of India—chicken, prawns, lamb. Vegetarian or meat curries as hot as or as mild as you like. It's one of several good Indian places in the Cross; try the **New Delhi Experience,** 229 Darlinghurst, 360–5623. Or in Darlinghurst, try the **Tandoori Palace,** 86 Oxford St.; 331–7072. All are moderately priced. Hours for the Bombay Indian: lunch noon–2:30 Monday–Saturday; dinner 5:30–10:30 p.m. seven days. Also has take-away.

Sydney Cover Oyster Bar • *Circular Quay East* • Little spot down from Writer's Walk with fresh oysters and snacks, great views of the Opera House. Writer's Walk is worth a stroll; it honors such authors as Charles Darwin, Banjo Paterson, D. H. Lawrence, Jack London and Henry Lawson. The oysters are moderately priced. Hours vary.

Away From Town

Mulligan's • *137 Cleveland, Chippendale; 699–5582* • Near the University of Sydney, supposedly the city's only Irish restaurant. Dinner comes with Irish fiddles and Ilian pipes. BYO. Dinner from 7 p.m. Tuesday–Sunday. *Moderate*.

Oasis Seros • *495 Oxford St., Paddington; 361–3377* • Award-winning licensed French restaurant, ready to entice you with such items as grilled crumbled pig's trotters with shitake mushrooms, glazed duckling with steamed ginger buns and a dessert of grilled figs with ginger custard. Truly decadent. Call for hours and reservations. *Expensive*.

Sails Harbourside Restaurant • *McMahaon Point across the harbor northeast of the Sydney Harbour Bridge; 955–5998 or 955–5793* • Fabulous view of the bridge and downtown Sydney, with inside or terrace dining. Pick live crayfish from a tank, snack on Sydney rock oysters, John Dory, or Aussie beef and lamb. You can drive or take a private ferry from the Number 6 Dock at Circular Quay. Reservations recommended. Lunch Monday–Sunday; dinner Monday–Saturday. *Moderate to expensive*.

Manly Pier Seafood Restaurant • *At the ferry dock; 949–2677* • View back toward the city, walking distance to the Pacific Ocean beaches. All sorts of finny and shelled critters. Hours vary. *Moderate*.

For budget diners: Find a newsstand and pick up a copy of *Cheap Eats*, which carries information and mini-reviews of hundreds of Sydney-area places. The reviews we've checked seem to be pretty good. The prices are too.

BEYOND SYDNEY ....

People—at least most sensitive people—cannot live by city alone and must, from time to time, escape the noise and hydrocarbons for smaller and less frantic scenes. New South Wales is filled with such oases of sanity, from the vineyards of the Hunter Valley to the raw nothingness of the desert country on the South Australia and Queensland borders.

If time is tight, however, there are many places of note outside the city proper that can be done in a day. A few worth investigation:

The Blue Mountains

Before early explorers found a way across the Blues, these rolling mountains were a terrifying barrier to colonial expansion, part of the Great Dividing Range that runs along the entire east coast of the continent. Even today, the steep mountains and heavily wooded valleys in the Blues are not completely tamed. The mountains get their name because, from a distance, minute oil droplets falling from the leaves in the thick eucalyptus forests turn sunlight blue.

The area became a popular summer retreat for Sydney's wealthy in the 1870s, and over the years since, has become a major tourist spot served by daily train and bus service from the city. (A train from the city to Katoomba is about A$10 round trip.) Driving, you take the Great Western Highway (Parramatta Road in the city) or the Hume Highway, which branches off Parramatta Road in the Sydney suburb of Ashfield.

About 500,000 acres of the area are included in the Blue Mountains National Park, which is filled with picnic spots, hiking trails and campgrounds. A gaggle of small resort towns is scattered around, most of them on the rail line from Sydney to Bathurst. Some of the once-grand housing is showing signs of wear, and some of the hotels and pubs are getting a tad grungy.

Still, the scenery and the cool air (crisp in the winter) are worth a day train trip or a longer visit. One stop should be **Katoomba,** the major town. If you're not averse to heights, check out the **Katoomba Scenic Skyway,** a cable car that dangles over the chasms of the Jamison Valley. The companion ride, almost as hairy, is the **Katoomba Scenic Railway,** a cog-rail beauty that drops at incredible angles into the valley. *Information: (047) 82–2699.*

At Katoomba is one of the Blue Mountains' most famous vistas, the **Three Sisters,** a set of sandstone columns stepping into the valley. If not driving, you can reach most of the scenic spots on the **Blue Mountains Explorer Bus,** which makes 18 stops on weekends and holidays. You can book the bus and pick it up at **Golden West Tours,** 283 Main St., Katoomba; tel. (047) 82–1866. Golden West Tours also runs special buses and four-wheel drive trips. In addition to the more staid excursions, a number of companies also offer rock-climbing, camping, horseback riding and other speciality trips in the park.

Another popular attraction in the area is the **Jenolan Caves,** about 50 miles southwest of Katoomba, a large system of limestone caverns that were the home of Aboriginals for centuries. The most popular caves are lighted and have stairs for easy walking; others require a guide.

Lithgow, basically a coal-mining and industrial town, is also the site of the famous **Zig Zag railway,** built in the late 1860s to allow trains to descend from the Blue Mountains to the Bathurst plains and, with its series of switchbacks and bridges, a real engineering marvel. The route has been restored and special steam trains run on weekends and periodically during school holidays. Information on times and fares is available from Golden West Tours in Katoomba. Information is also available from the **Zig Zag Railway Society,** P.O. Box 187, Lithgow, New South Wales 2790; tel. (047) 57–3061.

General information about the Blue Mountains is available from the Travel Centre of New South Wales in Sydney at 19 Castlereagh; tel. 231–4444. There are two tourist information centers in the mountains: Glenbrook, tel. (047) 39–6266, and Echo Point at Katoomba, (047) 82–1833. Brochures and general information are also available from the **Blue Mountains Tourism Authority,** P.O. Box 273, Katoomba, New South Wales 2780; tel. (047) 39–6266.

Among **bus companies** offering day tours are: **Pioneer,** Oxford Square, Darlinghurst, tel. 268–1331; **Clipper Tours,** 9–11 Alma Rd., North Ryde, tel. 888–3144; **AAT Kings Coaches,** Circular Quay and **Australian Pacific Tours,** 109 O'Riordan St., Mascot, tel. 693–2222. To give you an idea what to expect, one of Pioneer's trips leaves from Circular Quay around 9 a.m., tours most of the major spots in the mountains, and returns to the city by 7:30 p.m. The cost is about A$45, but if you have an **Aussiepass,** the fare is about half that. Meals are not included, and many of the tours stop outside Sydney at a koala farm so you can check out the furry little critters.

You will find the usual array of **accommodations** in the Blue Mountains communities, from motels to resort hotels. Among the latter is an old yellow heap called the **Hydro Majestic,** located in Medlow Bath just to the west of Katoomba. The Hydro Majestic, built in 1904, has good views of the Megalong Valley; rates are around A$60 a night double. There are a pool and tennis courts, and three golf courses are nearby. It's a good place for Devonshire tea, a fixture in the area: tea, scones, jam, polite chats. *Information: (047) 88–102.* Another grand hotel is the **Carrington** in Katoomba, the oldest in the mountains. Rates are about the same as the Hydro Majestic. *Information: (047) 82–1111.*

The good people of the region, in a plan that should be adopted by all civilized nations, have set up a "duty motel" program: weekly, one Blue Mountains hotel or motel is designated to help visitors seeking accommodations. The name and number of the duty hotel is listed at the tourist information center at Echo Point in Katoomba.

National Parks

There are 65 national parks in the state (including the **Blue Mountains.**)
Two others close in to Sydney are **Royal National Park** and **Ku-ring-gai Chase National Park.** Entry fees for both are around A$5 per car.
Information about parks in New South Wales, as well as any national
parks in the country, is available from the National Parks and Wildlife
Service, 189 Kent St., Sydney; tel. 237–6500.

Royal National Park became, in 1879, the second national park
in the world (Yellowstone was created a year earlier). The park, about
20 miles south of Sydney, sits on a peninsula just below Botany Bay.
It gives visitors a good idea of how the virgin bush area around Sydney
looked when the First Fleet arrived. The park's 31,000 acres include
Aboriginal artwork and relics as well as picnic areas, RV and tent camping
areas and beaches. It's reached easily by driving south on Highway 1,
the Princes Highway, which branches off Paramatta Road in Sydney.
It's also on a rail line. Park office tel.: 521–2230.

Ku-ring-gai Chase National Park is a watery park about 25 miles
north of Sydney in the Hawkesbury River delta. There are many hiking
trails, and boats can be hired by the day, no license required. You can
also rent a houseboat for a week; rates range from around A$500 in the
off-season to around A$1200 in the summer. Check with the Travel
Centre of New South Wales for rental agencies. The park headquarters
is reached by taking the Ku-ring-gai Chase Road turnoff from the Pacific Highway. The Pacific Highway starts in North Sydney across the
Sydney Harbour Bridge. The park is also accessible by train.

A cushy way to check out the park area is to hop the *Lady Hawkesbury,* a **60-cabin luxury boat** that runs four-day and weekend trips
up the river. The Lady is operated by **Captain Cook Cruises** in Sydney. A double deluxe stateroom costs around A$850 for a weekend
cruise; transportation to and from the port town of Brooklyn not included. Information: 27–4548. **Float planes** can also fly you in for the
day. Try **Vic Walten** at Aquatic Airways Ltd., Berrenjoy Boathouse,
Governor Phillip Park, Palm Beach, Sydney 2108; tel. 919–5638. The
national park office: 457–9853.

The Coasts

The basic dividing line between the upper and lower coasts of New
South Wales is Sydney Harbour, but you have to go a fair distance
either direction to get out of the Sydney suburbs. The entire coastline is
about 500 miles long. From the Hunter River north, it is basically semi-
tropical. South of Sydney, Highway 1, the major coastal route, is known
as Princes Highway; north of the city it's called the Pacific Highway.

The highway system—usually called "Australia One"—runs from northern Queensland around the continent to Western Australia.

Sydney to Tweed Heads

To the north, you are officially out of the Sydney metropolitan area once you pass the Hawkesbury River. Starting about 50 miles north of the city, the coastline encloses several large and popular lakes as it runs north, including **Tuggerah Lake, Lake Macquarie** and **Myall Lakes.**

An oceanside road runs up along the barrier islands separating Tuggerah from the sea. A long, narrow, and mostly deserted beach runs from the Entrance, a channel between the lake and the ocean, to Norah Head. You'll find **hotels** and **motels** all around the shores, with **cafes** and **restaurants** specializing in fresh seafood.

Lake Macquarie, the largest salt-water lake in the country, lies to the west of the Pacific Highway. The most famous spot on the lake is the village of **Wangi Wangi,** a mining village with dandy old architecture.

Next in line is the sprawling industrial city of **Newcastle,** the seventh largest city in Australia. It was here in early 1990 that Australia had a rare—and very upsetting—earthquake that leveled a number of buildings and killed several people. So rare are such incidents that locals thought a bomb had gone off or a plane had crashed. The city this century has basically been a company town for BHP, the giant Aussie conglomerate, which set up steel mills here. Despite this, there have been some comparisons between Newcastle and San Francisco because of hills with stately houses that run down to the harbor. The city is a gateway to the coal fields and vineyards of the Hunter Valley, which runs inland from the harbor along the Hunter River.

Just to the north of Newcastle is **Port Stephens,** one of the largest deepwater ports in Australia (twice the size of Sydney Harbour), known for great oysters, good fishing, and pleasant beaches. The main settlement in the harbor is **Nelson Bay.** Cruises and fishing charters are available, and there is a golf course.

Just across the narrow harbor entrance from Nelson Bay is **Hawks Nest,** a small resort village with a golf course and several RV parks. Hawks Nest also marks the southern tip of a 25-mile-long beach that goes up the coast to **Seal Rocks.** Right next door is the quaintly named settlement of **Tea Gardens,** which has accommodations.

The beach is part of **Myall Lakes National Park,** 77,000 acres in size and one of the best in the state. The shoreline areas of the park are lined with paperbark trees and palms, and the lakes and interior parklands are home to black swans, egrets and ducks, plus the usual assemblage of kangaroos, bandicoots, and swamp wallabies. Unlike Lake

Macquarie, Myall Lakes are freshwater, and stretches of the interior shore are rain forest. One way to enjoy the area is to take a **cruise** up the Myall River. **Boats** can be rented or booked at Tea Gardens or Bulahdelah, on the Pacific Highway. Canoe-camping trips are also available. *Information: Superintendent, National Parks and Wildlife Service, 28 Sturgeon St., Raymond Terrace 2324; tel. (049) 87–3108.*

The twin towns of **Forster** and **Tuncurry,** a few miles north of Myall Lakes, lie across Wallis Lake from each other. The area, popular for water sports, is also known for its seafood, especially prawns. **Taree,** a few miles farther north, is the agricultural center for the valley of the Manning River. For naturalists, there is a rain forest near town that is famous for its flying foxes, the huge Australian fruit bats that come out at night in masses to hunt.

About 45 miles north of Taree is the old penal settlement of **Port Macquarie,** which was set up in 1821 to take the worst felons from gaols farther south, and had a reputation as one of the cruelest prisons in Australia. It's now a major tourist center with a fair amount of ticky-tacky amidst the old sandstone buildings of the colonial past—look for St. Thomas Church, built by the convicts. The beaches nearby are rated as excellent for surfing. Just south of town is Sea Acres Sanctuary, which has tropical rain forest displays, including 1000-year-old strangler figs. How popular a town it is you can judge by the fact that there are 18 RV parks and at least 40 motels.

By the time you get to **Macksville,** about 80 miles north of Port Macquarie, you know you've entered the tropics—the place is surrounded by banana plantations, and the houses are starting to take on Queensland attributes: they come with verandas and tinned roofs, and many are built on stilts, all developments designed to cool things off in the summer and stay dry in the winter rains.

The old timber port-gold rush town-dairy center of **Coffs Harbour** 40 miles north is a popular base for exploring this stretch of the coast and thus has a fair share of motels, pubs, and amusements. About 10 miles north is the **Kumbaingeri Wildlife Park,** where you can rent horses—or if you haven't yet cuddled a koala, have a go. (How anybody could get this far from Sydney without holding the beasts at least once is a mystery.)

Also, we should mention that it is not Americans alone who have carried the art of roadside attractions to the point of nausea. Consider, if you will, the Big Banana, a huge concrete thing stuck in the middle of a plantation as a monument to bad taste. Inside its startling form is a souvenir shop and—here's the stopper—a display about the banana biz. Not to be missed.

Inland, to the west of the Macksville-Coffs Harbour area, are several parks where you can see expanses of rain forest and the wee beasties that inhabit them. Included are **Dorrigo National Park,** with excellent hikes and many waterfalls and picnic areas, and **New England National Park,** which has the largest preserved area of rain forest in the state.

The **Clarence Valley,** 50 miles north of Coffs, is pasture country and its population center, **Grafton,** is a genteel old town famous for its late-Victorian architecture and streets lined with stands of jacaranda. Within driving distance are two coastal parks, the closest of which is **Yuragir National Park,** and a bit farther up, **Bundjalung National Park,** which has a fair population of emus, wallabies, and koalas at the north end near Evans Head. Both parks have beaches, swimming, and hiking.

The two main coastal towns north of Grafton are **Ballina** and **Byron Bay.** Ballina is situated at the mouth of the Richmond River and has a maritime museum. Byron Bay is the easternmost point of land on the continent, which is why there is an old lighthouse there, still working. It also has one of the best surfing beaches in the nation.

The final stop on the coast before entering Queensland is the semi-tacky little settlement of **Tweed Heads.** Tweed Heads marks the beginning of one of the fastest growing tourist areas in the country, the so-called Gold Coast that runs from Tweed Head's sister (and connected) city, Coolangatta, to Surfers Paradise near Brisbane.

Sydney to Cape Howe

If you're heading south along the coast from Sydney, one place to stop, just for historical significance, is **Botany Bay.** It was here, you will recall, that Capt. James Cook landed in 1770 and so liked what he saw that 20 years later, His Majesty's Government decided to send all of England's felons along to take a look, too. The only problem was when they arrived 18 years later, they discovered Botany Bay was worthless as a spot to start a colony and went north a few miles to what is now Sydney Harbour.

It might amuse the good captain to realize that Botany Bay is now the site of Sydney's international airport and its shores are lined by container ship docks. At any rate, there is a **park** on the spot where Cook and his party landed. It's on the south spit of land at the entrance to the bay in a suburb called Kurnell, reached from Princes Highway. There are a museum, picnic area, and trails around the headland. The museum is open 10:30 a.m.–4:30 p.m. weekdays, 10:30 a.m.–5 p.m. weekends. The park itself is open 7:30 a.m.–7 p.m., admission charge about A$5 per car. *Information: 669–9923.*

The first major city south of Sydney is **Wollongong,** about 45 miles down, and the site of the state's largest steel plants. But there are also some fine beaches that draw Sydneysiders down by train on weekends. There are tours of the steel plants if you've a mind, and in **Mount**

Kembla Village, an old coal-mining town west of the city, is a monument to the 1902 explosion that killed about 100 miners. The area's coal mines still produce millions of tons a year.

One of the most famous attractions in the area is the **Blowhole,** located at **Kiama,** 10 miles south of Wollongong. It was discovered by explorer George Bass in 1797, and if sea, surf, tide, and wind are right, it can spray a fountain almost 200 feet high.

Between Wollongong and Kiama, the Illawarra Highway (Route 48) runs west to **Morton National Park** in the highlands, a big park that contains examples of most of Australia's native animals and miles of trails. The park, 50,000 acres, is noted for deep gorges and waterfalls. Near the northwest corner of the park is Fitzroy Falls, which drops 250 feet. Nearby is the hamlet of **Kangaroo Valley,** which has a pioneer museum and tea rooms.

South of Kiama, the coast road heads inland to cross the Shoalhaven River estuary at **Nowra.** At **Berry,** about halfway between, a coastal access road runs east to **Seven Mile Beach National Park.** Nowra, about 10 miles up the river from the coast, is growing as a tourist center, and is the commercial hub for this stretch of the coast.

To the southeast of Nowra on the coast are a group of **resort towns** centered around **Jervis Bay,** which has some of the best beaches on the whole New South Wales coast. For reasons that escape us, when the Australian Capital Territory was set up in 1911, it was decreed that the nation's capital had to have access to the sea, so about 18,000 acres around Jervis Bay were annexed to the ACT. The chunk of land is now home to the Royal Australian Naval College.

A group of coastal lakes and lagoons with white sandy beaches is centered around the town of **Ulladulla,** about 20 miles south of Jervis Bay. The town itself is a major fishing port, and the lakes offer water skiing, fishing, and boating activities. From this point to Bega, about 100 miles south, there are dozens of coastal access roads that cut east from the Princes Highway. The beaches are almost uniformly white sand, and in several areas, the waters and islands offshore have been set aside as wildlife sanctuaries. The **Tollgate Islands** near Bateman's Bay, for example, are a haven for penguins. From Bateman's Bay, there are cruises up the Clyde River and a bit farther south, there is a bird sanctuary with tours.

About 20 miles south you find **Moruya,** a farming and seafood center whose major claim to fame is as the spot where the pylons for the Sydney Harbour Bridge were quarried.

From Moruya south, most of the coastal towns and villages are in the dairy-seafood-lumber business, although bits and snatches of tourism are rearing their heads. **Central Tilba,** just outside of Narooma, has been declared a national historical village and has several fine examples of mid-Victorian buildings. Just behind town is **Mount Dromadery,** the highest peak on the New South Wales coast (2700 feet), which has a trail to the top and attendant views.

This is also **cheese country,** and you'll find many places that offer tastings. **Bega,** south of Narooma, anchors an area known for its cheddars, and the **Bega Cooperative Society Cheese Factory** has tastings and tours. West of Bega is **Kameruka Estates,** an agricultural center begun in the 1830s and now listed in the National Trust. You want to see sheep, they have sheep.

Tuna fishing and tourism are the mainstays of **Merimbula** and its sister town, **Pambula,** back on the coast south of Bega. There are also oysters and prawns, and for **Wind in the Willows** fans, an old building called Toad Hall (apparently no connection).

The last community of any size before reaching the Victoria border is **Eden,** an old whaling port with museum to match. It's also a lumbering community, and the harbor—Twofold Bay—is reputed to be one of the four or five deepest in the world. On the coast north and south of the bay is **Ben Boyd National Park,** which has red sandstone cliffs and lots of wildlife.

The Mountains

Inland from the fertile coast, the land steps up into the peaks and high tablelands of the **Great Dividing Range,** then down again onto the ranch country of the range's western slopes, then lastly into the flat and arid western plains.

Of all the sections of the Great Dividing Range, perhaps the most famous and most popular is the **Snowy Mountains,** the "Alps of Australia." Many North Americans at least recognize the name because of the successful Aussie movie, *The Man From Snowy River,* a horse-and-rider saga based on the poem of the same name by Banjo Paterson, who also wrote *Waltzing Matilda.*

By North American standards pretty small peanuts—the highest peak in the range, **Mount Kosciusko,** is only 7300 feet—the region nonetheless allows Australians to enjoy skiing and winter sports during the season, June–September. The total snowfalls can be iffy, however, and sometimes the skiing conditions are not very good. There are 10 peaks over 6800 feet, which, when you consider that most of Australia is flatter than a pool table, is geologically significant. The mountains are contained inside **Kosciusko National Park,** which sits at the state's southwest corner near the Victoria border. There are no day trips from Sydney, though, being about 300 miles away.

The best way to get into the mountains is to drive to Cooma, either on the coast highway to Bega and then over, or down Highway 23 from

Canberra. Once in Cooma, you can go northwest to Tumut or southwest to Jindabyne, Mount Kosciusko and the ski areas.

The two major downhill **ski areas** are located at **Thredbo** and **Perisher Valley.** Cross-country is allowed on almost all the snowfields. Most of the ski areas in the Snowies have accommodations, food, shops, and pubs. Rental equipment is available at all.

Thredbo is the oldest and one of the most developed of the resorts, with new snow-making equipment and all three levels of runs. It offers four chairlifts, three beginners' T-bars, and access T-bars near advanced runs. The chairlifts also run in the summer for gawkers and hikers, and the resort reportedly does a fair amount of conference business. From the end of the top lift station, hikers can get to the crest of Mount Kosciusko, a popular foray. (That's pronounced "koz-ee-AWS-koe," by the way.) *Information: The Thredbo Centre, 49 Market St., Sydney 2000; tel. 268–2681.* Or contact the resort at Thredbo Alpine Village, P.O. Box 92, Thredbo, New South Wales 2627; tel. (064) 57–6360. The resort has year-round accommodations.

Perisher Valley has more than 75 miles of trails and the capability of lifting around 30,000 skiers an hour on the highest lift in the area, rising to more than 6600 feet. All three levels of slopes are available, and new snow-making equipment has been installed. Lodges and luxury hotels are available. *Information: Perisher/Smiggins Resort Centre, Perisher Valley, New South Wales 2630; tel. (064) 57–5211.* Bookings also available in Sydney through World Travel Headquarters, 33 Blight Street; tel. 237–0300.

The northernmost resort is **Mt. Selwyn,** near Tumut, an area that has concentrated on cross-country but does have some downhill. There are snack shops, T-bars, and tow ropes, but no overnight accommodations. *Information: Mt. Selwyn Ski Resort, P.O. Box 363, Tumut, New South Wales 2720; (064) 54–9488 or 52–1108.*

Major population centers in the mountains are **Jindabyne,** at the east center of the park; **Kiandra,** to the north, and **Tumut,** which is the northern gateway. Jindabyne is next to a lake of the same name, stocked with trout. A shuttlebus runs from here to the ski resorts in the winter.

The Aussies have come up with a novel way to get skiers and hikers around the mountains. It's called the **Skitube,** and is an electrically operated train that goes through and into several mountains. It runs from the Alpine Highway (the road between Jindabyne and Thredbo) to the Perisher ski area and on to Mt. Blue Cow, one of the highest and newest of the Australian Alpine resorts. The Skitube runs all year so hikers can also take advantage of it, and mountain bikes are also available for rent. The tube costs about A$20 for a round trip; a one-day bike hire plus round trip on the tube is about A$40. If you want to try

Skitube, just stop at the terminal off Alpine Highway about 18 kilometers west of Jindabyne, or call (064) 56–2010.

The drive from Jindabyne to Thredbo is one of the loveliest in Australia. It follows a deep river valley most of the way, with the mountains on either side. Along the way are signs indicating "Wombat Crossings," and from the Skitube station on, the scenery gets even better. Thredbo is raw tourist town, full of resorts and ski shops. Many of the resorts are perched on a hill above the valley; access is on a tiny road closed to buses and trucks. The chairlift running out of Thredbo is a wonder, steep long and high, and lots of folks take it up to the top of the nearby peaks and then hike on to Mount Kosciusko.

The easiest way to get to the top of Australia's highest mountain is to drive from Jindabyne up the Kosciusko Road through the national park to a place called Charlotte's Pass—you can't miss the spot because the pavement ends. Park along the highway. You have two choices to get to the top—one goes right, one goes left. The easiest and shortest is to the left. At one time, you could drive to the top of the mountain, and this trail follows the old road. It's not at all hard, and it's not that far, maybe 8 or 9 kilometers, to the top. It gets a bit chilly, even in the summer, so wear a light jacket.

Once on top, you can go back the same way or complete a circle trip by taking the Lake Albina/Club Lake trail. It's a glorious hike, and the scenery rivals anything we've seen in Australia: hanging valleys, Alpine lakes, glaciated valleys, crisp air. The only problem is the last mile or so to Charlotte's Pass—the idiots paved the trail. First, it's very steep going down to a small river, then it's very steep going back up to the parking area. As any hiker can tell you, when it's steep like that, the last think you want is pavement. We assume it was paved for wheelchairs, but it's so steep we don't see how anyone could push a chair up the slope. Still, it's worth it just to say you've been there. We estimate the complete circle trip at about 20 kilometers; we did it in six hours, including an hour lunch break at the top of the mountain. (Food always tastes especially good when you've packed it in.)

There are several national forest campgrounds in the area, as well as a very nice RV park at Sawpit, about 15 kilometers from Jindabyne. It also has chalets and on-site caravans. Reservations and information: Alpine Accommodation Complex, (064) 56–2224. The headquarters for the national park is also at Sawpit.

Northwest of Kiandra on the Snowy Mountains Highway are the **Yarrangobilly Caves,** open all year. At **Cooma,** not really in the mountains, but the economic center of the area, there are food and beds. Museums in town have displays showing the work of the Snowy Mountains Scheme, a mammoth hydroelectric project that was built during World War II. During the ski season, Pioneer runs buses from the Cooma

airport to the resorts. Air service is provided to Cooma by Air New
South Wales; tel. in Sydney, 268–1678.

Snowy Mountain **information centers** are located at Cooma, Jindabyne, Thredbo and Tumut. Information about hiking, fishing and other
activities is available from the **Kosciusko National Park Headquarters,** (064) 56–2102. You can also try the **New South Wales Ski Association,** 157 Gloucester St., Sydney; tel. 24–1581, or the **Sydney
Snow Centre,** 74 Pitt St., Sydney; tel. 231–1444.

The Hunter Valley

A day trip to the Hunter Valley's **vineyards** is possible—but of course,
if you've ever been in the wine country of France or the Napa Valley
of California, you know that wine tasting is an endeavor best not rushed.
The two important centers of the wine area are Maitland and Cessnock,
which are also towns devoted to the huge coal industry that also exists
in the valley—the largest shaft mine in the Southern Hemisphere is located in Cessnock, they claim. And some of the world's largest open
pit mines (and a few of the ugliest power stations) are located in the
Singleton area of the Upper Hunter. The Hunter Valley harvest, by the
way, is usually in February.

There is daily **air service** to Maitland on Eastern Airlines (theirs,
not ours) for around A$200 round trip, or you can drive up from Sydney
in two or three hours.

Driving to the vineyards, take the Pacific Highway to Newcastle,
then hang a left onto the New England Highway, which parallels the
river from Newcastle. The **State Rail Authority** runs a one-day trip to
the vineyards from Sydney. Passengers ride to Newcastle, are bused
around the valley and then hop a return train that afternoon.

Several bus companies operate one- or two-day tours of the Hunter
Valley from Sydney. **Australian Pacific Tours** has a one-day that leaves
Circular Quay around 9 a.m. and returns about 7:30 p.m. The tour
includes free hotel pickup and drop-off, lunch at a winery, a drive through
the wine-growing areas and a chance to sample some wines and visit a
wine museum. The fare is about A$70. The two-day tour visits six
wineries, and includes accommodations, a wine appreciation course,
champagne breakfast and two lunches. The fare is about A$200. Con-
tact Australian Pacific at 252–2988 in Sydney; the trips can also be
booked through travel agents or Tourist Newsfront in The Rocks in
Sydney.

The one-day tour offered by **Great Sights South Pacific** visits four
wineries, stops at a museum, includes lunch and tastings and stops at a
farmers market. The fare is about A$70. The tour leaves around 9 a.m.

from Sydney, returns at 7:30 p.m. Free hotel pickup and drop-off. Book by calling 241–2294 or through Tourist Newsfront in The Rocks.

If you can get to Newcastle, Maitland or Cessnock, you can hop a tour bus that drives around the valley stopping at a range of wineries. The bus, billed as the **Hunter Vineyard Tour,** costs about A$50 with lunch. It can be booked through travel agents or the Tourist Newsfront in Sydney, or directly by calling (049) 91–1659 or 38–1011. The buses run daily.

Information about the vineyards, transportation, acommodations, restaurants and the wine biz in general is available from the Australian Wine Centre, 17–21 Circular Quay West, The Rocks, Sydney 2000; tel. 660–2066. Once in the area, there are tourist information offices at the Hunter Valley Wine Society in Cessnock (049) 90–6699; the Manning Valley Tourist Association in Taree and the Hunter Valley Tourist Association in Hexham. Complete information about the valley, plus bookings for accommodations, is available at the Cessnock Tourist Information Centre, corner of Mount View and Wollombi roads; phone (049) 90–4477.

The wine area is divided in two: the Upper Hunter and the Lower Hunter. In any event, expect to find wines made from *semillon, shiraz* (known as syrah in France) and *cabernet sauvignon* grapes with others thrown in here and there. The valley is primarily respected for its reds, although its whites have won fame at competitions.

Tastings at most Hunter Valley wineries are very much in the California style, meaning low-pressure sales tactics, a liberal pouring policy, and no insistence that you be a wine snob. Two vintages we would recommend are the 1985 Wyndham Estate cabernet sauvignon-shiraz blend and the 1985 Rosemount shiraz. In addition, you might try the 1987 Reserve Chardonnay from Rothbury Estate, the gold medal winner at the 1988 QANTAS Cup U.S.-Australia wine competitions held in the Napa Valley.

Probably your first stop in the area should be at the **Hungerford Hill Wine Village** at Pokolbin, a village close to several of the more well known wineries. Here you can see winemaking, do a tasting, eat at the Cellar Restaurant, and sleep at the Quality Pokolbin Resort, doubles about A$130. Heated pool, tennis court, laundry. Plus there are extensive playgrounds and picnic areas open 9–5 Monday–Saturday; 10–5 Sunday. *Information: Hungerford Hill, Broke Rd., Pokolbin, New South Wales 2321; tel. (049) 98–7666, or 98–7600.*

Among wineries to check out in the Lower Hunter are: **Rothbury Estate,** which has organized events all year. Open 9:30–4:30 seven days. *Information: Rothbury Estate, Broke Rd., Pokolbin, New South Wales, 2321; tel. (049)98–7555.*

McWilliams, one of the oldest and largest. Open 9–4:30 Monday–Friday; 10 a.m.–4:30 p.m. weekends. *Information: McWilliams Mount*

Pleasant Winery, Marrowbone Rd., Pokolbin, New South Wales 2321; tel. (049) 98–7505.

Wyndham Estate, with wine buildings dating back to the 1830s, now under the National Trust. Open 9–5 Monday–Saturday; 10–5 Sunday. *Information: Wyndham Estate, Government Rd., Dalwood, New South Wales 2335; tel. (049) 38–1311.*

Lindeman's, the Gallo of Australia, owned by Phillip Morris, comes with a wine museum. Open 8:30–4:30 Monday–Friday; 10–4:30 weekends. *Information: Lindeman's Hunter Valley Winery, McDonald's Rd., Pokolbin, New South Wales 2321; tel. (049) 98–7501.*

Tyrrell's, where public tasting is done amidst furnishings both woody and quaint. This winery was one of the first to assert the excellence of Australian wines, winning against the best Continental wines in contests. Open 8–5 Monday–Saturday. *Information: Tyrrell's Vineyards, Broke Rd., Pokolbin, New South Wales 2321; tel. (049) 98–7509.*

In the Upper Hunter Valley, try the **Arrowfield Winery** and **Rosemount Estate,** both just north of the town of Denman. This is white wine country, especially the chardonnays of Rosemount. *Information: Arrowfield, Jerry's Plains, New South Wales 2333; tel. (065) 76–4041; Open 10–4 seven days. Rosemount Estate, Rosemount Rd., Denman, New South Wales 2328; tel. (065) 47–2467, open 10–4 Monday–Saturday; noon–4 Sunday.*

Finally, the way it goes these days, you ain't a reputable wine-growing area unless you have **balloon flights,** and there are several companies offering trips in the Hunter Valley; expect to pay around A$125 to A$150 for an hour-long flight, and demand a champagne breakfast. Try **Balloon Aloft,** Branxton Road, North Rothbury, open seven days. *Information: (049) 38–1955, or toll free (008) 028568.*

Accommodations in the region, in addition to the inn at the Hungerford Hill Wine Village, include:

Peppers Guest House ● Probably the best in the area, almost always booked on weekends, with excellent licensed restaurant, pool, tennis, gym. Double around A$140. Peppers has a special Grape Harvest Package. If you stay at the inn between Sunday and Thursday, any night between about Feb. 1 and the end of March, you get full breakfast, a harvest dinner, a local vintner doing evening talks about the harvest, a winery tour and tastings. The package costs about A$200 a couple. Information: Peppers Guest House, Ekerts Rd., Pokolbin, New South Wales 2321; tel. (049) 98–7596.

Monte Pio Court ● Once a Catholic school; licensed restaurant, lovely pool, tennis courts, spa, bar. Very nice old building. A best bet. Doubles about $A120. Information: Monte Pio Court, Dwyer St.,

Campbells Hill, Maitland, New South Wales 2320; tel. (049) 32–5288; toll free (008) 02–5953.

Kirkton Park Country Hotel • Oakley Creek Road about a kilometer north of Pokolbin. All the comforts of home whilst in the wine country: saltwater pool, spa, tennis courts, laundry, gym, sauna, licensed restaurant. They'll deliver dinner to your room on the weekend. Rooms have mini-bars and hair dryers. There are three suites. Doubles A$145–175; suites A$270. *Information: (049) 98–7680.*

Hunter Country Lodge and Restaurant • Log cabin-style digs near Wyndham Estate and Rothbury Estate vineyards north of Cessnock on Highway 82. There are 16 units, all with private facilities, a saltwater pool, mini-bars and a licensed restaurant that has a very good international menu; it also serves breakfast and lunch. Doubles go for around A$140. The restaurant is moderate to expensive. *Information (049) 38–1744.*

Some other restaurants worth a nod are:

Buttai Barn • *Off the John Renshaw Road in Buttai* • This fun spot has a live bush band every Saturday night and good country tucker, moderate prices. *Information: (049) 30–3153.*

Paddy's • *Wollombi Road in Cessnock* • Live music on weekends. Specializes in char-grilled meats. Usually crowded, reservations advised. Lunch seven days; dinner Thursday–Saturday. *Moderate. Information: (049) 90–6699.*

Casaurina • *Hermitage Road in Pokolbin* • French and Aussie, with changing menu. There is also a country lodge with swimming pool, tennis courts and sauna; eight suites and a 3-bedroom cottage. Doubles from A$140. The restaurant is open for lunch on weekends from noon; dinner from 7 p.m. seven days. *Moderate. Information: (049) 98–7888.*

The Interior

To many Australians, the Outback is a state of mind, a mythical place which, like the long-gone American Frontier, somehow encapsulates all the truths and myths that surround the pioneering spirit of the country. The difference is that in the United States, once you got past the desolation of the Great Plains and the deadly wastes of the western deserts, there was a reward: California, Oregon, Washington. The early white settlers of New South Wales soon discovered that once they started into the Outback, about the only thing they had to look forward to was a bunch more Outback.

If you're of an adventerous bent, a trip to the real Outback of New South Wales will give you a glimpse of Australia that many tourists, either too strapped for time or simply ill at ease about all that flat nothingness, never get a chance to experience. You can drive, without any real trouble, or you can take a quick tour from Sydney.

Our suggestion is to head northwest over the Great Dividing Range toward what is called Corner Country, the bleak area where New South Wales, Queensland and South Australia meet.

A driving tour will take you over the old explorer's route through the Blue Mountains to Bathurst, then along the Mitchell Highway to Dubbo. From Dubbo, you can turn north on the Castlereagh Highway toward the Queensland border, or go to Nyngan. At Nyngan, you then turn due north toward Bourke or take the Barrier Highway to Broken Hill. Any of these routes will get you into the arid deserts of the outback. Do not, however, attempt a drive without the proper precautions, and if you truly want to get off the beaten path, join a 4-wheel-drive tour. Remember, check local conditions, availability of gasoline and stay home if it's raining. (See Driving section.)

After the first explorers pushed through the Blue Mountains and discovered good grazing on the other side, a road was built from Sydney to **Bathurst,** the country's oldest inland city. It was a pastoral center until 1851 when gold was discovered in the area and the rush was on. On **Mount Panorama** near town is the **Bathurst Gold Diggings,** a reconstructed mining village. Mount Panorama is also the location of the **Sir Joseph Banks Nature Reserve,** with native animals. Twice a year, the koalas are rudely awakened as bikers and race car drivers descend on the Mount Panorama race course. Easter is for motorcycles (often a fairly taut time, cops versus bikers), and in October, the Bathurst 1000 for production cars is held.

Famous for its fruits and livestock, **Orange** is also the birthplace of Australia's most famous poet, Banjo Paterson. About 20 miles north of town off the paved highway is **Ophir,** where the gold rush started. Farther up the Mitchell Highway is **Wellington,** where you'll see Burendong Dam and lake, the last big body of water for several thousand square miles. Also near town are the Wellington Caves, which claim to have the world's largest stalactite.

The area around Wellington and Mudgee, to the east, is becoming a fairly productive **wine area,** although the wineries are still small. The largest in the Mudgee area is the **Montrose Winery.** Others include **Platts, Huntington Estate** and **Miramar.** *Information:* Montrose Winery, Henry Lawson Drive, Mudgee, New South Wales 2850; tel. (063)

73–3853. Platts, Gulgong Road, Gulgong, New South Wales 2852; tel. (063) 74–1700. Huntington Estate, Cassalis Road, Mudgee, New South Wales 2850; tel. (063) 73–3825. Miramar, Henry Lawson Drive, Mudgee, New South Wales 2850; tel. (063) 73–3874.

Dubbo, about 260 miles northwest of Sydney (and about 125 miles from Bathurst) is in the heart of the wheat belt and is a main intersection for the interior part of the state. From Dubbo, you can keep going north and west into the harshlands, or head northeast or southeast on the Newell Highway, the fastest Brisbane-Melbourne route.

Just outside of town is what many Australians consider to be the finest wildlife park in the country, the **Western Plains Zoo,** about 700 acres of open range exhibits operated in conjunction with Sydney's Taronga Zoo. In town, check out the **Old Dubbo Gaol,** complete with gallows—a sure sign that Dubbo has been and continues to be the center of this part of Australia. Any colonial city worth its salt had at least one gaol and gallows to match. *Information: the Dubbo Visitors Centre, 232 Macquarie Street; tel. (068) 82–5359.* Dubbo has a half-dozen RV parks and about 30 motels.

If you're in a mad rush, you can get to Dubbo and the fringes of the outback by airplane. **Air New South Wales** operates *Jolly Swagman Tours* that fly from Sydney to Dubbo and several other Outback spots including Lightning Ridge. The all-day trip to Dubbo costs about A$400 per person, which includes lunch, sheep-shearing, boomerang demonstrations, a visit to the zoo, and a walk around town. Yes, it's a tad touristy, but if you're in a hurry . . .

Lightning Ridge is nowhere—or almost. It's about 250 miles north of Dubbo on the Castlereagh Highway, sitting next to the huge Lightning Ridge opal mines, said to be the only place in the world where you can find black opals. The remoteness of the town does not stop the city dads from cashing in on tourism, of course. There are opal showrooms, opal mine tours, and artesian baths. You can tell how far out you are: the nearest landmark marked on the highway map is a water tank. One thing you'll soon find out about the Outback towns, no matter where you are: the beer is ice cold. In this case, check out the **Diggers Rest Hotel,** where anybody who is anybody will be found. The Air NSW cost for the Lightning Ridge trip is about the same as the Dubbo excursion.

Information about these and other Outback flights: **Air New South Wales,** Kingsford Smith International Airport, Mascot, New South Wales 2020; tel. (02) 268–1678.

Driving between Dubbo and Lightning Ridge takes you through only two towns of any interest, **Coonamble** and **Walgett.** Coonamble is where things really start getting vacant, although not far to the west are the huge Macquarie Marshes, a major bird breeding area. Walgett, about 175 miles up the Castlereagh from Dubbo, is in the heart of a major opal mining area. In nearby **Grawin,** an opal weighing almost 500 grams was pulled from the ground in 1928. Walgett has an RV park, hotels and motels.

Going up the Mitchell Highway from Dubbo is a big citrus and cotton-growing area. At **Nyngan,** the Mitchell runs northwest toward Bourke and the Queensland border. **Bourke** has leant its name to an Aussie expression: Back of Bourke. If you're "back of Bourke," you're well and truly in the thules. This is sheep country, and from November to March, it's hotter than an old pistol and full of bush flies.

From Nyngan west, you're on the Barrier Highway for a long and lonesome 370 miles to Broken Hill. About 80 miles west of Nyngan is **Cobar,** a copper-mining town with one of the best examples of a grand bush hotel in the country: the Great Western hotel. The old heap, now protected by the National Trust, has the longest iron-lace verandah in New South Wales, and its rooms have been modernized. The bar is large and friendly.

About 25 miles west of Cobar are the Grenfell **Aboriginal cave paintings,** a group of very good animal and human figures. If you want to visit the caves, you'll have to turn off the Barrier Highway and drive about 20 miles north to the Grenfell station; the turnoff is marked. *Information: Cobar 36–4223.*

At **Wilcannia,** the highway crosses the Darling River and there are remains of an old wharf and buildings that were once part of a lively riverboat business when the town was the third largest river port in the country. It boggles your mind that paddlewheelers could come this far north, but the Darling runs into the Murray, and the Murray is the Mississippi of Australia. At one time, there were several hundred boats working the Murray-Darling rivershed.

Broken Hill is the mining center that gave rise to Australia's biggest conglomerate, **Broken Hill Proprietary,** or BHP, often called "the Big Australian." The hill that gave the town its name is the world's largest known deposit of silver, lead and zinc—a chunk estimated to be five miles in length, 500 feet wide, and 2,000 feet deep. That's one hell of a nugget.

One of the most striking things about Broken Hill (aside from its mines and the somewhat quaint idea of naming all the streets after minerals) is the abundance of greenery, supplied by water from Darling River dams. There is also an office of the Flying Doctor Service, which has airborne emergency medical service for the Outback, and the School of the Air, which provides shortwave classes for isolated school children.

Underground tours of an abandoned mine are available through Delprat's Mines; tel. (080) 88–1604. *General information is available at the Tourist Information Centre, corner of Bromide and Blende streets; tel. (080) 6077.* The town is run by labor unions (the Barrier Industrial Council) and is actually closer to Adelaide (315 miles) than Sydney

(725 miles). Just to prove something, the city runs on South Australia time, which is 30 minutes behind New South Wales.

Air New South Wales flies from Sydney Sunday, Monday, Wednesday, and Friday for about A$500 round trip. Air NSW also flies from Broken Hill to Ayers Rock for about A$600 round trip. Air service between Broken Hill and Adelaide is provided by Kendall Airlines for about A$250 round trip.

Bus service is also available from Adelaide and Melbourne. Smart travelers, however, will take the opportunity to go to Broken Hill on the Indian-Pacific, one of Australia's great train routes. It goes through Broken Hill on its way to Perth. The journey is about 18 hours and is made easier because the train has sleepers, dining cars and a lounge car. *Information: Rail Travel Centre of New South Wales, Transport House, 11–31 York St., Sydney 2000; or Railways of Australia, which represents the five state-owned rail systems in the country, at 85 Queen St., Melbourne, Victoria 3000; tel. (03) 608–0811.*

About 15 miles west of Broken Hill is **Silverton,** a once-thriving silver boom town which is becoming a feature in Aussie movies including being a set for a *Road Warrior* film and *A Town Like Alice.*

Two national parks lie north of Broken Hill. The smallest is **Mootwingee National Park,** where there are Aboriginal paintings believed to date back 25,000 years, many badly defaced by vandals. Farther up the Silver City track about 200 miles is a wide spot called **Tibooburra,** which is at the entrance to Sturt National Park. Tibooburra has some fine old period sandstone buildings dating from its heyday as a gold rush town. There is an RV park and one hotel, The Albert.

Sturt National Park is 465,000 acres of flood plains, rocks, sandhills, and lots of animals and birds. It's about five hours from Broken Hill. At Cameron's Corner, the northwest point where the three states come together, there is a monument proclaiming that fact, a dandy target to add to your personal accomplishment list. *Information about the park is available from the district office of the National Parks & Wildlife Service, Court House, Tibooburra, New South Wales 2880; tel. Tibooburra 8.*

If you're uncomfortable driving yourself, try the five-day 4-wheel-drive excursions that leave Broken Hill, go to the national parks, and also stop off at the White Cliff opal fields north of Wilcannia. The price of about A$700 includes meals, accommodations, and guides. The trips can be booked through Bill King's Australian Experience, which uses ATS/Sprint in Los Angeles as its North American broker.

If you're in a hurry, go with the mailman—in this case, the **Barrier Air Taxi Service,** which allows paying passengers on two flights, one to White Cliffs and one on its 25-ranch postal route. Contact the service in Broken Hill; tel. (080) 88–4307.

THE AUSTRALIAN CAPITAL TERRITORY

The Australian Capital Territory, the Aussie equivalent of the District of Columbia, is a very nice place to live and work, and, if you have time on your Australian jaunt, to visit. It is a planned area, born in the early part of this century, and as national capitals go, refreshingly clean and well-managed. But, and this is of course a biased but, you can visit Australia without going to Canberra and not feel a sense of loss. It's very much like going to Brazil and missing Brasilia. Comfortable and calm, that's Canberra.

Having said that, however, it remains that if you want to put the entire Australian experience in order, the tree-lined boulevards and stately federal buildings of the ACT are essential. Besides, as is said of many other places in the world, it's close to a lot of great stuff.

Being Australians, it was impossible to pick the national capital without a lot of shouting and carrying on, so when Australia decided to become an independent nation in 1901, the bickering started immediately. The loudest protagonists were Sydney and Melbourne, the new nation's economic and political centers, but it seemed as if every village on the continent wanted the honor of having the capital, as well. It took until 1908 for all the hoo-haw to die down enough to pick the spot, which turned out to be a grazing area in the Monaro Tablelands about 200 miles southwest of Sydney, 400 miles northeast of Melbourne. Thus you can say that both sides won—more or less Melbourne got its way because the capital didn't end up in Sydney. On the other hand, Sydney won because it's twice as close to the ACT as Melbourne. Ain't democracy grand?

When it came time to design the new capital city, a competition was held with a prize of $3500 for the winner. British architects, reportedly in a snit because of the way the bumpkin colonials had resolved the issue of location, opted not to enter designs, leaving the way open for one Walter Burley Griffin to snatch the honors. Griffin was, of course, an American.

What he had in mind was a city of around 75,000, but federal bureaucracies being federal bureaucracies, the present population hovers around 250,000. It is also worth noting that Griffin's grand scheme fell afoul of this and that (including World War I), and it wasn't until 1927 that Parliament first met in the new city. Between 1901 and the first session, the nation's leaders assembled in Melbourne. The Depression and the next war also took their tolls, and it wasn't until the 1950s and 1960s that major attention was paid to starting construction of the necessary facilities for the government. The first major building, Parliament House, was completed in 1927 as a temporary site, to be replaced at a later date—the later date, as it turned out, was 1988, when the huge new Parliament building was opened.

There was also a fairly strenuous debate about what the new capital should be called, and after a couple of years of pondering, the boys decided to use the name that had been there all along: Canberra (pronounced CAN-braw). One of the first settlers in the area started a station on the nearby Murrumbidgee River and named it Canberra, a form of the Aboriginal word for "meeting place," a fitting name for a seat of government.

The Founding Fathers of the United States, when they had their chance, chose to put the national capital in a swamp, which to this day draws quite nasty and thoroughly justified comments about its lousy climate, especially during one of the hot, muggy summers that so often descend on the White House and other centers of national enlightenment. Canberra, while not nearly as bad, does have a reputation for being uncomfortably hot in the summer and uncomfortably cold in the winter. Unlike the other major cities in Australia, it is not on the coast and is thus unable to cash in on the calming climatic influences of the ocean. So the time to visit Canberra is in the spring and fall. Autumn, with its change of colors and pleasant weather, is probably best.

The most striking feature of the city, and indeed its centerpoint, is **Lake Burley Griffin,** completed in 1964 by damming the Molonglo River. The lake, which created more than 20 miles of shoreline, lies just to the north of the major federal buildings, including the new **Parliament House,** the **National Library,** the **National Art Gallery,** and the **High Court of Australia.** With Parliament House as the center, a series of circular streets then radiates south into the suburbs, and that's where you find foreign embassies.

In the center of the lake, near the **Commonwealth Bridge,** which runs from Capital Circle and Parliament House to the downtown area, is the **Captain Cook Memorial Water Jet** (we'd call it a fountain) that spurts water 450 feet into the air and is reminiscent of the fountain in Lake Geneva. On Aspen Island, next to another bridge (Kings Avenue)

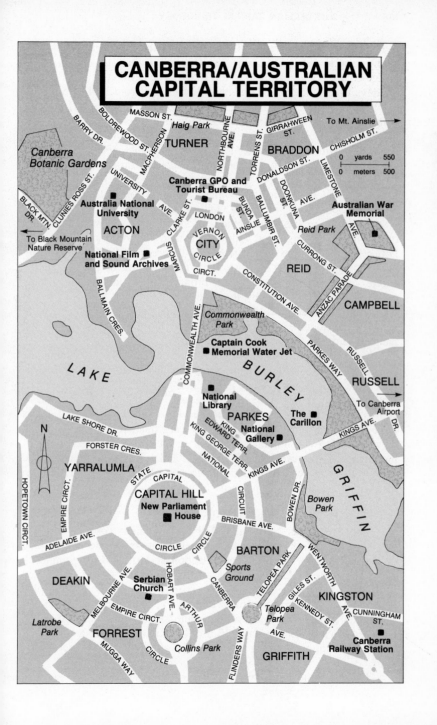

CANBERRA/AUSTRALIAN CAPITAL TERRITORY

MASSON ST.

Haig Park

BARRY DR.

BOLDREWOOD ST.

MACPHERSON ST.

TURNER

NORTHBOURNE AVE.

TORRENS ST.

GIRRAHWEEN ST.

BRADDON

To Mt. Ainslie

CHISHOLM ST.

DONALDSON ST.

DOONKUNA ST.

BALLUMBIR ST.

LIMESTONE AVE.

0   yards   550
0   meters   500

Canberra Botanic Gardens

UNIVERSITY

CLUNIES ROSS ST.

Canberra GPO and Tourist Bureau

CLARKE ST.

LONDON

BUNDA ST.

AINSLIE

CURRONG ST.

Australian War Memorial

Australia National University

ACTON

MARCUS

VERNON CIRCLE

CITY

CIRCT.

Reid Park

REID

BLACK MTN. DR.

To Black Mountain Nature Reserve

National Film and Sound Archives

BALLMAIN CRES.

CONSTITUTION AVE.

ANZAC PARADE

CAMPBELL

COMMONWEALTH AVE.

Commonwealth Park

Captain Cook Memorial Water Jet

BURLEY

PARKES WAY

RUSSELL

RUSSELL

To Canberra Airport

LAKE

National Library

PARKES

KING EDWARD TERR.

National Gallery

The Carillon

KINGS AVE.

DR.

N

LAKE SHORE DR.

FORSTER CRES.

YARRALUMLA

STATE

CAPITAL

KING GEORGE TERR.

NATIONAL

KINGS AVE.

BOWEN DR.

GRIFFIN

HOPETOWN CIRCT.

EMPIRE CIRCT.

CAPITAL HILL

New Parliament House

CIRCUIT

Bowen Park

CIRCLE

CIRCLE

BRISBANE AVE.

ADELAIDE AVE.

BARTON

Sports Ground

WENTWORTH AVE.

KINGSTON

DEAKIN

MELBOURNE AVE.

Serbian Church

EMPIRE CIRCT.

HOBART AVE.

ARTHUR

CANBERRA

TELOPEA PARK

GILES ST.

KENNEDY ST.

CUNNINGHAM ST.

Latrobe Park

FORREST

CIRCLE

Collins Park

Telopea Park

AVE.

FLINDERS WAY

GRIFFITH

Canberra Railway Station

MUGGA WAY

is the 53-bell **Canberra Carillon,** given to the city to mark its 50th anniversary in 1963, but opened by Queen Elizabeth in 1970. A footbridge connects the mainland to the island. The carillon bells are played Sundays from 2:45–3:30 p.m., and Wednesdays from 12:45–1:30 p.m.

The one place in Canberra that should be high on your list is the **Australian War Memorial and Museum,** the second-most visited spot in Australia after the Sydney Opera House. It's a moving display of Australia's participation in wars and conflicts from the 19th-century Maori wars in New Zealand to Vietnam, with emphasis on World Wars I and II. It shows clearly the out-of-proportion sacrifices the Aussies made to help out Great Britain and the United States on some of the worst battlefields of both wars, including Gallipoli and New Guinea.

Some Americans think the idea of inscribing a wall with the names of war dead was originated with the Vietnam Memorial in Washington, D.C., but the Aussies were there long before us. The **Canberra memorial** was completed in 1941, with the intention of placing all the names of Australian war dead on bronze plaques around the outside corridors of the building. By the time it was finished, Australia was at war again, so after World War II, and again following Vietnam, more names were added. A guide told us there are 102,000 names on the plaques—most from the First World War.

The memorial also has some interesting exhibits, including the **Aeroplane Hall,** which contains a number of aircraft including a complete Lancaster bomber. There is also a display about the 96 Australians who have thus far won the Victoria Cross, the British Commonwealth equivalent to the Medal of Honor. The view from the memorial, across Lake Burley Griffin to Capital Hill, is very nice, reminding us of the view from the Washington Monument to the Capitol. Guided tours of the memorial are available at 10:30 a.m. and 1:30 p.m. weekdays. The memorial, at the end of Anzac Parade east of the city center, is open daily from 9 a.m. to 4:45 p.m.; no admission charge. *Information: 243–4238.*

Other buildings worth a look include:

The Australian National Gallery—The gallery, opened in 1982, has more than 75,000 square feet of exhibition space and houses, and on the second floor, an excellent collection of Australian art going back 200 years. One of the most popular displays is the collection of Ned Kelly paintings by Sir Sidney Nolan. There is also a quite good display of Aboriginal art and some fine sculptures by such artists as Rodin and Modigliani. The gallery sits on the south side of the lake next to the High Court, and is open daily 10 a.m.–5 p.m. Tours are available. It has a restaurant overlooking the lake and a gift shop. *Information: 271–2411.*

The National Library—The library houses at least one copy of every book printed in Australia and in addition, has a wonderful collection of Capt. Cook's papers, including his diaries from the epic 1768–71 journey when he explored New Zealand and the east coast of Australia. In the foyer of the library is one of the cannons Cook threw overboard to lighten ship after *Endeavor* struck the Great Barrier Reef in 1770. The public areas of the library are open from 9 a.m.–10 p.m. Mon.–Thurs. and 9 a.m.–4:45 p.m. Fri.–Sun. Tours are available.

New Parliament House—Like the Opera House, the new edifice is not without its detractors, many of whom think the size—and the cost—were a tad much just to house a bunch of low-life politicians. The size is impressive—1500-foot-long granite walls—and so was the cost, somewhere in the neighborhood of a billion Australian dollars. The new structure is carved into Capital Hill behind the old building, and was officially opened by Queen Elizabeth during the Bicentennial. One of its major features—and points of artistic dispute—is a gigantic flagpole that rises almost 300 feet above the site. We would be unpatriotic if we failed to mention that the building was designed by—who else—an American. The overwhelming feeling you get when you walk into the entry hall is one of light and air—it has 48 greenish marble columns and two marble staircases going to the Senate and House of Representatives. Past the foyer is the Great Hall, the centerpoint of which is a huge tapestry on one wall, created by Australian artist Arthur Boyd. Of special interest in the Members Hall past the Great Hall is an original copy of the *Magna Carta*. The document, called the *Inspeximus Issue,* dates to 1297 and is one of only four known originals.

The building took 300,000 cubic meters of concrete, enough, we're told, to build 25 Sydney Opera Houses. Part of the total cost of the project went into artwork—the government commissioned 70 original pieces and purchased 3,000 paintings and other works. In excess of a million people a year are expected to visit the new facility.

Parliament House is open 9 a.m.–5 p.m. seven days. Guided tours are available when the houses are not in session; the tours start at 9:20 a.m. and run every 20 minutes, starting in the gallery of the Great Hall. Visitors are welcome in the galleries of the two houses when members are sitting. The most popular time is "question time" which begins in both houses at 2 p.m. This is when members, usually the opposition party, get to hack and chew on the prime minister and his cabinet. There is also a self-guided audio cassette tour available. The building has handicapped access and a cafeteria open from 9–5. There is a huge and free 6000-vehicle parking lot underneath the building; we parked our medium-size RV there. For information, contact Parliament's public relations section, (06) 277–5101.

Black Mountain—West of the city center, this is the site of the Telecom Tower, which rises about 650 feet above the ground and has viewing platforms and a revolving restaurant for the best views of the capital area. The tower is open daily 9 a.m.–10 p.m. *Information: 247–7371.*

Also at Black Mountain is the **National Botanic Gardens,** a display of native flora envisioned by Burley Griffin in his original design. The 100-acre site contains more than 600 species, including an Aboriginal trail showing how they used native plants. The gardens are open daily 9 a.m.–5 p.m. with guided tours on Sun. There is a BYO outdoor restaurant. *Information: 267–1811.*

Another good view is available from the top of **Mount Ainslie,** which rises 2700 feet above the city northeast of the city center. Both Black Mountain and Mount Ainslie can be reached by car.

Other sights include the **Royal Australian Mint,** west of Capital Hill, open for self-guided tours Mon.–Fri. 9 a.m.–4 p.m. and weekends from 10–3, no charge; the **Australian High Court** below Capital Hill, with 50-foot-high courtroom walls and oak panels, open daily 10 a.m.–4 p.m., and **Blundell's Cottage** on Parkes Way across the lake from Capital Hill, built in 1858 and kept around as an example of the sort of building that existed in Canberra before the Yank architects got going, open daily 10 a.m.–4 p.m. Nearby is the 260-foot-high aluminum spire of the Australian-American Memorial honoring U.S. efforts to help Australia in World War II.

Tours

The **Canberra Explorer** runs tour buses every hour from around 10:15 a.m. to 4:15 p.m. starting from the Jolimont Tourist Centre at the corner of Northbourne Avenue and Alinga Street. The buses stop at 19 locations, hitting all the high spots from Parliament to the war memorial. With ticket in hand you can get off and back on at any stop. A day ticket is about A$10; a one-hour ticket is about A$5. Free hotel pickup is available. *Information: 295–3611.* Or check with the Murrays Coachlines desk at the Jolimont Centre.

Monarch Tours has several good trips which take in the usual sights but also go to some sites outside the city such as the Tidbinbilla Nature Reserve and a national park. The city highlights tours, including admissions and lunch, is about A$70 per person. The wildlife tour, with admissions and lunch, is about A$70, and a city tour coupled with a barbecue at a local sheep station (complete with shearing demonstration) is about A$70. There are also half-day tours. Information: 259–1686 or see a local travel agent.

Outside Canberra

The diplomatic corps—at least those who can ski—must love being stationed in Canberra in the winter because it's next door to the Snowy

Mountains, a major skiing center in Australia. The ski resorts, located in Kosciusko National Park, Australia's largest, are about 100 miles from the capital and offer full services and ski equipment. The national park is also a summer playground with many miles of fine hiking trails. *Park information: (064) 56–2102. (See skiing information in New South Wales section).*

Other sights to check out around the Canberra area:

Tidbinbilla Deep Space Tracking Center—The hills west of Canberra used to be almost filled with U.S.-owned tracking stations, several of which were run by NASA. The only one still going is this station, operated for NASA by the Australian Department of Science. The station has spacecraft models, audio-visual displays, and radio telescopes. The visitors' center is open 9 a.m.–5 p.m. and is located 25 miles southwest of the city (on the same road you take to reach the observatory). *Information: 249–0818.*

Tidbinbilla Nature Reserve—Next to the space station, this 12,000-acre park offers hidden picnic areas and miles of trails through virgin bush. There's a special pen where you can ogle emus, roos, and wallabies. *The reserve information center is open weekdays 11 a.m.–3 p.m. and weekends from 9 a.m.–6 p.m.*

Lanyon—Here's your chance to see how gentlemen squatters lived in the Victorian Age. Lanyon is an old farmhouse begun in the 1860s, and is set in a green and tree-surrounded area in the middle of rich pastureland. It's filled with period furnishings and farm equipment. You reach it by taking the Monaro Highway south from Canberra (the road to Cooma) and turn off to Tharwa. Lanyon Homestead is open 10 a.m.–4 p.m. Tues.–Sun. and hol. There's a coffee shop. Admission A$2. *Information: 246–2176.*

The Essential Canberra:

INFORMATION • In Sydney, the tourist bureau for the ACT and Canberra is located at 64 Castlereagh Street; tel. 233–3666. In Canberra, the tourist bureau offices are in the Jolimont Centre, 61–65 Northbourne Avenue; tel. (06) 245–6464.

If you need them, the United States embassy and consulate are located at State Circle and Perth Avenue in Canberra, Yarralumla, 270–5000, and the Canadian embassy is on Commonwealth Avenue, Yarralumla 273–3844.

GETTING THERE • Canberra is one of the few national capitals in the world not served by an international airport, but it does have **air service** to and from major Australian cities. Australian Airlines, Ansett, East West Airlines, and Air New South Wales all serve the city from Sydney. The non-stop, one-way flights cost around A$100. The airport is about five miles outside of town. Bus service downtown is infrequent; a taxi ride will be around A$10.

There is a daily **express train** from Sydney that leaves at about 6:30 p.m. and arrives in Canberra at around 11 p.m. The return express leaves at 7:10 a.m. and arrives at 11:20 a.m. The one-way cost is about A$30, less with an **Aussiepass.** Regular service departs Sydney at 7:30 a.m., arriving in Canberra around noon and costs the same. Return service leaves Canberra at 12:30 p.m., arriving in Sydney around 5 p.m.

Getting to and from Melbourne is a bothersome job by train. There are several departures a day in both directions, but a chunk of the trip is by bus and takes most of the day—the 10:45 a.m. from Canberra, for example, arrives in Melbourne at 8:30 that night. Cost of the train/bus trips is around A$50. A one-way flight, by contrast, is about A$150.

The capital is also served by regular **buses** from Sydney and Melbourne on the Hume Highway and are priced around A$20 (Sydney) to A$40 (Melbourne). It takes about 9½ hours from Melbourne, 4½ from Sydney.

GETTING AROUND • Public transportation is casual in Canberra, and if you're serious about seeing the sights, renting a car is probably your best bet. Agencies include: **Avis,** 249–6088; **Hertz,** 257–4877, **Thrifty,** 247–7422, and **Budget,** 248–9788. For maps and other information, contact the National Roads & Motorists Association, 92 Northbourne Avenue, Canberra, ACT 2601; tel. (062) 243–8800.

If you must have a **taxi** and can't flag one, call 246–0444. Public **bus information** is available from ACTION, the municipal transportation authority, by calling 247–6185.

The city proper has about 70 miles of paved **bike paths,** a popular way to get around and generally regarded as the best urban bike facilities in Australia. If you feel inspired, you can rent bikes at the local youth hostel or at **Mr. Spokes Bike Hire** near the Ferry Terminal at West Basin on the lake. The cost will be around A$10 a day. The tourist office has special biking maps available showing the network of paths.

SHOPPING • The shopping center of Canberra is around Vernon Circle, straight across the Commonwealth Bridge from Capital Hill. Here you will find a pair of pedestrian malls, movie theaters, retail stores, and **David Jones,** the department store. You're probably better off buying souvenirs and such in Sydney—you have to go back there anyway.

ACCOMMODATIONS........................

Many hotels in the Canberra area have weekend specials. Among the best:

Lakeside • *London Circuit; tel. 247–6244* • Located close to downtown near the shore of Lake Burley Griffin. Airy white marble lobby, rooms with view of Parliament and the lake. The rooftop dining room—the **Burley Griffin Room,** what else—offers upscale dining with nice scenery. Indoor heated pool, business facilities, mini-bars. Six suites. Doubles A\$110–195; suites A\$180–500.

Hyatt Hotel Canberra • *Commonwealth Avenue, Capital Hill; tel. 270–1234* • Close to Parliament. The hotel restaurant—**The Oak Room**—was a winner of a 1989 National Tourism Award for restaurants. The Hyatt is a businessman/politicians hotel, one of the most expensive in town. Doubles from about A\$250.

The Pavilion • *Corner Canberra Avenue and National Circuit; tel. 295–3144* • Closest hotel to Parliament and one of the newest (opened in 1988). Almost Art Deco in style, with airy, glass-enclosed spaces and a central atrium. Indoor heated pool, sauna, spa and gym. Business center. Brasserie and bars. Among the 186 rooms are 40 suites with private spas. Doubles from A\$120; suites A\$180–500.

Canberra Rex Hotel • *150 Northbourne Ave.; tel. 248–5311* • About a kilometer from the lake, recently renovated. Rooms are fairly standard, but come with mini-bars and cable TV. Nice pool, French restaurant, 24-hour bistro, tour desk. Doubles from A\$120; suites from A\$220.

Capital Parkroyal • *1 Binara St.; tel. 247–8999* • Heart of downtown, close to the National Convention Centre. Pool, sauna, spa, mini-bars, seven suites. Elegant dining in Blundells—smoked beef with a bleu cheese mousse, red snapper chowder, venison in black current sauce. Expensive. Doubles A\$220; A\$400–800.

Canberra Forrest Motor Inn • *30 National Circuit; tel. 295–3433* • Close to Parliament in part of Embassy Row overlooking a park. Car wash, tour desk. Restaurant/bar. Doubles from A\$100; suites about A\$125.

Olims • *Corner Ainslie and Limestone Aves.; 248–5511* • Northeast of downtown, not far from the war memorial. Mediterranean-style facility with large courtyard, balconies, very nice lounge and a beer garden. Recently renovated, with some very nice split-level executive suites. Restaurant/bar, bistro. A good bet. Doubles A$125; Suites A$150–245.

The Chelsea Lodge • *526 Northbourne Ave.; 248–0655* • About five kilometers from the city center north of town. A very popular B&B with large rooms. Doubles A$40–50.

Gowrie and Macquarie private hotels • These are a good bet for the budget crowd. The **Gowrie,** 210 Northbourne Ave., is close to downtown; tel. 249–6033. The **Macquarie,** 18 National Circuit, is close to Parliament; 273–2325. Breakfast is included in the room rate. Both have large rooms with shared bath, TV lounges, off-street parking, laundry facilities and game rooms. Doubles at the Gowrie are about A$60; at the Macquarie, about A$65.

National Memorial Youth Hostel • *Dryandra St.; tel. 248–9155* • About six kilometers northeast of the city center. In the bush, not far from the city botanic gardens. Cooking facilities, bike rental. About A$15–20 per person.

RESTAURANTS.....................................

Jean Pierre le Carrousel • *Redhill Lookout, Redhill; tel. 273–1808* • Award winner with great views of the city. French, as the name suggests, almost always crowded. Here's a chance to try some national symbol: tender kangaroo filets with pink peppercorn and berry sauce; or veal scallopini with mango and wine sauce. Reservations a must. Lunch noon–2 p.m. Monday–Friday; dinner 6:30–10 p.m. Monday–Friday; 6–midnight Saturday. *Expensive.*

Hill Station • *Sheppard St., Hume; tel. 260–1393* • National Trust homestead, with an art gallery and antiques. A very popular watering hole, with five lounge and dining room areas with open fires and a verandah for outdoor eating. Fancy teas on weekends and traditional roast lunch on Sunday. Extensive Australian wine list. Lunch Thursday–Friday; dinner Wednesday–Saturday. Call for hours; reservations necessary. *Expensive.*

Imperial Court • *40 Northbourne Ave.; tel. 248–5547* • The best Chinese tucker in town, open late. Live music Friday and Saturday night. Open seven days for lunch and dinner; also has take-away food. *Budget to moderate.*

Campbell • *Blamey Crest near the war memorial; tel. 249–7333* • Old-fashioned steak and seafood house, but with some variations: pork filets with crab meat, rack of lamb with camembert and spinach in a port sauce, as well as crabs, lobster and oysters. Call for hours. *Moderate to expensive.*

Sheikh's • *On Bunda Street, three blocks north of Vernon Circle; tel. 257–6644* • Lebanese dine-in or take-out. Popular with the lunch crowd. Menu includes the standards: falafel, kebabs, baklava. BYO. Open from 10–10, seven days. *Budget.*

There are also four **McDonalds,** four **Pizza Huts** and seven **Kentucky Fried Chicken** outlets in the area.

QUEENSLAND AND THE GREAT BARRIER REEF

If you had time for only one stop in Australia, and were thus forced to make a truly horrible decision, we think your time would be best spent in Queensland. We do not say this lightly, because it is not easy to dismiss Sydney and the other great cities of Australia, nor is it easy to place the other great experiences to be found around the country in a secondary role.

But Queensland? Well, Queensland is the California of Australia, the perfect one-stop vacation destination. It has more going for it than any other single state, with a menu of activities available that ranges from the singular beauties of the Great Barrier Reef to the crocodile-infested jungles of the Cape York Peninsula to the sunny sandboxes along the coast to the raw and lonely Outback.

Queensland has the added attraction for North American visitors of being the first stopping place for many of the flights into Australia. The flights to Cairns, particularly, are opportune, because once on the ground, you're almost within rock-tossing distance of the Great Barrier Reef or a short drive away from the magnificent rain forests of the Atherton Tablelands and Cape York.

They call Queensland the Sunshine State, partly because of its subtropical and tropical climate, but also because of the string of glorious beaches stretching from the Queensland-New South Wales border north. The beaches have given rise to a series of resort communities where the air is filled with the smell of coconut oil and thousands of Australian families make an annual pilgrimage to spend a fortnight or two seeking fun and sun.

Queensland is huge—at about 667,000 square miles, the second largest state (Western Australia is the biggest) and more than twice the size of Texas. It takes up about a quarter of the Australian continent. There are about 2.5 million people living in the state, which is split about in half by the Tropic of Capricorn. Taking the Cape York Peninsula and the Gulf of Carpentaria into account, Queensland has an enor-

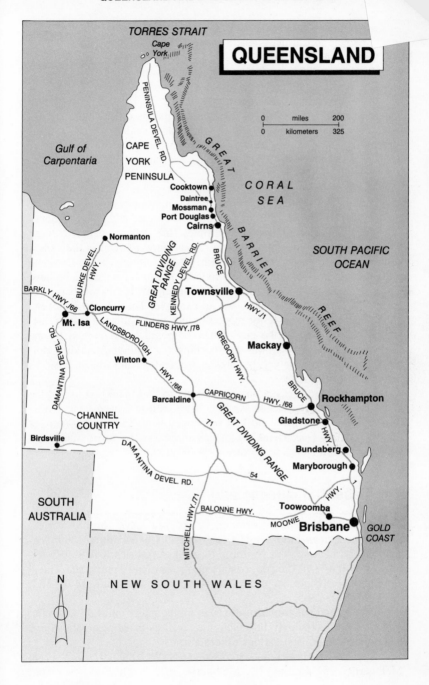

TORRES STRAIT

Cape
York

GREAT

QUEENSLAND

CORAL
SEA

Gulf of
Carpentaria

CAPE

YORK

PENINSULA

PENINSULA DEVEL. RD.

SOUTH PACIFIC
OCEAN

| 0 | miles | 200 |
| 0 | kilometers | 325 |

Cooktown
Daintree
Mossman
Port Douglas
Cairns

BARRIER

Normanton

BURKE DEVEL. HWY.

GREAT DIVIDING RANGE

KENNEDY DEVEL. RD.

BRUCE

BARKLY HWY. /66

Cloncurry

Mt. Isa

LANDSBOROUGH

Townsville

REEF

HWY. /1

FLINDERS HWY. /78

Winton

HWY. /66

GREGORY HWY.

Mackay

DAMANTINA DEVEL. RD.

Barcaldine

CAPRICORN

HWY. /66

BRUCE

Rockhampton

CHANNEL
COUNTRY

GREAT DIVIDING RANGE

71

Gladstone

Birdsville

DAMANTINA DEVEL. RD.

54

HWY. 1

Bundaberg

Maryborough

SOUTH
AUSTRALIA

MITCHELL HWY. /71

BALONNE HWY.

Toowoomba

HWY.

MOONIE

Brisbane

GOLD
COAST

N

NEW SOUTH WALES

1

mous coastline—something like 3200 miles—but only about half of that, from Brisbane to Cairns, is readily accessible by motor vehicle.

Queensland started out as part of New South Wales, founded as a penal colony in 1824. An influx of free settlers, many of whom entered illegally, changed its face from prison to agricultural center. In 1842, it was officially opened to free settlement, and by 1859, the population was large enough to justify its status as a separate colony. The settlers made their way with sheep, cattle, wheat, an abundance of natural resources, and cash crops—including bananas, which gave rise to the rather derisive name the rest of Australia uses for Queensland natives: "Banana benders."

The state is also a major producer of ores (bauxite, tin, and coal), and produces almost 100% of Australia's pineapple crop, as well as peanuts and sugarcane. But the allure of the climate and the semi-South Seas lifestyle of the Queensland tropics (the Aussies call it "going troppo") was just too much to ignore, and now tourism is the state's second-largest industry, raking in nearly A$10 billion a year. By some estimates, more than half of all tourists heading for Australia have Queensland as their major destination—much of the reason being, of course, the Great Barrier Reef. As an example, Tourism Brisbane, the public agency responsible for marketing the city, estimated that tourist-related construction in the city, either proposed or committed by the beginning of the 1990s, was approaching one billion Australian dollars—and Brisbane only gets about a tenth of all the tourist business that comes to the state.

Finally, it is at least a poetic necessity to remember that two of the country's most recognizable symbols were born in Queensland: *Waltzing Matilda* was written and first performed here, and Qantas Airlines first flew from Queensland's Outback airfields—the name stands for Queensland and Northern Territory Air Services.

The Essential Queensland

INFORMATION ● For information before you leave North America, contact the **Queensland Tourist and Travel Corporation,** 1800 Central Park East, Suite 330, Northrop Plaza, Los Angeles, CA 90067; tel. (301) 788–0997. In Canada, contact the Queensland Tourist and Travel Corporation, 2 Bloor St. West, No. 1730, Toronto, Ontario M4W 3E2; tel. (416) 922–2305.

Queensland has **tourism offices** in all the major cities of Australia. These offices can supply information as well as make reservations and recommend tours. The various offices are:

Sydney, 75 Castlereagh St., Sydney NSW 2000, (02) 232–1788; Melbourne, 257 Collins St., Melbourne VIC 3000, (03) 654–3866;

Adelaide, 10 Grenfell St., Adelaide SA 5000, (08) 212–2399; Brisbane, Adelaide St., Brisbane 4000; (07) 833–5255; Canberra, 25 Garema Pl., Canberra City ACT 2601, (062) 48–8411; Perth, 55 St. George's Terrace, Perth WA 6000, (09) 325–1600.

For information about national parks around the state, contact the **Queensland National Parks and Wildlife Service,** P.O. Box 190, North Quay, Brisbane 4000; tel. 224–0414.

GETTING THERE • Queensland has three **international airports** capable of handling wide-body aircraft: Cairns, Townsville, and Brisbane. For those planning a visit to the Great Barrier Reef, Cairns is the recommended destination, being close to the Reef and the Reef island resorts. The Townsville airport, developed and planned as the first international gateway to northern Queensland, has largely been bypassed in favor of Cairns and now receives only limited international service.

Among the international carriers flying to Queensland from the U.S. and Canada are **Qantas, United, Air New Zealand, Canadian Airlines International, Continental,** and **UTA French Airlines.**

GETTING AROUND • Internal **air service** to most major towns in the state is also available, usually on either Ansett or Australian airlines. *Information:* **Ansett Airlines of Australia,** 733 Ann St., Fortitude Valley, tel. 854–2222; **Australian Airlines,** 247 Adelaide St., Brisbane, tel. 223–3333. Service is also supplied by **Air New South Wales, East-West Airlines** (tel. 229–0455), **Air Queensland** (tel. 229–1311), **Sunstate Airlines** (tel. 229–0455), and **Lloyd Aviation.**

Traveling around the state by **rail** is a tedious process, with long hours involved between major population centers—speeds averaging less than 30 miles an hour are not unusual on many runs. Regular service between Sydney and Brisbane is provided by the **Brisbane Limited,** which leaves Sydney at 6 p.m. and arrives in Brisbane at 10 a.m. the next morning. The train has sleepers, a bar, and a dining car. A one-way, first-class berth is about A$150 per person; first-class sitting about A$110, economy sitting about A$80.

From Brisbane, a number of trains provide service to outlying communities. These include the **Westlander,** which runs to Cunnamulla in the Outback west via Charleville with connections to Quilpie. The trip to Charleville takes about 17 hours; to Cunnamulla, about 22 hours, and to Quilpie (change of train), about 22 hours. The Westlander has berths, a bar and dining car, and one-way costs are comparable to the Brisbane Limited.

There is regular **daily service** between Brisbane and Coolangatta, the south end of the Gold Coast. The service is a combined bus/rail trip taking about 2½ hours. A popular service to the Gold Coast from Sydney is the **Pacific Coast Motorail,** an overnight (17 hours) that lets the natives ship their cars up to the Gold Coast on the same trip. The train goes to Murwillumbah, leaving Sydney at 6:30 p.m. and arriving at 11 a.m. The return trip leaves Murwillumbah at 4:30 p.m. and arrives in Sydney the next morning at 9 a.m. A one-way first-class berth is about A$125 per person; first-class sitting, about A$90, economy sitting, about A$60.

Another Gold Coast train from Sydney goes to Surfers Paradise, also about 17 hours. It leaves Sydney at 6 p.m., arriving in Surfers at 11 a.m.; return service leaves Surfers at 1:30 p.m., arriving in Sydney at 7 a.m. The one-way costs are comparable to the Pacific Coast Motorail.

Three trains go north along the coast from Brisbane, all of which are equipped with berths, dining cars, and bars. The **Capricornian** leaves Brisbane around 7 p.m. and arrives in Rockhampton at 8:30 a.m. First-class berths are about $110 per person; economy-class berths are about $70, economy sitting about A$45.

The Queenslander and the Sunlander both go from Brisbane to Cairns, with stops in Townsville and other cities along the way. The **Queenslander** leaves Brisbane with Sunday-only service at around 8:15 a.m., arrives Townsville about 30 hours later, and reaches Cairns at around 6 p.m.—a total of almost 34 hours and 1000 miles from Brisbane. A first-class berth and meals between Brisbane and Cairns is about A$290 per person; economy sitting, about A$100, no economy sleepers. By contrast, a one-way flight from Brisbane to Cairns takes only a couple of hours—but costs about A$300.

The **Sunlander** offers service to Cairns Mon.–Thurs. and Sat. It leaves Brisbane at 7:15 a.m. and arrives in Cairns 37 hours later. A first-class berth is about A$180 per person; economy berth, A$115; economy sitting, A$100.

From Rockhampton, the **Midlander** runs inland to Winton, with stops at Barcaldine and Longreach. The train leaves Rocky about 6:30 p.m. and arrives in Winton around 1:15 the next afternoon. The return train leaves Winton about 4 p.m. and arrives in Rockhampton at 9:50 a.m. A first-class berth runs about A$110 per person; economy-class berths, A$80.

From Townsville, the **Inlander** runs to Mount Isa in Queensland's Outback. The train leaves Townsville Wed. and Sun. at 4 p.m., arriving in Mount Isa the next morning at 9:45 a.m. The return leaves Mount Isa Mon. and Thurs. at 2 p.m., and arrives in Townsville at 7 the next morning. A first-class berth is about A$110, economy sleeper about A$75.

For information on railroad service in Queensland, contact the **City Booking Office,** Queensland Railways, 208 Adelaide St., Brisbane 4000; tel. 225–0211. Information is also available from **Railways of Australia,** 85 Queen St., Melbourne 3000; tel. (03) 670–8808. Intrastate trains leave the city from the **Brisbane Transport Centre** on Roma Street beneath the Brisbane Travelodge. The centre is also the main bus station, and tickets for both rail and bus trips can be purchased there. There is a tourist information desk, and for the budget traveler, a special desk with information and bookings for backpackers, open from 7:30 a.m.–7:30 p.m. *Information 225–0211.*

Two other sources of information about railroads, as well as other services, are the **Public Transportation Information Centre,** Brisbane City Council, Brisbane Administration Centre, 69 Ann St., tel. 225–4444, open Mon.–Fri. 8:15 a.m.–4:45 p.m., and the **Public Transport Information Centre** at the Central Station in Ann St., open Mon.–Fri. 8:15 a.m.–5 p.m.

Bus service from Brisbane to outlying cities is regular, fairly inexpensive, and often faster than the trains. The 34-hour train trip from Brisbane to Cairns, for example, only takes 24 hours by bus.

Service into Brisbane is on **Greyhound, Pioneer, McCafferty,** and **Deluxe;** from Sydney, the trip takes between 15 and 17 hours and costs about A$50 one way. The costs of bus travel around the state can be significantly reduced by getting a pass with one of the companies. The bulk of service in the center of the state is on Greyhound; the other companies run regular service along the coast. There is also regular bus service between Brisbane and the nearby resort coasts. *Information on all services is available from the Public Transportation Information Centre.* Information for the various companies: **McCafferty**'s, 221–8555; **Greyhound,** 240–9300; **Pioneer,** 226–1184, and **Skennars,** 832–1148.

For RV fans, there are a couple of hundred **caravan parks** around the state, with rates generally in the A$10–A$20 per-vehicle, per-night range. For a guide to many of them, look for the *Caravan Parks & Regional Tourist Guide* issued by the Caravan Parks Association of Queensland, available through government tourist offices. It's also handy for auto drivers, because it contains gasoline station locations and tourist site information.

Driving in Queensland can be boring or very dangerous, depending on where you are and what you're driving. Generally, the coast road between Brisbane and Cairns is adequate, but once you turn inland, roads tend to get narrow and shoulders tend to disappear. Rental car agencies are generally available anywhere there is air service—but watch out for drop-off charges if you're not planning to return to the city where you rented the car.

For general road information and other help—particularly if you're a member of the CAA or AAA—contact the **Royal Automobile Club** of Queensland, 300 St. Paul's Terrace, Brisbane 4000; tel. 253–2444.

CLIMATE • As befits a sub-tropical/tropical state, annual temperature ranges generally tend to be kind to humans, with highs along the coast ranging from 70° in the winter to 90° in the summer. Inland, it gets a bit beastlier: Mount Isa, way out in the Outback, gets about 30 days a year in the 100° range. Rainfall is also varied, with Cairns receiving between 80 and 100 inches a year, and Longreach getting under two inches—farther west is even dryer. In the Wet (Dec.–March) it can get pretty swampy north of Cairns in the Cape York area, but it might make you feel better knowing that the Queensland tourism folks assure us that a lot of the rainfall comes during the night. Reef resorts and islands offshore tend to be cooler than the mainland, with steady sea breezes. The sea can get so rough at times, however, that it's impossible to visit the Reef in safety.

One very serious note about the North Queensland coast: swimming. Australia has several species of deadly coelenterates, such as physalia and chironex—what we'd call jellyfish and the Aussies call box jellyfish, sea wasps, or stingers. Every year when the jellyfish come out (Nov.–March), it seems there's at least one death from these creatures, although most beaches are clearly marked. Forget about being eaten by sharks—more people have died in Australia from contact with jellyfish than any other animal. And even though there are some anti-venoms for some species, the chances of a fatality due to anaphylactic reaction or pulmonary edema are very strong, even in healthy adults. The problem is that some of the deadliest species are tiny, almost invisible. Some resort areas try to use special nets to keep the critters out, but uninhabited beaches and even some freshwater rivers rely solely on a swimmer's common sense. Some swimmers, male and female, claim pantyhose will protect them, but our advice is if you're not totally sure, don't go swimming. And watch where you're walking on the beach because even the stingers of a dead jellyfish can harm you.

TIME • Queensland is on Australian Eastern Time, meaning it's 18 hours ahead of Pacific Standard Time on the U.S. West Coast; when it's noon Saturday in San Francisco, it's 6 p.m. Sunday in Brisbane. Queensland does not go on daylight savings time, and probably won't, at least for a while. In the spring of 1992, there was a very expensive, often rancorous referendum on the question, which saw the pro-daylight savings forces go down in a resounding defeat. This, despite predictions that the Brisbane/Gold Coast business factions would out-vote the rest of the anti-light rural areas of the state.

BRISBANE

Flowers, gardens, palm trees, and the river—that's what you mostly remember about Brisbane. The city has a manageable population, about 1.2 million, and sits about 20 miles up the Brisbane River from Moreton Bay on the coast.

The climate, Brisbane's greatest asset, is mostly pleasant, normally ranging from highs of about 85° Fahrenheit in the summer (Dec.–Jan.) to lows in July of around 50°. The highest point of land in town is about 135 feet above sea level.

The city center is nicely placed, sitting on a peninsula carved by the meandering river, with several large parkland areas to break up the urban skyscape. The city's external appearance is not much to get excited about, being mostly efficiently designed banks and high-rises.

The city got a shot in the arm from the 1988 Expo, which saw the city develop several new hotel and office areas around town, and, more importantly, the Expo site itself. The site, on the river directly across from the city center, had been an old and ugly warehouse district. After Expo moved out, the city started developing the site as part of a larger plan to increase attention to the river, which until recent years, had been mostly ignored.

Several projects have begun along the river, including the Beaufort Hotel, opened in 1989 and built on a plot of land on the river near the corner of Margaret and Edward streets next to the Botanic Gardens, and the Waterfront Place development on the river off Market Street.

Another water-directed project is the **Gateway Marine Centre,** located near Fisherman Islands at the mouth of the river. The center, primarily designed for sports fishing, will eventually have a hotel, tavern, and ferry terminal.

In addition, expansion of the city's international airport runways and facilities is being undertaken. Some planning estimates see an annual increase in passenger loads of around 13.5 percent, with about 7 million passengers clearing the airport by 2000.

The housing areas spreading out from the city center are basically just comfortable suburbs. Driving around will give you a chance to study Queensland architecture—verandas, houses up on stilts, iron grillework, tinned roofs, and front yards filled with flowers and palm trees. The urban area goes on forever—the city limits contain about 470 square miles of country.

Brisbane cannot rival watery Sydney in beauty or attractions, but it is one of the most comfortable of the large Australian cities. The city showed off its friendly ways and vitality well enough when it held the Expo, and judging from the amount of development already begun and what is planned, it seems there will be no keeping the city down. The name, by the way, is pronounced "BRIZ-bun." Or, if you're feeling Australian, you could call it Brissie (that's Brizzie).

DOWNTOWN.................................

Queen Street Mall

The best part of the city is its heart, which centers on the Queen Street Mall. Almost every city of any size in Australia has a pedestrian mall, and this is one of the best in the country. It's casual and easy, a place where you can get a coke and a hamburger or a suite in a five-star hotel. The mall was begun in 1982 to show off for the Commonwealth Games, and was expanded and gussied-up again in time for Expo 88. Part of the expansion was an underground bus station.

The mall runs for two long blocks from near the river to Edward Street. Many of the best hotels, important offices, and good restaurants are either on the mall or within a short walking distance of it. A first stop in the city should be at the **Queensland Tourist and Travel Corporation** on the 36th floor of the Riverside Centre, 123 Eagle Street just off the mall; tel. 833–5400.

Anzac Square

The Australians are thorough when it comes to remembering their war dead, and Anzac Square is Brisbane's chief monument to the fallen. Located at the northeast end of Ann and Adelaide streets, the monument has an eternal flame and bronze tablets to commemorate European battlegrounds where Anzac forces were involved. In a vault underneath the flame is the **Shrine of Memories,** which has soil from countries where Australian armed forces fought. Directly across Adelaide Street from the war memorial is Post Office Square, which contains one of Brisbane's prides and joys, the **General Post Office.** The old stone hulk was built in the late 1870s on the site of what had once been the quarters for female convicts, and has been restored to its Victorian excellence. Inside is a museum with displays of 175 years of Aussie postal history. It's open 10 a.m.–5 p.m. Mon.–Fri., Sat. until noon. *Information: 224–1215.*

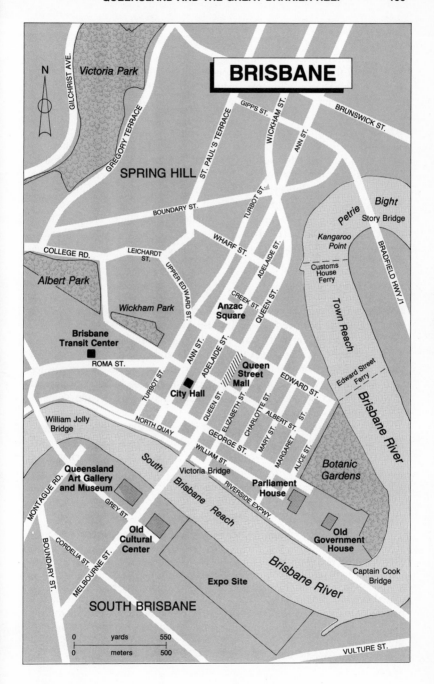

The City Hall

This is probably the public building that Brisbaners prize the most. Construction of the massive stone structure began in 1920 and took 10 years to complete. The building was refurbished in 1988–89. Its centerpoint has always been the 300-foot-high clock tower, for its early years the tallest structure in the city. The tower has an observation platform and is included on conducted tours of the facility. The tower was officially reopened in 1988 by Andrew and Fergie—the Duke and Dutchess of York. The building also houses a concert hall and what is considered to be one of the finest pipe organs in the Southern Hemisphere. Inside are the **City Hall Art Gallery and Museum.** The building faces King George Square, which is highlighted by small gardens and a fountain—and as befits its latitude (27 degrees, 28.3 minutes south), there are palm trees all over. The building is open 10 a.m.–4 p.m. daily. *City Hall information: 225–4360; museum information, 225–4355.*

The Convict Past

Most of the convict-labor buildings from Brisbane's penal past are long gone. One that does remain is the **Old Windmill,** also called the Observatory, located on Wickham Terrace, a quiet residential street on a hill above the city. The tower dates to 1828 and was built as a windmill under the orders of Capt. Patrick Logan, the infamous prison master who was slain by an Aboriginal. In this century, the building was used in the 1930s to broadcast some of the world's first television signals. It's not open to the public.

The oldest stone structure in town is the **Old Commissariat Store,** 115 William St., which sits on what was once the town's original wharf. It was built in 1829 and now houses the offices of the Royal Historical Society of Queensland. *Information: 221–4198.*

OTHER BRISBANE SIGHTS ....

Parliament House

Queensland's Parliament House dates from 1868 and is done in a style called French Renaissance. It sits next to the river on the city center's peninsula adjacent to the Botanic Gardens. The building, copper-topped and built of stone, contrasts nicely to the groves of palm trees surrounding the site. Tours of the building, at the corner of George and Alice streets, are available Mon.–Fri. 9:15 a.m.–2:45 p.m. *Information: 226–7111.*

Botanic Gardens

The Botanic Gardens are a favorite spot for picnics and weekend concerts. The gardens date from 1865, and while not spectacular, are still a breath of green in the increasingly urban nature of the downtown area. The concerts are part of the city's **FREEPS** programs—Free Recreation and Entertainment for Everyone in the Parks). *FREEPS information: 832–5552.* The gardens are open 24 hours. *Information: 221–4528.*

Near the gardens and Parliament House is **The Mansions,** a set of restored townhouses now used as a shopping center. The buildings are the best example of 1890s colonial architecture in the city. One of the stores in the complex is the **National Trust Gift Shop.** *Information for The Mansions: 221–4965.*

Queensland Cultural Centre

If you're an art or science fan, the center of things in Brisbane is the Queensland Cultural Centre, located directly across the river from downtown, and adjacent to the Expo site. The centre houses the Queensland Art Gallery, the Performing Arts Complex, a museum, and a state library. The gallery has an impressive collection, including works by Picasso, Toulouse-Lautrec, and Renoir, plus a number of works by Australian artists. The museum has a fine display on the exploits of aviation pioneer Sir Charles Kingsford-Smith. The performing arts area has three theaters and is home to the Queensland Symphony Orchestra. Tours of all the facilities in the cultural centre are available. *Information: 240–7200 or 240–7229.*

CLOSE TO THE CITY..........................

Lone Pine

The most famous attraction in the Brisbane area is the Lone Pine Koala Sanctuary, the largest private reserve in the country. Here's your chance to have your photo taken with a koala. There is strong evidence to suggest that the eucalyptus-leaf diet they exist on keeps them stoned out of their minds most of the time, leading one Australian travel writer to describe them as ''grotty little dope fiends.'' Well, you decide for yourself.

The newest koala kid on the block, last we checked, was named Corvette, and he and his mates will pose with you for A$7 per person per Polaroid shot. After you pay the fee, you can take photos with your own camera.

What Lone Pine does offer—and this is one of the best-kept secrets of Australian animal life—is a chance to meet kangaroos up close and personal and to discover that they, unlike koalas, are intelligent, friendly creatures with great personalities. The Lone Pine roos have life made. All they do is lie around in the shade all day and let tourists feed them. To give you an idea of what you're dealing with in a tame kangaroo, just watch them with children—even when the little monsters pull their ears and walk on their tails, they just get up and walk away. If they wanted, they could open the kids up like a tin of sardines—they have claws like a saber-tooth tiger's teeth. The park also has emu, platypuses, dingoes, Tasmanian devils, and deer.

Lone Pine makes for a pleasant day in the country. You can get there either by bus, boat, or a combination of both. There is a **Lone Pine express** (BCC 518) that leaves from a bus stop on Roma St. across from the Mayfair Crest International Hotel, and starts running at 7:35 a.m., and costs about A$3 per person one-way.

The boat, run by **Koala Cruises,** leaves downtown around 1 p.m. and arrives at Lone Pine around 2:15 p.m. The boat returns to the city at 3:50 p.m. Tickets for the boat back to the city can be bought at Lone Pine. The one-way trip is about A12 per person. The boat has a bar and snacks. The company offers a transfer service from downtown hotels to the quay for some trips. *Information: Koala Cruises, Queens Wharf Road, North Quay, Brisbane 4000; 229–7055.* Tickets are also available through the Queensland Government Tourist Bureau.

Lone Pine is open from 9:30 a.m.–5 p.m. The platypus tanks are open for view from 11:30 a.m.–noon and 2:45–4 p.m. There is a souvenir shop, cafe, and refreshment kiosk. Ticket costs are about A$10 per person. *Information: Lone Pine Koala Sanctuary, Jesmond Road, Fig Tree Pocket, Brisbane; tel. 378–1366, or 222–7278.*

Mount Coot-tha

The Brisbane City Council is developing this bush area about eight kilometers west of downtown into what is expected to be Australia's largest sub-tropical gardens. A winding road leads to the top, where excellent views of the city are available. In the park are the **botanical gardens,** the **Sir Thomas Brisbane Planetarium,** and the **J.C. Slaughter Falls.** Information: 377–8898. Planetarium information: 377–8896 noon–7 p.m. On the road to the top is the **Mount Coot-tha Summit Restaurant,** a licensed place that serves light meals and Devonshire teas as well as lunches and dinners. *Information: 369–9922.*

The planetarium honors the city's namesake, who was governor of Australia in the 1820s. It offers shows twice a day Wednesday–Sunday. The BCC runs its Gardens 39 bus from Ann Street on King George Square hourly to the park.

Newstead House

The oldest residential building in the city is Newstead House, which was built in 1846 as the home of pioneer squatter Patrick Leslie. The carefully restored and furnished house sits on a hill above a bend on the Brisbane River about 2.5 miles north of the city center in the Newstead area. Sunday is a good day to take a look and have a Devonshire tea at the same time. Admission to the house is A$1; children free. It's open Mon.–Thurs. 11 a.m.–3 p.m. and Sun. 2 p.m.–5 p.m. Buses run from downtown. *Information: Newstead House, Breakfast Creek Road, Newstead; tel 252–7373.*

Chinatown and Fortitude Valley

Northeast of the city center is Fortitude Valey, a modest shopping and eating area with a few department stores and the renovated Chinatown that serves as the city's center of Asian cuisine. The main shopping/eating area is centered around Brunswick Street between Wickham and Ann streets. The valley keeps the same store hours as downtown Brisbane, and is serviced regularly by BCC buses.

ON THE WATER ....

In addition to the cruise upriver to Lone Pine, there are several other tours available on the Brisbane River, as well as trips to Moreton Bay and some of its vacation islands.

A paddlewheeler, the ***Kookaburra Queen,*** has restaurant facilities and offers morning and afternoon teas, lunches, and dinners. The teas are in the A$15 range; lunch from A$17 to A$40, and dinners from $A20 to $A50. Dinner cruises are about four hours long. *Information: Kookaburra Queen, The Pier at Waterfront Place, Eagle Street; phone 221–1300.*

The **Golden Mile Ferry Service** offers daily trips up and down the river, starting at the Botanic Gardens. It's the best bargain on the river, costing about A$2 for a round trip that takes about an hour. Sundays, the ferry goes all the way to Moreton Bay on a three-hour trip that costs about A$10. *Information: Golden Mile Ferry, Riverside Centre, 123 Eagle St., Brisbane; tel. 229–7055 or 832–4795.*

Brisbane City Ferries, the way a lot of folks spend a weekend afternoon in Brisbane, also offers a chance to see the city from the river. Ferries stop along the way to inspect some of the sights, including Newstead House (Saturdays) and the Queensland Cultural Centre (Sundays). Reservations necessary. *Information: Brisbane City Ferries, tel. 399–4768.*

Moreton Bay, 20 miles from downtown, is a large (410 square miles) protected ocean area with several hundred islands, the largest of which are North Stradbroke, South Stradbroke, and Moreton. At the south end of the bay is the beginning of the Gold Coast and its resorts and long sandy beaches.

At the north end of the bay is **Birbie Island,** a wildlife sanctuary with several small settlements and a permanent population of several thousand. The island, about 20 miles long, is connected to the mainland by a bridge from Bongaree. Campgrounds and RV facilities are available on the island.

Moreton Island, 24 miles long and six miles wide, forms the northeastern part of the bay. Its chief geological feature is Mount Tempest, at 920 feet, one of the highest stable sand dunes in the world. The island is home to 125 species of birds and has several freshwater lakes in its interior. Most of the island is a national park, although there is a hotel on the west side of the island, the **Tangalooma Moreton Island Resort.** It has space for about 250 guests, with rooms running around A\$99–170 per person a day full board. The resort is a deep-sea fishing center. *Information: Tangalooma Resort, Moreton Island, Queensland 4004; tel. (07) 268–6333.* The national park ranger can be contacted in care of the resort or by calling (07) 548–2710. The beach is about 25 miles long and there is a lighthouse at the north end of the island that is still in use. Only four-wheel-drive vehicles can drive on the island. There are day trips to the resort that leave from the Hamilton Wharf (near the airport) at 9:30 a.m. and return at 5 p.m. The cost is about A\$30 per person. Information available from the resort.

Passenger launches leave regularly for the island from the wharf at Hamilton; from Redcliffe, north of town, and from Bribie Island and North Stradbroke Island. The one-way cost, depending on port, ranges between A\$20 and A\$30. There are also two small airstrips on the island. Campsites must be reserved and supplies are available on the island.

North Stradbroke, the largest of the Moreton Bay islands, is also a sandy barrier island with freshwater lakes and several impressive headlands. There are three settlements on the island, which is a popular fishing and surfing destination for city dwellers. There are camping areas at all three locations. At Point Lookout, on the ocean side of the island, is the **Anchorage Village Beach Resort,** which offers a variety of accommodations, from small units to suites. There is a pool, tennis courts, and a licensed restaurant. Price range for the rooms runs between A\$100–130 double. *Information: (07) 549–8266.*

There is regular **barge service** to Dunwich, on the island's west side, from Cleveland and Redland Bay. *Information in Cleveland, (07)*

286–2666; in Redland Bay, (07) 358–2122. There is also helicopter service from the Brisbane airport.

A plusher way to see the sights of Moreton Bay and the Gold Coast area is aboard the *M.V. Brisbane Explorer,* a 170-passenger, four-deck cruise ship that runs two-night and four-night cruises around the area. Cost of the four-night in high season (Sept.–Apr.) is between A$550–A$650 per person, all meals and teas included. *Information: Captain Sturt Marine, tel. (07) 844–3533.* The ship leaves from downtown Brisbane Mondays and Fridays.

The Essential Brisbane

INFORMATION • For general help and brochures about activities around the state, contact the **Queensland Tourist and Travel Corporation,** 36th Floor, Riverside Centre, 123 Eagle St.; tel. 833–5400.

There are several offices that offer information about the city itself, including the **Greater Brisbane Regional Tourist Association,** located on the pedestrian mall at the Brisbane Transit Centre on Roma Street near downtown; tel. 221–1562. If you're downtown, try the **Brisbane Visitors and Convention Bureau,** with offices in the City Hall, open Mon.–Fri. 8:30 a.m.–5 p.m.; tel. 221–8411. You can also make use of the **Brisbane City Council information booth** located on the Queen Street Mall, just northeast of Albert St., open Mon.–Fri. 8:30 a.m.– 5 p.m. and 8:30–11:30 a.m. Sat.

GETTING AROUND • **The Brisbane City Council bus system** (BCC) serves the city and suburbs, running up and down both sides of the river as well as crossing back and forth. Buses normally run from 5:30 a.m.– 11 p.m. daily. Normal fares within a zone are about 75 cents. The BCC, however, offers a **Day Rover Pass,** which allows unlimited travel on BCC facilities for A$5. A Circle Bus travels in the downtown area from Riverside Centre to City Hall. The buses run every 5 minutes from 7:55 a.m. to 5:47 p.m. The fare is 45 cents. Information and timetables can be obtained from the **Brisbane City Council Transport Information Counter** at the Brisbane Administration Centre, 69 Ann Street; tel. 225–4444. The city's information offices also have bus and ferry information.

There is regular **ferry service** at more than a half-dozen spots along the river. The two main routes in the downtown area are between Edward Street (next to the Botanic Gardens) and Kangaroo Point, and the Customs House Ferry, which also runs to Kangaroo Point. Fares are the same as buses. *Information: Brisbane City Ferry Cruises, located at the transport information center, 69 Ann St.; tel. 399–4768.*

There are several radio-operated **taxi services** in the city, the largest of which is **Black and White.** Fares start at $1 and meters rack up fees at a rate of about 60 cents a kilometer; no charge for luggage. *Information: 229-1000.*

Getting into the city, seven miles from the airport, is possible by **airporter bus** for about A$5, or by taxi for around A$15. The bus, run by **Skennars Coaches,** stops at several major downtown hotels, and runs every half hour or so; *information: 832-1148.* A major site at the airport is the Southern Cross, the Fokker tri-motor that made the first crossing of the Pacific under the control of Australian aviation pioneer Sir Charles Kingsford Smith. (The Sydney airport is named in his honor). The Brisbane airport, located in the suburb of Eagle Farm, is in the process of being updated, but currently has all expected amenities. *General information: 268-9511.*

POST OFFICES • The General Post Office in Brisbane is at 261 Queen Street and is open, as is the case for most Queensland post offices, 9 a.m.–5 p.m. Mon.–Fri. The GPO does have 24-hour vending machines. *Information: 224-1215.*

TELEPHONES • The area code for Brisbane is (07).

BANKS • Normal banking hours are 9:30 a.m.–4 p.m. Mon.–Thurs. and until 5 p.m. Fri. There are foreign currency exchanges at all banks as well as the airport.

CONSULATES • In Brisbane, the U.S. Consulate is at 383 Wickham Terrace, tel. 839-8955.

SHOPPING • Normal hours are 8:15 a.m.–5:30 p.m. Mon.–Fri. and 8:15 a.m.–4 p.m. Sat. Most city stores stay open to 9 p.m. Fri.; 9 p.m. Thurs. in the suburbs.

With a **Day Rover bus pass,** you can hop the BCC's Great Circle Line, a route that covers about 50 miles and hits eight major shopping complexes as well as the Mount Coot-tha Botanic Gardens. The buses run every half hour.

Downtown shopping is primarily centered around the **Queen Street Mall,** where you will find three large department stores: David Jones, Myer, and C.J. Coles. **David Jones,** the most upscale, is at 194 Queen St. **Meyer,** which has just undergone a major renovation, and in the process created a shopping center with movie theaters, parking, and 200 speciality shops, now takes up a city block along the Mall. **Coles** is a supermarket/variety store at 210 Queen St. There are several shopping centers in the area, including the **Wintergarden,** on the mall, **Post Office Square,** and the **City Plaza,** next to City Hall. The **Rowes Arcade,** 235 Edward St., follows in the footsteps of Sydney's Queen Victoria

Building and lets shoppers glory in Victorian ambiance, complete with native woods and lots of glass. It houses about two dozen shops. Another place to shop in period architecture is at **The Mansions** next to the Botanic Gardens. A new shopping area is located in The Pier, part of the Waterfront Place river development near Eagle Street. There's a McDonald's there.

Unfortunately, there are few places around the city where you can get good Aboriginal artwork. About the best is **Queensland Aboriginal Creations,** 135 George St. Amidst the hokey stuff for tourists (do you really wanna buy a boomerang?) there are also some authentic pieces. *Information: 224–5730.*

The city's duty-free shops, like those in Sydney, offer the usual array of electronic and photographic goods, along with souvenirs and booze. Among the several are **City International Duty Free,** 86 Queen Street, tel. 229–2556; **Downtown Duty Free,** corner Edward and Queen sts., tel. 221–5666, and **Orbit Duty Free,** 136 Queen St., tel. 229–2922. These stores usually require proof that you're a tourist; a passport works, and sometimes even a driver's license.

If you're a compulsive flea market fanatic, check out mounds of used Aussie junk at **Paddy's Market** in New Farm, east of the city center across from Kangaroo Point. The market, corner of Macquarie and Florence sts., is open daily 9 a.m.–3 p.m. You can find produce and milk in addition to the oddiments. Admission is free Mon.–Fri.; weekends there's a A$5 entry charge. *Information: 252–7211.*

In addition, there are two Sunday markets. One, the **Closeburn County Market,** is about 15 miles north of the city in the community of Petrie. Craft items are a speciality. It's open 9 a.m.–2 p.m. *Information: 289–4291.* A more urban scene is the **Cat's Tango Market,** 123 Eagle St. in the city (near the wharf area), where you can see artisans at work—glassblowers, painters, potters. It's open 9 a.m.–4 p.m. *Information: 371–1452.*

Outside of the city center, in the western suburbs, is **Paddington-Circle,** a five-mile stretch of shops, restaurants, and stores housed in restored Queensland houses. It's worth a drive, and is about two miles from downtown. Most of the shops are located along Given Terrace and Latrobe Terrace.

ACCOMMODATIONS......................

One thing to always check in Brisbane is weekend specials at many hotels. Sometimes these can result is substantial savings; sometimes these deals are advertised, sometimes not, so always ask.

Hilton International Brisbane • *190 Elizabeth St.; tel. 231–3131* • Faces onto the Queen Street Mall. The lobby has a 25-story atrium. There are three floors of shops. Pool, sauna, spa, tennis courts, gym, night club, handicapped facilities. Victoria's Fine Dining Room is the hotel's white-linen eatery; more relaxed is the Tropicana pool deck restaurant. And one of our favorite budget/moderate restaurants is here, the New Orleans Restaurant, which is in the Wintergarden Shopping Center inside the hotel. It's a big food hall. Trey the hotel's Americas Cup Bar. Doubles A$280; executive floor, A$300; suites from A$500–950.

Sheraton Brisbane • *249 Turbot St.; tel. 835–3535* • The hotel sits in the middle of the financial district with nice views overlooking the river and downtown. Sauna, squash courts, parking, pool, coffee shop, two restaurants, five bars, a nightclub, fitness center, mini-bars. Doubles A$200–230; suites from A$380. The top two floors of the hotel are executive: private lounge, butler service, business facilities, separate registration. Doubles here are A$325; suites from A$500.

The Heritage • *Corner Margaret and Edward St.; tel. 221–1999* • This is the new kid on the block, with one of the best locations in town, right on the water near the new Waterfront Place development. All 232 rooms and the 19 suites have river views and butler service. What sets this hotel apart is its use of the Port Office, a 19th century building that was renovated during Expo and now has the main hotel restaurant, a wine cellar and a shopping arcade. The restaurant—Siggi's—is supposed to recall images of the places you find people like Somerset Maugham, and it comes close. It's marbles and dark wood, antiques scattered around. Very good and very expensive. The main hotel has a heated outdoor pool for views of the world, plus a fitness center. Doubles start at A$300; suites from A$400–1800.

Mayfair Crest International • *Corner of Ann and Roma sts.; 229–9111* • Right across from the Roma Street transportation center, this hotel has been our Brisbane base several times. It was recently sold to a Singapore-based company, and was extensively refurbished, which it needed. Pool, sauna, parking, handicapped facilities, mini-bars. Large, airy lobby with cafe/restaurant. Spillane's, a nightclub, is popular. Three restaurants, six bars. Doubles A$180; suites from A$250.

Lennons Hotel • *66–76 Queen St.; tel. 222–3222* • Lennons—the name—has been around Brisbane since 1880. That's when John Lennon (no relation, we think) built the first Lennons Hotel. The 1880 version was demolished in 1940, and a new one rose in 1941—this one became the headquarters for Gen. MacArthur and his staff during the war. The hotel moved out of that building in 1972 and opened at its present location. Just before Expo, the hotel company spent around A$5 million refurbishing rooms and public areas. Over the years, everybody has stayed in the hotel (wherever it was): Lyndon Johnson, Diana Dors, Chuck the Prince, Louis Armstrong . . . us. Pool, sauna, spa, barbecue area, free paper, parking, mini-bars, two restaurants—the Hibiscus Room, famous for a luncheon seafood smorgasbord; and the Traditions Restaurant, which is French. Check out the picture of Dugout Doug in the cocktail bar. Doubles A$150; suites A$260–375.

Brisbane City Travelodge • *Roma Street, on top of the transit centre; 238–2222* • You can't get any closer to the bus and train station than this. There are two non-smoking floors, handicapped facilities, the Drawing Room restaurant/bar, plus other bars and a cafe. Sauna, spa, parking, mini-bars. Doubles A$155–175; suites from A$475.

The Gazebo • *345 Wickham Terrace; tel. 831–6177* • In the leafy hilltop area above the main city, down the street from the Old Windmill. Some rooms have balconies with city views, some have cooking facilities. Mini-bars, pool, free undergound parking, three non-smoking floors, restaurant/cocktail bar with good views, 24-hour brasserie. Doubles A$125–150; suites A$170–200.

Albert Park • *551 Wickham Terrace; tel. 831–3111* • The hotel was undergoing major surgery in 1992, expanding and refurbishing. It, like the Gazebo, has city views and also one of the city's better small restaurants, Aldo's on the Park, closed Sundays. Pool, parking. Doubles about A$80.

Tower Mill Motor Inn • *239 Wickham Terrace; tel. 832–1421.* •Built in a round-tower shape, the hotel has spacious rooms and suites, 24-hour room service, and views of the city from the top-story restaurant. It sits next to Albert Park and across the street from the Windmill, one of the oldest buildings in Brisbane. Covered parking. Doubles from A$100.

Chancellor on the Park • *Corner of Leichhardt Street and Wickham Terrace; tel. 831–4055* • The newest and probably the best of the hilltop hotels. The Chancellor has a rooftop pool with the usual stunning views, 24-hour reception, a business center, drive-in bottle shop, guest laundry, five bars, four restaurants, barbershop, sundeck and barbecue areas. The rooms are all suites with business folks in mind, and have fax lines, kitchens with microwaves, separate dining areas and mini-bars. Spa, sauna and gym. It also has some of the best weekend deals in town—once it was charging 90 bucks a night for a suite that usually goes for A$170. Regular prices for the suites (there are four categories) start at A$100 and go to A$270. The place is a good bet.

Coronation • *205 Coronation Dr., Milton; tel. 369–9955* • About two kilometers west of town toward Mount Coot-tha. Each room can sleep four people, and come with TV and mini-bars. The hotel seafood restaurant has won more awards than any other seafood place in the state. Free taxi from the airport. Live jazz five nights a week. Babysitting, tour desk, parking, guest laundry. Great weekend specials. Doubles A$90 weekdays, A$80 weekends.

Airport International • *528 Kingsford-Smith Dr., Hamilton; tel. 268–6388* • Five kilometers from the airport. Bar/restaurant, pool, kitchens, TV, guest laundry, courtesy van, car wash, handicapped facilities. Doubles $A80.

Annie's Shandon Inn • *405 Upper Edward St.; tel. 831–8684* • B&B started by the owner's grandmother in the late 1800s. The 20 rooms are in an old three-story house; some with shared bath. TV lounge, limited parking. Doubles A$55–65.

Emuroo • *58 Mollison St., South Brisbane; tel. 844–6045* • B&B. The morning brekkie is full continental with lots of Queensland fruit. Backpackers welcome. Doubles A$55.

Story Bridge Hotel • *200 Main St., Kangaroo Point; tel. 391–2266* • Across the river from the Botanic Gardens, easily reached by ferry. Kitchen, laundry, free pickup, free beer when you check in. Try the all-you-can-eat pasta nights; live music six nights. Shared and double rooms starting at A$15 per person.

City YHA Hostel • *53 Quay St.; tel. 236–1004* • One of the newest hostels in town, open in 1990, and one of the best locations, next to the transit center. A$15 for members; A$20 non-members.

Backpackers Bridge Inn • *196 Bowen Terr., New Farm; tel. 358–5000* • Next to the river near the Story Bridge and the Carlton Brewery. Large porch to watch the river, free pickup from transit center, kitchen, laundry, tour desk, TV lounge, barbecue area, close to bus stop. Shared and doubles starting at $A15 per person.

RESTAURANTS......................................

This is Brisbane, remember, and that means seafood, especially a wonderful little sea critter called the Moreton Bay Bug, which is downed in immense quantities by the locals. Before you start running for the door (Eat bugs? Me?), relax. The bug is really a crustacean; some call it a lobster, some a crayfish. Whatever, it's delicious and served in hundreds of different ways, from curried bug to bug with drawn butter.

They also serve up mud crabs (big hummers) and a wide variety of fresh catches from the bay and ocean, including Australia's answer to fancy European fish, the barramundi. Add that to the list of tropical fruits available, and the Brisbane eating scene can be fun—and fattening. You won't find as wide an ethnic mix as in Sydney or Melbourne, but there are enough choices to keep you busy.

The city also has its share of Singapore food halls if you like your dining less formal and inexpensive—one of the best is in the Hilton Hotel. As is the case elsewhere in Australia, many restaurants are closed Sundays, so call ahead to make sure. In addition to the hotel restaurants we've mentioned, some other ideas:

Michael's Riverside • *Riverside Centre, 123 Eagle St.; tel. 832–5522.* • One of the best locations in Brisbane, right on the river, especially nice at night. Actually two restaurants. The Garden Room is more formal, Continental-style dining; the popular Waterfront Cafe is more casual and serves home-made pasta and other Italian dishes. The complex has already won several awards. Open for lunch and dinner; closed Sundays. Moderate to expensive.

Daniel's Steakhouse • *145 Eagle St.; 832–3444* • Part of the Riverside Centre. The decor features Aboriginal carvings and paintings. Famous for big grain-fed steaks, it also has fresh lobster and other seafood as well as your basic chook. Open lunch and dinner Monday–Friday. Moderate to expensive.

Breakfast Creek Hotel • *Kingsford-Smith Drive; tel. 262–5988* • There are several restaurants in the Breakfast Creek area near the airport, and the hotel is the most famous. It was built in 1889 and has won many awards over the years for its barbecued steaks. It also has a beer garden. You get to pick your own cut and size of steak before grilling, and if beef is not your bag, they also have chicken, lamb and fish. Open seven days for lunch; dinner from 5:30 p.m. Try it, you'll like it. Expensive.

Jimmy's • Two locations on the Queen Street mall. Jimmy's started as Jimmy's on the Mall, one of our favorite cafe-style places in the city, very handy when in the mall area. It got so popular, a second cafe, Jimmy's Uptown, has been opened at the Edward Street end of the mall. Both outdoor places specialize in good cafe food—burgers, steak and chips, soup and the biggest cappuccinos in town. Prices are still good; so's the food. Budget to moderate.

Jo-Jo's • *Queen and Albert sts.; 221–1221* • Our first love in Brisbane (it was the first place we ate in town). It's a small food hall with assorted ethnic cuisines and one of the friendlier bars around. It's on the second floor with open windows and a breeze. Always fairly crowded, a good place to sit down after a strenuous day walking around. The food remains good and low-cost. There's a happy hour Monday–Thursday from 4–6 p.m. It's open early to late.

Friday's • *123 Eagle St.; tel. 832–2122* • Another Riverside Centre facility, this one along the lines of Jo-Jo's but a lot newer. Large complex with three restaurants, four bars and a nightclub, all overlooking the river. Watch the paddlewheelers sail by and get your chow from an ala carte menu, buffet, ethnic stuff or just light snacks. There's live music every night, and it's open seven days a week all day and into the night. Budget to expensive.

Asian food • Two good bets are the Oshin Japanese Restaurant and the Golden Palace Chinese Restaurant. The **Oshin** is on the second floor of Koala House, corner of Adelaide and Creek sts.; tel. 229–0410. Near Anzac Square; specializes in barbecues at your table and high-quality Aussie beef dishes. Licensed. Lunch noon–2:30 p.m. Monday–Friday; dinner 6–10:30 p.m. Monday–Saturday. The **Golden Palace** is at the corner of Ann and Duncan; tel. 252–8872. It's in the Chinatown area of Fortitude Valley about three kilometers northwest of the city center. A new place, with really good food and live entertainment and dancing Friday and Saturday nights. Being Brisbane, there is, of course, a tank with live mud crabs and lobsters. Licensed and takeaway. Open seven days for lunch and dinner. Budget to expensive.

Pasta Joke • *100 Commercial Rd., Fortitude Valley; tel. 852–1394* • Pasta, pasta and more pasta. Popular hangout for students and folks who like big portions and moderate prices. Licensed. Lunch noon–2 p.m. Sunday–Friday; dinner from 5:30 p.m. seven days. Good bargain.

Mount Coot-tha Summit Restaurant • *Sir Samuel Griffith Dr.; tel. 369–9922* • Probably the best views in town and arguably some of the finest food. The decor is tans and blacks, and the menu offers the full range of Queensland goodies, from Moreton Bay bugs to vegetarian specialities to one we always try to forget: lamb's brains. The bugs are the best we ever had—butterflied with garlic, tarragon and wine. Whoa. Mushroom caps with cheese and crab, rabbit, quail. An added incentive is the hours: morning to late, seven days. If you're out on a tour, try the morning or afternoon teas. A delight and worth the drive out, which is under 10 kilometers. Not to be missed. Expensive.

THE GOLD COAST

The Gold Coast is Australia's answer to California, Atlantic City, and Miami Beach rolled into one. It's a 20-mile stretch of beach from Southport (about 50 miles from downtown Brisbane) to the New South Wales border. In many parts, unfortunately, it has become tacky, beach-front ugly, a prime example of everything bad that can happen to a quiet, beautiful resort area: high-rise apartments, hokey attractions, bikini emporia, fast-food joints, waterslides—you get the idea. It was probably inevitable, when you realize that the center of things on the coast is a place called Surfers Paradise.

But one critic's tourist disaster is another's delight, and annually, more than three million souls flock to the Gold Coast to drink in the sun and fun—and donate something like A$600 million a year to the local coffers in the process. It's popular with families from all over the country, as well as becoming a growing mecca for Japanese honeymoon couples. We are, quite frankly, not sure why North Americans would come this far to do what they could do just as easily in Florida, California, Mexico, Hawaii, or the Bahamas.

The Gold Coast, at least for us, is not a major Queensland attraction. Given the delights of other parts of the state, we would go to the coast only if we were in the Brisbane area and were dying from beach withdrawal. There is another side to this part of the coast, however: not far inland, there are some very nice rain forests and watery areas far removed from the beach madness. More of this later.

But if you're a surfer or a true beach freak—or perhaps just a sociologist looking for new forms of tribal behavior—the Gold Coast will probably draw you like a moth to a bug zapper. And in all honesty, the beaches themselves really are excellent, and there are more golf courses than you can shake a four-iron at. Green fees here, even though it's a resort area, are a steal by American standards, mostly around A$30 for 18 holes.

Our favorite memory of the coast is the beach outside Grundy's entertainment center in Surfers Paradise. Here, tanned the color of old horsehide, stood a gent operating a paint sprayer on a much paler gent (obviously a tourist). The sprayer was full of Coppertone, 50 cents a spray. Somehow it all made sense, because the whole atmosphere of the coast is that way—you will, by God, have fun, as efficiently as possible.

Southport, the original settlement in the area, is at the northern end of the coastal strip. It's a lot more city-like than the rest of the strip, and doesn't actually sit on the coast—a sand spit separates it from the ocean. It is the commercial and administrative center of the coast.

Across from Southport on the spit (in what is called Main Beach) is the **Fisherman's Wharf tourist development** with shops, fishing fleet, bars, and restaurants—supposedly modeled after its namesake in San Francisco (which, depending on how you look at it, is either a good idea or purgatory). Nearby is **Seaworld,** with marine animal attractions and shows, said to be the largest such in Australia. There are also some killer water slides, fast-food joints, and a bar or two. Next to the wharf is a place for "Jaws" fans, the **Great White Shark Expo.** *Information; Fisherman's Wharf, 32–2990; Seaworld, 32–5131; Great White Shark Expo. 32-7230.* The admission charge to Sea World is around A$30. The area code on the Gold Coast is (075).

On the spit, fronting both the ocean and the Broadwater (the inlet between the spit and the mainland), is one of the coast's newest and snazziest resort hotels, the **Sheraton Mirage.** It has shopping, a marina, butler service, restaurants, and hovercraft service to and from the Brisbane airport. It has 300 rooms, with doubles from A$300–500; suites A$625–A$2100. *Information: 91–1488.* Reservation information: Sheraton Corporation, (800) 325–3535 USA and Canada. Southport is also a popular camping spot—it's full of **caravan parks,** many with rental units. Most of them also allow tent campers.

Surfers Paradise, where it's happening on the Gold Coast, is the most crowded stretch of beach on the coast, the place to see and be seen. It rocks and rolls with the best of the world's beach resorts, and being Australian, and thus a close cousin, it always reminds us more of Fort Lauderdale than anything else.

Whatever, you can do just about anything in the Surfers area that humans have devised to amuse other humans.

One of the most popular family spots is **Grundy's Paradise Centre,** loudly self-billed as the largest family entertainment center in Australia, with three air-conditioned acres of games, rides, and attractions, plus food halls and live entertainment. It's a great place to grab a good meal and get out of the sun, even better if you have the kids along. As a for instance, a three-course meal (picking from the various ethnic outlets) and wine is about A$15. Grundy's sits right next to the beach. *Information: 38–9011.*

Nearby is the setpiece of the whole Gold Coast, the **Conrad International Hotel** and its glass-enclosed **Jupiters Casino.** The hotel, part of the Hilton chain, sits on its own island in the Nerang River, 15 acres of park and resort where you can sleep in style and lose the family fortune any night of the week at the 24-hour casino. The hotel has 600 rooms, four licensed restaurants, and a 1000-seat showroom for Las Vegas-style revues. Double rooms start at around A$180 and go up; suites $A625–2100. *Information: 92–1133.*

Other entertainment areas along the Gold Coast Highway include **Magic Mountain,** an amusement park with more than 20 rides plus entertainment and a magic and illusion show. Unlike the other major attractions, which are open every day, the Mountain closes Friday and Saturday. *Information: 52–2333.*

The latest development along the coast is the posh new **Sanctuary Cove,** sited on the Coomera River north of Southport, about 20 minutes by car from Surfers Paradise, being developed by Shinko Australia, the Australian arm of Shinko Limited, one of Japan's major golf-course and resort companies. The development includes expensive single-family homes for a population of about 1500, a marina, the Marine Shopping Village with 100 stores, two golf courses (including one designed by Arnold Palmer), harborfront restaurants, and a recreation center. The anchor for the development is the new **Hyatt Regency** resort, modeled in classic Outback-mansion style. Rates at the hotel (including free golf) begin at around A$220 double; suites up to A$1700.

Not far from Sanctuary Cove, on the Pacific Highway just inland from the coast, is another major attraction, **Dreamworld,** Australia's answer to Disneyland. There are about 30 rides, including the Thunderbolt, claimed to be the world's largest double-loop rollercoaster. The park has a number of theme areas based on Australiana—Gold Rush Country, Koala Land, etc. Entry fees are about A$30, which lets you ride everything. *Information: 53–1133.*

For the naturalists in the crowd, the Gold Coast does have two quiet areas away from the sandy bustle. **Burleigh Heads National Park** has walking trails and views of the coast, and the **Currumbin Sanctuary** has an aviary with daily feedings of Aussie birds as well as koalas and kangaroos. *Information about the national park—as well as other regional parks, is available at the National Parks and Wildlife kiosk at Tallebudgera. For information about the sanctuary, call 34–1266.*

The Gold Coast has one thing going for it: plenty of places to stay, from tent sites to the Hyatt and its ilk. During the high season, it might be hard to find a place, but there are so many between Southport and Coolangatta that something is always available. It helps, of course, to book in advance.

Information is available from the Queensland Government Travel Centre in Brisbane, or from the Gold Coast Visitors and Convention Bureau, 115 Scarborough St., Southport; tel. 91–1988, or by mail to P.O. Box 878, Surfers Paradise, Queensland 4217; tel. 36–7765. On the coast, there are information centers at the Cavill Mall in Surfers Paradise, tel. 38–4419; or at the Beach House, Coolangatta, tel. 36–7765.

Getting to the Gold Coast is easy, either by driving yourself, taking a bus, or going on a tour. There is also a small airport at Coolangatta. **Skennars, Greyhound, McCafferty's** and **Coachtrans Pacific West** buses run about A$15 one way and leave from the city transit center on Roma Street in Brisbane. Buses also run from the Coolangatta airport to Surfers for about A$5 one way. On the beach itself, the Surfside bus makes regular trips between Southport and Tweed Heads for about A$5 for an all-day ticket. *Information: 36–7666.* **Sunstate Tours** runs a number of all-day tours to the coast from Brisbane with free pickup at your hotel. One, for example, leaves the city at 9:15 a.m., visits Sanctuary Cove, the beaches, Surfers Paradise, the casino and other stops, then returns at around 5:30 p.m. The cost is about A$35 for adults. *Information: (07) 229–2577.* Similar tours are run by **Boomerang Luxury Day Tours,** with offices in the Roma transit center. *Information 221–5235.*

Near the Coast

Within easy driving distance of the surf madness and the high rises are several bush areas well worth a visit if you like rain forests and green calm. They are generally situated in the string of low mountains that begin to rise about ten miles inland. Some are getting cluttered with boutiques and galleries, but there are still plenty of places to take a walk by yourself in the silence.

One of the most popular areas is **Tamborine Mountain,** about 15 miles west of Coomera. In a ten-square-mile area are seven small national parks, filled with waterfalls, ancient stands of palms (they claim some are 15,000 years old), and hiking trails. *Information on the area is available at the Tamborine Mountain Visitors Centre in Doughty Park, North Tamborine.* The center is open daily 10:30 a.m.–3:30 p.m. except in "very wet weather." Day trips to the area are available through both **Boomerang** and **Sunstate Tours** from Brisbane, both in the A$40-per-person range.

Farther south is the **Springbrook** area, about 25 miles west of Coolangatta. Near the small town are two national parks, **Gwongorella** and **Warrie.** In Gwongorella is the famous **Purlingbrook Falls,** with many trails, including one that goes behind the falls. Also in the area, are stands of 3000-year-old Antarctic beech trees which grow in only four places in the world. A good drive is the **Lyrebird Ridge Road** near town, with great views of the coast.

To the west of Springbrook is **Lamington National Park,** about 30 miles from Southport. The 50,000-acre park is in an area formed by volcanic activity, and the result is a wild mix of deep canyons, water-falls (500 by estimate), and a dense jungle filled with ferns, mosses, and 700 species of orchids. The streams are home to platypuses (count yourself very lucky if you spot one), and the air with rare Australian lyrebirds and hordes of rosellas. You will also see bowerbirds as well as ring-tailed possums. There are several excellent bushwalks, one in the Green Mountains section of the park, the other in the Binna Burra area. There is a camping area at the Green Mountains. There are two ranger stations in the area, the easiest of which to reach from the Gold Coast is at Beachmont on the main road into the area. *Information (075) 45–1734.*

There are two resort facilities in the park. **O'Reilly's Mountain Resort** in the Green Mountains has wheelchair trails, four-wheel-drive excursions, a licensed restaurant, and 30 units. Rates, including all meals, run around A$100 per person; camping available. Check road conditions before driving to the resort. *Information: (075) 45–1611.* The second facility is the **Binna Burra Mountain Lodge and Campsite,** ten kilometers south of Beachmont. The resort has a licensed restaurant and the campsite has hot showers and a supplies kiosk. Rates, including all meals, are about A$110 per person. *Information: (075) 33–3622;* for lodge reservations, toll-free, call (008) 074–260. The lodge can also be booked through ATS/Sprint, (800) 423–2880 USA or (800) 232–2121 Canada.

Up the Coast

It is about 1100 miles from Brisbane up the coast to Cairns, and much of the highway is rural boring—long stretches of sugarcane fields, small towns, and farms. The coastal road, which north of Brisbane changes names from the Pacific Highway to the Bruce Highway, is in really nasty condition in places (holes, no shoulders), and farm vehicles and heavy trucks add to the fun. Still, if you have the time, a drive along the coast will at least let you see how Queensland got its start as an agricultural and mining area. Also, many of the major towns along the way have services out to offshore islands or the Great Barrier Reef.

Just north of Brisbane is the state's next major beachy playground, the **Sunshine Coast,** probably fated to end up looking just like its ugly stepsister, the Gold Coast. The Sunshine Coast runs roughly 45 miles, from Caloundra to Noosa Heads. The attraction here is fine beaches with things not yet as hectic as Surfers Paradise. The Queensland government says the Sunshine Coast is the fastest-growing area in the state, but at present, there is relative calm available. You get a feel for the future, however, by looking at the solid residential and tourist developments that have sprung up along the beaches from Maroochydore to

Mooloolaba. For instance, on the A$200 million Eden Twin Waters resort at Maroochydore opened in 1990.

The Sunshine Coast is as close to Brisbane as the Gold Coast, and is served by a number of buses, trains, and tour companies. Driving up from Brisbane is about an hour's effort—turn off for the coast at the Caloundra road, then follow a small coast road all the way to Noosa. **Skennar's Coaches** run daily trips from the Roma Street transit center in Brisbane for around A$10–A$20 depending on destination. *Information: Skennars, 832–1148.* Train service is available by catching either the **Queenslander** or **Capricornian,** which run to Nambour. **Sunstate Tours** and **Boomerang** also run day tours to the Sunshine Coast. *Information about attractions and accommodations is available from the Queensland information center in Brisbane, or from the Sunshine Coast Tourism and Development Board, P.O. Box 246, Mooloolaba, Queensland 4557; tel. (071) 44–5655.*

The major population centers, going north, are Caloundra, Maroochydore, Nambour (inland a ways and the largest), Tewantin, and Noosa Heads. The **Heads** are internationally known among surfers as the site of some of the world's most perfect waves, and it's also an area of lush private retreats as well as the rain forest quiet of **Noosa Heads National Park.** Just north of the Heads is **Teewah** and the **Colored Sands,** a beautiful 30-mile-long stretch of almost uninhabited beach.

There is a wide range of **accommodations** on the Sunshine Coast, from motels and RV parks to resorts. Many of the best are at Noosa, including **Noosa International,** a 65-unit resort with rooms in the A$200 a night double range; *information (074) 47–4822.* In the same price range is the **Netanya Resort Hotel,** which sits on the beach and has about 50 suites; *information (074) 47–4722.* It's a big U-shaped building, with rooms starting around $A170–300; suites $A350–700. The 170-room **Sheraton Noosa Resort,** a A$60 million project, claims to offer the largest standard guest rooms in Australia; *Information: (074) 49–4888.* Also at Noosa is **Accom Noosa,** a rental agency that handles several properties in the area and can make bookings. *Information (071) 47–3444.*

Two of the more popular tourist attractions in the area back of the coast are the Glasshouse Mountains, southeast of Caloundra, and the Sunshine Plantation. The **Glasshouse Mountains,** so named by Capt. Cook on his 1770 exploration because they reminded him of the glass furnaces of his native Yorkshire, are craggy volcanic remains and figure prominently in Aboriginal lore. The highest peak is about 1800 feet. You get to the mountains, and the three national parks in the area, by turning off the Bruce Highway near Beerburrum. The area around the peaks is mostly pineapple plantations.

The **Sunshine Plantation** is another one of those roadside tourist spots so beloved of tacky places collectors. The main feature of the facility (in addition to a collection of Aussie fauna) is the Big Pineapple, a two-story fruit-cum-souvenir stand. There is also a train available to take you around the sugarcane fields of the area. Admission to the plantation, at Woombye just south of Nambour, is free; hours are 9 a.m.–5 p.m. every day. *Information: (071) 42–1333.* We probably should not overlook the Big Cow, a giant bossie in the same spirit as the pineapple, which celebrates the dairy industry with farm animal displays and hiking trails. It's near Nambour. *Information (071) 46–7144.*

From Nambour, the Bruce Highway cuts inland past Gympie to Maryborough and Hervey Bay, the main population centers near Fraser Island. **Gympie,** an old Gold Rush town, is the gateway to **Cooloola National Park,** for our money one of the most scenic stretches of the whole coast. The park, a 97,000-acre mixture of deserted sandy beaches, freshwater lakes, swamps, rain forest, and stands of eucalypts, is a popular hiking and four-wheel-drive area. It is criss-crossed by numerous tracks and trails, and there are several campgrounds with toilets, fresh water, fireplaces, and showers. Advance booking for all campsites is required. Mainland hotel and motel accommodations are available at Rainbow Beach, Pomona and Boreen Point.

One of its most famous spots is the *Cherry Venture,* a 3000-ton freighter that was blown high on the beach during a hurricane in 1973. It's a fairly easy stroll from Rainbow Beach southeast along the coast to Double Island Point, where the beached ship slowly rusts in the Queensland sun. Another popular destination is **Teewah Coloured Sands,** a stretch of beach at the far southern edge of the park, noted for 650-foot-high cliffs composed of earth-toned deposits. The easiest way to get to the area is by renting a boat at Boreen Point, crossing Lake Cootharaba, and hiking over to Teewah. Although the park itself is closed to non-four-wheel-drive vehicles, you can drive from the Bruce Highway to Tin Can Bay, Rainbow Beach, and Boreen Point near the park. Tin Can Bay Inlet, a popular fishing and prawning area, marks the southern edge of the range of one of Australia's most dangerous animals, the saltwater crocodile. Several companies in Brisbane and Noosa offer four-wheel-drive rentals or tours to Cooloola National Park as well as Fraser Island. Check with **Trekabout Tours,** GPO 2637, Brisbane 4001; tel. 357–5741. Or try **Sunrover Expeditions,** 11 South Pine Rd., Alderley, Brisbane 4051; tel. 352–5888. Tour information is also available at the Sunshine Coast information center in Mooloolaba. *For information and reservations in Cooloola National Park, contact the Queensland National Parks and Wildlife Service, P.O. Box 350, Gympie, Queensland 4570; tel. (071) 82–4189.*

Fraser Island, north of Cooloola National Park and due east of Maryborough, is said to be the largest sand island in the world. The island is a naturalist's feast, offering everything from 800-foot-high sand dunes to thick forests and 40-odd freshwater lakes nurtured by an annual rainfall of around 60 inches. The island is large enough (about 75 miles long, nine miles wide) to sustain small herds of brumbies (wild horses) and packs of what are believed to be the purest strains of dingos in Australia. There are also 250 species of birds and large stands of satinay trees that reach 250 feet in height. The island was the scene of a bitter and successful environmental fight in the 1970s when sand mining was damaging the fragile island ecology. The island is now managed by the federal government and permits are required to visit and camp on the island. Most of the northern end of the island is taken up by **Great Sandy National Park,** which is about 26 square miles in area.

Access to the island is by boat or small aircraft. **Charter aircraft** leave from Brisbane, Hervey Bay, Rainbow Beach, and Maryborough. Travel on the island is by four-wheel-drive vehicle or by foot. Car ferries run from Inskip Point near Rainbow Beach to the only paved road on the island, which heads north toward the Eurong Beach Resort. Boat service also is available from Urangan and from North Head, south of Urangan. In addition to campgrounds, there are several resorts and tourist centers on the island. At the north end is the **Orchid Beach Re-Resort,** with individual cabins, a swimming pool, and licensed restaurant; rates are around A$350 double, meals included. Bookings are available through Ansett Travel, Oxford Street, Sydney 2000; tel. 268–1555, or the nearest Ansett office; information: (071) 279–185 or (07) 221–6399. Accommodation information, as well as general information about the island and tour operators, is available from the Hervey Bay Council Office, 10 Bideford St., Torquay 4657; tel. (071) 28–2855. Information about Great Sandy National Park is available from the Queensland National Parks and Wildlife Service, Rainbow Beach Rd., Rainbow Beach 4570; tel. (071) 86–3160. Island permits are available at the Hervey Bay Council Office or the district forestry office in Maryborough; tel. (071) 22–2455.

Maryborough, the major port for the area's Gold Rush, was built on the backs of "blackbirds," black slaves imported to work in the cane fields, many of them from Fiji. It still shows some vestiges of the golden past, including the city's pride and joy, an iron lacework bandstand. **Hervey Bay,** about ten miles from Maryborough, is a middle-class seaside community sometimes called the "caravan capital of Australia"— there are at least a dozen RV parks in the area. The park service is trying to create a marine environmental area off Hervey Bay to protect humpback whales, which swim through during their annual migration along the Queensland coast between August and October.

Bundaberg, the next major community up the coast, is a sugarcane processing center and home to the most famous rum in Australia, named after the city. Once, in the Northern Territory, we stopped at a bottle shop to pick up a case of XXXX beer for ourselves and a bottle of Bundaberg for the mem-sahib's cuba libras. The clerk accused us of being Queenslanders who, he said, are notorious for combining XXXX and Bundaberg to make incredibly wicked boilermakers. We decided not to even think about trying one.

From Bundaberg north, you start getting into **Great Barrier Reef** country. The first chunk of the reef, now set aside as part of the **Great Barrier Reef Marine Park,** is due east of Gladstone and Rockhampton. **Gladstone,** once a quiet rural town, is now a major seaport and mining center, and has paid the price in smokestacks and industrial sprawl. The world's largest bauxite processing plant is here, as well as coal-handling facilities.

Rockhampton, about 60 miles north, is the capital of what is called the Capricornia area, so named because it sits astride the Tropic of Capricorn. The tropic, in fact, goes right through the city's tourist information center on the Bruce Highway at the south entrance to town. Rockie is a major beef-shipping center, with an estimated 2.5 million cattle feeding on ranges within 150 miles of the city. It has some fine old pioneer buildings preserved along the Fitzroy River, including some pubs. The Capricorn Highway, a major route to the Outback via Winton and beyond, starts in Rockhampton.

Near Rockhampton, at Yeppoon, a Japanese industrialist, Yohichiro Iwasaki, has been in the process of creating a huge resort supposedly catering to Japanese tourists. The resort, the **Capricorn Iwasaki Resort,** now more than a decade in the building, has been embroiled in controversy from the start. Some Australians objected to cattle being raised on the resort property, seeing them as a threat to the Australian beef business, and others, still remembering World War II, were less than enthused at having a huge Japanese settlement on the Queensland coast. The project has been in and out of courts and construction delays have put the whole affair in hot water. When last heard of, the project was back before the Queensland Parliament for more discussion on land use in the resort area. It has also changed names since the first phase was opened in 1987: it's now the Capricorn International Resort. The change was made, hotel spokesmen said, because the bulk of the resort's clients are Australians and Europeans. The present 400 units are one- and two-bedroom apartments plus motel rooms. The 21,000-acre resort has three licensed restaurants and a golf course, and also boasts it has the largest freshwater swimming pool in the Southern Hemisphere, plus a 15-kilometer beach. Rates are in the A\$100–A\$250 range. *Information: Capricorn International Resort, Farnborough Rd., Yeppoon; tel. (079) 39–0211 or 39–7550.*

Mackay (pronounced muck-EYE), about 190 miles north of Rockhampton, is the sugar capital of Australia and the southern end of the Whitsunday Coast. The buildings in town are relatively new, courtesy of a cyclone that destroyed everything in 1918. About 50 miles west of Mackay is **Eungella National Park,** one of the largest undeveloped parks in the state. It's a vast expanse of rain forests and low mountains, with no roads, but plenty of trails. *Information: Queensland National Parks and Wildlife Service, P.O. Box 623, Mackay 4740; tel. (079) 57–6292.*

The small cities between Mackay and Townsville—Proserpine, Bowen, Ayr—are basically agricultural centers that are also jumping-off places for visits to the Whitsunday Islands and the Reef itself. On the coast near Proserpine is a peninsula extending into **Repulse Bay,** where resort and tourist development is on the increase because of its close proximity to the Whitsundays. Here you will find boat charters, small airlines, and tour companies servicing the islands. The main departure point for day trips is **Shute Harbour,** next to Circular Quay in Sydney, the busiest passenger port in Australia—currently Shute Harbour sees 6000 people a day in the high season. Five miles away is **Airlie Beach,** a growing resort community with accommodations, RV parks, restaurants, and a growing assortment of T-shirt and souvenir shops. As an example of the growth in the area, a new A$251 million marina/resort facility is being developed at Airlie Beach, complete with hotel, condos, golf course, and ferry terminals. Meanwhile, there are plans afoot to upgrade the passenger and cargo facilities at Shute Harbour, an undertaking estimated to cost around A$100 million. Also at Shute Harbour, Seair Pacific has opened a new airport terminal for service to Mackay as well as reef trips and charter flights. Of interest to bushwalkers is **Conway National Park,** on the end of the peninsula, with hiking trails and some small beaches. A new national park just north of Airlie, **Dryander,** includes six prominent headlands and 11 islands. Of interest at **Bowen,** which hosts the annual Festival of Murals, is the Ken Done mural used in the United Nations Pavilion at the 1988 Expo in Brisbane.

TOWNSVILLE ....

Townsville, the first of the northern Queensland coastal cities to start into the tourist business in a big way, has a population of more than 100,000, making it the state's second-largest city. The first international airport capable of handling jumbos was built in Townsville, and for some years the city got a major share of the Great Barrier Reef tourism business from North America. The international airport at Cairns has changed that to a certain degree, and Townsville now handles mostly Asian traffic. This does not mean the city is fading away, however. The state tourism authority reports that close to A$650 million in proposed and approved tourist development is under way in Townsville, and there are plans to extend the city's international airport runways to handle

747-400s. Townsville is a more or less typical coastal Queensland city, with wide streets, a prosperous pedestrian mall downtown, good restaurants, and a casual tropical lifestyle.

One of the major tourist attractions near the city is **Magnetic Island,** a tall island about seven miles offshore that is increasingly being developed into a resort area. Fortunately, more than half of the island has been turned into a national park, and at **Horseshoe Bay,** a small area has been designated as a waterfowl refuge. *Information for the park is available from The Queensland National Parks and Wildlife Service, Northern Regional Centre, (077) 74–1411.*

Included among the accommodations on the island are **The Latitude 19 Resort** at Nelly Bay, currently the largest on the island, which offers rooms ranging from lodges in the A$90 double category to suites in the A$100 and up range. There is a pool, restaurant and cocktail lounge. *Information: (077) 78–5200.* Another major lodge is the **Arcadia Holiday Resort,** operated by Hayles Cruises, which runs a ferry service to Magnetic Island from the city. Rooms at the Arcadia are in the A$70–100 range, and there are shops, two pools, two bars, and a restaurant. *Information: (077) 78–5177.* Hayles has at least 10 services a day to the island all year long. A round-trip ticket is about A$10 per person. Both resorts will arrange a pickup at the island dock if notified ahead of time. There is also air service from the city airport to the island. Once on the island, you can rent mokes (the Aussie cross-breed of a dune buggie and golf cart) or motorbikes for getting around on the paved roads between the residential and shopping areas on the island. *The island has an information service; call 78–5117.*

Offshore island resort areas served by Townsville transportation services include **Orpheus, Hinchinbrook, Dunk,** and **Bedarra** islands. Townsville was also the jumping-off place for guests heading for the now-defunct Four Seasons Barrier Reef Floating Hotel, anchored on the John Brewer Reef about 50 miles offshore. Townsville is also a major transportation hub, connecting with a major Outback-bound route, the Flinders Highway, as well as the rail line that runs to Mount Isa. Although many international-grade hotels and tour operators have located in the Cairns areas, Townsville has its share, including several diving outlets and some very good hotels.

Townsville is a center for marine research, with major studies of coral life being done by **James Cook University** as well as the **Australian Institute of Marine Science,** both located in the city. Of major interest to Townsville scientists has been the decimation of the reef near the city by crown-of-thorns starfish, a major threat to the entire reef because they eat huge chunks out of the living coral. James Cook also has the National Centre for Studies in Travel and Tourism, which says something about the popularity of the Queensland coast.

A quite good introduction to the Great Barrier Reef is available at the new **Great Barrier Reef Wonderland,** where an artificial section of reef has been created, complete with tides and spectacular examples of the animals that inhabit the reef. The facility, near the Flinders Mall pedestrian shopping area, has a 70-foot-long transparent underwater tunnel to see the marine displays up close, as well as an Omnimax theater, a food arcade and a gift shop. It's open weekly from 9 a.m.–5 p.m., entry fee about A$20. *Information: (077) 72–4249.*

Townsville also has one of the best-equipped dive shops near the Reef, **Mike Ball Watersports.** The shop has a diving tower where you can learn deep diving, and offers SCUBA certification as well as bookings on Reef-bound dive and snorkeling boats working out of Townsville. *Information: 252–256 Walker St., Townsville: (077) 72–3022.*

As befits its role as tourist boomtown, Townsville has acquired some first-rate hotels during the last decade, including the **Sheraton Breakwater,** which now has the only casino in Northern Queensland. *Information about the city, the surrounding area and the state in general is available from the Townsville Information Centre located in the center of the Flinders Mall; tel. 71–2724.* For an overview, either drive, bus or taxi to the top of **Castle Hill,** the 950-foot peak that sits behind the city. Once there, you can also chow down at **Panorama House** which has seafood dinners and snacks. *Information: 72–4555.*

ACCOMMODATIONS......................

Sheraton Breakwater Casino-Hotel • *Sir Leslie Theiss Dr., Townsville 4810; tel. (077) 22–2333* • In addition to the casino, the hotel has a pool, health club and two licensed restaurants. The hotel won the Sheraton group's Pacific region hotel-of-the-year award in 1988. All 200 rooms have color TV, in-house movies, mini-bars, and direct-dial phones. Rates run from around A$165 double; one- and two-bedroom suites are A$290–700.

Townsville International Hotel • *Flinders Mall, Townsville 4810; tel. (077) 72–2477* • This cylindrical structure, hated and loved and sometimes called the "Sugar Shaker," is in the heart of downtown Townsville. It features a rooftop pool, two restaurants, and three bars, and rooms with mini-bars, direct dial, and color TVs. Double rooms run about A$130; suites up to A$230.

Townsville Ambassador • *75 The Strand, Townsville 4810; tel. 72–4255* • One of the first and best of the city's hotels, it has a pool and a licensed restaurant and bar. Rooms have mini-bars and color TVs. Doubles are in the A$115; suites A$160 range. Reservation information:

Southern Pacific Hotel Corporation, (800) 421–0536 USA; (800) 252–2155, California; (800) 251–2166 Canada.

Reef International • *63 The Strand, Townsville 4810; tel. 21–1777* • Situated on the waterfront, the Reef is a newer hotel with spacious rooms, equipped with color TV and direct-dial phones. The hotel has a licensed restaurant and bar, parking garage, and pool. Rooms are in the A$80–A$90 range depending on view; suites A$110.

Bessell Lodge • *38–42 Bundock St., Belgian Gardens; tel. 72–5055* • Pool, licensed restaurant (closed Sunday), mini-bars, courtesy van, guest laundry. Doubles about A$75.

Colonial Rose • *23 Bowen Rd.; tel. 25–1422* • Licensed restaurant, pool, spa, guest laundry, handicapped access. Doubles from $A55–70; three suites, A$75–100.

Seagulls Holiday Inn • *74 The Esplanade; tel. 21–3111* • Most with kitchens, room service, licensed restaurant, pool, half-court tennis, guest laundry, handicapped access, courtesy van. Doubles about A$70.

Raintree • *Corner of Bowen Road and Carmody Street; tel. 75–3066* • Licensed restaurant (closed Sunday), pool, spa, guest laundry, handicapped facilities. Doubles A$60.

Civic House Backpackers Inn • *262 Walker St.; tel. 71–5381* •Free pickup and return to bus, train or ferry. Free laundry, free beach bus, BBQ. Dorms, singles, doubles and some units with private facilities. Shared rooms about A$15 per person; doubles about A$30.

Reef Lodge • *4 Wickham St.; tel. 21–1112* • Two-story, 27–room house. Lounge, games room, BBQ, kitchen, guest laundry, snack bar, free bus pickup. Shared rooms are about $A15 per person; doubles about $A40. Motel units from $A50 double.

A few hour's drive inland from Townsville you start running into cattle country and old towns that were created by the gold rush in the 1870s. The two major tourist spots are **Charters Towers** and **Ravenswood.** The diggings around Charters Towers, about 90 miles southwest of Townsville on the Mount Isa highway, produced millions of ounces of gold before they went dry in the 1920s. With those proceeds, the locals built some very fine residences, many of which still stand, and also erected the Stock Exchange, the Queensland National Bank, and other historic buildings that have been restored. **Ravenswood,** due south of Townsville, is more ghost town than Charters Towers, with lots of old mining equipment and slowly collapsing boomtown buildings scattered around. You can still find gold in the creek beds around town. To get there, take a turn at Mingela on the Mount Isa highway.

Continuing up the coast from Townsville are huge areas of rain forest, sugar cane fields, small coastal cities, and many access points to the Great Barrier Reef.

About 30 miles inland from Ingham, 60 miles north of Townsville, is **Wallaman Falls,** which has the longest drop in Australia: 911 feet. Offshore between Ingham and Cardwell are several island resort areas, including **Orpheus** and **Dunk** islands, and a favorite naturalist's destination, **Hinchinbrook Island. Cardwell** is the last coastal town on the Bruce Highway until you reach Cairns. The highway south of Cardwell climbs through a small coastal range offering great views of the offshore islands and the reef.

Tully, about 60 miles north of Ingham, is the wettest spot in Australia, receiving something in excess of 10 feet of rain a year. The area around town is made up of dense rain forests, and the Tully River is a popular whitewater canoeing spot.

Near **Innisfail,** an important sugar center, is **Mt. Bartle Frere,** at 5300 feet, the highest peak in Queensland. Also close to town is Australia's only tea plantation, about 20 miles west at the small settlement of **Nerada;** open daily except Mondays. For nine days, starting the last Saturday in August, Innisfail is home to a large sugar festival. The town is also a deep-sea fishing center and is on the Palmerston Highway, which connects to the Kennedy Highway to the west and thus allows a back-door approach to the Atherton Tablelands.

About nine miles north of Innisfail is the turnoff to the headquarters of **Bellenden Ker National Park,** which contains **Mt. Bartle Frere.** The park, largely undeveloped, is a hiker's feast. Here and there, you'll see huge gaps in the forest. These were not caused by loggers, but by the cyclones that frequently hit the coast and cause widespread damage. A popular track goes from the ranger's offices to the summit of the peak. Another popular hike, nowhere near as strenuous as the peak, is a half-mile jaunt to **Josephine Falls,** a popular swimming spot where the fun is sliding down slippery rocks in Josephine Creek. Another approach to the park is from **Babinda,** about five miles north of the headquarters turnoff. From Babinda, there's a road that goes about six miles into the park to **The Boulders,** a popular swimming and picnic area. Camping is allowed in the park, but permits must be obtained. *Information is available at the ranger office at the Josephine Falls trailhead or from Bellenden Ker National Park, P.O. Box 93. Mirriwinni, Queensland 4871; tel. (070) 67–6304.*

From **Gordonvale,** about 20 miles north of Babinda, the Gillies Highway runs west into the **Tablelands.** The road is a piece of work, with almost 300 tight curves along the way. It's a scenic drive through the rain forests and volcanic crater lakes.

CAIRNS

Cairns, with a new international airport, new hotels, and millions of dollars in developments taking place, is rapidly becoming the capital of the Great Barrier Reef and the center of one of the fastest-growing tourist areas in Australia. This is one of those Aussie cities you'd better pronounce as they do or no one will understand what you're saying: it's Cans, with no "r." The city area code is (070).

The city, like some other coastal Queensland settlements, started life as a Gold Rush settlement, followed by emergence as a remote sugar port. It was an ore-shipping terminus and is the last stop on the railroad north from Brisbane. The present population of about 75,000 is expected to double by the early 2000s as the coast from Cairns north to Cape York continues to expand as a major vacation destination. At this writing, the city dads estimate that something like 1.5 million people pass through Cairns every year, about 200,000 from overseas.

Cairns is a pleasant enough city, and we like it a bunch. But in and of itself, it's not very exciting. What makes it special is its proximity to the Reef and the Cape York Peninsula, as well as being a gateway to Papua New Guinea. Its group of high-quality hotels and restaurants are a definite plus, and it offers just about any travel or tourist service you will ever need to explore what is one of Australia's premier vacation areas. It is the first place many North American visitors ever see in Australia due to the non-stop flights to Cairns. The city really got into the air business in a big way in 1988 when the Australian and U.S. governments, which had been sniping at each other for some years, finally agreed to allow Continental and United Airlines to fly to Cairns; in return, Qantas was allowed to expand its service to interior U.S. cities. About 50 flights from all over the world arrive in Cairns each week. The city is also an internationally recognized fishing center, considered to be one of the best marlin areas in the world. It is also close to all the new resort settlements being built at Port Douglas and other spots north along the coast, and is near the splendid Atherton Tablelands, a farming/forest area with some of the prettiest scenery in the whole country. We encourage anyone coming to Australia, even those connecting to Sydney or other places in the country, to take two or three days at least and check out some of the wonderful experiences to be had on day trips from Cairns.

It is a city of wide, wide streets, palm trees, tin-roofed houses, marinas, new high-rise hotels, and many shops. It is also an orchid-growing center, and the bulbs are so packed and purified that they can be taken back with you to the United States. Try **Lonne's Nursery,** 15 Hoad Street, Earlville, about four miles from the city center; tel. (070) 54–1746.

Around Town

Cairns is flat and wide, sitting with its north end facing the **Coral Sea** and the center and south of the city facing **Trinity Bay** and **Trinity Inlet,** where mangrove swamps abound. One of the main centers of activity in town is at **Marlin Jetty,** where the large fleet of sports fishing boats is based. The jetty is also the base for several of the larger boats that run trips to the reef and resort islands.

Just to the side of the jetty is The Pier, a new shopping center which also has the new Radisson Plaza Hotel. The shops range from pushcarts filled with nicknacks to clothing stores and jewelry stores, plus food night clubs and a pub or two. It's open 9 a.m.–9 p.m. seven days. Further down the harbor, past the Hilton Hotel, is Trinity Wharf, another shopping complex. Try the Trinity Wharf Bar for a cold XXXX and some pub grub; decent view, as well. Next door is the cruise ship terminal.

A long waterfront stretch along the center of the city, the **Esplanade,** is the location of many restaurants and hotels. If you're looking for beaches, you'll have to go north of Cairns. Off the Esplanade you have high tides and mudflats.

If you know your Australian history, you'll know about the **Royal Flying Doctor Service,** and there's a branch in Cairns. There are tours of the facility every day, including a video show and museum. The RFDS station here, as in other parts of the country, also operates a shortwave school for isolated children and also serves (for a price) as a radio, telegram, and radio-telephone communications service. The service is located at 1 Junction St. in the Edge Hill section of the city, not far from the international airport. The admission charge is A$2.50. It's open from 9–4:30 daily. *Information: Royal Flying Doctor Service, 1 Junction St., Edge Hill, Cairns; tel. 53–5687.*

Cairns City Place, at the intersection of Shields and Lake streets, is the central downtown square of the city, where people-watching is in full flower. Situated in an old art school on City Place is the Cairns Museum, which has displays on the early history of the city as well as a good section on the Aboriginal people who lived in the nearby rain forests.

In North Cairns, on the way to the Flying Doctor offices, is the **Flecker Botanical Gardens,** where you can see Queensland's tropical

Collins Ave, west off Sheridan St (Cook Highway) 3km N
Also Saltwater Creek boardwalk + Whitfield Range Environmental Park

flora up close. There are lakes, walking trails, and gardens. If you're feeling lazy—or extravagant—you can try a three-hour pedicab picnic in the gardens. For about A$60 for two people, a pedicab driver will pick you up at your hotel, take you to the gardens, give you a champagne and chicken lunch, let you wander around, and then take you back. *Information: Pedicab, tel. 31–2046.* There is a restaurant at the gardens that specializes in Devonshire teas.

If you'd like a waterborne tour of the Cairns area, you could try a half-day excursion aboard the *Terri-Too,* which goes around the harbor and down the inlet into the mangrove swamps, and around Admiralty Island. There are three trips a day. The fare, which includes coffee or tea, is about $A15 per person. The 2 p.m. cruise offers a prawn lunch for $A20. The boat has a bar. *Information: Terri-Too, The Pier, 31–4007.*

Among the many shops in Cairns, you might try **Fred Jones Men's and Boy's Wear** at the corner of Shields and Sheridan streets downtown. The store has a good selection of Australian wear, including Akubra hats, Speedo swimwear and a variety of luggage. We finally found an Akubra for Joan here that would fit her, the Snowy River model, for about US$60.

For New Guinea and Indonesian artifacts, try the **Asian Connections Emporiums,** 51 Abbott St.; tel. 51–7392. The **New Guinea Adventure Centre** has some artifacts for sale and is also a major travel agency handling adventure travel to New Guinea—four-wheel-drive, dugout canoe, rafting, you name it. The center is located at 44B Aplin St.; tel. 51–0622.

Aboriginal and New Guinea artworks can be found at **Gallery Primitive,** 26 Abbott St. downtown; tel. 31–1641. It's open 9–6 seven days. **Anuaka Arts & Crafts,** in Portsmith, south of the city center, is an art store managed and staffed by Aboriginals. The store is at the corner of Palmer and Toohey streets in Portsmith; tel. (070) 51–7786.

There are a couple of duty-free shops in the city; **City International Duty Free,** 29B Shields St., 51–2338, and **Downtown Duty Free,** 18 Abbott St., 51–0211.

A popular shopping area weekdays, as well as Saturday and Sunday mornings, is **Rusty's Bazaar,** a group of speciality shops located in the block between Grafton and Sheridan streets and Shield and Spence streets. There's a Mexican restaurant there as well as shell, opal, and T-shirt places. If you're looking for camping or hiking gear, try the **Outdoor Equipment Centre** at Rusty's.

Fishing

The average cost for hiring a boat to go pursue the wily black marlin (best done between September and December) is around A$100 to A$300 per person per day depending on season, tackle, and niceties, but can be lower or much higher. The marlin grounds are between 50 and 60 kilometers offshore and if you're lucky, you might hook into a 1000-pounder. But the reef and the open ocean areas around Cairns offer far more than just marlin. If you're a fisher, this is Heaven. Know, however, that the marlin boats are so popular, many are reserved years ahead of time. If you're thinking about going fishing, try to book your boat from North America in advance of your trip.

Any of the Queensland Tourist & Travel Corporation offices in North America or Australia should be able to supply information on companies that handle fishing vacations or individual fishing outfits all along the coast. One company that can arrange charters out of Cairns from North America is **So/Pac,** which also handles hotel reservations all over Australia. *Information: So/Pac 1448 15th St., Suite 105, Santa Monica, Calif. 90404; (800) 551–2012 USA; (800) 445–0190 California; (800) 235–8222 Canada.* One Cairns outfit to try is **John and Barry Cross Fishing Safaris,** P.O. Box 84, Earlville, Cairns 4870; tel. 55–1641. Or Peter Bristow at 32–1744.

In Cairns, one way to try for a marlin trip is just to walk down to the jetty and check the boats; many will have chalkboards out listing prices and availability. If you like to fish but don't like oceans, try **Dolphin Boat Hire,** in front of the Hilton, which hires aluminum outboards and tackle for fishing the inlet and mangrove areas for perch, snapper, and coral trout. If you want tackle, deep-sea or otherwise (and even if you don't), go to **Jack Erskine's Tackle Shop** at 51 Mulgrave Rd.; tel. 51–6099. You have to see if Big Momma, which they claim is the world's largest captive barramundi, is still around or whether they finally decided to eat her. Feeding times for the big fish were 4 p.m. Mon.–Thurs. and 7 p.m. Fri. For general Cairns-area fishing and bookings, call Blackboard Travel and Charters 31–4444 or 53–4803. Or contact the Cairns Professional Game Fishing Association at 31–4742.

For information about reef diving and snorkeling, as well as services to the resort islands off the coast of Cairns, please refer to our section on the Great Barrier Reef.

The Essential Cairns

GETTING AROUND ● The best way to do the Cairns area is by car, and there are plenty of rental agencies to pick from, with prices as low as about A$20 a day at **Sheridan Rent-A-Car,** 196A Sheridan St.; tel. 51–3942. Other rental agencies include **Avis,** 135 Lake St., 51–5911; **Hertz,** 147 Lake St., 51–6399; **National,** 143 Abbott St., 51–4600; **Budget,** 153 Lake St., 51–9222; and **Cairns Rent-a-Car,** 147 Lake St., 51–6077. The big names have offices at the airport. RVs can be

AMAX 1A Lake St , Topless Cat Rentals 13A Sheridan St

rented at Budget. Note that these rental agencies do not want you going any farther north than Daintree because the roads disappear and your insurance is worthless.

There is **airport bus service** to most downtown hotels for about A$5; tel. 53–4162. The main **taxi service** is **Black & White,** tel. 51–5333.

Direct internal **airline service** from Sydney and other major Australian cities is provided by **Australian** and **Ansett** airlines. **Rail service** is provided by the two major Queensland coast routes, the **Sunlander** and the **Queenslander.**

Tourist information about Cairns and the area is available at Far North Queensland Promotion Bureau, corner of Sheraton and Aplin streets, P.O. Box 865 Cairns 4870; tel. 51–3588, 3371 or 3392. Also available is the Welcome North Australia office at 105 W. Lake Street in City place; tel. 51–8177.

A good place for **maps** of the area (as well as the whole state) is the **Sunmap Centre,** 36 Shields Street; tel. 52–3221.

Walkers 96 Lake St , Absalli Newsagency Lake St.

ACCOMMODATIONS......................

High internal air fares, or long driving distances, mean that when most Australians take vacations, they tend to stay put in the same spot and rent an apartment-style unit for a week or two. Which is why all over the country, you have budget and moderate apartment or villa rentals available. If you're planning on spending some time in the Cairns area you might want to try this idea. Any travel agent in town can fix you up. Some of the nicer places are north of the city toward Port Douglas. Depending on the unit, you're probably looking at something like $A500 a week or so for a two-bedroom unit with kitchen. Most international tourists don't hang around that long, so they park in one of the city's bigger hotels. We like the Hilton and the Pacific International, but there are several other good ones as well. The city and the beaches to the north are also great for backpackers.

Hilton International • *Wharf Road; tel. 52–1599* • On the waterfront, halfway between the Marlin Jetty and Trinity Wharf. Some parts of the Hilton are showing their age, but we think the service is the best of any hotel in town. The concierge desk is staffed by young eager guys who seem to know everybody in Queensland—you want a tour, a trip or whatever, they can organize it. The lobby bar is airy and nice, and the pool has a nice bar and sandwich service. There are times when service overcomes glitter, and this is one. Get a room on the harbor side, if possible. Doubles A$200–260; suites $A400–600.

Cairns International • *17 Abbot St.; tel. 31–1300* • One of the newest in town, it is now fairly famous for its lobby, which is resplendent with acres of native Queensland woods. Opened in 1988, the hotel is to our eyes a tad sterile despite all that wood, but the amenities are world-class. It has a rooftop pool, parking, handicapped access and is next door to a small shopping arcade. If you care, it's not on the waterfront. Doubles start at A$160; suites from A$320 to A$1200.

Raddison Plaza • *At The Pier; tel. 31–1411* • Another new hotel, this one also not one of our favorites. It has a great location, as previously noted, but it's just another hotel. Maybe time will change our impression. We admit that the suites are nice, equipped as they are with private spas. It has parking, a pool, sauna, spa, handicapped access and is close to all those shops in the arcade. Doubles A$200–250; suites A$380–1200.

Pacific International • *Corner of The Esplanade and Spence Street; tel. 51–7888* • The Pacific has the distinction of being the only major hotel in town not owned by foreign companies, should you care. It, like the Hilton, is a bit worn at the edges, but again the service more than makes up for the decor. The parking lot is a bit small and you might end up parking in the street. The second-floor bar is very nice, as is the first-floor coffee shop. There is a rooftop pool, spa, three restaurants, several other bars. Doubles from $A165.

Harbourside Quality Inn • *209 The Esplanade; tel. 51–8999* • The hotel sits away from the action a bit, toward the residential end of The Esplanade and a long walk or short drive to the downtown area. It faces the park that runs along the mudflats; rooms have balconies. Pool, spa, restaurant/bar, mini-bars, parking, handicapped access. Good hotel, nothing special. Doubles from A$120–140; suites A$150.

Holiday Inn Cairns • *Corner The Esplanade and Florence Streets; tel. 31–3757* • Opened in 1990. Open plaza with a waterfall, rooms with ocean and non-ocean views. Pool, spa, restaurant/bar, coffee shop, bottle shop. Holiday Inn quality. Doubles around A$200.

Outrigger • *Corner Florence and Abbot streets; tel. 51–6188* • A block up from The Esplanade. The Outrigger is awash in jungle growth; it almost takes a machete to get to the pool. The rooms are also very tropical, with rattan furnishings and sliding louvered doors. More than half the rooms are suites. Spa, licensed restaurant, parking. Good bet for the money. Doubles A$105–120; suites A$175.

Four Seasons • *Corner of The Esplanade and Shields Sts.; tel. 51–2311* • One nice thing about this hotel is the lobby bar/cafe, which is open from 10 a.m.–10 p.m. seven days, and the Coral Brasserie, which is open from 6 a.m. to 10 p.m. You won't starve or die of thirst. Rooms have mini-bars; suites have kitchens. Pool, sauna, BBQ, spa, tennis courts, parking, courtesy van, handicapped access. Doubles from A$140; suites from A$145–200.

Acacia Court • *223–227 The Esplanade; tel. 51–5011* • Yet another new hotel (1989). Despite the architecture (sort of Iron Curtain blocky), the Acacia is nice digs, offering views of the mountains or the sea, and the price is definitely for the cost-conscious. It, like the Harbourside, is away from the action, about two kilometers from downtown. Sauna, pool, spa, tennis court, parking, restaurant/bar, tour desk. Ocean-view doubles $A85; mountain view, $A80.

Lyons Motor Inn • *Corner of The Esplanade and Alpin; tel. 51–2311* • Up the street a long block from The Pier. You have here a hostelry for most pocketbooks. Rooms include 80 tower suites and 50 motel units. Some of the rooms are budget with shared baths. Restaurant/bar, bistro. Rooms have mini-bars. Tour desk, BBQ area, handicapped facilities. Doubles from A$100; budget doubles from A$65.

Cascade Gardens Apartments • *Corner of Minnie and Lake Sts.; tel. 51–8000* • The sort of place we were talking about for budget-minded Aussie families on holiday. The apartments are fairly large, with kitchens, small dining areas; they come in studio or one-bedroom units. Pool, spa, guest laundry, BBQ area, travel desk, baby-sitting, guest lounge. Studio doubles A$100; one-bedrooms for A$110–120.

Adobe Motel • *191 Sheridan St.; tel. 51–5511* • Here we have 15 motel and 17 apartment units. More of the family/budget scene. Pool, guest laundry, BBQ, parking. The motel units are A$65 double; the one- and two-bedroom apartments start at A$65 a day or A$330–365 a week.

Uptop Downunder • *164–170 Spence St.; tel. 51–3636* • One of the many hostels hovering around the downtown area. Garden with pool, tour desk, courtesy van. Twins, doubles and dorms starting at A$15 per person.

Dreamtime Travellers Rest • *4 Terminus St.; 31–6753* • As the name suggests, it's close to the train station, and is one of the city's newest hostels. Kitchen, laundry, BBQ area, TV lounge, garden, tour desk, courtesy car. Shared rooms for A$12 per person; doubles from A$30.

Cairns YHA McLeod • *20–24 McLeod St.; 51–0772* • One block off the main highway. Pool, garden, tour desk, always crowded so call ahead. Dorm beds for A$15; doubles also A$15 per person.

Out of town:

Mrs. Miller's Original Kuranda Hostel • *In Kuranda; tel. 93–7355* • It's across from the famous Kuranda Victorian train station. Salt-water pool, single, double and family rooms. Doubles and family A$40; dorms A$15.

Pioneer Valley Holiday Ranch • *Lake Eacham; 96–5882* • This place is up in the Atherton Tablelands near Lake Eacham National Park, and gives the budget folks a chance to stay down on the farm for cheap. You can either stay in an old farmhouse for $A15 a night, or in ranch units for $A20 a night. There's lots of activities nearby: horses, biking, hang gliding, water skiing and what is our all-time favorite, platypus-spotting (you get your clothes off and go into the woods at night; sighting a platypus is optional). The ranch offers free pickup from Cairns.

RESTAURANTS.....................................

A number of restaurants in Cairns are BYO. Thus, you might want to check out the **Liquor Barn** in the Barrier Reef Hotel, which is one of the largest discount liquor outlets north of Brisbane. There's a large wine cellar (tax-free if you're from overseas) and seven-day-a-week hours.

Being as close to the Barrier Reef as it is, it's not surprising that the Cairns area is awash with seafood, as well as freshwater fish from the mangrove swamps and rivers. Restaurants also throw a lot of tropical fruit at you, especially pineapple, for which Northern Queensland is famous. A few suggestions:

Breezes • *Wharf Rd.; tel. 52–1599* • In the Hilton Hotel, one of the better hotel restaurants in town. Open and airy, overlooking the hotel gardens and the Trinity Wharf area. Seafood buffet Friday and Saturday nights starting at 6: the tab, including dessert and coffee, is A$35. There's also a Sunday champagne brunch. Moderate to expensive.

Barra's Seafood Restaurant • *Conservatory Shopping Village on Abbott and Lake next to the Cairns International Hotel; tel. 31–4343* • This is one of the newest and best seafood places in town, offering the aforementioned range of finny delights. Open for lunch and dinner, licensed, reservations essential. Moderate to expensive.

Swiss Inn • *221 Sheridan St.; tel. 51–6020* • BYO. Bruno, who runs the place, is an old Cairns tradition. The continental menu changes regularly. Seafood also high on the list, although a fondue might show up now and then. Open from 6 p.m. to late, Tuesday–Sunday. Reservations essential. Moderate to expensive.

Dundee's • *Corner Sheridan and Alpin Sts.; tel 51–0399* • Well, we couldn't resist, given the name. It's a licensed family restaurant, with grain-fed beef, seafood, pasta and fresh garden salads. A good bet for basic Aussie tucker. Lunch Tuesday-Friday; dinner seven nights. Moderate.

Cock and Bull • *Corner Grove and Digger Sts.; tel. 31–1160* • Belly up, chaps, for some Olde English fare, with such offerings as bangers with mash and peas, steak and kidney pies, fish and chips, ploughman's lunch and Cornish pasties. Also 50 kinds of beer, both local and imported. If you like English food, here's the spot. Lunch noon on Friday, Saturday and Sunday; dinner from 5:30–midnight seven days. Budget to moderate. We like it.

Damari's • *171 Lake St.; tel. 31–2155* • Italian fare, specializing in pizza and pasta—there are 16 varieties of pasta and 26 different sauces. Inside candlelight dining, or on the open-air balcony. Live entertainment some nights. Licensed. Take-away and deliveries. Lunch noon–2 p.m. weekdays; dinner from 6 p.m. seven nights. Budget to moderate.

Buffalo Bill's • *252 Sheridan St.; tel. 51–1122* • Old Cairns tradition. Here's your chance to eat stuff you can brag about later—including buffalo and crocodile. There is also seafood, steaks, pasta and a large salad bar. Indoor or outdoor dining. Licensed and very popular. Dinner from 5 p.m. seven nights. Moderate to expensive.

Margie's • *Corner of Abbot and Wharf Sts.; tel. 51–4245* • In the Barrier Reef Hotel. Inespensive Aussie pub food. Licensed. Lunch specials about A$3.50; dinner specials around A$8. Lunch and dinner Monday–Saturday. Budget.

Fuji • *Corner of Abbot and Minnie sts.; tel. 31–1134* • Teppanyaki, seafood tempuras, sushi and shabu-shabu. Very nummy Japanese food. Dinner from 6 p.m. Tuesday–Sunday. Reservations necessary. Moderate.

BEYOND CAIRNS.................................

Your traveling choices from Cairns include going up the last stretch of paved highway along the coast to Mossman or hanging a left and heading inland to the Atherton Tablelands. Either choice leads to some great Aussie adventures. The area code for all phones in the Far North is the same as Cairns, (070).

About 16 kilometers north of Cairns is the intersection of the Cook and Kennedy highways. The Kennedy angles up into the Tablelands to Kuranda, the Cook goes on to Mossman. At the intersection is a large shopping mall, the **Smithfield Shopping Centre,** which has a major grocery store, bottle shop, clothing stores, fast-food outlets and the **Smithfield Tavern** (live music Fridays and Saturdays). Just the spot to stock up on sandwich materials or traveling needs.

The Atherton Tablelands

Because of its proximity to Cairns, the northern part of the Atherton Tablelands is probably the best explored and most popular part of the huge rain forest and timberland area that rises a few miles inland from the coast. The Tablelands runs south from Mossman, all the way past Innisfail, and from just west of the coast to the center of the Great Dividing Range. The forests get wetter and wetter as you travel from the Range east to the ocean, with rainfall ranging from 30 inches a year in the west to more than twice that on the eastern edge.

The Tablelands rises about 2300 feet above sea level, hence the rainfall, and the area's granite valleys and hills are filled with animals and plants seen nowhere else on the planet. Here you can find most of Queensland's huge butterflies. Birds are all over the place, but because of the high forest canopy, are sometimes difficult to spot. One of our favorites is a Victoria's riflebird, which makes a loud cracking noise and which we have heard many times—but never seen. One of the more interesting animals is the tree kangaroo, two species of which inhabit Queensland rain forests. The major mammals in the Tablelands are possums, including several ring-tailed species. The other major mammals are rats, which range all the way north to the tip of the Cape York Peninsula. Of all the vegetation, among the most impressive are strangler figs, which in some cases grow hundreds of feet high. Pine trees also reach high into the air, and there are big ferns everywhere—not as large as the monsters you find in Tasmania, but impressive nonetheless.

There are several national parks in the Tablelands, the largest of which is **Bellenden Ker** (see description under Innisfail notes). Another is **Palmerston National Park,** at the south end of the area, reached by taking the Palmerston Highway west from Innisfail. Here is a chance (slight) to see platypuses in the wild (near the Henrietta Creek campground) and something like 500 species of trees and more orchids than you can believe. Especially interesting are the trees that have giant buttress roots, some big enough to stand behind. *Information about the park is available from the ranger at Palmerston National Park, P.O. Box 800, Innisfail 4860; tel. 64–5115.*

The most pleasant way to see the Atheron Tablelands is by private car, although many companies run day trips. The drive from Cairns into the Tablelands is remarkably short; from the Smithfield turnoff, you can be in Kuranda in less than an hour. You will be able to see many of the highlights of the area in one day if you hustle a bit. And if you dawdle, there are places to stay (mostly inexpensive motels in the A$25- to A$40-a-night range) and restaurants to visit at any of the many settlements in the area. If you have time and interest, try renting an RV and exploring; the woods are full of caravan parks.

We suggest a **circle trip** starting in Cairns up to Kuranda, north to Mareeba, then along the route to Atherton, Ravenshoe, Millaa Millaa, Malanda, Yungaburra and back to the coast south of Cairns. This does not include everything, of course, but it will show you why the Tablelands is so popular.

Kuranda is one of the more touristed villages in the area, one reason being the famous **Cairns-Kuranda railway,** an engineering marvel and one of the prettier rail trips around the globe. The line is only about 20 miles long, but has 15 tunnels and almost 100 curves, which took 1500 men four years to build in the late 1880s. Along its climb toward Kuranda, the train passes many waterfalls, including **Stoney Creek** with its impressive bridge, and **Barron Gorge,** where the train stops for photographs of **Barron Falls.** How great a vista that is depends on the season—sometimes almost no water comes over the falls. (Sit on the right side going up). A one-way trip takes about an hour and a half, counting waterfall stops. At the end of the line is the almost too-quaint **Kuranda Train Station,** a restored Victorian edifice festooned with hundreds of orchids and other plants.

There are several **rail trips** a day starting from Cairns, including non-tourist trains that regularly serve the highlands. Several ticket choices are available. Straight fare is about A$15 one way. Also available are cars that have guides giving commentary on the route. These seats, reserved, run about A$20 one way and A$30 round trip. *Ticket information is available from Queensland Railways, McLeod St., Cairns; tel. 51–0531.* **Freshwater Connection,** a tourist company that runs a restaurant in a reconstructed railway station about six miles from Cairns, and is a stop on the journey, has several choices available including reserved commentary seats or "royale service," which offers drinks, lunch, souvenirs, Atherton tours and commentary in a special coach, for around A$60 round trip. *Information: Freshwater Connection, Kamerunga Rd., Freshwater, Cairns; tel. 55–2222.*

In addition, there are several companies that run Tableland trips by bus that include riding the railroad one way. Try **Australian Pacific Tours,** 51–9299, which offers a full-day trip for about A$45, or **Down Under Tours,** 31–1355, which has a tour that includes the train, the Tjapukai Aboriginal dance company, and free hotel pickup for about A$65 per person. One of the largest outfits running trips around the area, including the Reef and the Cape York Peninsula, is **Tropic Wings,** 54 Lake St., Cairns; tel. 51–8433. The company's Tablelands trip runs about A$50.

Kuranda, as small as it is, has several interesting attractions. One that should not be missed is the **Tjapukai dancers,** a group formed to show the public the dances, music, and ceremonies of the Aboriginal people of the Tablelands. This might be the only chance you have in Australia to see authentic Aboriginal dances—and listen to a didgeridoo played as it should be. The performances are held at 11 a.m. and 1:30 p.m. daily; three times daily when the Kuranda markets are open. The dancers are a real success story, the brainchild of Don Freeman and David Hudson. Freeman's background is theater; Hudson, an Aboriginal, is one of the country's premier didgeridoo players, born in Cairns, and has a degree in recreation. Once, Hudson (tribal name, Dwura) was a major part of the act. But the group became so popular, he spends most of his time being an administrator. After we first saw them in 1988, the Tjapukai Dancers became so successful Hudson was able to build a new, 300-seat theater for the performances. The group did a world tour and has performed all over Australia, winning national and international tourism awards. Every performance is full, seven days a week. "We used to have to beg our dancers to work for us," Hudson says, "now they stand in line." The dancers (the name is pronounced JAPU-guy) are one of the most popular attractions in Queensland, well worth a stop. Try to book in advance. Tickets are about A$15; information (070) 93–7544). There is a gift shop at the theater with Aboriginal artworks. And for a price, Dave will custom make you a didgeridoo—just tell him what key you want it in.

Another interesting stop is the **Australian Butterfly Sanctuary,** where you can see Australia's largest butterfly—the female birdwing—as well as the country's most beautiful species, the brilliant blue Ulysses butterfly. On a guided tour of the small facility, you'll see the insects being fed and tenderly cared for. If you want a few memorable photos, wear a red shirt—the critters love red, and you might end up with a half-dozen nesting on your chest. Tickets to the sanctuary are about A$10 per person; tours are run from 10 a.m.–3 p.m. daily. *Information: Australian Butterfly Sanctuary, Kennedy Hwy., Kuranda; tel. 93–7575.*

Another major draw in Kuranda is the open markets held every

Wildlife Nocturum

Sunday and Wednesday mornings, where you can buy everything from worthless trinkets to food to good clothing. The markets are in an area just across the road from the village center.

There are several places to sup or sip in Kuranda. Just up from the train station as you make your way into town is the **Bottom Pub,** with a garden bar and good pub lunches; live music at night. In the center of town, look for **Frogs,** where you can get a beer or great Devonshire teas (A$3.50). The **Trading Post Restaurant** has good dampers and excellent cappuccino. Good Italian food is available at **Monkey's,** a BYO that has an outside deck and a fine example of a fish-tail palm tree. If you find yourself short of Aussie money, look for the **chemist's shop,** the only place in town that will change U.S. travelers checks. Kuranda is short on accommodations, but a good bet is the Kuranda Rainforest Resort out of town on the Greenhills Road, which has a wide range of accommodations from backpackers to rustic-style lodges. It has a very nice natural rock pool, tennis court, guest laundry, rental cars, spa, shops, scuba courses and baby-sitting. Larger lodge units have balconies with view of the rain forest area. In addition to motel rooms, the lodge has a couple of two-bedroom units with cooking facilities; there is also a hostel. Free pickup from Cairns is offered. Doubles go for about $A100; the bunkhouse section for about A$15 per person. Backpackers have free use of all lodge facilities. Information: (070) 93–7555. The lodge restaurant, popular with some bus tour companies, has good, moderately priced meals and a terrific breakfast with Queensland fruits. And the bar is friendly.

Mareeba, up the road from Kuranda, is the biggest commercial center in the area. In July, the town goes nuts with one of Australia's biggest **rodeos.** Around town are tobacco fields and, south of town, the remains of a U.S. Army Air Force base built during World War II. About six miles west of town is **Granite Gorge Park,** with swimming, camping, and picnic areas.

Down the Kennedy Highway between Mareeba and Atherton is the tiny village of **Tolga,** where there is a good restaurant and bar at the **Corn Cob Motel,** which also has rooms. Or you can snarf down pub meals and icy beer (also rooms) at the elderly but nice **Tolga Hotel.** At Tolga, you can take the Tinaroo Road, which heads for Lake Tinaroo.

Lake Tinaroo was created by damming the Barron River for hydroelectric power, and is a popular sailing and fishing hole, especially for Australia's favorite fish, the barramundi. If you want to haul in, the **Lake Tinaroo Pines RV park** has cabins, and seafood is available at the **Tinaroo Licensed Restaurant,** open seven days a week.

Next to the dam wall, for flower lovers, is yet another orchid garden. At the north side of the dam begins the 20-mile-long **Danbulla Forest Drive,** a scenic woodsy trip that passes some nice overlooks with picnic areas and also takes you past one of the two Big Figs. The

600m botanical walk to L. Euramoo. Also Mobo Creek

fig in question here is the rare **Cathedral Fig,** a parasitic plant (ficus virens) that has dropped vines from high above to the ground. This is also riflebird country. Much of the road is narrow, dirt or gravel, and can be a pain in The Wet. In dry conditions, a normal car can make it with no problem. The road joins the Gillies Highway southeast of Malanda.

Just west of Tolga is **Atherton,** the center of a peanut and maize-growing area. *dull* It has five motels and five campground/RV parks. If you're hungry, there is the **Fu Wah Chinese Restaurant** and the **Continental Pizza House,** both open seven days. From here, you can either keep on *MH Hydroponic* the Kennedy Highway to Ravenshoe or cut down to Yungaburra. **Rav-** *Crater* **enshoe** is significant for two reasons. First, it's in the heart of a contro-*Herberton* versy about logging in the Tablelands, and you'll see signs here and *Tin* there saying "Greenies Suck." It's probably not a topic you want to *Festival* raise in a local pub. Secondly, if you know how to pronounce it, the locals will figure you're a straight bloke: it's Ravens-hoe, not Raven-shoe, as we tried it the first time. *Millstream Falls*

Just before reaching Yungaburra, you come to the other Big Fig, this one the **Curtain Fig,** so named because it has toppled its host tree and dropped vines like a curtain to the forest floor. In **Yungabarra,** *pretty village* you'll find our favorite Tablelands pub, the **Town and Country** in the **Eacham Hotel,** which also has reasonably priced rooms. Downtown 'Burra has been listed by the National Trust, and has a number of oldies and goodies to look at. Being close to Lake Tinaroo, there is water-sports equipment for rent. Also, there is a growing artists' colony in town.

West of Yungaburra is **Malanda,** which has a few of what pass as *pleasant spot to stay, old building* upscale digs in the Tablelands. Try the **Malanda Lodge,** with pool, golf course, and licensed restaurant, rooms in the A$50 range; tel. 96–5555. Or, nearby, the **Park Lodge,** a two-bedroom cottage facility with kitchenette, laundry, and linens, within walking distance of tennis and golf. Rates are about A$50 a night, A$250 a week; tel. 97–2223. If you like traditional Aussie ambiance, try the **Malanda Hotel,** which they say is the largest wooden hotel in Australia. It has a nice bar and rooms in the A$25–A$40 range; tel. 96–5101. Budget travelers should call in at the **Gondwanaland Hostel,** with dorm rooms in the $A10 range; tel. 96–5046.

A bit farther west is **Millaa Millaa** (mill-AH mill-AH), the water-fall capital of the area, with at least a half-dozen worth a look. The best is probably **Millaa Millaa Falls,** which looks like it was imported from Hawaii. Others of note are **Zillie Falls, Elinjaa Falls,** and **Mungali Falls.** While you're in the area, try to find a store and pick up some Millaa Millaa cheese, which, you must forgive them, is touted as The Great Australian Bite. *16 km circuit*

Heading toward the coast on the Gillies Highway from Yungaburra, you come to two of the more popular lakes in the area, Barrine and Eacham. Both are in the remains of ancient volcanic craters, now surrounded by pleasant walking paths and picnic areas. **Eacham** has a swimming area set aside for small kiddies. At **Barrine,** the bigger of the two, there is a boat that takes folks on excursions around the shoreline to look for platypuses, pythons, herons, and tortoises. Around the edge of either lake, you can also spot cassowaries and bush turkeys. At Barrine is the **Lakeshore Restaurant,** which has Devonshire teas and shops, and on the shore below it, a mostly tame herd of Australian pelicans, whose bright colors make American brown pelicans look like ugly step-sisters.

Farther down the Gillies Highway at the Mulgrave River, just a few miles from the coastal road at Gordonvale, you'll find a nice spot for lunch or a beer at the **Mountain View Hotel.**

The Far North Country

The other major onshore touring area near Cairns runs north along the Cook Highway to Mossman and Daintree. Just north of the city you begin to run into some nice beaches that have a wide range of accommodations ranging from RV parks and tenting grounds to super-deluxe resorts. The stretch between Cairns and Port Douglas is virtually one long beach, and the area is referred to as the **Marlin Coast.**

Within an hour north, there are the small communities of **Holloways Beach, Yorkey's Knob, Trinity Beach, Kewarra Beach, Clifton Beach,** and **Palm Cove.** Almost all the beach areas have protected swimming areas (but don't forget the dangerous jellyfish), and most have picnic areas. At each settlement, there are a number of apartment and condominium units for rent, usually by the week, but also by the day. There are also a slew of small resorts. As an example of what is available, there is the **Kewarra Beach Resort,** about five miles north of Cairns, which has two restaurants, cooking facilities, a pool, and tennis, with doubles running A$170 to A$275. Information: (070) 576–666. Or try **Chantal Garden Condominiums** at Yorkey's Knob, with pool, spa, private laundries, and private parking, doubles for around $A600 a week depending on season. Or visit the **Ramada Reef Resort** at Palm Cove, with big pool, bars, barbecues, tennis courts, and tons of palm trees, with doubles running between A$150 and A$250. Almost all the units can be booked in Cairns or through the Queensland Tourist and Travel Corporation offices in North America. Ask for a copy of the *North Queensland Sunlover Holidays* book, which has booking information and details.

If you don't mind a fairly heavy dose of gee-whiz tourist stuff, there are a couple of animal farms along the route to Mossman where you can see birds and snakes and flowers and stuff, including "croco-

— 3pm (Paradise Travel 25 Spencer St $14)

dile attack shows,'' which while pretty hokey, do give you some idea
of how big a saltwater croc can grow. There's **Wild World,** just north
of Palm Cove, and **Hartleys Creek Zoo,** north of Ellis Beach. For the
more scenery-minded, the 35-mile drive from Palm Cove, about five
miles north of Smithfield, to Mossman is one of the better beach drives
in Australia. It's lined with white-sand beaches, mostly deserted, and
the highway folks have built some overlooks with great views. Be sure
to stop at the **Rex Lookout,** about halfway up, where you'll get your
first really good look at how huge the Great Barrier Reef really is.

1¼ hours To reach Port Douglas, you have to take a cutoff, about five miles,
to the ocean. South of town is **Four Mile Beach,** a perfect tropical
paradise. If they take care, developers might not destroy its charm, but
there are already bites being taken here and there, including the new
and very posh **Sheraton Mirage Hotel,** which opened in the winter of
1987 and won the "Best Resort Award" from the Australian Tourist
Commission in 1988. It's a low-rise, expansive place, complete with an
18-hole golf course, tennis courts, rooms for the disabled, jogging tracks,
a marina, shops, restaurants, and bars—all the goodies you'd expect at
a high-quality resort, including butler service. There are 300 rooms and
suites, with prices starting at around A$300 double and rising to around
A$1700 for the royal suite. Local information and bookings, Sheraton
Mirage, Port Douglas Rd., Port Douglas 4871; tel. 99–5888. Reservation information: Sheraton Worldwide, (800) 325–3535 U.S. and Canada.

Across the road from the Sheraton is the new **Radisson Royal
Palms,** which opened in 1989. The resort has a waterfall-bedecked pool,
golf courses, restaurants, and bars. Rooms range between A$130 and
A$260 double. Local information by writing the hotel at Port Douglas
Rd., Port Douglas 4871; tel. 99–5577.

Near the Sheraton Mirage is a new attraction, Habitat, a three-acre
enclosed zoo/aviary with many native Australian animals and birds on
view. Ever see a fruit bat up close? There's a tame one or two hanging
around the guides—literally. There are roos, koalas, crocks, emus—the
whole range. At 8 a.m. Wednesday and Sunday, you can have "breakfast with the Birds," a champagne and orange juice buffet for A$20,
which includes admission to the facility. The regular admission price is
$A10. As these things go, it's OK; if you haven't seen the animals
anywhere else, give it a try. To get to Habitat, drive north on Captain
Cook Highway (Highway 1) to Port Douglas and the turnoff to the Sheraton. Hours at 8–5 daily.

For the cost-conscious, there are a number of other places around
Port Douglas that will let you soak up the sun and sand without pecu-
niary strangulation. In the A$80 to A$150 range, these include self-
contained units such as the **Coral Sea Villas,** 68 Macrossan St., Port
Douglas, tel. 99–5677; the **Rusty Pelican Inn,** 123 Davidson St., Port

Douglas, tel. 99–5266, and the **Whispering Palms,** Langley Rd., Four Mile Beach, Port Douglas, tel. 99–5128. So far, the developments around town haven't destroyed its South Seas, small-town charm. But hurry.

Information about the Port Douglas area is available at the Port Douglas Tourist Information Office, 27 Macrossan St., Port Douglas 4871; tel. 99–5599. The office can make hotel or lodge bookings, and has information about fishing, reef trips, jungle excursions, and other activities.

Mossman, about nine miles north of the Port Douglas turnoff, is the gateway to **Daintree National Park** and has, as yet, escaped any major developments. The 140,000-acre park is a splendid way to examine the vegetation and wildlife of the Main Coast Range that rises west of town. Among its more spectacular attributes is **Mossman Gorge,** a deep, 10-mile long canyon carved through the granite by the Mossman River. The trails through the rain forest are some of the best in the state, and getting to the lower reaches of the gorge is an easy hike. To get to the parking lot, take the park road, which starts near the post office in Mossman. It's a three-mile drive. There are swimming holes in the river, and one short loop trail takes you over a suspension bridge, then past some huge fig trees. All in all, a great place for a hike. Serious back-country hikers must register with the rangers. *Information: Ranger, Daintree National Park, Cairns Regional Office, P.O. Box 2066, Cairns 4078; tel. 51–9811. Or if you're in Cairns, stop off at the office at the Far Northern Regional Centre, 41 Esplanade.*

We confess to not much appreciating the mega-resort look of the hotel developments around Port Douglas. The Sheraton Mirage, despite it's faintly reminiscent Queensland look, could be on any beach in Hawaii. If you're looking for a place that is almost completely rainforest in its look and feel, we urge you to try Silky Oaks, a few miles inland from Mossman. The lodge is surrounded by World Heritage rain forest, and has won several environmental awards for the way it has been integrated into the forest. Silky Oaks, along with the Coconut Beach Resort near Cape Tribulation, is showing others how you can have first-class hotel complexes and still not either destroy the environment or end up looking like the Kauai Lagoons.

Silky Oaks sits on a hill above the Mossman River, which is a wonderful place to have a swim or sunbathe. The river, by the way, is safe—no crocs. There's also a regular pool. The lodge units are separated by rain forest growth, and the large dining room is open air with a view of the river gorge below. The service is impeccable. The restaurant, which has won heaps of dining awards, is open to non-guests. If you don't want to spend the money for a night's lodging, you can reserve breakfast, lunch or dinner ahead, which also gives you full use of the resort's facilities—including the river.

Lunch courses run around A$9–15, and include such items as prawn and buffalo brochettes, country style terrine or just burgers and gourmet open-face sandwiches. Dinners are in the A$18–20 range, and are excellent. Try fresh barramundi, or a rack of lamb, or for A$60, a seafood platter for two. Breakfast is from 7–10:30 a.m.; lunch noon–2:30 and dinner 6:30–9:30 p.m. If you're coming up for the day, bring a towel and swimming suit.

The lodge goes for about A$300 a night double, not including food. There are hiking trails, canoes and a kangaroo nursery. Tell Moss and Theresa we said howdy. To get to the lodge, drive north from Mossman and watch for a small sign on the left side of the road; then follow the road. *Information: (070) 98–1666.* Note: kids under six not allowed.

North of Mossman, the road beomes a dirt track to the tiny settlement of **Daintree;** after that, it's four-wheel-drive all the way. But it's an easy drive to the Daintree River ferry crossing, where there is a parking lot and a small restaurant. Here is where the Daintree River trips begin. A number of outfits run river trips and can be booked either in Cairns or Port Douglas. The most popular, and our favorite, is **Daintree World Heritage Wilderness Tours,** which operates a "river train" that carries passengers along the river for views of the forests—and close-up looks at saltwater crocodiles that inhabit the river. Please note the "no swimming—crocodile" signs and pay heed. There are 27 species of mangrove on the river and 250 species of fish. It's also the spawning grounds of box jellyfish, which then float out to sea to grow up. After spawning, it takes them about two weeks to grow to adult size and each one has enough poison to kill 200 people. There are also feral pigs, left over from the original porkers put ashore by Capt. Cook. The trip, with great guides (the boats are quite safe, as well), is about A$25 per person; there are two daily. You can book the trip at any of the information offices, or the manager of the lodge or hotel where you're staying will give them a call. You can also arrange to be bused to the Daintree dock; a total package cost of about A$80 per person from Cairns, or A$70 from Port Douglas. *Information: 98–7676 in Daintree, or 51–9533 in Cairns.*

North of Mossman

Beyond Daintree, there is only one more spot of civilization on the coast near Port Douglas: **Cooktown,** the place where Capt. James Cook repaired his crippled *Endeavor* during the 1770 exploration of Australia. During a gold rush in the 1870s, the town reportedly had more than 90 pubs and 30,000 people. Today, there are under 1000 living here, and the last time the pubs were counted, the total was down to four. Getting to Cooktown can be fairly easy or a pain, depending on weather conditions. Indeed, the only time to do any exploring in the Cape York Peninsula is in the Dry, between June and December. The trek to Cooktown can be made in a normal car or small RV (with difficulty) but that's not recommended—and your insurance is likely to be no good, either. The road, mostly a gravel track, runs out of Mossman, through Mt. Molloy, and crosses several riverbeds and flood plains. An easier way is to call the **Quicksilver** people, who run an excellent Barrier Reef trip from Port Douglas. *Information: Quicksilver, Port Douglas, tel. 98–5373; Cairns, 51–8311.* **Coral Coaches** also runs daily bus service from Cairns to Cooktown via Ellis Beach. Information: (070) 98–1611. The one-way fare is in the A$50 range. **Air Queensland** also has regular flights to Cooktown from Cairns, with fares around A$60. If you want to hang around, check out the **Sovereign Hotel** on Charlotte Street, with doubles going for around A$120 a night. There are also budget rooms. It has a licensed restaurant and baby-sitting. *Information: 69–5400.*

A popular day trip from Daintree is to **Cape Tribulation National Park,** on the coast about 16 miles from Daintree. The 42,000-acre park has the state's third-highest peak, **Mt. Thornton** (4500 feet) and a wide array of flora and fauna, including strangler figs, tree kangaroos, ferns, orchids, pythons, forest dragons (a species of lizard), and saltwater crocodiles in the Daintree and Bloomfield rivers, which flow into the ocean in the park. Camping is allowed in the park, with permits available from the Parks and Wildlife service in Cairns; tel. 51–9811. There are also private developed campgrounds at Thorntons Beach.

There are a bunch of companies that offer four-wheel-drive trips up to Cape Trib and Cooktown, or farther. Among these are:

Australian Wilderness Safaris, Mossman Gorge; tel. (070) 98–1766. This one-day tour hits it all, including a trip on a Quicksilver boat from Cairns to Port Douglas; morning tea and hikes at Silky Oaks; a Daintree River Cruise, barbecue lunch, and tours around Cape Tribulation National Park. The daily tours will pick you up at your Cairns hotel; you can, if you wish, stay overnight in the Cape Trib area and join a later return bus. Fares are about A$120 per person.

Strikie's Safaris • *Cairns (008) 179–090, or Port Douglas 99–5599* • Rain forest hikes, Daintree river cruise, Bloomfield Falls, kangaroo feeding. One-day trip from Cairns A$90; from Port Douglas, A$80; two-day trip with night at Cooktown, A$190. Food and accommodation not included.

Reef and Rainforest Coast Connections • Book through the Port Douglas & Cooktown Tourist Information Centre, Marina Mirage, Port Douglas; tel. (070) 99–5599. Guided rainforest walks, lunch at the Coconut Beach Resort, swimming hole in the heart of the forest, beach stop at Cape Tribulation, Daintree River cruise. Fares are about A$60; food not included.

Kangoala Australian Safaris • *268 Mulgrave Rd., Cairns; tel.; 31–5030* • A one-day trip, including a stop at the Hartley Creek Crocodile Farm, Daintree River Cruise, an Aussie barbecue lunch with wine and a tour around the national park, is about A$100 per person. Tours go every day starting at 7:30 a.m. The trips, in air-conditioned Mercedes-Benz buses, included optional overnight stays at either the Coconut Beach Resort or the Heritage Lodge. A very good outfit. It is a half-owner of the Habitat attraction at Port Douglas.

Or you can do it yourself. We rented a 4-wheeler in Cairns for about A$90 a day (plus a credit card deposit charge of A$1000). You can make it to the Daintree in plenty of time to do the cruise (the first trip is at 10:30 a.m.). After the 2½-hour cruise, you take the ferry across the river (A$2 per person) and start up the Cape Tribulation Road. It's rutted and bumpy but we've been on worse in The Outback; it is subject to flooding in spots during the wet season (January–June). The first thing you realize is that this stretch of road is very busy and is far from being nothing but jungle. All along the way, clear to Cooktown, there are motels, resorts, restaurants and pubs. But mostly it still remains the oldest rainforest in the world, and development is being restricted. There is no doubt about it's popularity.

By mid-afternoon, you can haul in at your selected accommodations, or depending on how far north you have gone, return to Port Douglas or Cairns. One thought is Cape Kimberley, reached by taking a right turnoff about five kilometers north of the ferry crossing. The Daintree Rainforest Resort offers budget accommodations. There is a restaurant/bar, fishing boat, tours of nearby Snapper Island and swimming—remember the jellyfish. There are cabins, tent and RV sites, laundry, pool, showers and two kilometers of beach. Cabins are A$35 a night; tent sites A$5. Information in Mossman: (070) 90–7500.

Or, you can try the Heritage Lodge, about 20 kilometers north of the ferry crossing. Individual bungalows with private facilities; licensed restaurant open seven days, laundry, tour desk. Full or continental breakfast. Swimming in a pool or freshwater creek. Guided rainforest hikes, horseback riding, reef trips. Adjoins the national park near a 530-foot waterfall. Doubles about $100. Information: (070) 98–9138.

About 30 kilometers north of the ferry crossing is our favorite, the Coconut Beach Resort. The resort, as noted before, is one of the more progressive environmental lodges in the Cape Trib area, and has won several national and international awards. It sits on 50 acres of land in the middle of the national forest and next to a lovely beach. You can't spot the resort from the road, and units are built around and among the tall vegetation of the forest. The rooms are in blocks, with verandas. Presently, there are 30 units, but the number is being expanded, as are conference facilities. New units will include budget accommodations as well as hillside suites. The new development was scheduled to be completed in late 1992. The resort is not air conditioned, it being felt that the noise of the machines at night would intrude on the feel of the place (ceiling fans instead, very loud frogs out the back door). The main restaurant and bar are housed in a beamy, wooden building next to the pool and close to the beach. It's a wonderful place to sip a cold one or eat some of the excellent luncheon buffets. It is definitely worth the drive.

Or if you don't want to drive, you can take the Quicksilver to Port Douglas and be bused from there; come up on a four-wheel drive vehicle for about A\$60 round-trip, or fly into Cow Bay south of the lodge and be bused in (about \$65 one-way). Current rates are A\$230 double including breakfast and guided bushwalk. Information: (070) 52–1311.

CAPE YORK PENINSULA.....................

Most of the Cape York Peninsula, until recently, was the least-disturbed natural area in Australia, a huge tongue of forests and rivers and crocodiles and marsupials left untouched since the days of Captain Cook. It is also a land of natural resources, including timber and the world's largest deposits of bauxite. There have been several skirmishes between environmentalists and those not so inclined, notably a battle over putting a road through the Daintree forest, which was a defeat for the Greens. As yet, the development of major tourist areas in the cape has been very slow, but there are many in Australia who see the increasing numbers of people hopping four-wheel-drive buses and trucks on safaris to the top of the peninsula as just the first drops in an eventual flood. Would you believe there are even plans afoot to build a spaceport on the peninsula's west coast? True. Australia has created the **Cape York Space Agency** to develop a facility at Weipa, which is also the site of those huge deposits of bauxite. But it's far away from the rain forests, so nobody much has made any complaints yet. The space folks tell us, by the way, that a geostationary satellite launched into orbit from Cape York would require less fuel than one from Cape Canaveral, and thus be able to stay up longer—and also be cheaper to put up.

The peninsula is divided into two basic climatic zones, created by the **Great Dividing Range,** which starts in Cape York and runs along the Australian coast all the way to New South Wales. From the mountains east, there are the huge expanses of rain forests. To the west of the range, things are a great deal drier, with stands of eucalypts. There are two seasons on the peninsula: wet and dry. In the Wet, creeks and rivers flood, the roads often disappear under water, and about the only way anyone gets around is by air. In the Dry, the roads north are dusty, rock-strewn, and often filled with safari vehicles. The east coast areas get something like 60 to 80 inches of rain a year.

You could, if you wish, drive from the Mossman area to the top by yourself, and many hardy adventurers do. But if you're not an experienced bush traveler, we suggest you don't. Even in the Dry, things along the route can get very dicey indeed, and a busted axle in the middle of nowhere is not conducive to a good vacation.

Instead, grab a place with one of the outfits that regularly run trips up the peninsula. These safaris can range from pretty basic to cushy, depending on how much time and money you are willing to invest. But if you are even a bit adventurous, this is one of the great adventure trips in Australia, not to be missed.

Most **safaris** leave from Cairns, go up through Cape Tribulation, then back down through Mossman, then up the Peninsula Developmental Road to Lakeland, then Laura, then to Coen (about halfway up), then to a fork in the road where they either go to the Gulf of Carpenteria coast at Weipa or on north to Bamaga and Thursday Island. Along the way, there are several national parks to explore, including **Lakefield,** one of Queensland's largest, plus ample opportunities to check out the things that go bump in the night. The number of people on the trip can vary from a half-dozen or so to 30 or 40, and vehicles range from air-conditioned buses to LandRovers. The average length of a round trip is two weeks, but some of the safaris are only one-way—you fly back to Cairns. In most, the cost of the trip includes food, camping equipment (not including sleeping bags, which are usually for rent), and air fares. Trips can be booked in major cities in Australia, or in Cairns. But if you're smart, you'll book ahead from North America.

Several examples:

New Look Adventures, 129A Lake St., Cairns 4870, tel. 51–7934, runs a variety of trips including a 16-day round-trip for about A$1300 per person, which includes touring Thursday Island and the Barrier Reef; group size six to 18. A ten-day, one-way trip is about A$1200, including air back to Cairns; group size four to ten.

The founding father of adventure travel in Australia is **Bill King,** who runs wild and woolly trips all over the country. His company, **The Australian Experience,** has several Cape York trips, including a 14-day safari for about A$1700; group size four to 12. An eight-day trek is about A$1300 including air fare to Cairns; group size four to 12. King's trips can be booked through ATS/Sprint, 1101 E. Broadway, Glendale, Calif. 91205; tel. (800) 232–2121 California, (800) 423–2880 USA. In Australia, call toll-free (008) 33–1373.

It might be that all that bouncing around over rocky tracks and creeping through sodden rain forests is not your bag. Not to worry. You can hop a plane and fly up to Bamaga and then hop a bus for the 15-mile trip to the very tip of Australia, where you will find the **Cape**

York Wilderness Lodge, another fishing camp of the upscale variety owned by Air Queensland. Rates run between A$170 and A$200 a day, and include all meals and sporting activities, including fishing and guides; booze extra. There are 24 cabins, a pool, ceiling fans, and no kids under six. The air fare will run you around A$400. Bookings can be made through a Queensland government tourist office or by contacting Australian Resorts, 441 Kilda Rd., Melbourne, Victoria 3004; tel. (03) 829–2301. Or contact Australian Airlines in Cairns; tel. 50–3766.

Another novel way to do the Cape York trip is by DC-3, the world's most venerable aircraft. A company called **DC-3 Queensland** has a variety of flights all over the peninsula, from one-day affairs with stops at Cooktown and a ride on the Kuranda railroad (about A$200 including lunch and hotel pickup), to a three-day jaunt that hits just about every place of interest in the area, including Thursday Island, a glimpse at the spaceport, a visit to the Reef at Lizard Island, lodging in Weipa, and several memorable pub stops. The three-day flights, run only in August and September, cost about A$950 per person. If you've never flown in a DC-3, it's a fascinating experience, a far cry from seeing a country from 35,000 feet. They're noisy, bouncy and wonderful. The company also runs trips to the western Outback. Information: DC-3 Queensland, Cairns Airport, General Aviation Section; tel. 53–7819, or toll-free in Australia (008) 07–9026.

THE QUEENSLAND
OUTBACK ....

Well, there's Outback, and then there's Outback. In eastern Queensland, the Outback more or less starts when you leave the lush coastal plain and pass over the Great Dividing Range going west. In western and southern Queensland, the whole country is Outback. And then, there's the Channel Country of southwest Queensland, which is about as far as you can get from somewhere and still find a beer—down in that corner is one of the most famous out-in-the-middle-of-nowhere places in Australia, **Birdsville,** and brother, to drive far enough to drink a beer at the **Birdsville Hotel,** you really have to want to be away from it all.

The vast chunks of Queensland beyond the coast are not all sandy desert. Some of the Outback is cattle country, some is rock outcroppings, some is miles of flat scrub with no trees, and some is, indeed, sandy wastes. Because even a harsh land must have some compensation, a huge selection of western Queensland sits atop mammoth deposits of artesian water, and annual rains can turn parched mudflats into lush pastures overnight. Sometimes, though, the rains don't come, and cattle die and fields burn up. Being a rancher or sheepman in Queensland can be a painful occupation.

There are several major highways that serve the towns and cities of the Outback, but many of the tracks Out There are dry-season only, and even then, not to be undertaken lightly. The country out around Birdsville is what caused the famous Australian explorers, Burke and Wills, to lose their lives in 1861.

Rural Queensland is friendly country because people are few and far between, and the spirit is very reminiscent of northern Arizona or southern Utah, where a harsh environment seems often to create gentle people. Much of the area is also cowboy country. At Longreach, on the Capricorn Highway west of Rockhampton, is the **Stockman's Hall of Fame,** a very popular museum and national monument to the Aussie cowboy.

Outback Queensland also gave birth to two of Australia's national symbols: Qantas airlines and *Waltzing Matilda*. If you like to camp by yourself and get away from it all, or simply would like to meet a breed of Australian a bit less complex and more down to earth than the sophisticated mob down in Sydney, the Queensland Outback will be just your ticket.

How far you go into the Outback depends on your frame of mind— and the frame of your four-wheel drive. Many of the more interesting spots can be reached by passenger car, but it gets hot and dusty—lordy, does it get dusty—and getting off the main tracks is for the adventurous. (See our section on driving in Australia, with particular attention to bulldust.) Your best bet is to do the Outback between April and October.

The major highways from the coast run west from Brisbane, Rockhampton, and Townsville, and of the three, the **Flinders Highway,** which cuts across the country from Townsville, is probably the most traveled. The Flinders Highway makes its way from the lushest of rain forests to the driest of deserts, ending up at the isolated mining community of **Mont Isa.** From there the highway changes names (becoming the Barkly) and goes another 520 miles to **Tennant Creek,** halfway between Darwin and Alice Springs in the Northern Territory.

Between Townsville and the old Gold Rush settlement of Charters Towers is an area called the **Anthill Plains.** The reason will become clear as you start passing mile after mile of termite mounds along the road—in Australia, termites are called white ants. You'll also see herds of cattle, big groves of eucalypts, and rocky hills. Going down into the plains west of **Charters Towers,** you start running into grasslands, where you can spot wild kangaroo and bustards, and now and then, a windmill next to a stock pond. Cars and towns are few and far between. The road basically follows the tracks of the Townsville-Mount Isa railroad, the Inlander.

Hughenden, about 150 miles west of the Towers, is a major intersection. From there, you can go southwest to Winton or continue on west to Cloncurry. Hughenden has about 1800 people and is the nearest town to **Porcupine Gorge National Park,** about the only national park for several thousand square miles and sometimes called the Grand Canyon of Australia—but a lot smaller than the original. To get to the park, which has camping areas and some rugged trails, take the **Kennedy Developmental Road** (dirt and washboarded) about 30 miles north. **Porcupine Gorge** lies at the extreme southern tip of the mountain range that runs north through the Atherton Tablelands to the Cape York Peninsula. There are four motels and several pubs in Hughenden, which also has gasoline.

From Hughenden you can either keep on the Mount Isa road or head down the Kennedy to Winton. Toward Mount Isa, there are three settlements of note, Richmond, Julia Creek, and Cloncurry. Around **Richmond,** a small agricultural center, are some of the richest grasslands in Australia. At **Julia Creek,** another 100 miles west, there are several motels and hotels. From the town north runs a paved highway to Normanton and Karumba, fishing and agricultural towns on the Gulf of Carpenteria. **Cloncurry,** 80 miles more, was once a copper boomtown, but now gets along quietly as an agricultural center. Of interest is **Scarr Street Museum,** which has relics from the Burke-Wills expedition, as well as artifacts from the fierce Aboriginal tribe that once ruled here. Cloncurry also has the honor of being the site of the first Flying Doctor service base. Another paved road runs north to Normanton.

Mount Isa is a mining town, plain and simple, sitting atop some of the world's richest deposits of silver and lead, as well as major veins of copper and zinc. The population is around 30,000, a fifth of whom work directly for Mount Isa Mines, and everybody else depends on the miners for a livelihood. Tours of the mines are available, either above or underground. North of town are two man-made lakes, including **Lake Moondarra,** about 12 miles away, which is a popular boating and recreational area. **Lake Julius,** the town's main water supply, is about 60 miles out. Tours are also available at the **Royal Flying Doctor Base** on the road to the airport (the Barkly Highway, also known as Camooweal Road). With the flying doctor is the **School of the Air,** which runs short-wave classes for children isolated all over the Outback.

There are about a half-dozen motels in town, plus RV parks.

A couple of suggestions:

Burke and Wills Mt. Isa Resort • *corner Grace and Camooweal sts; tel. (077) 43–8000* • Licensed restaurant, mini-bars, pool, spa. Doubles A$80–100.

The **Overlander** • *119 Marian St.; tel. 43–5011* • Some units with kitchens, laundry. Doubles A$60–70.

The **Winton-Longreach** area, to the south of Hughenden, is one of the most interesting parts of the Outback. In the bush about halfway between Cloncurry and Winton (bad road) is a place called the **Combo Waterhole,** where Banjo Paterson supposedly wrote *Waltzing Matilda.* However, we have it on good authority that at least three other billabongs in the region were the true site of the deed. Whatever, Winton has adopted the anthem as its own, and in the middle of town, there is a statue of the Swaggie made famous in the song. Winton also has the distinction of being the birthplace of Qantas Airlines—which stands for Queensland and Northern Territory Air Service. Qantas rose to fame and power from its base at Longreach, however.

THE GREAT BARRIER REEF

If you have ever dived on the Great Barrier Reef, or at least snorkeled it, you know that written descriptions of its incredible allure are hopelessly inadequate. In the whole world, there is probably no place so singularly beautiful as the Reef. The Australians call it the Eighth Wonder of the World, and that's an understatement. Of all Australia's attractions, the Great Barrier Reef is probably the most famous—and one of the most visited. It is why Queensland is the important tourist destination it has become. Despite this, we have to say in all honesty that over the years, the Australians have been pretty cavalier about protecting the reef. All manner of ecologically damaging schemes have managed to become reality, including actually anchoring a floating hotel above the living reef. (This dumb development, we are delighted to say, was a failure; a Japanese company bought the hotel and towed it to Ho Chi Minh City.) Many of the islands of the reef system have been exploited, and it seemed in the past that only the constant hue and cry of environmentalists kept the Queensland government from doing something new to despoil the reef. In addition, there have always been natural threats, such as cyclones and coral-eating predators. Despite it all, however, the reef today seems to be holding its own.

The reef is often called the largest living organism on earth, a vast group of interrelated marine creatures living in an oceanic community that runs more than 1400 miles down the east coast of Australia, from the Torres Strait southeast of Papua New Guinea to a spot east of Gladstone on the Queensland coast. There are more than 700 islands involved in the system, which also includes some 2000 individual reefs. Nowhere does the reef make contact with the shore. The Great Barrier Reef, as Capt. James Cook discovered in 1770 (see the History section), generally resembles a funnel, with its wide mouth to the south and its ever-narrowing spout at the far north. Some parts of the reef are more than 200 miles off shore; near the tip of the Cape York Peninsula, you can almost throw a stone and hit the reef.

The reef is not a single type of coral structure, but rather several main groups, including what are called "ribbons," the long narrow strips of barrier reef that caused Capt. Cook so much trouble on his voyage. Farther south, coral is often found in circular formations, often surrounding a continental island. One thing about coral makes it great for us tourists; it has trouble growing much below 100 feet, and large chunks of it are in the 20- to 30-foot-deep range, making it ideal for diving and snorkeling. There are more than 400 separate species of coral in the reef, the largest such grouping on the planet. The reef supports an abundance of other life, including something like 1600 species of fish and hundreds of other reef dwellers, such as crustaceans, molluscs, marine worms, and algae—all of which come in every hue of the palette. The reef is so colorful, as a matter of fact, you will not believe it's real even when you're looking at it. The scores of uninhabited reef islands in the system are important nesting areas for many species of sea birds and amphibians. Reef waters, as well as the deeper waters that surround them, provide some of the richest sport fishing in the world. The best fishing is on the outer reefs, where the coral formations sit next to deep drop-offs and the big gamefish come to play—marlin, tuna, and billfish. The combination of warm water and high visibility makes the reef and its lovely islands a perfect destination for stressed-out tourists. The scuba diver of our duo, just as an example, decided he'd finally reached Heaven the day he was able to stick his bare hand out and stroke the soft and gentle lip of a three-foot-wide giant clam, sitting on the bottom of a coral formation in warm, quiet water with at least 150-foot visibility.

In this section, we list all the major island resorts and attractions along the coast, although many of them are technically not part of the reef. But they are all off the Queensland coast and generally offer the same sort of adventures. How you get to the reef and the resorts depends on which group you're heading for. The main Barrier Reef centers are in the north, at Cairns and Townsville, while the gateways to the Capricorn section of the reef (including popular Heron Island) are Gladstone and Rockhampton. The major reef and island gateways on the mainland can be reached by train, plane or bus. If your stay in Australia is brief, we suggest you make some arrangement to fly to Cairns or Townsville and do your reef explorations from there. Cairns is especially attractive because not only does it have regular international air service to Hawaii and North America, it's closer to the reef than Townsville and is also close to some other fascinating areas.

The Great Barrier Reef Park

In 1983, the Australian government created the Great Barrier Reef Marine Park, the largest marine preservation area in the world. Run by an agency based in Townsville, the park extends the entire length of the reef (plus some non-reef areas), and is divided into a number of parts, including the **southern section,** which takes in the far-offshore reef running from east of Mackay to east of Bowen; the **Capricornia section,** which is off Gladstone and Rockhampton; the **inshore southern section,** which contains the close-in islands and reef from Gladstone to Cairns; the **central section,** which takes in the far off-shore formations from roughly east of Bowen to Innisfail; the **Cairns and Cormorant Pass section,** from Innisfail to Lizard Island; and the **northern section,** which runs from Lizard Island to the tip of the Cape York Peninsula. In all, something like 98% of the reef is in the park.

The **Great Barrier Reef Authority** has the unenviable job of trying to oversee all the possible uses of the reef, from tent camping on deserted islands to commercial fishing. Information: P.O. Box 1379, Townsville, Queensland 4810. One of its toughest jobs is trying to gauge the effect coastal development might have on coral growth, and also of balancing tourist dollars against over-use—when do too many people become too many people? Working with the authority are other agencies, including the Queensland government and a number of private and public agencies. In late 1988, for example, the Centre for Studies in Travel and Tourism at James Cook University in Townsville undertook a study of algae on reefs between Cape Tribulation to Innisfail to see what effect boats and moored structures might be having on reef formation. James Cook is also running a study of the crown-of-thorns starfish, which has denuded big chunks of the reef off Townsville.

Another sign of the increased attention being paid to the reef came along in 1989, when the National Parks and Wildlife Service announced plans to increase aerial inspection of the park. The new flights now cover the Dunk Island to Whitsundays section of the reef. The area around Cairns and the Capricorn section were already being patrolled. The flights look for park rules violations, including illegal fishing and oil spills.

Any Australian tourism office, especially the **Queensland Tourist and Travel Corporation,** can supply information about the Great Barrier Reef. The reef authority in Townsville has a number of publications available, including an excellent overview of the reef called the *World Heritage Nomination Book,* which has history and science information, as well as management policy and strategy. For information, contact the Great Barrier Reef Marine Park Authority, P.O. Box 1379, Townsville, Queensland 4810; tel. (077) 71–2191. Another general information source is the **Queensland National Parks and Wildlife Service,** MLC Centre, corner of George and Adelaide streets, Brisbane 4000; tel. (07) 224–0414. For information about fishing licenses and regulations for coastal areas as well as inland, contact the **Queensland Fish Management Authority,** P.O. Box 344, Fortitude Valley (Brisbane) 4006; tel. (07) 224–4335.

Finally, before you start out on a reef adventure, a few words of caution. First and foremost, do not go scuba diving unless you've had the proper training. We know of no dive shop or training center in Australia that is not reputable, but we haven't seen them all. We are suspicious of hotels in some tropical ports around the world that offer to teach you to scuba dive in two hours. The mechanics of using scuba gear can be deceptively simple, but there are enough things involved that proper training is essential. You can get into some serious—and possibly fatal—situations if you haven't had proper scuba training, even in shallow water. You can easily get your scuba card in Canada or the United States through dive shops or often the local YMCA. If you have time, you could take the training in Australia. But you should have a card from either **PADI** (the Professional Association of Dive Instructors) or **NAUI** (National Association of Underwater Instructors) certifying that you have had the requisite hours of training. The Great Barrier Reef is not a place to learn things the hard way. If you ever go into a dive shop in Australia—or anywhere else in the world—and they offer to sell you air without asking for your dive card, just walk on by.

Secondly, and we are not trying to make a big deal about this, the Great Barrier Reef, with all its beauty, has some very nasty critters, some perfectly capable of killing you. So, even if you're an experienced diver, the first time out on the reef should be with an Australian buddy, or with a local group. Sharks are probably the least of your worries, but among the evil cast of characters, there's a small seashell that is deadly, and there's a dandy species of poisonous octopus, as well as fire coral and sea snakes. Snorkelers probably won't get into too much trouble floating above the reef—but again, if you're inexperienced or new to the reef, go with a local group or agency—and don't leave home without a pair of old tennis shoes. Walking around a coral head barefooted is just asking for major-league problems. Having said all that, we now insist that you move heaven and earth to get underwater on the reef. Otherwise, you will have missed one of the greatest sights in this or any other solar system.

The Southern Islands (Capricornia Section)

North of **Fraser Island** (the world's largest sand island) is the Capricornia section of the Great Barrier Reef Marine Park, a group of coral reefs and islands about 340 miles up the coast from Brisbane. The area is divided into two parts, the Capricorn group and the Bunker group. (Bunker was a Yankee whaler who passed by in the early 1800s). The most popular of the islands in the group is **Heron,** which is a true coral island about 50 miles offshore. The island, only about 30 acres in size, is the home of a resort hotel and a marine biology station, and more than half of it is a national park. In addition to being close to some excellent diving, the island is also filled with birds, is a breeding spot for green sea turtles, and is one of the most heavily forested keys on the reef. There are usually daily lectures from staff members of the research station and reef walks. The fastest way to get to the island is by helicopter, **(Lloyd Air Services)** which costs about A$300 per person round trip. There are also daily launches, which cost about A$70 per person one way and take about 90 minutes. The launches allow the island to be done on a day trip. They leave the mainland at 8 a.m. and 1:30 p.m., returning from the island at 11 a.m. and 4:30 p.m. There are no camping facilities on the island.

The **resort** itself is built into the forest, and offers accommodations for about 300 guests in several ranges, including beach houses (around A$350 double), lodges (about A$200 double), and suites (about A$300 per person). All rates include meals. Reservation information is available from SH Enterprises, 520 Monterey Dr., Rio Del Mar, Calif. 95003; tel. (800) 225–9849 USA or (408) 685–8902. The resort operates a fully equipped dive shop, and scuba instruction is available.

Information about the island and its flora and fauna is available from the **Queensland National Park and Wildlife Service,** P.O. Box 1395, Rockhampton 4700; tel. (079) 27–6511. There is regular air service from Brisbane to Gladstone, as well as regular train service.

Another popular island in the Capricorn section of the reef is **Lady Elliot Island,** which marks the southern tip of the reef. The island has an airstrip, reasonably priced accommodations, and is a major target for divers. The reef formations at Lady Elliott are widely regarded as being some of the best in the whole system, and there are also turtles and sea birds to enjoy. The island is around 100 acres in size, and, like Heron, is a true coral island. It is famous for schools of huge manta rays. The accommodations come in two styles: **beachfront cabins** (about A$145 a day per person, including meals) or **safari tents** (about A$100 per person a day, meals included). The resort operates a glass-bottomed boat, and scuba lessons are available. Air service to the island is available from Bundaberg for about A$155 per person round trip, and day-trip packages are offered.

IntAussie Tours offers special packages to Lady Elliot from Brisbane. A three-night stay, including meals, accommodation and round-trip transportation, is about $A700 per person in cabins, $A550 in tents. Tour information and brochures are available from IntAussie Tours, 350 N. Crescent Dr., Suite 114A, Beverly Hills, Calif. 90210; (800) 635–5641 8 a.m.–6 p.m. West Coast time. Or in Brisbane, contact the company at 355 Queen St.; tel. 221–5301.

Also in the Capricornia group are several small islands, including **Lady Musgrave, Northwest Island,** and **Tryon Island,** which are available for campers. None have water or firewood, and transportation is up to you, available from services in Gladstone and Rockhampton. *Permits and information are available from the Queensland National Park and Wildlife Service, Roseberry St., Gladstone 4680.*

Opposite Yeppoon, northeast of Rockhampton, is **Great Keppel Island,** only eight miles offshore and a long boat ride from the reef, but popular because of its great beaches and fringe reefs. Most of the island is a national park, crisscrossed by trails. At one time the island was a sheep ranch, and the old ranch house still stands. The island, one of the five owned by Australian Airlines, caters to a young, hard-drinking clientele, and has room for hundreds of guests in a variety of accommodations. The official motto of the island is: "It's a great place to get wrecked." There *is* a baby-sitting service, however. The recently expanded and renovated accommodations are either beachfront or back in the bushes, and run between $A300–345 per person a day, meals included. There are also small cabins and camping available. Access to the island is either by launch from Rosslyn (about A$20 per person round trip) or by air from Rockhampton for about A$100 round trip. Booking information is available through Australian Airlines offices in North America: (800) 922–5122 U.S. or (800) 448–9400 Canada. Reservations are available through So/Pac, (800) 551–2012 USA, and Goway Travel in Canada, (800) 387–8850 Ontario and Quebec.

The other island of the group, **North Keppel,** is an uninhabited national park. It has camping facilities with limited water supplies and some firewood in designated sites with toilets. *Information is available from the parks and wildlife service in Rockhampton.*

General information about the area is available from the **Queensland Tourist and Travel Centre,** 119 East St., Rockhampton 4700, (079) 27-8611; the Capricorn Tourism and Development Organization Inc., Curtis Park, Gladstone Rd., Rockhampton 4700, (079) 27–2055, and Reef Adventureland Information, 100 Goondoon St., Gladstone 4680, (079) 72–4000.

The Whitsundays

This group of islands, opposite the cities of Mackay, Proserpine, and Bowen, is probably the single-most popular destination on the whole reef, as the dozens of resorts and lodges strewn about prove. The Whitsundays, so named by Captain Cook, are not true coral islands; rather they are part of the mainland, with steep slopes and forests. Most of the islands do have coral reefs around them, however, and are excellent for diving and snorkeling. The islands offer just about any style vacation you want, from the five-star plush palaces on Hayman and Hamilton islands to beach camping on uninhabited islets. One thing to keep in mind is that most of the resorts have **stand-by rates;** if they have cancellations, you might be able to sneak in at a reduced rate, so give them a call if you're in the neighborhood. For general information, contact the Whitsunday Tourism Association, P.O. Box 83, Airlie Beach 4802; tel. (079) 46–6673.

The main access point for trips to the islands is **Shute Harbour,** the developing tourist area near Proserpine. In addition, air service is available to the larger settlements. Some of the island resorts, in fact, are owned by airlines. A rare treat would be to hire a bareboat yacht, and do the islands at your own speed. (If you're interested, contact **Australian Bareboat Charters,** P.O. Box 357, Airlie Beach, Queensland 4802; tel. (079) 46–9381, or **Queensland Yacht Charters,** 16 McLachlan Ave., Rushcutters Bay, Sydney, NSW 2011; tel. (02) 331–1211.

If you're ecologically minded, the development of **Hamilton Island** will make you grind your teeth. The 1500-acre island, the largest resort in Australia, looks like a clone of Waikiki and got that way with what seems to be little or no regard for nature. The island is unique because it is owned outright by one man—Keith Williams—rather than being in the public domain as most of the barrier reef is. Williams is infamous in Queensland for the way he built the resort. First, he dynamited the top off a mountain to put in a helipad, dredged the harbor, and dynamited another peak to extend the island's jet landing strip. He says he wants to develop only about a quarter of the island, so the newest buildings are going high rise. The privately owned airport, already equipped to handle jets, is becoming an international facility with flights coming in from Japan, New Zealand and Singapore. The airport recently expanded.

The resort has everything from Mexican fast food to exclusive penthouse apartments. You can rent VCRs, hire a motor buggy, cook your own food in a kitchenette, or drop a foot in one of the resorts's eight swimming pools. It's enough like a Hawaiian resort to leave us wondering why anyone from North America would bother coming this far, when the beaches are better and much closer on Maui. There is the nearby reef, of course, but there are less populous and more attractive places to hang your hat on a reef trip. Having said that, we do acknowledge that Hamilton does make life easy with all the activities it offers, as well as the range of accommodations and food outlets. There is even 24-hour medical service and a health center.

The island has space for 1100 guests. The newest facility is Hamilton Towers, opened in 1990. There are 411 rooms in the 20-story tower, which has a 24-hour coffee shop and a 2000-seat tennis stadium. Daily room rates are between A$175–275; suites $675 and up for a double. Whitsunday Towers, an earlier development, has one-bedroom units for A$275 a night or beachfront units for A$360. All have kitchens. The Polynesian hut units at the Outrigger section of the resort go for around A$220–250 a day double. At Catseye Beach, you can rent almost any form of water vehicle, including bareboats or canoes. There is a marina, with docking fees around A$50 a day. If you've a mind, you could also visit the Fauna Park, home to kangaroos and koalas (A$5 a head), or hike on several trails in the mountains. The resort offers boat trips to the reef, with snorkeling and reef walks, lunches, and bar service, all for about A$70 per person for a half day. The island is popular with day-trippers, who take a launch from Shute Harbour for about A$20 each way. The one-way airfare is A$65.

Reservation information in North America for Hamilton Island is available by calling (800) 426–4753 USA or (800) 663–1118 Canada. Brochures and information are available by writing Hamilton Island, 9841 Airport Blvd., Suite 418, Los Angeles, Calif. 90045.

Remote Lindeman Island, home to flying foxes, great bushwalking, Ulysses butterflies, tons of birds and an inland lake. A national park with seven white sandy beaches, mangrove swamps and stands of eucalypts. Remote Lindeman Island? Naw. Club Med is planning its first Australian resort on the island, set to open in late 1992. And there goes the neighborhood. The club will have an 18-hole golf course and accommodations for 500 guests. A pox on their house, and the house of whomever decided to expand the tourist facilities on the island.

The Old Lindeman Island Resort, done over in the late 1980s, has 104 rooms, new bars and restaurants, and a nine-hole golf course. In contrast to Great Keppel, the emphasis on Lindeman is family atmosphere, with prices to match. Several grades of accommodations are available, and run from A$320–400 a day double, including meals, depending on season. There are two restaurants, three bars, tennis, and a disco. Access to the island is by launch and air from Proserpine, Mackay or Shute Harbor; launch A$50 round trip; air $55 one way. Reef trips and fishing are available. *Information: Lindeman Island Resort, Lindeman Island, Queensland 4741; tel. (008) 77–7322 (toll free).* Booking information: (800) 445–0190 California, (800) 551–2012 USA, (800) 663–1118 Canada.

The northernmost resort island in the Whitsundays is **Hayman Island,** which was closed down for two years in the late 1980s for a A$200-million facelift. The resort, owned by Ansett Airlines, is generally regarded as the snazziest in the Whitsundays and has space for about 500 upscale souls, with rooms starting at A$250 a night double (no meals) and rising rapidly. The place is awash in marble and antiques, with separate reception areas in each wing of the facility. Here is the land of dress codes for dinner, a huge wine cellar, and underground service tunnels so you can't see the gnomes who provide the first-class service. There are five restaurants, including an elegant French abode where prices are on a par with Sydney's best. There are nightly cabaret shows and a late-night disco. If you get tired of all the fluff, you can take advantage of the resort's tennis facilities, a huge swimming pool, or watersports. There are trips to the reef, and if you're in the mood, some spectacular hiking trails. Along with all this is other normal big-money resort hotel stuff you'd expect, such as a hairdresser, pharmacy, and an art gallery.

Access to the island is by air from Proserpine or Shute Harbour, (about A$50 one way) or aboard the elegant *Sea Goddess* ferry from Hamilton Island, which connects to flights from Brisbane and other mainland cities (about A$40), where you can snack on champagne and canapes and watch the ocean go by. Helicopter service is also available from Proserpine (about A$160). Booking information: Ansett Airlines, 9841 Airport Blvd., Suite 418, Los Angeles, Calif. 90045; tel. (800) 366–1300 USA and Canada.

At the south end of the Whitsunday Passage is **Brampton Island,** another spot owned by Australian Airlines; (079) 51–4499. The emphasis here is on couples, with prices for the 200-odd units starting at around A$125–A$150 per person, meals included. Two of the local inhabitants to watch out for are scrub hens and green tree ants. The birds are one of Australia's mound-building species; the ants are famous for their huge melon-sized nests. The resort offers the usual watersports, and has nightly parties and frequent barbecues. Most of the island is a national park, with gentle trails. No camping is allowed. Launch from Mackay A$30 round trip; air A$70 one way. Booking information is available through Australian Airlines or So/Pac, (800) 551–2012 USA.

Daydream Island, just two miles from Shute Harbour, was closed until late 1990 for redevelopment. It had been a popular hangout, done in a Polynesian style, and the beach at the north end of the island is magnificent. Now it looks like a motel, with units in blocks; doubles from A$250. Information: (079) 46–9433.

Other Whitsundays worth a look include Hook and South Molle. **Hook** is close to some of the best diving and snorkeling areas in the area and has an underwater observatory where, for A$5, you can peek through one of the three dozen or so windows at the fish. Camping is available nearby, and there is a place to get food and beer. *South Molle,* another Ansett Airlines property, has a casual air, with bungalows and motel-style units stuck in tropical gardens. One of the best views of the island group is available from the top of the island's peaks. It can hold around 500 guests, and has two restaurants, tennis, a very nice golf course, scuba equipment and lawn bowling. There are reef and fishing trips as well as day trips to other spots in the Whitsundays, including Hook Island, now owned by the airline. Rooms go for about A$175 per person, including all meals. *Information: Ansett Airlines.*

Campers should take note of these Whitsunday islands, which are among the 100 or so uninhabited islands in the group: **Saddleback, North Molle, Shute, Tancred, Rabbit** and **Outer Newry.** Most have toilets, picnic areas, firewood and camping areas. The islands are all within 10 miles of Shute Harbour and are administered by the **Queensland National Parks and Wildlife Service,** P.O. Box 623, Mackay 4740; tel. (079) 57–6292.

North of the Whitsundays, the barrier reef starts coming closer and closer to shore, and the resort islands get fewer and farther apart. In their place, however, are the numerous resort hotels and restaurants on the mainland at Cairns and Townsville, plus the dozens of tour operators that run day trips or longer excursions out to the reef.

About 15 miles offshore from Ingham, on the coast north of Townsville, is **Orpheus Island,** part of the Palm Island group. The island is a mix of exclusivity (only 50 guests at a time) and low-key, with camping available in the national park areas of the island. James Cook University has a facility on the island, and the snorkeling is excellent right in front of the resort. Rooms are in bungalows and studios with terra-cotta tile floors and South Seas furniture. Some rooms have enclosed gardens with sunken tubs. Rates, including all meals, range from about A$300 to 350 per person a day. The place is very light and airy, and its proximity to the reef makes it a nice place to haul in while you're exploring. NB: Kids are frowned on. The resort offers the usual array of watersports equipment and daily trips to the reef. The park portion of the island (about 3300 acres) has a large rain forest, as well as hiking trails. Camping by permit is available through the Cairns office of the park service, P.O. Box 2066, Cairns 4870; (070) 53–4533. Access to the island is by air from Cairns (about A$130 one way) and Townsville (about A$100 one way). Booking information is available from RHC International, (800) 663–8889 USA and Canada.

Near Cardwell, north of Ingham, is the largest island national park in the world and one of the largest islands on the Queensland coast— **Hinchinbrook,** which is something like 145 square miles in area. It is one of Australia's premier wild and scenic areas, with volcanic peaks, dense rain forests, mangrove swamps, and important breeding areas for a wide variety of waterfowl. The tallest peak on the island is **Mt. Bowen** at about 3650 feet. There is only one resort on the island, with room for only 30 guests. The island is hard to get to and they plan to keep it that way, and the facilities at the resort are water-oriented. Although there are several well-maintained trails (including a boardwalk through the mangroves) most of the island is rugged and fit only for experienced bushwalkers. The treks are worth it, however, because the bush is filled with pools, waterfalls, and hardwood forests. There are secluded beaches and giant sea turtle nesting areas. All in all, for a camper, Hinchinbrook is ground zero. Camping is allowed (for 14 days at a time) at two spots, with permits from an on-duty ranger.

The **resort,** at Cape Richards on the northern tip of the island, has rustic units set into the forest, a pool, dining room with great food and a bar. It was expanded and renovated in 1989. Rooms are around A$170 a day per person, meals included. There is a tribe of tame wallabies and some largish goannas running around. The beach is fantastic, and not far away you can spot Ulysses butterflies and orchids. Access to the resort (and the camping areas) is by launch from Cardwell (about A$40 per person round trip) or by seaplane from Cairns (about A$125 one way) or from Townsville (about A$100). *Information on the national park is available from Queensland wildlife service offices in Cairns or Townsville.* Resort booking information: So/Pac, (800) 445–0190 California, (800) 551–2012 USA.

Next in line are two more Australian Airlines properties, Dunk and Bedarra islands. Of the two, Dunk is the most traditional, a nicely meshed mix of high-quality resort and tropical island laziness. Bedarra is—well—designed for rich folks to get away from the rest of us slobs.

The advertising logo for **Dunk** is a Ulysses butterfly, not surprising because the island is full of butterflies and orchids. The bulk of it is a national park, with camping facilities. There are some excellent beaches, and the sports activities at the resort are abundant. You can, if you wish, shoot skeet with a $3000 shotgun (you pay for the shells and the skeet), or play tennis, go walkabout, waterski, or go sniff orchids. The immense bar/dining area is now one of the most attractive we've seen, and the food comes in prodigious quantities. The resort can handle about 320 guests at a time in several grades of rooms, including beachfront cabanas for about A$230 per person double, meals included, and rooms in two-story units for about A$190 per person. Day-long trips to the reef are available for about A$70 per person, which includes lunch.

Camping on the island is limited to three-day stays, and facilities include toilets, but no water. Permits are required and are available from the Cairns parks and wildlife service. Access to the island is by air from either Cairns or Townsville (about A$80 each way), or by launch from Clump Point Beach near Tully (about A$15 round trip. Booking information for the resort is available from So/Pac, (800) 551–2012 USA; (800) 235–8222 Canada.

Dunk's sister island, **Bedarra,** is the home of a small and exclusive resort whose sole aim seems to be pampering a maximum of 32 gilt-edged guests. Accommodations in the two sections of the resort property are in apartment-like units (small villas, they say) set into the foliage, with great views and airy space. Everything here is taken care of—including an open bar and a resident gourmet chef—and total isolation is the key. You halfway expect to see Joan Collins or Marlon Brando wander by. Rates reflect the exclusivity: about A$400 a day per person, weekly packages somewhat lower. Some sports activities for Bedarra guests are available at Dunk, and a free lunch is available for guests. Getting to Bedarra is via Dunk. Reservation information is available through Australian Airlines or So/Pac. In Australia, call Bedarra at (070) 68–8233.

Two island resorts near Cairns are Fitzroy and Green islands. **Fitzroy** is a continental island, not a true reef structure, but it has beautiful coral beaches and heavy vegetation. The **Fitzroy Island Resort** has space for about 160 guests in villa units and also in a hostel area where you can share cooking facilities. The villas go for A$150 per person, some meals included. The hostel-style bungalows are A$25 per person. The island is a popular day-trip destination, and is on a catamaran route that runs from Cairns to Green Island. It's possible to hit both islands the same day, and there is late service on weekends. **Big Cat Tour Services** in Cairns runs daily trips to the two islands on several itineraries, including a few that give you a chance to snorkel on the reef. The price, no meals, no equipment, runs about A$30 per person for a four- to five-hour trip. *Information: Big Cat Tour Services, 111 Lake St., Cairns 4870; tel. 51–0444.* The catamaran leaves Cairns at 8:30 a.m. and 10:30 a.m. daily and takes about 45 minutes to get to Fitzroy. It then leaves for Green at about 1 p.m. Fitzroy offers trips to the close-by reef and also excursions in a semi-submersible submarine for reef viewing.

Nearby **Green Island,** which is partly a national park, is a true coral island that sits on the inner part of the reef system and has typical coral island foliage such as casuarina and dune plants. It's a marine fowl nesting area and sea turtles are often seen. No camping is allowed. The Green Island Reef Resort at the west end of the island has doubles for about A$300, with breakfast and dinner included.

Finally, opposite Cooktown north of Cairns, is **Lizard Island,** where Captain Cook climbed a peak and spotted a path through the reef after his unfortunate experiences. There is a trail you can follow to the exact spot where he stood. The island is a national park, noted for a profusion of wildlife including three-foot-long monitor lizards and dugongs, huge sea mammals that look like giant pigs and which were almost hunted to extinction for their oil. Camping by permit is allowed for one-week stays. A launch from Cairns is A$20 round trip; the Big Cat is about

A$30 round trip. *Information available from the Cairns parks and wildlife service.*

The **Lizard Island Lodge** is small (room for 64 guests) and expensive, with rooms going for around A$300–A$580 per person a day, meals included. The emphasis, again, is on service and seclusion, with a good wine list and an excellent food service. Activities are water-oriented and every year the resort is a focal point for marlin fishing. Within a half-hour of the front door are several excellent snorkeling and diving spots, and small boats are available for guests to rent. Near the resort is a marine research station where you can enjoy lectures on reef life. Lizard Island is one of the best places to enjoy a pampered tropical getaway next to some of the most beautiful parts of the reef. Access to the island is by air from Cairns (about A$250 round trip) and the scenic flight takes you over great chunks of the reef. Booking information: So/Pac, (800) 551–2012 USA; (800) 235–8222 Canada.

Reef Adventures

It would take a whole book just to list all the companies that provide reef trips. Almost any community of any size along the Queensland coast has a tour operator or boat/diving service available, and the range of options available is immense, from helicopter overflights to two-week long camping excursions. Here are a few to consider:

Bill King's Australian Experience has a 5-day reef diving trip on a dive boat running from Shute Harbour. The trip, for students or qualified divers, costs about A$750 per person, and includes all meals and diving equipment. The boat has an air compressor. Booking information: ATS/Sprint, 1101 E. Broadway, Glendale, Calif. 91205; tel. (800) 232–2121 California, (800) 423–2880 USA.

One of the best dive shops we ran into along the reef, in terms of trips available—and friendly folks—is **Down Under Dive Travel** in Cairns. The shop can get you aboard a dive boat or arrange a snorkeling trip for any age group. A two-night excursion for snorkelers, for example, meals included, is A$250 per person. Information: Down Under Dive Travel, 93 Esplanade, Cairns 4870; tel. (070) 31–1288.

One of the best ways to get a quick, comfortable and satisfying first look at the reef is aboard one of the **Quicksilver catamarans** that run from Port Douglas to Agincourt Reef, a ribbon formation about 90 minutes offshore. The boats offer huge smorgasbord lunches with a licensed bar, free snorkeling equipment, lectures by reef biologists, a stop at an underwater observatory and, for an extra cost, snorkeling trips guided by a marine biologist, divemasters, and scuba equipment. The one-day trip costs A$100 per person. Coach transfers are available from Cairns to Port Douglas for A$10. If you only have time for one trip to the reef, this might be your best bet. In Port Douglas, information is available from Quicksilver Connections, P.O. Box 171, Port Douglas 4871; tel. (070) 99–5500. To pre-book from North America, call (800) 445–0190 California; (800) 551–2012 USA, and (800) 235–8222 Canada. A comparable trip is offered by **Great Adventures,** which runs catamarans from Cairns to Green Island and several offshore reef areas. In Cairns, contact, Great Adventures at (070) 51–0455.

The best way to get an overall look at what's currently available (including prices) of Great Barrier Reef services, including everything from day trips to week-long cruises on tall ships, is available in a magazine-format release offered by Queensland Government Tourist and Travel Corporation offices both in Australia and North America. Ask for the *Sunlover Holidays* book.

If you'd like to see a range of what's available on Great Barrier Reef diving/snorkeling trips from North America, try these companies:

Adventure Center, (415) 654–1879, (800) 228–8747; Dive in Australia, (415) 421–5588; IntAussie, (213) 858–7383 (collect from Canada), (800) 635–5641; Poseidon Venture Tours, (714) 644–5344, (800) 854–9334; P&O Resorts-Heron Island, (408) 685–8902, (800) 225–9849 outside California; Sea & Sea Travel, (415) 434–3400, (800) 348–9778; Sea Safaris, (800) 262–6670 California, (800) 821–6670 USA and Canada, and Tropical Adventures, (206) 441–3483, (800) 247–3483 USA and Canada.

NORTHERN TERRITORY

Red, as far as you can see, red. And flat. And hot. And desolate. And magnificent. One-sixth of the land mass of Australia, 480,000 square miles in all, twice as big as Texas. You could stick a bunch of Europe in here and still have room left over. A huge chunk, some 95,000 square miles, is all sand dunes and claypan desert. But the Northern Territory is more than just desert—it's also a land of monsoons, with heavy rains, tropical vegetation, deep river gorges, and crocodile-infested coastal wetlands. All in all, you're faced with a vast and empty place with a total population of only about 160,000.

If you travel around the Northern Territory, that's what you remember—the seeming lack of human life, a land where nature, at least for now, seems to be in charge. The Territory is for those who like their views unobstructed, their pleasures at a leisurely pace, and their adventures on the peculiar side. Where else, for example, can you ride a camel to a wine tasting? Or watch a boat regatta down a dry stream bed? Or see an emu getting a shampoo? Or take a drive on a highway infested with trucks measuring a half-football field in length?

The Territory, which got self-government in 1978, is split geographically (and philosophically) into two parts: The **Top End** and the **Red Centre.** Each area has one of the Territory's major attractions. In the Red Centre is the nation's most celebrated hunk of stone—**Ayers Rock**—and in the Top End are the wonders of **Kakadu National Park,** which has one of the richest storehouses of ancient human art in the world. The Red Centre is the home of **Alice Springs,** the settlement made famous in the Neville Shute novel *A Town Like Alice,* and the Top End is the home of one of the seasonally most humid cities around, **Darwin,** the territorial capital—which gets something like 300 inches of rain during the rainy season. For all its red desert and lack of water, the Territory is amazingly lush with animal and plant life, clinging to oases and river banks and coastal rain forests and ecozones. There are at least 100 mammal species (including 40 marsupials), 400 species of birds, 100 species of butterflies, and more reptiles and frogs than you can throw a textbook at. The rangers at Kakadu claim there are at least 250 species of birds in the park alone.

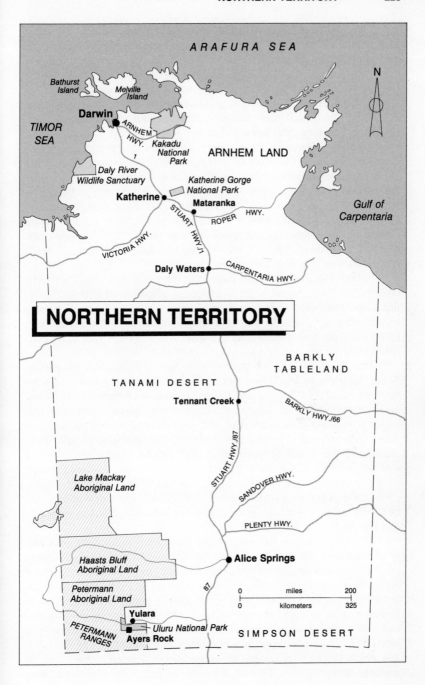

The original inhabitants of the Territory were Aboriginals who came to Australia on an island-hopping expedition at least 40,000 years ago. They first settled around Kakadu, and over the course of about 30,000 years, made their way to Uluru—the Aboriginal word for Ayers Rock. One of the first Europeans to pass by was Dutch sea captain Jan Carstensz, who came calling in a ship named the *Arnhem,* after which the huge Aboriginal land mass called **Arnhem Land,** at the northeastern tip of the Territory, was named. The bay where Darwin sits was named after Charles Darwin in 1839. The early 19th-century explorations of the Territory were the stuff of legends, with the doomed Burke and Wills expedition passing by, as well as Capt. Charles Sturt, who went from Adelaide to the Tropic of Capricorn near Alice Springs before he was forced to give it up. In 1862, a member of Sturt's original party, John McDouall Stuart, tried it on his own and became the first white Australian to traverse the continent north to south. The early telegraph line and the present Adelaide-Darwin highway follow his route. Indeed, it's even called the Stuart Highway.

Construction of the 1760-mile-long telegraph line, itself a daring undertaking, was begun in 1871 under the direction of Charles Todd, the South Australian superintendent of telegraphs. The Todd River was named after him, and the site of a telegraph station and watering hole along the route was named after his wife: Alice Springs (not to be confused with the present city.)

The Territory was first part of New South Wales, became part of South Australia in 1863, then became a federal territory in 1911. Self-government allows Territorians to control their own finances, but Canberra retains control of uranium mining and Aboriginal affairs. The two major population centers are **Darwin,** with around 80,000 people, and **Alice Springs** (widely known as "the Alice") with around 23,000. They are two of the fastest-growing cities in Australia. Any other towns of size are located along the Stuart Highway, although the large tourist center at **Ayers Rock** could qualify as a town in its own right. About 25% of the population is Aboriginal, living either in small communities in the Outback or—often unfortunately—in poor conditions in the Alice and Darwin.

The long-standing isolation of the Territory is rapidly disappearing as tourism raises its ugly head—now the Territory's second-largest source of income after mining. Visitors to the area, most of whom head for Ayers Rock, seem to be increasing geometrically every year, with international traffic accounting for about 25 percent of the total. Annual revenues from tourism are approaching A$500 million. In the last decade, the number of guest accommodation spaces has risen something like 150%. Darwin's airport is a true international facility, and the Alice and Ayers Rock are reachable by either air-conditioned motor coach or regional airline service. One of the most important developments, long awaited, was paving the Stuart Highway all the way from Adelaide, 1700 miles north to Darwin. The Territory recognized the growing importance of tourism in 1980 when the **Northern Territory Tourist Commission** was formed. It's an aggressive and well-managed agency, with headquarters in Alice Springs and offices overseas.

Many foreign visitors to the Territory see only the tourist village at Ayers Rock, which is a shame. The drive from Darwin down the Stuart to the Alice and then to the Rock is one of the most rewarding in all Australia. Towns are nicely spaced, and there are scenic spots along the route that will blow you away. You haven't really experienced the Territory until you stand in a village pub, covered from cheek to toe in red dust, snarfing down an icy beer and telling tall tales about the rigors of the Outback. If time is short, our suggestion is to forget the Rock—although climbing it is a big deal—and head for **Kakadu.**

The Northern Territory might well be the first place you'll encounter Australia's oldest inhabitants, in this case, the Aboriginal peoples of the Top End and Red Centre. Their lives have changed enormously since white settlers came, and some have not been able to handle the pressures of a lifestyle totally alien to their own. White history was not kind to the First Territorians. Gold rushes, ranchers, and cattle drives throughout the Territory pushed them off their traditional lands, and when they fought back, many were killed in a protracted war that continued on into the late 1920s. Christian missionaries came in to help, but basically made things worse—this time causing mostly psychological problems—and the tribal patterns that had ruled Aboriginal lives for thousands of years started to disappear.

Many Aboriginal leaders think the best way to solve many of their people's problems—alcoholism, crime, poverty, and illiteracy—is to move back into the bush and leave the white world alone, and there are a number of tiny, isolated Aboriginal communities all over the territory. Access to Aboriginal lands is restricted, with permits from the owners required to enter. Permits are rarely given to casual tourists, although arrangements have been worked out with some white tour operators. (This is true all over Australia.) Entering Aboriginal land without a permit can result in a fine of A$1000. It is possible to drive across Aboriginal lands if the highway is public, but before taking off, check with the lands councils.

Three **land councils** are in charge of Aboriginal holdings in the Territory, under provisions of the Aboriginal Lands Act of 1976. If you want to try for a permit, you must fill out a proper application form, either in person or by writing (enclose a SASE). The three councils are:

Darwin, Nhuulunbuy, and Katherine regions: Permits Officer, Northern Land Council, P.O. Box 39843, Winnellie 5789; street address, 47 Stuart Highway, Stuart Park, Darwin; tel. 81–7011.

Alice Springs and Tennant Creek: Permits Officer, Central Land

Council, P.O. Box 3321, Alice Springs 5750; street address, 33 Stuart Highway, Alice Springs; tel. 52–3800.

Melville and Bathurst islands: Permits officer, Tiwi Land Council, Nguiu, Bathurst Island, via Darwin 5791; tel. 78–3957 or 81–4111.

One of the provisions of the 1976 law created methods of returning Aboriginal lands to their traditional owners. A very symbolic return took place in 1985, when Ayers Rock and the Olgas were returned to tribal land councils. The federal government, of course, was not about to let the highly profitable Rock get too far away, and it was immediately leased back to the commonwealth for 99 years.

Some Aboriginal efforts, however, are very mainstream, such as a new Aboriginal-owned hotel at Kakadu National Park, a radio/TV station in Alice Springs, plus a number of Aboriginal owned or operated tour companies offering walkabouts, guided tours into Arnhem Land, or corroborees (tribal get-togethers, complete with food, music, and storytelling). In 1984, the Northern Territory Tourist Commission created a position for an Aboriginal liaison officer, and since then tribal tourism activities have expanded greatly.

Among the **Aboriginal-oriented tours** available in the Territory are these:

Ipolera tour: This tour departs Alice Springs on a one-day trek that visits the Ipolera Aboriginal outstation, about 75 miles west of the Alice, where community leaders Herman and Mavis Malbunka give you a cuppa and a chunk of damper and then take you off to learn—men in one group, women in another—and to study sites of significance and discuss Aboriginal lore. Don't feel like it's sex discrimination: some traditional knowledge is only for women, some only for men. Cost is about A$100 per person. *Information: (089) 52–2350 in Alice Springs.*

7-Day Top End Adventure: Offered by Australian Kakadu Tours, this trip goes to Kakadu and winds up with a stay on Bathurst Island. The cost is about A$1200 including meals and transportation. The company also offers shorter and longer trips around the Territory. *Information: Australian Kakadu Tours, Smith Street Mall, Darwin 0800; tel. 81–5144; toll-free, (008) 89–1121. North American bookings and information: (800) 445–0190 California; (800) 551–2012 USA, (800) 235–8222 Canada.*

Melville and Bathurst islands: A trip to these islands in the Timor Sea about 30 miles north of Darwin is becoming very popular. The islands, the traditional home of the Tiwi people, cannot be visited by individuals, but are open to tour groups. Tiwi, by the way, means either "People, we the people" or "the chosen people." The major population center is Nguiu on Bathurst, where you can watch islanders make pottery, clothing, and silk screens. Day or half-day tours are available, which include air transportation and visits to one or both islands. The major company offering island trips is **Tiwi Tours,** Darwin Airport, (089) 81–5444. full day, about A$200 per person. Longer stays can be arranged. Three days for example, is A$560. All rates include air, meals, guides and accommodation. North American information and reservations from ATS/Sprint, (800) 423–2880 USA; (800) 232–2121 California. **Australian Kakadu** will also fly you from Darwin to Putjamirra, at the tip of Melville Island, for two- or three-day tours and stays with the Tiwis. The cost, including airfare, is around A$700 per person double for the three-day trip. Accommodations are in an African-style safari camp.

The Dreamtime Tour: One of the best quickie Aboriginal tours in Australia, this comes highly recommended by Burnum Burnum (he wrote the definitive book on Aboriginal Australia.) The tour is run by Rod Steinert, and goes near Alice Springs to hear Aboriginal people explain how life was before the Europeans came. They even feed you bush tucker. On other Steinert tours, the Aboriginals will explain the magic meaning of an ancient ceremonial ground and rock paintings. On Wednesdays, there is a corroboree. The Dreamtime cost is about A$60 in the summer, less in the winter. The trip takes a half-day, leaving the Alice around 8 a.m. every day. There is also a one-day trip that will teach you rudimentary bush survival skills, using Aboriginal teachers. Wanna try snacking on a witchetty grub (a big caterpiller that is a favorite canape of the bush folks)? *Information: Rod Steinert Tours, P.O. Box 2058. Alice Springs N.T., 0871; Phone (089) 555–000.*

Bamurru Djadjam trip: This one does Kakadu with the added lure of having an Aboriginal guide: Mick Alderson, who owns Wild Goose Tours, will show you his view of the park and its wildlife and history. Mick takes you on a six-hour trip (starting at Cooinda) through his traditional lands near Kakadu not open to the public, for about A$80 per person. *For information contact Wild Goose at the Four Seasons Cooinda, 79–2545.* Terra Safari, associated with Wild Goose, does a five-day Arnhem Land trek for about A$700 per person in the winter, less in summer. *Information: Terra Safari Tours, 5 Moil Crescent, Moil, Darwin; tel. 45–0863 or 27–0881.*

One of the few people allowed to come and go into Arnhem Land is a wonderful guy named Max Davisdson, who runs tours to a private lodge at a place called Mt. Borradaile, where you get a safari-tent experience at Max's place, which is near to Aboriginal rock art and has fishing, bird watching or just lying in the sun. It's a very special place, but it ain't the Hilton. It's mosquito nets at night, strange noises in the dark, *Out of Africa* sort of stuff. There's a close-on billabong infested with birds, and there's always a chance to see a croc, a dingo or a wild pig. The fee of A$300 per person includes payments to the Aboriginal land owners, all meals, accommodation, guides tours and fishing. A tremendous experience. You can often find Max at the Four Seasons Cooinda, where he takes folks out for fishing trips. Otherwise, contact him at (089) 27-5240 or 41–1394.

The Northern Territory Tourist Commission offices have a booklet outlining Aboriginal tours. The free booklet is called *Come Share Our Culture*. Another quick look at Aboriginal culture is in another booklet, *People of Two Times*.

The Essential Northern Territory

INFORMATION • The main North American office of the Northern Territory Tourist Commission is located at 2121 Ave. of the Stars, 12th Floor, Los Angeles 90067; tel. (213) 277–7877. For information and some bookings, call (800) 468–8222 USA; (800) 661–6882 Canada.

NOTE · · · Tour companies and services without North American contact numbers can often be booked through a travel agent; lacking that, book them yourselves through the Territory tourist offices in North America. Or, if you're playing it by ear, book when you get to the Territory. There is almost always space available today—or tomorrow. The NT tourist office in Sydney is at 89 King St., Sydney 2000; tel. (02) 235–2822. In the Territory, the headquarters are in the Ford Plaza Building, Todd Mall, Alice Springs 5750; tel. (089) 51–1299. Other bureaus are located at 31 Smith St. Mall, Darwin 5790, (089) 81–6611; corner of Stuart Highway and Lindsay Ave., Katherine 5780, (089) 72–2650, and corner Paterson and Davidson sts., Tennant Creek 5760, (089) 62–3388.

GETTING THERE • Unless you have lots of time—and patience—driving to the Territory is probably just not worth it. There are three major interstate roads into the area: the **Stuart** from Adelaide; the **Barkly Highway** from Tennant Creek to Mt. Isa in Queensland, and the **Victoria Highway** from Katherine to Western Australia. They're all long and arduous. The best way is to fly in.

There are no direct flights from North America to the Territory, but there is regular interstate service to Darwin, Alice Springs, and Ayers Rock. The two major national carriers going to Darwin and the Alice are **Ansett** and **Australian Airlines. Ansett,** serves Ayers Rock. In addition, a number of tour companies operate small plane services. Within the Territory, there is service between the major settlements on a subsidiary of Ansett, **Ansett NT.** Probably your best bet is to buy one of the **air passes** available that will allow you to include the Territory on a tour of Australia. **East-West,** for example, has two passes starting at US$525 that allow flights either from Sydney to Ayers Rock and

Alice to Brisbane, or from Brisbane back around. Once you're in Australia, you'll find that booking internal flights between cities is quite expensive, although most airlines offer stand-by fares if you have the time. Without a pass, expect to pay in the neighborhood of A$450 for a one-way ticket from Sydney or Brisbane.

One of the most popular ways to get to Alice Springs is on the **Ghan,** a weekly 23-hour run from Adelaide. The train is equipped to take automobiles, so you can avoid those long stretches on the Stuart but still have a car when you get to the Red Centre. First-class sleepers go for around A$300 per person one way; taking a car is about A$200 extra. There is a dining car and a bar and—would you believe—an entertainment car with video games, a bookstore, and poker machines.

There is also **bus service** into the Territory, but guys, it's a long haul. The **Greyhound** bus from Brisbane to the Alice takes about 44 hours; Brisbane–Darwin is about 50 hours; Adelaide–Alice, 20 hours, and Adelaide–Ayers Rock around 22 hours. If you want to try the bus bit, we urge you to get a pass on one of the major carriers so you can get off once in a while and relax. **Deluxe** has several passes, including the **Great Divide,** which lets you do the Stuart Highway (plus the Queensland coast) for around A$600 per person, good for 12 months. A similar pass, **Aussie Highlights,** is offered by **Greyhound** for about the same money.

Once in the Territory, there are a slew of **charter companies** that can either fly you or drive you around to the sights. **Deluxe,** for example, has a number of tours from the Alice to Ayer's Rock and the Olgas, or from Darwin to Kakadu. Prices vary according to itinerary, but a week trip around the Alice Springs area, including accommodations, can be as little as A$500 per person.

Renting a car in the Territory is a snap, with at least a dozen rental agencies on hand, including the biggies. Almost all allow one-way hires, allowing you to fly into Darwin, say, then drive to Ayers Rock and fly out. Many have special weekly rates, with the tariff, depending on size of car, going for around A$50 to A$70 a day. There are also campers and mokes (the little dune-buggy-sized cars) for hire. You can get cars in Darwin, Katherine, Yulara, Tennant Creek, Jabiru (Kakadu National Park), or Alice Springs. (See the DRIVING section for a few cautionary notes on Outback motoring.)

CLIMATE • If you don't time it right, the Northern Territory can bake your buns—or give you a terminal case of mildew. Maximum temperatures in the Top End in the summer (Nov.–March) are in the 90s. In the Red Centre, it gets ghastly, with highs above 110°. A couple of years ago, a German Boy Scout wandered off by himself near Ayers Rock and died within a few hours from exposure to temperatures reported to be around 140 degrees, so it's not something to take lightly. In the winter, high temperatures around Darwin are in the 80s, around 65° in the Ayers Rock area. Spring, with its incredible bloom of wild desert plants, is the best time to see the Red Centre. You should know, also, that Alice Springs gets damned cold in June or July, with temperatures sometimes below freezing.

Darwinians take a certain perverse pride in their lousy climate. "Nobody ever drowns here," a local told us, "they just rust." The Aussies have succinctly described the climatic conditions near the Timor Sea as "the Wet" and "the Dry," and when it's wet, it's wet. The Red Centre, by contrast, gets around 90 inches a year, a lot of that during torrential downpours. The monsoon Wet is generally from October through April, the Dry is from May through September. During the Wet, rivers overflow, waterfalls get humongous, and road conditions can get very dicey. The Todd River through Alice is normally dry, but recently has overflowed its banks and flooded the downtown part of the city.

TIME • The Northern Territory is on Central Standard Time, meaning it's a half-hour behind Queensland and New South Wales. The telephone area code for the Territory is (089).

THE TOP END

Gone troppo—the Aussie expression for becoming a lotus eater—is a fair description of the whole area around Darwin. The whole town is about as uptight as a rock lizard, and pretense and big-city running around is met with quiet derision. Detractors would have you believe that Darwinians are as relaxed as they are because the heat has melted their brains, but the good folks around town seem bright enough. Part of their personality results from being so far away from what passes as civilization in Australia—Darwin is closer to Asia than Sydney. As the crow flies, Sydney is about 1800 miles; Jakarta is 1500, Manila, 1700, Singapore, 1900. Even other places in the Territory are a fair jaunt there—the Alice is 700 miles away, for example.

The Top End's proximity to Asia has not been without its perils. Darwin was the first Australian city to be bombed by Japanese aircraft in World War II. Between February and November 1942, it was bombed

64 times; 243 people were killed, including the postmaster and his family. They have a saying around town: "Darwin—blown up and blown away." The latter because of Cyclone Tracy, which roared into Darwin on Christmas Eve 1974 and virtually flattened the city. The hurricane's 140-mile-an-hour winds destroyed more than 5000 buildings in a four-hour period. More than 60 people died in what has been recorded as Australia's worst natural disaster. As a result, Darwin is a brand-new city. Only a few colonial buildings managed to survive both the Japanese and the cyclone.

The modern result is a wide-avenued, tropical settlement where shade is found beneath bamboo and mango trees. This is not to suggest that visitors are forced to rack out in palm-thatched hovels on the beach, because, in fact, there are some nicely upscale digs. But the combination of palm trees and wet air, and sun and clear skies (when it's not raining) is a balm to a frazzled mind. And, in truth, the weather between May and October can be very pleasant, with sunny days and cool nights. But Darwin's greatest lure, to be honest, is as a base to check out the other delights of the Top End.

DARWIN

Disneyland on the Timor? Not hardly. But if the kids are getting out of hand (or you have a thing for fish), direct yourself to **Doctor's Gully** where, at high tide, a swarm of finny devils come in to snatch a free meal from all the tourists. For A$2.50 an adult head (A$1.50 for kids) they give you free bread and you can feed the critters. It's a pleasant enough way to kill an hour, and you'll get to see, among others, milkfish, mullet, toad fish, catfish, and gar. Feeding times vary according to the tide. The feeding grounds are in the Aquascene on the city's waterfront Esplanade.

If you're a World War II buff, or just curious, the city has set aside an old military bunker area at East Point, northeast of the city center, with displays of old tanks and other equipment, plus photographs of the bomb damage. Admission is A$2.

For colonial buildings, check out **Government House,** a house of seven gables built in 1869 (and rebuilt every time a cyclone comes through). The administrator of the Northern Territory, what passes as a governor in the USA, lives in the old relic, built on a point of land on the southeast corner of the Esplanade.

At **Indo Pacific Marine,** next to Cullen Beach near Myilly Point, you'll find large seawater tanks filed with coral animals. Small by some aquarium standards, it is nonetheless a dandy place to check out some of the sea denizens that inhabit Australia's oceans. It's open all week. Admission A$5 for adults.

Not far away is the **Diamond Beach Hotel and Casino,** where you can play 10- or 20-cent slots or go after bigger game. Shoreward of the casino is the city's botanical gardens, started in 1891, but, like Government House, rebuilt every time a big blow comes along. It has 400 species of tropical and sub-tropical plants.

A good display of Aboriginal and Southeast Asian art and history is available at the **Northern Territory Museum of Arts and Natural Sciences** near Bullocky Point north of the gardens. There's a restaurant and art gallery as well. A memorial worth a look honors the completion of the telegraph line (finished Aug. 22, 1872), located in a small area just to the north of Government House. And, because Australians seem fascinated with jails and executions, you can visit the **Fannie Bay Gaol** in the Fannie Bay area of the city, where the National Trust has preserved a 100-year-old prison, compete with gallows. The jail was last occupied in 1979. Free admisison; open daily 10–5; phone 41–0341.

Darwin claims to have at least 40 ethnic groups living in town, including a healthy number of Greeks and newly arrived Southeast Asians. This leads to a good variety of food in the city, and the best time and place to check it out is Thursday nights along Mindil Beach, when local cooks offer their wares—everything from grilled lamb and pita bread to hot satays from Indonesia. Things get hopping around 5 p.m. and the party—very popular with Darwinians—lasts past 9 p.m.

Darwin holds several festivals every year, the most outrageous of which is the **Beer Can Regatta,** a wet affair requiring all entrants to make boats out of beer cans, held every June. There is also the August **Mud Crab Tying Championships,** another blast of frivolity, which sees contestants tying up huge mud crabs with their bare hands. There is also the **City-to-Surf** run in April, a **bougainvillea festival** in May or June and an **international boat race** in July.

Finally, a note about swimming. Darwin's excellent white sand beaches are plagued by deadly box jellyfish (called stingers) between October and May, and swimming on most beaches is prohibited. In one area off Nightcliff, there is supposedly a stinger-free net, but use care.

The Essential Darwin

TRANSPORTATION • Darwin Radio Taxis can be contacted at 81–8777. The main downtown taxi rank is on the Knuckey Street end of the mall. The main city bus terminal is in Harry Chan Avenue near the

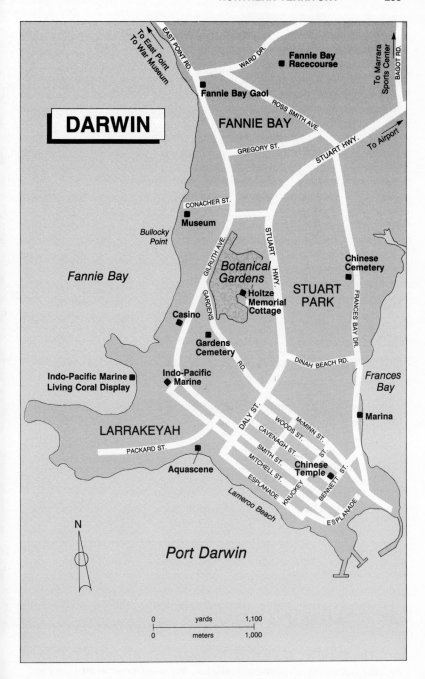

Bennett Street end of the city mall. Buses run throughout the city except on Sundays. Information: 89–6540; there is also airport bus service; tel. 81–2000. For highway conditions (in case you're heading someplace and it's been raining heavily, contact either the AANT (Automobile Association of the Northern Territory), 81 Smith St.; tel. 81–3837; or the NT Emergency Service 84–4455.

Every major rental car company is represented in Darwin. The rates are pretty good, often in the A$25-a-day range (plus insurance and a kilometerage charge). Our favorite used to be Cheapa Rent-A-Car, but the company changed its name to the more distinguished Territory Rent-A-Car. The rates are still good, however, and the company now has agencies all over the territory. In Darwin, the office is at 149 Stuart Highway; tel. (089) 81–8400. If it's an RV you want, we urge you to try Budget. They have been great to work with, including one terrible day when the generator went out on our RV in the middle of the no-where in above-100-degree temperatures; they rescued us, gave us a cold beer, fixed us up with another vehicle and were totally profes-sional. *Information: Budget Campervans; tel. 41–1187.*

Darwin is served internationally by Qantas, Royal Brunei, Garuda, Merpati and Singapore Airlines; internal air is available with Ansett, Australian, Ansett Airlines WA and Ansett NT. There are also com-muter and charter flights all over the territory and to nearby islands.

SHOPPING • Many stores in Darwin are open weekdays from 9 a.m.– 5 p.m., but stay open to 9 p.m. Thursdays; Saturday hours 9 a.m.–1 p.m. The major shopping area in the central city is the mall, which is situated on Smith Street between Bennett and Knuckey streets. If you're looking for Aboriginal art, try the Raintree Aboriginal Art Gallery on Knuckey Street; tel. 81–2732; for Australiana, try It's Australian on the mall, open seven days; tel. 81–5246.

INFORMATION • The Northern Territory Tourist Bureau is on the Smith Street Mall; tel. 81–6611. Hours 9–5 Monday–Friday; 9 a.m.–1 p.m. Saturday. The Conservation Commission has a booth at the same spot, invaluable if you're planning unguided bush treks; tel. 89–4408.

BANKS • Banking hours are Mon.–Thurs. 9:30 a.m.–4 p.m.; Fri. un-til 5 p.m.

ACCOMMODATIONS......................

The Beaufort Hotel • *The Esplanade; tel. 82–9911* • The city's premier hotel, not an architectural gem, but done in pleasant pinks and blues with Japanese and French restaurants, several bars, a pool, spa, health club and business facilities. Rooms, most of which have harbor views, start at A$200 double; suites A$300–1000.

Sheraton Darwin ● *32 Mitchell St.; tel. 82–0000* ● Located downtown near the mall, with Flinders and Mitchell's restaurants, both licensed. Pool, spa. Doubles A$195; suites A$400–1000.

Diamond Beach Hotel/Casino ● *Gilruth Ave., Mindil Beach; tel. 46–2666* ● Next to tennis courts and golf course, across from botanic gardens. The large white building, a hallmark of the city, contains a casino with disco Friday–Saturday. Hotel has a lounge, recreation room, sauna, pool, spa, handicapped facilities and some cooking facilities. Doubles A$180; suites A$220. The casino is open from midday to around 3 a.m.; dress code (no jeans, no thongs, no T-shirts).

Darwin Travel Lodge ● *122 Esplanade; tel. 81–5388* ● Close to shopping and the beaches. Licensed restaurant, pool, barbecue area, good city views from one of the few tall buildings that survived Tracy. Doubles A$139; suites A$190.

Atrium Hotel Darwin ● *Corner of Peel and the Esplanade; tel. 41–0755* ● One of the newest in town, with a seven-story atrium. Suites have kitchens. Mini-bars, licensed restaurant, pool, barbecue area, laundry, garden pool, spa, parking. Doubles $A150; suites from A$165.

Four Seasons Darwin ● *Dashwood Crescent; tel. 81–8200* ● Located about a mile from downtown near Mindil Beach, the casino and the botanic gardens. Older hotel, renovated. Pool, licensed restaurant, barbecue area, laundry. Doubles A$115; suites from A$120–140.

Poinciana Inn ● *Corner McLachlan and Mitchell sts.; tel. 81–8111* ● Motel-style units, with doubles and family rooms. Licensed restaurant, pool, tour desk, rental cars, parking. Doubles A$90.

Darwin Hotel ● *10 Herbert St.; tel. 81–9211* ● Motel-style near the Esplanade. Licensed restaurant, pool, laundry. Doubles A$90.

Top End Frontier ● *Corner Daly Street and the Esplanade; tel. 81–6511* ● Disco Wednesday–Saturday; pool, laundry, kitchens, licensed restaurant. Doubles A$105.

Boulevarde ● *38 Gardens Rd.; tel. 81–1544* ● In the botanic garden-casino area. Has apartments or motel units. Licensed restaurant, indoor/outdoor bar, laundry, pool, barbecue area, tennis courts. Motel units A$80 double.

Crest Townhouses • *88 Wood St.; tel. 81–1922* • Two-bedroom, split-level apartments downtown. Barbecue area, laundry, dishwashers, pool. Good place if you plan to stay a while. Doubles A$80–100. You can book the townhouses and the Boulevarde, as well as the Transit Centre hostel through a toll-free number, (008) 89–1128; or information at the Peninsular Apartments, tel. 81–1922.

Darwin City YHA • *69A Mitchell St.; tel. 81–3995* • Open all day, pool, all-twin rooms. A$14 per person members; A$20 non-members.

Tops Transit Centre Hostel • *69 Mitchell St.; tel.81–9733* • Located at the bus depot; some rooms air conditioned, some with fans. TV lounge, kitchen, laundry, barbecue area, pool, sauna, game room, luggage storage, parking; more than 200 rooms, some with private baths. A$15–30 single; A$30–40 double.

KOA and Malak Caravan Park • *McMillan's Road south of town; tel. 27–2651.* • Next to shopping plaza and a golf course. All 327 sites are paved; laundry, store, barbecue area. A$15 per person.

RESTAURANTS....................................

The Beagle • *In the Northern Territory Museum of Arts and Sciences at Fannie Bay; tel. 81–7791* • Eighteenth century atmosphere, named after Charles Darwin's ship which called here in the 1830s. If you like sunset views with your food, here's the spot. Specializes in seafood, also popular smorgasbord lunches. Lunch from noon Monday–Friday and Sunday; dinner from 6:30 Monday–Saturday. Reservations. Moderate to expensive.

Peppi's • *84 Mitchell St.; tel. 81–3762* • Opposite the Beaufort Hotel, specializing in international cuisine. Special business lunches (three courses, A$20), good wine list. Lunch from noon Monday–Friday; dinner from 6:30 p.m. seven nights. Moderate.

Orchid Room • *First floor at the casino; tel. 46–2709* • Cantonese cuisine, with ala carte or buffet. Seafood a speciality. Has won several dining awards. Lunch noon–2:20 Monday–Friday; dinner 6:30–11 p.m. seven nights. Moderate.

Rafferty's • *Beaufort Centre, Mitchell Street; tel.41–2555* • Territory specials—buffalo, seafood, grain-fed beef; home-made desserts, large selection of wine and beers. Casual family-style dining. Italian night Saturday and Sunday from 10 p.m.–late. Dinner from 6:30 p.m. seven nights.

Jessie's Family Bistro • *Casaurina Tavern, Trower Rd., Casaurina (south of town); tel. 27–9155* • Award-winning steak house; also serves seafood. Also has a blackboard menu. Lunch Monday–Friday; dinner from 6 p.m. seven days.

Arabian Nights • *41 Cavenagh St.; tel. 81–9322* • BYO. Darwin's original Lebanese restaurant—the usual Near Eastern fare, complete with Arab music in the background and camels on the window. Try the warra da walle (ground beef and rice with spices wrapped in grape leaves) or shurab (soup of lentils and spinach, peppers and nutmeg with a touch of lemon). Belly dancing some nights. Take-aways, also vegetarian dishes. Lunch 11 a.m.–2:30 p.m.; dinner 6–11:30 p.m. seven days.

Victoria Hotel • *Smith Street Mall; tel. 81–4011* • More lives than a cat, this old wreck was built in 1890, and was damaged in cyclones in 1897, 1937 and 1974 and was damned near burned to the ground by rioting soldiers in 1942. Rebuilt after Tracy, the Vic is probably the closest Darwin has to an authentic old-style Aussie pub. Buffalo burgers are a luncheon special; basic pub and family food. Open from midday–2 a.m. Monday–Saturday.

Finally, for those who want to do the Top End experience in real style, there is the Seven Spirit Bay resort on the Cobourg Peninsula in Arnhem Land. The lodge has 24 cottages with louvers and screens to keep the mozzies out. Each cottage has a private garden and private bathroom. They come with two double beds, ceiling fans, hair dryers and bathrobes. The lounge is air conditioned, with a restaurant and bar, outdoor decks overlooking the pool. The resort area is near the ocean, and the emphasis is on getting close to the remoteness of the area. There are naturalist-led bush walks, and the resort has its own photo lab to process film you shoot on treks. There are boats, bikes, four-wheel-drive vehicles. Note: no ocean swimming: crocs, sharks, stonefish, etc. This is definitely off the path, and there has been some grumbling about it having been built in the area at all. Just getting there is half the sport: an air charter from Darwin (about A$200 round trip), then a one-hour ride in a catamaran and a bumpy ride on a jeep. The resort will soon have a small airstrip for light aircraft flights from Darwin. Doubles are about A$550, meals and activities included. Information: Seven Spirit Bay, P.O. Box 4721, Darwin 0801; tel. (89) 79–0277.

Toward Kakadu

The main route to **Kakadu National Park** is the Arnhem Highway, which runs for about 120 miles, ending at the park's boundary at East Jabiru. You catch the Arnhem by taking the Stuart south of Darwin about 20 miles.

About 10 kilometers south of town on the Stuart Highway you'll come to the Big Pink Buffalo, which houses a souvenir shop and, more importantly, a Northern Territory information office that's open seven days. The buff is really ugly, the folks inside are friendly and can book tours. Along the way to the park on the good pavement of the Arnhem road, you come to one of the friendlier spots in the Territory, the **Humpty-Doo Hotel.** The pub comes with a bull that drinks beer, barramundi and buffalo meals, and a very popular Sunday barbecue. *Information: 88–1372.* A few miles on past the Humpty-Doo is the turnoff to **Fogg Dam,** a waterfowl nesting area. Thirty miles from the Stuart turnoff, you come to the **Bark Hut Inn,** which has rooms, meals, gasoline, and an RV park. *Information: 76–0185.* As you drive between the two pubs, you'll come alongside some enormous termite nests, which provide a dandy photo op.

KAKADU ·································

If you've seen the first Crocodile Dundee movie, you've seen a lot of Kakadu National Park. The park, about 20,000 square kilometers in area, is a mixed bag of ecosystems and land forms, composed chiefly of flood plains highlighted by the dramatic cliff edges of the vast Arnhem Land escarpment, which runs for about 250 miles through the Territory. Its wetland, billabongs, streams, gorges, grassland, and eucalypt forests are home to a huge variety of animals: 250 species of birds, 1000 different plants, 75 reptiles, 50 mammals, 25 frogs, and 55 fish, plus 16 different vegetation zones. Its popularity is increasing by the minute: in 1980, about 40,000 visitors came through, but by the end of the decade, the number was in excess of 200,000 a year.

The park is named after the traditional owners of the land, the Gagudju, who leased the park area to the federal parks and wildlife service in 1978. Tribe members still have a voice in the park operation, and a number of them are park rangers. It became a national park in 1979 and is on the World Heritage list. The rocks in the park are very old, dating in some cases back two billion years. Indeed, a full third of the park area is rock, but the annual monsoon rainfall allows wild orchids and other exotic plants to flourish. The whole area is alive with flowering plants between December and March.

The park very nearly never came to be. When Frank Woerle, the park's first ranger, arrived in 1970, he found the area overrun by water buffalo. In the 1830s, a herd of 150 of the voracious critters were introduced into the area; by the time Frank and his wife arrived, there were more than a quarter of a million, and the delicate environment of the Kakadu area was in deep trouble. Water buffalo remain a problem in the Territory even today, as you will note by seeing the number of dead buffs on the sides of the Stuart Highway, the victim of trucks. He was able to cull out the herd at Kakadu and begin the slow task of bringing the park to the condition it enjoys today.

Here, we think it prudent to discuss the mightiest of Kakadu's inhabitants: crocodiles. Around the park, and on the roads leading to it, you will see signs warning people not to swim because of crocodiles. This is not a publicity stunt based on Paul Hogan's movie—it's deadly serious. Both species of Australian crocodiles are present in the park: the estuarine, or saltwater variety (Crocodylus porosus, called "salties"), and the freshwater species, (Crocodylus johnstoni or "freshies.") The saltwater species grows to huge lengths and is very dangerous. Common throughout the park, these crocodiles live mostly in tidal rivers, billabongs on the floodplains, and in coastal waters. But they are also found in freshwater streams, so the basic rule is, don't swim. It's not even safe to get close to the water in some places, because the big reptiles are not averse to coming ashore to grab a meal, and they can move incredibly fast. The freshwater variety, not as large or as hungry, is generally regarded as safe to be around, but why take a chance on being the first exception to the rule? The various tours around Kakadu provide plenty of chances to see the crocs in safety, so try to avoid meeting them on your own.

The park has provision for campers, RVers, or folks who want to stay in top-grade hotels. You can tour by yourself or go with one of the many excellent adventure tour groups offering Kakadu trips. From June through October, the park ranger staff offers a number of free guided tours and evening programs. The tours include Aboriginal painting sites, wetlands hikes, and forest walks.

The **park information center** is located near Jabiru at the intersection of the Arnhem Highway and the road that cuts off to Yellow Water. In addition to park information, the center shows an excellent slide and sound show with a general overview of the park, well worth a look. *Information on the park is available from the National Parks and Wildlife Service, P.O. Box 1260, Darwin 5794; tel. 81–5299; or from the park headquarters, P.O. Box 71, Jabiru 5796, tel. 79–2101.*

There are more than a dozen designated **camping areas** in the park, which are free and range from the very primitive to sites with showers and flush toilets. Two campgrounds, owned by **Kakadu Holiday Vil-**

lage and **Cooinda Four Seasons,** have powered sites. Bush camping is allowed, but requires a permit from the park ranger's office. Many of the camp areas are closed during the Wet.

Accommodations in the park are available at four facilities. There is the 48-room **Four Seasons Cooinda Hotel,** centrally located at Yellow Water, with rooms going for about A$150 double. *Information: 79–0145.* Second is the **Kakadu Holiday Village,** on the Arnhem Highway about 25 miles west of the park headquarters, with rooms for about A$130 double during the May–Oct. season. *Information: 79–0166.* Finally, there is the new **Four Seasons Kakadu,** a 110-room hotel in Jabiru built in the shape of a crocodile, with doubles at $A140 to A$170. *Information: 79–2800* The Cooinda Hotel and the Four Seasons Kakadu are owned by the Gagudju people.

Recently opened is the Kakadu Frontier Lodge and Caravan park, a big complex on the South Alligator River near the park headquarters. In addition to the 100 serviced RV sites, the facility has a pool, general store, barbecues, laundry and a tour desk. The lodge is designed for families and backpackers. The units have four bunks to a room, which go for A$70; or if you're sharing, A$20 a person. The powered RV sites are A$20 for two persons; the tent sites are A$7 per person. Linen can be hired. *Information: 79-2422.*

In addition, there is a **youth hostel** on the Ubirr road just past the Border Store at the northeast edge of the park. Rates are about A$8 per person. *Reservations and information: 84–3902.* It's subject to closure during the rainy season.

The small village of Jabiru has food, gasoline, supplies, and a shopping center. Gasoline and water is also available at the **Kakadu Holiday Village** and the **Border Store.**

High on your list of things to do at Kakadu must be a visit to the **Aboriginal art sites** that are open to the public. There are at least 120 artwork locations in the park, some of which are classed as sacred sites. As part of the Aboriginal land rights legislation in 1976, a law was passed creating the Aboriginal Sacred Sites Protection Authority, which is empowered to keep a record of such sites around the country and to handle Aboriginal claims about sacred tribal places. Disturbing sites under protection of the authority can result in heavy fines, as you will see on signs here and there in Kakadu. *For information about the sites, contact the Aboriginal Sacred Sites Protection Authority, P.O. Box 1890, Darwin 5794; tel. 81–4700.*

The **artwork** you see at Kakadu represents three distinct areas in Top End Aboriginal history. First, there was **pre-estuarine,** a period that lasted until the sea level rose to flood the present-day tidal area of the park, which took place about 7000 to 8000 years ago. One famous painting, the yam figure at Nourlangie Rock, is believed to be about 25,000 years old. The second period, or **estuarine era,** lasted from the sea level rise until the arrival of European settlers. From this era is the famous painting of a thylacine—the Tasmanian wolf—believed to have become extinct on the Australian mainland about 4000 years ago. Some of Australia's most famous Aboriginal artworks—the so-called X-ray paintings—were created during this era. The unique style of art shows the inner organs and bones of animals and is quite striking. The most common animal in the paintings is a barramundi. The third era is called the **contact period,** because artwork reflects the results of association with the white colonists. Here you see paintings showing rifles and steel axes.

The two main visitor sites at Kakadu are at Nourlangie Rock and Ubirr. Near **Nourlangie** are the so-called **Blue Paintings,** the only ones in the park in that color—the ancient Aboriginals had no blue pigments. These paintings are modern, completed in 1964 using laundry bluing. The rock itself is on the edge of the escarpment and has a great view of the floodplains. The area might be closed soon, however, because the local Aboriginals say the spirits of the dead in the area are restless and angry, and are not leaving as they should. (Even on parklands leased to the government, sites may be closed down if the owners feel things are not right with the spirit world.)

Ubirr is the most popular and accessible site, with part of the trail able to accommodate wheelchairs. Among the paintings on view are the X-rays, the thylacine, and the early monochromes done in red ochre. The trail past the major galleries is about a kilometer long. At the end is a moderately steep path to the top of Obiri Rock for another great view of the escarpment.

The other must in the park is to take a **water trip** to check out the birds and beauties of the wetlands—and see a few crocodiles in the process. We recommend the two-hour **Yellow Water boat cruise** at A$25 per person. Among the beasties on view is the jabiru, also known as the black-necked stork, which is the Northern Territory symbol. The tours can be booked at the Four Seasons Cooinda. There are 6 trips a day, starting at 6:45 a.m. From January–March during the floods, there's a 3½-hour wetlands tour. Probably the best of the year if you're there in the rainy season. Another boat trip takes visitors on a five-hour **tour of the South Alligator River** aboard the *Kakadu Princess,* complete with a barbecue of buffalo or barramundi. The charge is about A$50 per person; bookings at Kakadu Holiday Village.

There are also some excellent **day trips,** the best of which is the 35-mile trek to **Jim Jim Falls,** which tumbles 700 feet down the edge of the escarpment, truly awesome when the streams are running high. The road to the falls is strictly four-wheel drive. Tours can be booked either in Darwin or at the hotels in the park.

If you're **driving** yourself—even in a regular car—and are heading south on your stay, try taking the Kakadu Highway out of the park. It's in the process of being paved, but long stretches are still dirt and you might have to ford a couple of streams along the way—don't try it between November and March without checking with the park rangers. There's a new **gasoline station** at the Mary River crossing, and the road is paved at least 50 kilometers in from Pine Creek, where it meets the Stuart Highway. We made it with a small RV, no worries.

There are scads of Kakadu **tours** available, everything from a one-day jaunt to canoe trips or tent camping expeditions. A couple of companies you might check are **Dial-A-Safari** and **Bill King's Australian Experience.** Dial-A-Safari has a one-day tour, which includes visits to the rock paintings and a boat trip, for about A$100 including lunch and free hotel pickup in Darwin. The company's two-day trip adds a stay at Cooinda and some back roads; price about A$340 per person. Bill King offers a bunch of four-wheel drive treks around the park, anything from three to nine days, staying either in tents or in one of the park hotels. The seven-day trip, for example, includes Jim Jim Falls, Yellow Water, and a trip down to Katherine for a boat trip through Katherine Gorge. Cost is about A$1500 per person, including lunches and accommodations. *Information on both companies—as well as others—is available from ATS/Sprint, 1101 E. Broadway, Glendale, Calif. 91205; tel. (800) 232–2121 California, (800) 423–2880 USA.*

Another company, this one of the largest, is Australian Kakadu Tours, which has a wide variety of Kakadu experiences, from one-day trips from Darwin to 10-day treks that do Kakadu, Melville Island and the Katherine area. The one-days run around A$90, and include the Yellow Waters cruise and other Kakadu highlights; the 10-day Melville Island excursion goes for about A$1850, which includes airfare and accommodations. You can get information about the company and its programs by contacting one of these North American companies: Newman's (800) 421-3326; Austravel Inc. in New York, (212) 972-6880, or Goway Travel Toronto (416) 322-1034; or Goway Travel Vancouver (604) 687-4004. In Australia, the tours can be booked through Northern Territory tourist bureaus.

Finally, if you're going to do Kakadu in a camper, in our opinion the only way to fly, there are several **RV outlets** in Darwin and Alice Springs. You can rent everything from a VW pop-top to a rig able to handle six adults. Pop-tops go for around A$80 a day plus insurance and taxes; the big rigs go for around A$200 a day plus insurance and tax. Note that insurance does not cover you on unpaved roads unless you get prior approval from the company. We suggest either **Koala Campers** or **Budget Campervans.** Koala has an office in Darwin at 90 Mitchell St., Darwin 5750, tel. 41–0877; or in Alice at the Melanka Lodge, 94 Todd St., Alice Springs 5750; 52–2233. **Budget's** office in Darwin is at 1427 Stuart Highway, Winnellie 5789, tel. 84–4575; in the Alice, 64 Hartley St., Alice Springs 5750, tel. 52–7644. A third choice is **Trans Australia Caravan Hire** in Darwin at 3 Streeton St., Parap, tel. 81–3955. Campers are very popular in the Territory, so you're advised to book them in advance from North America through a travel agent or the NT tourism offices.

DOWN THE STUART ....

As you drive down the Stuart, gathering up red dust in every pore and counting the number of kangaroos and water buffalos left dead in the wake of lumbering road trains, the last thing you'd ever expect to encounter is a spectacular river gorge able to handle large tour boats. But there it is, **Katherine Gorge,** a miniature Grand Canyon and one of the Territory's more photogenic spots.

The city of **Katherine** is about 200 miles south of Darwin, in what is called the "Land of the Never-Never," so named because once you live here, you'll never, never leave it. But the name is more often associated with *We of the Never-Never,* a book written by a pioneer woman named Mrs. Aeneas Gunn who set up life on a station near Mataranka, south of Katherine, in 1902. It's a great book for capturing the spirit of the white Australians who settled the desolate lands of the Territory. Katherine, named after the daughter of one of the men who financed Stuart's expedition, is the third largest city in the Territory, with about 7000 population. The region languished for many years, but the enlargement of a Royal Australian Air Force base near the city, plus the general increase in Territory tourism, has created a mini-boom that will probably double Katherine's population by the turn of the century.

The **gorge** is actually a series of gorges, cut over a period of 25 million years by the Katherine River, which starts in Arnhem Land, flows south to Katherine, then joins the Daly River, which turns northwest and empties into the Timor Sea southwest of Darwin. The whole gorge area is now a large **national park,** situated 20 miles north of town on a paved highway (hang a left at the police station in downtown Katherine.) The gorges, 13 in all, sprawl along a ten-kilometer system and in some spots are more than 200 feet deep. In places, high on the canyon walls, are large Aboriginal paintings, some dating back 10,000 years. Most visitors take a boat trip into the gorges, which start from a landing located near the RV campground in the park. (It was next to the camp headquarters where we watched a guy give his pet emu a bath, a truly remarkable sight. The bird ate it up.)

The **boat tours,** which are booked at the campground, are for two hours, a half day, or a full day. The trip is a ride-and-walk arrangement because the gorges are entered through a series of waterfalls, exposed down to bare rocks during the dry season. The two-hour trip goes to the first two gorges; the longer ones will go back to the seventh or eighth gorges. The cost of the two-hour trip is A$15 per person. In the Wet, the water level in the gorge system can rise 40 feet. If you're lucky on your trip, you might spot freshwater crocodiles, who share the river with 40 species of fish. *River trip information: 72–1253.* The gorge area is also a favorite bushwalking area, with more than 60 miles of trails. Canoeing is also popular, although there is a lot of portaging involved. If you're interested, contact **Kookaburra Canoe Hire** at the park near the boat dock; a full day's rental starts at A$20. *Information: Greg Wood, P.O. Box 2068, Katherine 5780; tel. 72–3604 or 72–3301.*

Information on the park is available from Katherine Gorge National Park, Katherine 5780, tel. 72–1886, or from the Conservation Commission of the Northern Territory, Katherine Terrace, Katherine 5780, tel. 72–1799.

Among **accommodations** available in Katherine are the **Katherine Hotel-Motel,** with bar, restaurant, and pool. *Information 72–1622;* the very nice **Paraway Motel,** also with bar, restaurant, and pool, *information 72–2644;* and the **Katherine Frontier Motor Inn,** outside of town with pool, tennis courts, restaurant and bar, *information 72–1744.* Rates for all three are in the A$75–A$90 double range, depending on season. For information about the city, including other lodging and food, contact the Community Information Centre, First Floor, TIO Building, Katherine Terrace, tel. 72–3904. **Note:** there's a **coin laundry** in Katherine on Kintore Street.

Sixty miles down the pike from Katherine, put there because God took pity on the heat-stroke victims passing by, is **Mataranka Homestead,** where you will find one of the truly fine watering holes on the continent, the **Mataranka thermal pool.** The pool, a Territory park, is located behind a privately owned caravan park, and is always a pleasant 93°, with a daily flow of five million gallons. Words fail us remembering the glorious feeling of dipping bodies into the pool after a rugged day wandering around in the heat. (If you go, get on the down-flow side of the footbridge and sit in one of the deep pools. It almost beats sex.) **Accommodations at Mataranka** include a motel, caravan park, and campgrounds at the **Mataranka Homestead Tourist Park,** with licensed bar and cafe, and a youth hostel (right next to the thermal pool.) Most nights, there is a live country-western music show. *Information: 75–4544.* There is also the Territory Manor motel, which also has RV and tent sites. *Information: 75–4516.* Next to the campground is a replica of the Gunn family house, complete with verandah and some furniture. Then, about seven kilometers south of Mataranka is a turnoff that goes another seven kilometers to the graveyard where Jeannie Gunn and her husband are buried at the Never-Never homestead.

About 100 miles south of Mataranka is an historic wide spot in the road called **Daly Waters,** which was founded by Stuart on his successful trip north, and has served over the years as a drover station, pony express stop, telegraph station, and World War II base. It's also the home of the self-proclaimed **Historic Daly Waters Pub,** which features, among other things, a Taffy Special—don't ask Taffy, the barkeep, what's in it; just make sure you have a designated driver. The pub has good lunches for a buck and a night barbecue for A$8.50. There is a moldy but serviceable motel for A$30 a night double. There's also a gasoline station.

From Daly Waters south, the country gets drier and drier, the vistas more and more bleak. This is the north end of the Red Centre, and humans are few and far apart. Between Daly Waters and Tennant Creek, 250 miles away, there are two villages, **Elliott** and **Renner Springs,** which have gasoline and motels. About ten miles north of Tennant Creek is **Three Ways,** the junction of the Barkly Highway that runs east to Mount Isa in Queensland.

This is the land where many of the Big Myths of Australia were born: tiny towns, wild and woolly one-horse pubs, huge cattle ranches, and hopeful prospectors. The area around is known as the **Barkly Tablelands,** and is desert in climate (freezing at night in the winter, 110° in the shade in the summer.) **Tennant Creek** (about 4000 population) is the largest town between Katherine and Alice Springs, and word has it the smallest settlement is **Rabbit Flat,** population two, out in the Tanami Desert near the Western Australia border.

Myth? Well, legend has it that Tennant Creek was founded by the drivers of a beer wagon that broke down, who then decided to stay put and drink up all their cargo. Tennant Creek is a place to stop only if you have to, being basically a sleepy village. But it does have three motels (check the **Eldorado,** named after a nearby gold mine) and an RV park. If you want to call the whole thing off and go home, Tennant Creek does have an **airport,** with service by **Ansett NT** to Darwin and Alice Springs. It's also a stop for bus companies.

Between Tennant Creek and Alice Springs, distances are calculated, not in kilometers, but in beer stops. At **Wauchope,** population about ten, there is the colorful **Wauchope Hotel,** which, according to usually reliable sources, has an annual cricket match, taking on the rest of the world—but also gasoline and lodgings. Just north of town is a strange rock formation called the **Devil's Marbles,** a bunch of huge granite boulders strewn about, worth a photo or two. Next along comes **Barrow Creek,** with another great Outback pit stop, the wide-verandahed **Barrow Creek Pub.** (Population, around ten; gasoline and lodging available.) **Ti Tri,** a bit farther on, also has gas and rooms.

ALICE SPRINGS

So, after 700 miles of noble trek, you have now arrived in Alice Springs, where, as you will immediately discover, there ain't no town like Alice. Alice Springs, because of Neville Shute's book (and a certain amount of hot air from the local tourism people), has an international reputation as the original wild and colorful Outback town, full of hard-drinking drovers, a pub every 10 feet, sand and bulldust and fallen women, camels in the streets, and cattle in the bathrooms. Tain't so, folks. The Alice looks like just what it is: a rapidly growing, quite successful commercial center, the gateway to both Kakadu National Park and Ayers Rock, a place with libraries, churches, supermarkets, nice hotels, and even a car wash. There are bits and snatches of the old Alice here and there, but if you came here hoping to see raw Australia at its best, you're about 60 years too late. As the 1980s ended, the city dads took a look around and counted more than 300,000 tourists a year going through town—and not a stampede or lynching to be seen.

The Alice started life at a small springs about three kilometers north of the present town, where a repeater station for the overland telegraph station was built in 1871. The waterhole was discovered by William Mills, one of the surveyors pushing the telegraph line north to Darwin from Adelaide. But the village that grew up near the waterhole in this century (at first named Stuart) was mostly isolated until the late 1920s, when a rail link finally arrived from Adelaide. The train was called "the Ghan" to honor the Afghan cameleers who had been the main source of supplies and transportation for years. Camels were first introduced into Australia in the 1830s; the Burke and Wills expedition, for example, relied heavily on the beasts to carry supplies—not that it helped. Camels played a big role in many early pioneering efforts, including hauling supplies to gold fields all over the country as well as working on railroads.

Camels are still a big part of the myths about Alice Springs. The Australians say they have the only wild herds of dromedary (one-humped) camels left in the world, and the folks around the Alice say half of all the wild camels in Australia are in the Territory. As a matter of fact, Australia is now exporting camels back to places in the Near East where the beasties have become almost extinct. One of the groups most interested in the export business is the Aboriginal Central Lands Council. And, just so the local camels won't feel lonely, there is even an outfit

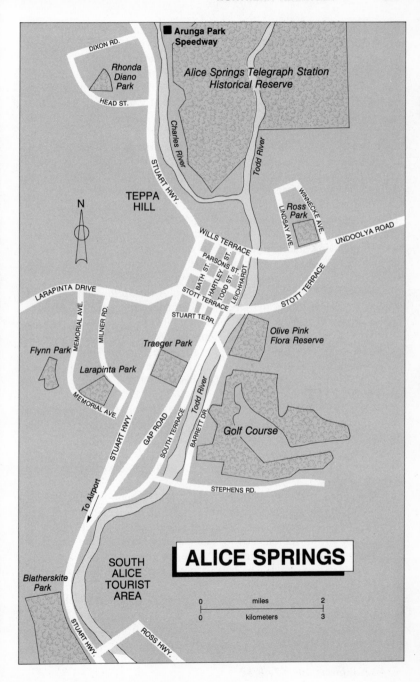

in Alice Springs growing date palms, and the Territory is thinking about expanding the industry. But although camel activities are a major tourist attraction around Alice Springs, the Territory has not cornered the market on dromedary tourism. There are camel tour operators in at least three other Australian states, all eager to get you humping. In Alice Springs every year in May, there is the **Camel Cup,** a hell-for-leather race right out of Lawrence of Arabia. If all these dates palms and camels make things around town sound like you're in East Fez, Morocco, not to worry. Alice Springs is about as Australian as it gets.

The heart of Alice Springs is the **Todd River,** a usually dry watercourse that fronts the downtown area. But in March 1988, a huge storm dumped so much water, the Todd overflowed its banks and flooded the city. The sandy riverbed is famous as the site of the annual **Henley-on-Todd Regatta,** where every October, bottomless boats propelled by runners gallop down the Todd for money and glory. Apparently, nobody was paying attention to the flood waters, because two of the city's premier hotels are built—and are being expanded—on the Todd River floodplain south of the business district.

One of the things to take a look at in Alice Springs is the **Royal Flying Doctor Service,** the legendary outfit that was begun to provide free emergency medical care to folks in trouble in the Outback. During the day, the service is used as a telephone system, patching in calls all over the area. Two hours a day are set aside for emergency medical communications. Tours of the base are available every half hour during the day for A$1.50 per person. The base is located at the corner of Stuart Terrace and Hartley Street.

That other great Outback invention—the **School of the Air**—is also open for inspections. The school, which has taught generations of Outback kids via shortwave classes, is located on Head Street, west of Stuart Highway near the Telegraph Road turnoff. The school is open for visits 1:30 p.m.–3:30 p.m. Mon.–Fri.; closed between Dec. 9 and Feb. 1. *Information: 52–2122.*

To get to Alice Springs—the real Alice Springs—you head back up the Stuart Highway at the north edge of town to Telegraph Road and drive east to the springs and restored repeater station and its outbuildings. Entry to the station, now a national park, is free. The area near the springs is great for picnics, and there are emu, wallabies, and peacocks wandering around. The park is open 8 a.m.–9 p.m. Oct.–Apr., and 10 a.m.–6 p.m. May–Sept.

South of town near the Ross Road turnoff to the MacDonnell Ranges is the **Pitchi Richi Sanctuary,** a large outdoor museum and botanical garden that displays the wonderful sculptures of Aboriginals by Victorian artist William Rickets (whose works are also on display near Melbourne.) Admission to the park, which is open 9 a.m.–7 p.m. all week, is A$2. *Information: 52–1931.*

If you are at all interested in **Aboriginal art,** Alice Springs is one of the best places in Australia to pick some up, particularly paintings. The area has a long tradition of art. One of Australia's most famous artists, the Aboriginal Albert Namatjira, lived at the Hermannsburg Mission about 90 miles west of Alice Springs. He painted the Outback in European-style watercolors, and his works sold all over the country. The Alice is now a magnet for Aboriginal artists living throughout the Red Centre, who create works in traditional tribal style. The Australian government has established an art gallery in the Alice where Aboriginal artworks are sold, and it's not unusual to meet one of the artists wandering in to drop off a work or pick up a commission. The **Aboriginal Art Gallery,** located at 88 Todd St., is open 9:30 a.m.–6 p.m. Mon.–Fri. and 9 a.m.–2 p.m. Sat. *Information is available by writing the gallery at 88 Todd St., Alice Springs 5750; tel. 52–3408.*

While most of the stock is paintings, there is also a selection of jewelry, purses, bags, and carvings done in mulga wood. One of the artists to look for is named (honest) George Bush, a member of the Walpiru tribe. He is said to be the first man to take tribal sand paintings, created on the ground for ceremonial use much like the Navajo sand paintings of the Southwestern United States, and reproduce them on canvas. Bush (tribal name Tjanpala) has works on display in the National gallery in Melbourne. His paintings and others range in price from about A$100 and up, depending on size.

If you're really interested in a camel trek, go to the **Frontier Camel Farm** on Ross Highway about five kilometers east of the Stuart Highway intersection. There's a camel ride for all tastes, from a five-minute jaunt around a corral to full-day safari. Also at the farm is **Graeme Gow's Reptile World,** where for A$5 a head (which includes a camel ride) you can eyeball some of Australia's deadliest snakes. The admission charge also lets you use the farm's barbecue and picnic area.

By far the most popular camel excursions are the rides to **Chateau Hornsby,** the home of Australia's most unlikely winery. A full-day trek to the winery, which goes down the dry Todd River bed, is A$50, including a barbecue lunch and a wine tasting. The price includes a gander at the snakes, plus pickup at your hotel or RV camp. Also for A$50 is a dinner trip to the winery, with wine tasting and a dinner of Territory buffalo or fish. It also includes pickup at your hotel. Overnight treks in the area are also available. *Bookings and information; Frontier Tours Pty. Ltd., P.O. Box 2836, Alice Springs 5750; tel. 53–0444.*

You can avoid the camels and still do the winery, of course. Chateau Hornsby, owned by Dennis and Miranda Hornsby, is reached by taking the Stuart Highway south of town toward the airport, then turning east on Colonel Rose Drive. About five kilometers along Rose Road, turn left on Petrick Road to the winery. The place is open air and sunny, and schedules lunches and dinners on request. The Hornsbys produce shiraz, moselle, and riesling-semillon wines. A couple of bottles of shiraz (they're really not bad) will run you around A$20. *Information Chateau Hornsby, Petrick Rd., P.O. Box 107, Alice Springs 5750; tel. 52–5771.*

If you want to get into the camel thing a lot more intensively, there are a number of tour operators around the Territory who offer week or longer treks. Among these are **Alice Springs Camel Outback Safari,** P.O. Box 3244, Alice Springs 5750, tel. 56–0925; **Central Australian Camel Treks,** P.O. Box 84, Alice Springs 5750, tel. 52–7611; **Camel-Time Walking,** P.O. Box 2764, Alice Springs 5751, tel. 52–8466. These tours normally can be booked through Bill King's Australian Experience company, which in turn is booked through ATS/Sprint, (800) 423–2880 USA; (800) 232–2121 California. For these long trips, including meals, camping equipment, guides—and of course, the camel—you can expect a price of around A$100 a day per person, twin share.

The Essential Alice Springs

INFORMATION • The **Alice Springs Regional Tourist Association** is located in the old Hartley Street school on Hartley Street downtown next to the post office behind the Todd Mall. *Information: P.O. Box 2227, Alice Springs 5750; tel. 52–5199 or 52–5362.*

The Northern Territory Tourist Commission offices are on the Todd Mall in downtown Alice. *Information: Ford Plaza Building, Todd Mall, Alice Springs 5750; tel. (089) 52–1299. It's open weekends.*

GETTING AROUND • **Taxis**—Alice Springs Taxis, tel. 52–1877; 24 hours, seven days.

Airport shuttle—Alice Springs Airport Shuttle Service, 113 Todd St., tel. 53–1011 or 53–0310; pickup at hotels, motels, and caravan parks, about A$7 per person, reservations required. The airport, by the way, is too small for the number of flights going in and out, and there's often a mob scene, so be prepared.

ACCOMMODATIONS......................

Sheraton Alice Springs • *Barrett Dr., tel. 52–8000* • On the Todd River about 1.5 miles from downtown. In addition to an 18-hole golf course, the hotel has tennis, a pool, several bars, coffee shop and two restaurants; handicapped facilities, non-smoking rooms. Doubles from A$195–210; suites from A$350.

Lasseters Casino • *93 Barrett Dr.; tel. 52–5066* • Gambling from midday to early in the morning; the disco runs from 11 p.m. Sunday–

Wednesday; from 9 p.m. Thursday–Saturday. Pool, restaurants. Doubles about A$150; suites from A$200.

Red Centre Resort • *North Stuart Highway, about four kilometers from town; tel. 52–8955* • About a third of the rooms have kitchens; also have four-person backpacker units and camping facilities. Pool, spa, restaurant/bar, store, laundry, photo service, courtesy van. Cook-your-own meat in the barbecue area; Mexican cantina, casual open fire with good margueritas. Doubles A$100–115; backpacker units A$20 per person.

Oasis Frontier Resort • *10 Gap Rd.; tel. 52–1444* • Near downtown with restaurant/bar, pool, sauna, spa, squash courts. Barbecue dinners several times a week. Doubles A$80–90. A good bet.

Alice Springs Pacific Resort • *34 Stott Terr.; tel. 52–6699* • On the banks of the Todd River downtown. Pool, laundry, recreation room, mini-bars, licensed restaurant. Doubles from A$110.

Four Seasons Alice Springs • *Stephens Road; 52–6100* • Opposite the casino. Pool, waterfall spa, tennis courts, barbecue, licensed restaurant, handicapped facilities. Doubles A$120.

Elkira Motel • *65 Bath St.; tel. 52–1222* • A good restaurant, the Terrace, licensed French/Australian (moderate); bar, pool, barbecue, laundry, handicapped access. Doubles A$80.

Desert Palms Resort • *Barrett Dr.; tel. 52–5977* • Near the casino and golf course. Kitchenettes, laundry, pool, barbecue, tennis. Doubles A$75.

Alice Tourist Apartments • *Corner of Gap Rd. and Gnoilya St.; tel. 52–2788* • One- and two-bedroom units with kitchens. Pool, barbecue, laundry, parking. Doubles A$60–100.

The Swagman's Rest • *67 Gap Rd.; tel. 53–1333* • Self-contained units with kitchens. Pool, barbecue, laundry, handicapped facilities. Doubles A$70.

Melanka Lodge • *94 Todd St.; tel. 52-2233* • Pool, restaurant/bar, TV lounge, recreation room, barbecue, laundry. Doubles A$50–65; backpackers dorms A$18 per person.

Alice Springs Pioneer YHA Hostel • *Corner Parsons St. and Leichhardt Terr.; tel. 52–8855* • Center of town, closest hostel to transit center. On the grounds of a former outdoor movie theater. Air-conditioned rooms, pool, barbecue, laundry, tour desk, kitchen, 24-hour access. A$14 per person members; A$20 non-members.

Toddy's Backpackers • *41 Gap Rd.; tel. 52–1322* • Free pickup, air-conditioned rooms, pool, store, barbecue, laundry, two kitchens, bike hire, tour desk. Must rent crockery and linens. Dorms start at A$15 per person; cabins A$50 double.

RESTAURANTS......................................

Alice is not generous in its variety of eating establishments. What you basically have to choose from, outside the good but not yet great hotel restaurants, is family-style food with a traditional Australian approach—Territory meats, fried fish, Italian, sandwiches. It's not a culinary desert, exactly, but if you're looking for 5-star food, fly back to Sydney. Still, it's the Territory, meaning good value for the money and generous portions. To name a few:

Melanka Steak House • *94 Todd St.; tel. 52–2233* • Part of the Melanka Lodge; good pub food. Salad bar, buffalo steaks, regular beef steaks and burgers, schnitzels and some seafood. Most items are fried, unfortunately, but the servings are often enormous. Dinner 6–9 p.m. seven nights.

Terrace • *134 Bath St.; tel. 52–1222* • In the Elkira Motel. A mixed menu: French, Italian and Asian. Nice cocktail bar for pre-dinner drinks. Dinner from 6:30 p.m., seven nights a week.

Golden Inn • *9 Undoolya Rd.; tel. 52–6910* • Wide range of Chinese and some other Asian dishes. Take-aways. Lunch noon–2 p.m. Monday–Saturday; dinner 5–midnight seven days.

La Casalinga • *105 Gregory Terr.; tel. 52–4508* • Italian fare and pizza. Dinner 6–10 p.m. seven days; the pizza parlor open from 5 p.m.–1 a.m. seven days.

Alice Springs Eating Centre • *Diarama Village, Larapinta Dr.; tel. 52–2964* • Food hall, sorta. Pizza, steaks, fish and chips. Indoor and outdoor eating. Noon–late seven days.

In the Alice Area

There are dozens of tour operators offering trips in the Alice Springs area, everything from tours of town to flights over Ayers Rock and extended safaris in the bush. If you haven't booked ahead, one place to stop is the **Alice Springs Tour Booking Centre** at 74 Todd St.; tel. 52–6266. The company has a 24-hour tour booking service for a group of companies offering trips all over the Red Centre. The service includes free hotel pickup.

Ansett Trailways, which offers a number of Red Centre fly/coach packages in the Red Centre, has a couple of Alice Springs-area tours that can be booked in town. The two-day package takes you through some Outback cattle stations, and includes a trip to the Olgas and a sunset stop at The Rock. The next morning, you have enough time to climb Ayers before heading back to the Alice. Rates, depending on where you stay at Ayers Rock Resort, are around A$200 per person, including accommodations and food. *Information: Ansett Trailways, Todd Mall; tel. 52–2422.* Deluxe Coaches runs a day tour to Ayers Rock and the Olgas for around A$100. The Deluxe office in the Alice is on Gap Road; tel. 52–4444.

If you're more adventurous (and more laden with gilders) you could fly to and over Ayers Rock and the desert. **Alice Springs Air Charter** will fly to Ayers via Palm Valley and Kings Canyon for around A$175 per person, including lunch and some ground touring. *Information: 52–1250 or 52–5086.* **Skyport** takes the same route for about the same money. *Information; 52–3059 or 52–3105.*

You can look down on it all at a slower pace from one of the balloons available in the Alice. Check with **Toddy's Balloon Safaris,** 41 Gap Rd., Alice Springs 0870; tel. 52–1322 or 52–5999. A sunrise champagne flight will run you about A$150 for an hour. Toddy's also has week-long trips, ballooning at Ayers Rock and visiting tourist areas near the Alice. The safaris or sunrise trips can be booked ahead through ATS/Sprint.

Two highways going east and west out of town get you to a number of historic sites and territorial or national parks. The **Ross Highway,** going east, is paved almost all the way to the hamlet of Ross River. You pick it up south of town on the way to the airport. Along the route are **Trephina Gorge Nature Park,** with good MacDonnell Ranges scenery, and **Corroboree Rock Conservation Reserve,** an area of significance to the Aboriginals in the area; overnight camping allowed. N'Dhala Gorge Nature Park, with Aboriginal rock carvings in the two gorges, requires four-wheel drive.

West of the Alice, on Larapinta Drive, are some of the more popular spots around town. Catch the road by turning west at the intersection of Stott Terrace and the Stuart Highway (look for the K mart.) The first biggy is **Simpson's Gap National Park,** an area eroded over 60 million years by river action with a dramatic but small gorge in the cliffs. There are rock wallabies about and the area is filled with ghost gums. It's a popular picnic area. The park (free entry) is open 8 a.m.– 8 p.m.

One of the more dramatic places in the Red Centre is about 24 kilometers farther west from the gap: **Standley Chasm,** also carved by river action, has a wonderful walking trail back to gorges cut 100 feet deep into the ocher and yellow rocks. The chasm is owned by the Iwup-ataka Aboriginal Land Trust. There's a $1.50 per person entry fee. It has a food kiosk and picnic area. The best time to do the chasm is around noon, when the light is at its best in the gorges; it's mostly shady all the way. The park is open 8 a.m.–5 p.m. A bit farther along are **Serpentine Gorge Nature Park,** more of the same only less, and **Ormiston Gorge and Pound National Park,** a dramatic waterhole where you can cool off with a swim. Overnight camping allowed at both parks. Finally, you come to the end of the non-four-wheel drive road about 80 miles west of the Alice at **Glen Helen Gorge Nature Park,** more river-cut topography with majestic red cliffs. Nearby is the **Glen Helen Lodge,** which has rooms and a pleasant RV park. Doubles are A$70; backpack-ers, $A10. If interested, you can book through the NT tourism office or by writing the lodge at P.O. Box 3020, Alice Springs 5750; tel. 56–7489.

Other scenic spots around, such as **Kings Canyon, Finke Gorge National Park** (in which you find the famous **Palm Valley,** where palm trees bloom in the middle of a furnace-blast desert), and the **Redbank Gorge Nature Park,** are for four-wheel drive when things are dry. If you're interested, contact **Brits Rentals** on the Stuart Highway in town. *Information: 52–8814.* Again, it's probably a good idea to book them ahead from North America.

Information about all the Alice-area parks, as well as Ayers Rock and the Olgas, is available from the Conservation Commission of Australia offices on Gap Road in town; tel. 50–8211.

AYERS ROCK AND THE OLGAS ....

Make sure you top off with gasoline before you head south toward Ayers Rock—there's no gas for 125 miles between the Alice and Erldunda, where the Lasseter Highway cuts west from the Stuart. There are a couple of stations along the 150-mile stretch between Erldunda and the

Rock, but there are lots of other drivers with same idea—we stopped at a station on the Lasseter once and they were out of gas.

Your first look at the famous rock shows that it's a strange pebble, indeed, sticking up a thousand feet and more into the air, looking like a huge red-orange bagel. The minerals the rock is made of act like an artist's pallette, changing colors throughout the day from a light tan to a deep orange as the sun sets. The Olgas and Ayers are made of a sandstone with a rich iron content, so rich the rocks actually rust when they get wet. Because the surrounding landscape is so flat, both formations are striking, and Ayers, particularly, is so strangely beautiful it's easy to understand why people come from around the world to stare.

The rock got its Christian name in 1873 when William Gosse, the first European to see the rock, named it in honor of Sir Henry Ayers, then chief secretary of South Australia and later premier of the state. The Aboriginal people have inhabited the area around the rock for at least 10,000 years. The traditional owners, the Pitjantjantjara, Yunkantjatjara, and Ngaanyatjara peoples, call it Uluru, which means "giant pebble," and it has great spiritual significance for them. Several areas of the rock are sacred sites and off-limits to tourists.

Ayers, and the Olga Mountains, about 20 miles west, are basically part of the same geologic formation. They are conglomerate, part of a sandstone formation between 600 million and 700 million years old that was folded and pushed up as part of a mountain chain. Erosion of the range left the three formations that now rise above the desert: Ayers Rock, the Olgas, and nearby Mount Connor. Some geologists say Ayers took the form it has now about 40 million years ago. It is thought that the Olgas, a system of 36 domes spread over an area of about 15 square miles, were once a giant single dome, much larger than Ayers, that eroded into its present form. Ayers is believed to be the tip of a formation that extends at least 6000 meters below ground. There is a slight difference in texture between the Olgas and Ayers, because Ayers is arkosic sandstone, a finer grain than the Olgas. The rangers at the park say the top of Ayers is 348 meters above the surrounding landscape, or 1141 feet.

At first blush, especially from a distance, it looks impossible to climb the thing. From some angles, the cliff faces look vertical. But there is a trail, and it's well used. Between 1931 and 1946, when just getting to the area was an adventure, only 22 people climbed the rock. Now about 300,000 people a year visit, and many of them make the 1.6-kilometer climb.

The route up is on the west face of the rock, a short drive from the ranger station. The first 200 yards are very steep, and for most of that distance, a chain and metal posts have been set into the sandstone so you can pull yourself up. Toward the top, the trail becomes a series of ups and down as it wanders through the wind- and water-cut mini-canyons. At the end of the trail there is a cairn that has a guest book to record your epic. The trail, while not technically difficult, is very strenuous. In hot weather, you should do the climb early in the morning, and when it's raining, stay off. The normal time for the trip to the top and back down is around two hours, but a crazy New Zealander made it to the top once in 12 minutes. **A word of caution:** a number of people have died climbing Ayers Rock, many from heart attacks, but a few—including a young woman not long ago—by slipping off the sheer sides. Stick to the trail, and if you have kids along, watch them like a hawk.

In addition to the climb, there are several hikes along or around the base of the rock. Ayers Rock is about six miles in circumference at the base, and a four-hour walk should get you around. The rock itself is about 1.3 square miles in area. There is also a paved road that circles the rock if you want to see it from all sides. If you turn left at the intersection with this road and the road past the ranger station, you'll come to **Mutitjulu,** also known as Maggie Springs, where a trail takes you back to an area at the base of Ayers Rock where there are Aboriginal paintings.

There are daily **ranger walks** around parts of the base. The schedule for these is located on a bulletin board at the parking lot at the base of the climbing trail, or available at the ranger headquarters on the road into Ayers Rock. The rangers operate a small museum at the station with information about the area. And next door is an Aboriginal display area and museum which also has artworks for sale. **Note:** taking photographs of the Aboriginals, anywhere in the park, is not allowed. The rangers also stage dune walks around the Ayers area, and a 2½-hour jaunt across the desert from the ranger station to the rock is escorted by Aboriginal guides.

The most popular spot in the whole park to watch the sun set on Ayers Rock is on the paved road that runs from the Resort to the ranger station. You'll see a sign about seven kilometers past the Olgas turnoff that says: "**sunset viewing,**" and near it is a parking lot, usually filled with tour buses and camper vans. Find a spot, get out about 30 rolls of film, and have at it. If you're feeling like a swell, you can hire a limo and liveried chauffeur to get you to the rock on time, complete with champagne and canapes. The price is about A$70 an hour. Call 56–2283 in Yulara for details. If you're not the limousine type, but still want to see your rock and eat too, try the bus-dinner trip, which parks you at the sunset viewing area and serves Aussie meals for around A$50 per person. It leaves the Ayers Rock resort around 4:30 p.m. and gets back two hours after sunset. *Information: 56–2171.* And, if you want to fly around the area, you can take a half-hour helicopter tour of the Olgas and Ayers Rock for about A$130 per person.

The Olgas are higher (some peaks are about 1800 feet high) and spread out. They were discovered by explorer Ernest Giles, who spotted them in 1872 and named them after the then-Queen of Spain. Together with Ayers Rock, the Olgas comprise **Uluru Aboriginal National Park,** about 500 square miles in area. The Aboriginal name for the Olgas is Kata Tjuta, or "Many Heads." The road from the resort to the Olgas is terrible, and unless you're keen on busting the springs of your rental car, take a bus. A number of tours are available.

There are several **hiking trails** in the Olgas, relatively easy but potentially dangerous in hot weather without proper precautions. The most popular trail goes from a parking lot up past Mt. Olga into Olga Gorge; it's about two kilometers to the trail end. A bit more strenuous, but an emotional high is the **Valley of the Winds** walk, about four kilometers, which goes through narrow gorges. In hot weather, the rangers suggest you have a pint of water for every hour you plan to hike. Detailed hiking maps are available at the ranger station.

In addition to its rocky lures, Uluru National Park is also recognized as a fine example of arid-zone Australian ecosystem, which despite a low annual rainfall (7 to 12 inches), supports a large variety of plant and animal life. Some of the animals—70 reptiles, 42 mammals, and some amphibians—are the usual strange critters you expect in Australia. On the one hand, there are perenties, the largest lizard in Australia, which can grow to eight feet long. On the other hand, in depressions worn into the top of Ayers Rock, you find shield shrimp, which lay eggs that can lie around for years in the sun waiting for rain so they can hatch.

A valuable lesson for Australians (and for the folks who live in the mountains of California) was learned in 1976, when lightning storms started fires that burned more than 75% of the vegetation around the park. The ancient Aboriginal practice of starting small fires to burn out brush and other tinder had been stopped at Ayers Rock, but after the fires, it was begun again.

In spring, after the rains, the desert around the area is full of wildflowers, particularly rose dock, a non-Australian plant introduced as ground cover, which is slowly killing off many native species. Old Ayers Rock hands say that one of the best times to visit is during a rainstorm when the usually-dry waterfalls are full and Ayers is covered with huge streams falling down the sheer sides of the rock.

The Northern Territory Tourist Commission alleges that the Ayers Rock area has the clearest skies in the world, and offers a chance to prove it. The Southern Skies Observatory, operated by the Sydney Observatory, allows day and night use of its facilities, which include three telescopes, video screens and adaptors that allow some models of 35 mm cameras to take photos of both the sun and the night sky. During the day, the charge is a modest A$2; evening sessions are about A$10. Check with the Visitors Information Centre adjacent to the Four Seasons Ayers Rock hotel.

Ayers Rock Resort

Large questions of morality are still being discussed about this A$160 million resort complex near Ayers Rock, the same sort of questions you get discussing the Black Hills with a member of the Oglalla Sioux. But, for better or worse, the resort is there and it's an oasis for tourists who want to sweat and strain hiking up the rock or through the Olgas and then come home to a hot shower, tennis, or a swim. Counting all the hotel and lodge rooms, plus camper spaces and tent sites, the resort can accommodate around 5000 tourists at any one time. The resort, which also includes a school, police station, fast-food joints, restaurants, bars, and an interpretive center, is laid out in a sand dune area about 18 kilometers from the base of Ayers Rock. There is an airport, served by **Ansett,** and **Australian,** as well as car and moped rentals and a service station.

There are five accommodations choices available:

Sheraton Ayers Rock • *Yulara Dr., Yulara 0872; tel. 56–2200* • This hotel is at the top end. All amenities, including the licensed Kunia Room Restaurant, mini-bars, pool, tennis, spa, three bars and non-smoking rooms, around A$225–275 double; suites A$360–420.

The Four Seasons Ayers Rock • *Yulara Dr., Yulara 0872; tel. 56–2200* • Around 100 rooms, with the Stuart Room licensed restaurant, pool and the Oasis Bar. Rooms begin around A$200 double. Reservation information:

Red Centre Hotel • *Yulara Dr.; 56–2170* • Offers a range of accommodations from hotel units and a lodge to backpackers bunkhouse. Pool, barbecue area, laundry. The hotel units start at A$190 double; the lodge units, which are air conditioned and can sleep four, are $A75, and the air conditioned bunkhouse units are $A20 per person, linen hire $A8.

Yulara Maisonettes • *Yulara Dr.; 56–2131* • One-bedroom units with some cooking facilities; heated pool, disco, barbecue, laundry. Doubles A$95.

Ayers Rock Campground • *Lasseter Highway, Yulara 0872, mailing address P.O. Box 96 Yulara 5751; tel. 56–2055* • There is space for 3600 campers, including powered sites, tent sites, pool, barbecue, store, public phone and areas for bus tour groups. There are also permanent RV units for rent. Five amenity blocks, with showers and laundries. Rates start at around A$20 for a tent site; RV sites A$30, rental RVs around A$70 a night double.

For accommodation information, contact the Northern Territory Tourist Commission: 2121 Avenue of the Stars, Suite 1203, Los Angeles, Ca. 90067; (800) 468–8222, or 489 5th Ave., 31st Floor, N.Y., N.Y. 10017, same 800 phone number. In Australia, call (089) 56–2144.

VICTORIA

Victoria had a tough time getting started. Somebody back in the Foreign Office in London, taking note that the French were sniffing around, tried to start a convict colony in 1803 on the Mornington Peninsula at the outlet of Port Phillip Bay, but bad soil and lack of support stopped the effort within a year. Another quarter-century passed before another attempt at colonization was made, this time in 1835 at a spot far inside Port Phillip where John Bateman, a land speculator, found acreage more adaptable to grazing and agriculture. Like the Dutch in Manhattan, he came laden with trinkets and baubles and conned the local Aboriginals out of 600,000 acres of prime real estate. In 1836, the tiny settlement was named after Lord Melbourne, the English prime minister at the time. It should be noted that the first successful attempts at founding settlements in what would become Victoria were not as a result of the penal system. Meanwhile, enterprising graziers and explorers had succeeded in crossing the Blue Mountains in New South Wales and discovered the vast and gentle pastures of what would become northern Victoria. It was the great Gold Rush of 1851, however, which established Victoria—and Melbourne—as permanent Australian fixtures. The strikes began in New South Wales and worked their way along the topography into what is now Victoria. In September 1851, the biggest field of all was found at Ballarat, a mere 75 miles northwest of Melbourne, and within seconds, the area was flooded with diggers from all over the world, including a bunch of 49ers fresh from the gold fields in California. While all this was going on, the leaders of the Melbourne area had been agitating to create a separate colony from New South Wales, with emphasis on making transportation of prisoners illegal, and that same year, the separation was granted and the new colony was named after the Empress Queen back in London. The gold strikes faded, depressions came and went, but the colony had received instant population. By 1860, Melbourne was a city of 600,000 and had become the largest city in the country.

Today, in addition to farming, manufacturing, and industry (Victoria accounts for a full third of the nation's GNP), the state is a popular domestic tourist target, especially the Murray River basin and the ski areas in the Victorian Alps. Victoria is also outlaw country, the Deadwood and Whitehorse of Australia, where bad guys roamed up and down the Hume Highway, which runs across the state and then north to Syd-

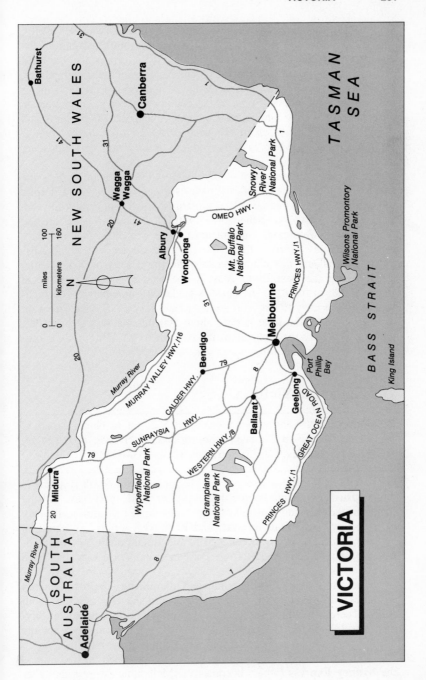

ney. The most famous of the bushrangers, of course, was Ned Kelly, Australia's Jesse James. Whole towns up in the northeast part of the state thrive on Kelly-based tourism. Northeast Victoria is also the heart of Victoria's growing wine industry. The Rutherglen area, particularly, is well-known for its reds, and the Milawa-Glenrowan district is a major producer of table wines. Some of the country's major producers are in this part of the state, including Lindeman's and Brown Brothers and Seppelt's. *Information about the wine areas all around the state is available from the Victoria Wine Industry Association in Melbourne, (03) 614–5811.*

Victoria's compact size—only about 85,000 square miles, the smallest of the mainland states—makes for easy touring. And despite its small area, it has some of the most diversified topography in Australia. In the east, along the border with New South Wales, are the rugged Snowy Mountains, and for most of the way along that boundary flows the mighty Murray. In the west, on the border with South Australia, are flat and dry plains leading into the deserts of central Australia. Along the Bass Strait coast in the west is the dramatic Great Ocean Road; in the east, the coast is backed by mountains. The highway system is easy to manage, and you can see most of what you want in a short while; the state is only about 500 miles across at its widest point. If you have the inclination, it's possible to go skiing in the morning and walk the beach that afternoon.

The Essential Victoria

INFORMATION • For information about Victoria in North America, contact the **Victorian Tourism Commission,** 2121 Ave. of the Stars, #1270, Los Angeles, Calif. 90067; tel. (213) 553–6352.

GETTING THERE • Air service to Melbourne from North America is direct, usually with one stop either in Queensland or Sydney. All the major airlines serving Australia fly to Melbourne. In addition, the city is served by **Australian, Ansett,** and **East-West** airlines. Without an air pass, expect to pay between A$150 and A$200 one-way from Sydney, around A$225–A$300 from Brisbane, and A$350–A$450 from Cairns.

The city's international terminal, **Tullamarine Airport,** is about 12 miles outside of town, and cab fares into the city average about A$20. There is a shuttle service that will drop you off downtown: Skybus, tel. 338–5136. The fare is about A$10 per person. Look for the bus every half-hour outside the domestic section of the terminal.

Rail service into Victoria from Sydney is provided on two routes, the **Sydney Express** (which becomes the Melbourne Express the other way) and the **Intercapital Daylight.** The Express operates seven days, leaves Sydney (or Melbourne) at 8 p.m., and arrives in Melbourne (or Sydney) at 8 the next morning. The trains are parked at the stations by 7 p.m., so you can have dinner aboard before you leave if you wish. The Express has sleepers, a buffet car, dining car, and lounge. Without an Australpass, the one-way fare is about A$110 plus sleeper fare. The Daylight runs through some great scenery on its way between the two rival state capitals. It leaves Sydney at 7:45 a.m., arriving in Melbourne at 8:20 p.m. Fares are about the same as the Express; note that the Daylight doesn't run on Sundays. There is also rail service to Canberra and Adelaide. Trains within the state are run by **V/Line.** Information on interstate service is available from Railways of Australia, 85 Queen St., Melbourne 3000; tel. 608–0811. For service within the state, contact V/Line Travel, Transport House, 589 Collins St., Melbourne 3000, tel. 619–1500; reservations, 620–0771. Interstate trains leave from the Spencer St. Station; suburban trains leave from the Flinders St. Station.

A variety of **bus lines** service Melbourne. The two main routes from Sydney are on the Princes Highway, which hugs the coast as it turns a circle toward Victoria; the other uses the Newell and Great Western Highways to cut over the Great Dividing Range. The Princes route takes about 18 hours; the mountain route about 16 hours. A third route goes through Canberra on its way between the cities. Without a bus pass, expect to pay around A$50 one way. Information: **Greyhound** Australia, Greyhound Terminal, corner of Franklin and Swanston Streets; tel. 668–2666. **Deluxe,** 58 Franklin St.; tel. 663–6144. **Pioneer Express,** 465 Swanston St.; tel. 668–2422.

CLIMATE • Outside of the much-maligned Darwin up in the Top End, Melbourne arguably often has the worst weather in urban Australia. Weather wags—probably from Sydney—say the city has four seasons, to be sure; the only trouble is, they all come the same day. It's usually cooler in the winter (Apr.–Sept.) than Sydney, and hotter in the summer. Statistically, the city receives less rainfall than Sydney, but the problem is, it can come at any moment—few Melbournians leave home without an umbrella, even when the dawn is clear. Summer highs are around 75°; winter lows can get down to near freezing.

TIME • Victoria is on Eastern Standard Time, the same as Queensland, Tasmania and New South Wales, putting it 18 hours ahead of San Francisco.

MELBOURNE

The easiest way to get into a fight in Melbourne is to suggest, however marginally, that Sydney really is the Number One city in Australia. The debate about which of the two Australian biggies is best has been going on almost as long as white Australia has been around, and it's not likely to be settled soon. Sydneysiders look upon their cousins in Melbourne as stuffy, conservative, and dull, and caustically point out that the reason the streets in Melbourne are so wide is because they were designed so herds of sheep could pass freely. The folks in Melbourne, on the other hand, think all the citizens of Sydney are flaky extroverts with big mouths and no sense of propriety. Melbourne is also a tad bent out of shape because it remembers when it served as the capital of Australia between 1901 and 1927, before political compromises forced all the bureaucrats to move to Canberra. For visitors, the differences in the two cities are great enough that you miss a big chunk of what makes Australia Australia by not seeing them both.

Melbourne (pronounced MEL-burn) is a city of diverse ethnic backgrounds. It has, for example, the third largest urban Greek population in the world after Athens and Thessaloniki. It's a place of wide-wide avenues, rich stands of Victorian architecture, and a streak of madness when it comes to any form of sports. This is, after all, the home of that most Australian form of athletic insanity, footy—Australian Rules Football. But it is also the home of the richest and most prestigious horse race in the country, the Melbourne Cup. The city's new, international-grade tennis facilities are the site of the Australian Open. Across the Yarra River, is the Melbourne Cricket Ground, which also serves as the footy stadium, and is the largest cricket facility in the world, capable of holding 120,000 fans. It served as the main stadium for the 1956 Olympics and every year is the site of a variety of international cricket matches.

Melbourne, with about 4.1 million people, is also the commercial and manufacturing center of the country, sometimes called the Detroit of Australia because of its motor vehicle plants, refineries, and industrial parks, and the city's port is the busiest in the nation. But it's also called the Garden City, because parks account for about a fifth of the city's acreage. Like San Francisco, it is famous for maintaining a fleet of historic public transit vehicles—in this case, the famous Melbourne trams, which flit like green insects around the downtown area. Also,

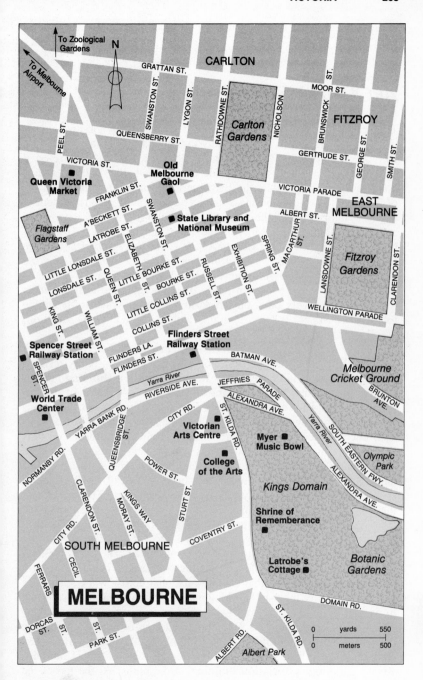

the city is home to the company that brews Australia's most famous beer, Foster's.

AROUND MELBOURNE......................

The heart of the city, and target of much derision from non-dwellers, is the Yarra River, which splits the city in half and flows into Port Phillip Bay. Because of its silt-laden waters, the Yarra is sometimes referred to as the "river which flows upside down," but it's silt-laden waters don't look any worse than the Brisbane River up in Queensland. Most of the city's downtown business district and shopping area is laid out in a grid system north of the river. To the south are the arts complexes and large garden areas. Most of the major hotels are in a 16-square-block area near Parliament House. *NB: It's sometimes almost impossible to find a place to hang your hat in town during the annual Melbourne Cup race in November; plan ahead.* The downtown area is a combination of highrises and Victorian relics. There is supposed to be a pedestrian mall, like every other city in Australia, but the one in Melbourne (on Bourke Street) is open to trams and if you don't pay attention, you'll get nailed proper.

Many of the finest old Victorians around the city are the result of the Gold Rush, and include such noble works as the carefully restored **Windsor Hotel** (1883); the gaudy **Royal Exhibition Building** (1880), and the biggest and best, **Parliament House** (1854). Most of the important old buildings are now protected by the National Trust. The city's two main shopping strands are Collins Street and Bourke Street. **Collins,** once likened to a boulevard in Paris, runs up and down on hills between Spring and Swanston streets and is the site for many of the city's—and the nation's—major financial houses. The northeast end of the street, near Parliament House, was once an area of small exclusive shops; a few remain, but skyscrapers have taken over. **Town Hall** and the **City Square** are at the intersection of Collins and Swanston. Aside from **St. Paul's Cathedral** at the south side of the square, the square is worth a miss, but nearby is the city's most infamous pub, **Young and Jackson's Hotel,** at Number One Swanston St. The bar is home to one of Australia's most beloved paintings, the naked but demure form of lovely Chloe, a work that caused a national uproar when stiff-necks arrived in the city for the 1880 Melbourne Exhibition and just happened to wander by in herds to gawk—and then protest.

Along Collins there are several old buildings of note, including the massive **ANZ Bank Building,** 386 Collins; the **Melbourne Stock Exchange,** 351 Collins, open Mon.–Fri. for visitors, and the **Commonwealth Banking Association building,** 335 Collins. At the top of the street is the sandstone mass of the **Old Treasury,** built in the 1850s, where most of the gold from the Ballarat fields was stored during the Rush.

Bourke Street, containing the aforementioned mall, is the site of the city's major department stores, including **David Jones, G.J Coles,** and **Myer.** The Myer building is reputed to be the largest department store building in the Southern Hemisphere. The mall, which runs between Swanston and Elizabeth streets, is awash with small boutiques as well as big stores. At the Elizabeth Street end is the Melbourne General Post Office.

In addition, there are hundreds of shops and stores along side streets, many of which, just to add to the confusion, are named after the bigger lanes: Little Bourke, Little Collins, Little Russell, etc. Here you can find at least a dozen small shopping arcades, including the **Royal Arcade,** built in the 1870s, where small shops bask in restored elegance in a smaller version of Sydney's Queen Victoria Building.

OTHER MELBOURNE SIGHTS...............

Museums

The Aussies have a peculiar fascination with jails and executions, caused, no doubt, by their colorful penal past. You find restored jails and gallows all over the country, and none finer or more grisly than the **Old Melbourne Gaol,** which has a particularly revolting display of death masks from just-hanged prisoners. In its day (1841–1929), more than 100 prisoners were executed in the gaol. The star of the show is Ned Kelly, who was hanged here in November 1880. the immortal bushranger's famous bullet-dented suit of armor is here, as is the gallows they used to send him to his reward. There are also a few restored cells so you can see how prisoners were housed. The museum, at the corner of Franklin and Russell streets, is open daily 10 a.m.–5 p.m., admission charge about A$5. *Information: 663–7228.*

Downtown, the **Museum of Victoria** and **State Library** complex stretches about a block between Swanston and Russell streets facing La Trobe street. Access to the museum is from Russell Street, the science museum section from Swanston. The complex houses a rich stew of Australiana, from Aboriginal weapons to a stuffed racehorse. The complex is open 10 a.m–5 p.m. Mon.–Fri. and 10 a.m.–6 p.m. Sun.; no admission charge. *Information: 669–9888.*

The Chinese who came to Australia to work or to hunt for gold had about the same experience as their brothers and sisters who came to North America at about the same time, and the persecution, racial bigotry, and brutality shown to them in Australia is displayed with no holds barred at the **Museum of Chinese Australian History** in the heart of Melbourne's Chinatown. The museum is open weekdays (except Fri.) 10 a.m.–4 p.m., weekends from noon to 4:30 p.m. The museum is at 22 Cohen Pl., off Little Bourke St. *Information: 662–2888.*

The Arts Scene

The cultural heart of the city is a complex of three buildings on South Kilda Road on the south side of the Yarra River. Here are found the **Melbourne Concert Hall,** the **National Gallery,** a **theater complex** and the **Performing Arts Museum.** The gallery houses some of the finest Australian art in the country, everything from Victorian land-scapes to Aboriginal works less than a decade old. It also has a formi-dable display of foreign works, including Picasso and Durer, and, surprisingly, a good selection of pre-Colombian and Asian art. The gal-lery is open daily, admission about A$2; free on Mondays; guided one-hour tours of the whole complex, called the **Victorian Arts Centre,** are available 10 a.m.–5 p.m. daily for A$5. *Information: 617–8151.*

The theaters in the complex offer performances by the **Australian Ballet,** the **Australian Opera,** the **Victorian State Opera,** and the **Melbourne Theatre Company.** The concert hall is the home of the **Melbourne Symphony Orchestra.** The arts complex is immediately recognizable because of the tall spire that sits on top of the theater building. Detractors say it looks like a TV tower; admirers, that it soars into the air as a symbol of artistic freedom. Whatever.

Gardens

As noted, a big chunk of Melbourne is green, with large and well-tended parks on both sides of the Yarra. On the north side, near down-town, are the **Carlton Gardens,** the **Flagstaff Gardens,** the **Fitzroy Gardens,** and the **Treasury Gardens.**

In the Fitzroy Gardens northeast of the downtown grid is **Captain Cook's Cottage,** hauled board by board from its home in Yorskire by a public-spirited Melburnian in 1934. Take a look, but know that it was the home of the bold explorer's parents and he apparently never lived in it. The house is open 9 a.m–5 p.m. daily; admission about A$2.

At the center of the Carlton Gardens, northwest of Parliament House, are the **Royal Exhibition Buildings,** a huge fluffy Victorian complex opened in 1880 and still used as a convention and trade show area. Part of the complex was used by the Victorian Parliament after it moved out, when its quarters were taken over by the federal government before the capital was moved to Canberra. *Information: 663–5000.*

The major parkland in the city is the **Kings Domain-Royal Bo-**

tanic Gardens area on the south shore of the river. In all, the area is about 600 acres of huge lawns, flowerbeds, and recreation facilities. You can rent a **bicycle** near the Botanic Gardens and check out the six-mile **Yarra River Bikeway.** There is also an outdoor **amphitheater,** which is used as an ice rink in the winter. In the center of the Domain, is the **La Trobe Cottage,** the state's first government building. The Botanic Gardens have around 12,000 species of plants, plus gardens and lakes with at least 50 species of birds. The gardens are open from sunrise to sunset daily; free guided tours are available. *Information: 650–5037.*

The major **sports activity** in Melbourne takes place in two parks on the north bank of the river opposite the Kings Domain: **Yarra Park,** which houses several cricket fields including the immense **Melbourne Cricket Ground,** and **Olympic Park,** with the **Melbourne Indoor Sports and Entertainment Centre,** and the **National Tennis Centre.** There are a couple of **sports museums** at the cricket grounds. The field is open for a look if no games are on. Information on matches (cricket or footy) 654–6066.

More Sights

The biggest flea market in town (and maybe the country) is held Sundays at the **Queen Victoria Market** at the corner of Willam and Franklin streets from 9 a.m. to 4 p.m. On Tuesday, Friday, and Saturday mornings, starting in the wee hours, it's a fresh produce and fruit market.

The **Greek area** of town is centered around Lonsdale Street between Swanston and Russell streets. In the summer, it's outdoor eating time at a variety of cafes and restaurants with typical Greek fare. **Chinatown,** as mentioned, is on Little Bourke Street and is connected to the Greek quarter at Heffernan Lane. In addition to lots of first-class restaurants, there are also a number of Chinese grocers and artisans doing business.

The *Polly Woodside,* an 1885 commercial sailing ship, is the main attraction at the **Melbourne Maritime Museum** on the south bank of the Yarra across from the World Trade Centre. The ship and museum are open weekdays 10 a.m.–4 p.m., weekends 10 a.m.–5 p.m. Admission is A$6. *Information: 699–9760.*

The Essential Melbourne

INFORMATION • In Melbourne, the **Victoria Tourism Commission's offices** (it's called Victours in Australia) are located in Building D of the World Trade Centre, corner of Flinders and Spencer sts., Melbourne 3005; mailing address P.O. Box 279, Melbourne 3005; tel. 619–9444.

Also check the **Melbourne Tourism Authority,** with an office at Nauru House, 80 Collins St.; tel. 654–2288. Budget travelers can check with the **Youth Hostels Association of Victoria,** 122 Flinders St., Melbourne 3000; tel. 654–5422.

GETTING AROUND • The historic **trams** really are the best way to get around Melbourne, and the ticket cost of around A$1.80 (depending on destination and how many zones you pass) also lets you ride trains and buses. The basic fare applies for a three-hour period; other tickets are available for longer periods. If you plan to ride a lot, buy a A$7 **City Saver Card,** which allows 10 trips on the city's transport system for 24 hours. Tram, train, and bus route **maps** are available from Victours or from the Metropolitan Transit Authority bus terminals, train stations and tram depots. *Information on transportation schedules is available by calling 617–0900; hours 7:30 a.m.–8:30 p.m. Monday–Saturday; 9:15 a.m.–8:30 p.m. Sunday.*

A quick tour of the city is available on the **Melbourne Explorer Bus,** which leaves the Flinders Street Railway Station every hour with stops at seven major sites around town, including the Old Goal, Captain Cook's Cottage, the Polly Woodside, and the Victorian Arts Centre. A day ticket is A$13 per adult. Hours 10 a.m.–4:45 p.m.

TELEPHONES • The area code for the Melbourne area is (03).

SHOPPING • Normal shopping hours in the city are 8:30 a.m.–5:30 p.m. Mon.–Wednesday; 8:30 a.m.–9 p.m. Thursday and Friday and 8:30 a.m.–5 p.m. Sat.

In addition to the large department stores and arcades already mentioned, you might want to look at these shops:

The **Opal Mine,** 121 Bourke St., for jewelry made from opals and other Aussie gems, prices moderate to astounding; the **Aboriginal Artists Gallery,** 12 Liverpool St.; the **Meat Market Craft Centre,** 42 Courtney St., North Melbourne, for crafts in progress, and the **Victorian Tapestry Workshop,** 260 South Melbourne, for internationally recognized weavings (some of the works have sold for A$400,000).

Some of the city's more upscale fashion outlets are in South Yarra, where prices are high and so is quality. Toorak Road, which runs through South Yarra and Toorak (also on tram lines) is sort of an antipodean Rodeo Drive in spots, a lot longer but with the right mix of fancy stores and expensive cars. Elegant restaurants are on hand, as well.

ACCOMMODATIONS........................

Our favorite hotel in all Australia is located in Melbourne, the grand and elegant Windsor. The Victorian style and grace of this hotel, especially the excruciating elegance of the Grand Dining Room, puts the Windsor in a class all by itself. But it's not the only great hotel in town; we put the Menzies at Rialto second. They are worlds apart in tone and atmosphere, but each in its own way is a wonderful experience.

Part of the charm of the city's central hotel district is the tree-lined sidewalks and broad boulevards, always compared to Paris (close, but no seegar), but offering a more genteel atmosphere than most of Sydney and all of Adelaide. And if you don't feel like plunking down $A800 a night for a butler-serviced suite at the Windsor, there are digs for all pocketbooks.

The Windsor • *103 Spring St.; tel. 653–0653* • The Grand Old Lady of Spring Street, as it's known, was built in 1883 and has been completely refurbished and gussied up, from the top of its twin towers to its elegant lobby. You are greeted by top-hatted doormen (last time it was James of the Windsor), and the service goes uphill from there. It's near parks and Parliament House and the whole thing is part of the National Trust. The pride of the hotel is its suites (there are 20), furnished in Victorian style and fitted with antiques. The other rooms, more modern, are still excellent. The Grand Dining Hall is right out of a movie, all chandeliers and thick carpeting, orchestral trio, silver service and tuxedo-attired waiters. It is, of course, very expensive. There are also a more casual cafe and the Windsor Lounge where you can have morning or afternoon tea (cucumber sandwiches and such). Truly one of the premier hotels in the world.

Regular doubles start at $A300; small suites $A400; or the Victorian Suite (private dining room with butler service, separate lounge, festooned with works of art), about $A800.

Menzies at the Rialto • *495 Collins St.; tel. 620–9111* • The hotel complex is an excellent example of what a good architect can do. Half of it is an old Victorian building, half is modern, but blended in so you can't really tell them apart. Between the old and new wings is a vast, 10-story atrium, with hotel room balconies looking over, and the Portego, a popular garden-like dining and bar area. The Portego has breakfast from 6:30 a.m. Monday– Saturday, and a A$30 per person Sunday brunch from 10 a.m.–2:30 p.m. Sunday. It also has lunch and afternoon teas and dinners from 6:30–11:30 p.m. daily; moderate to expensive. The Chandelier Room, which is one of the best restaurants in the city, has a business lunch from noon–3 p.m. Monday–Friday (about A$50);

dinner from 7–10:30 p.m. Monday–Saturday (jacket and tie required). Expensive.

Doubles at the hotel from A$275; suites from A$380. If you're a sporting soul, the Menzies complex also contains Tabaret, an electronic gambling/game facility where you can bet on international sports events as well as wager with electronic games. It's open from 11 a.m.–3 a.m. daily; dress code (no jeans, no tennis shoes, no T-shirts). Information: 612–2900.

Hilton on the Park • *192 Wellington Parade, East Melbourne; tel. 419–3311* • East of downtown near the Fitzroy Gardens and the cricket grounds. Glass and marble, antiques everywhere. Several restaurants, including the Clivedon Room, one of the best in town (expensive). Pool, sauna, spa, handicapped facilities, parking. Doubles A$235–295; suites A$350–1100.

Hyatt on Collins • *123 Collins St.; tel. 657–1234* • Huge marble foyer, lots of art, to us a discordant Art Deco flavor—pink lit ceilings, sterile feel. Collins Chase is an atrium-like complex of bars and international food outlets. The rooms have marble-top desks, mini-bars and the bathrooms are all marble and mirrors; great views. The Regnecy Club floor has guest lounge, free breakfast, evening cocktails and snacks; comes with a butler and concierge. The hotel has two restaurants, bar, nightclub, health center including a golf driving range, tennis courts, sauna, pool and a business center, kosher kitchen, parking. Doubles from A$330; Regency Club from A$400; suites from A$620–2000.

Regent • *25 Collins St.; tel. 653–0000* • North end of Collins near Parliament, occupying part of the 50-story Collins Tower—soaring interior, atrium lounge. Health center, two restaurants, the Black Swan bar. Rooms have original art, great views, fresh fruit and flowers, marble bathrooms. Pool, tennis, business center. Doubles A$310–360; suites A$460–2000.

Rockman's Regency • *Corner of Exhibitoin and Lonsdale sts.; tel. 662–3900* • Smaller luxury hotel; spacious rooms with separate dressing rooms, movie library, mini-bars, umbrellas (it's Melbourne, remember). Also one- and two-bedroom apartments and suites with spas. The restaurant—Memories of the Mediterranean—has won awards as one of the city's best new places. Pool, spa, sauna, health center, free valet parking. Doubles A$300–315; suites A$450–900.

Eden on the Yarra • *Corner of Flinders and Spencer sts.; tel. 629–5111* • Situated in the World Congress Centre, the city's new and ponderous convention complex. The hotel is modernistic, sterile, about as far from the grace of the Windsor as possible; still it's popular and carries a five-star rating. Two restaurants, two bars, business facilities, outdoor heated pool, valet parking. Rooms have mini-bars, hair dryers, irons. A number of special weekend packages called Temptations are available. Doubles A$245; suites A$320–385; penthouse A$775.

Old Melbourne Hotel • *5–17 Flemington Rd., North Melbourne; tel. 329–9344* • Mock-English building near the University of Melbourne. Restaurant and bistro bar; pool. parking, mini-bars. Doubles A$175; suites A$265–420.

Melbourne Airport Travelodge • *Center Road; tel. 338–2322.* • Opposite the international terminal, 20 kilometers northwest of the city. Restaurant, pool, courtesy airport van. Doubles A$100–175; suites $A360.

St. Kilda Road Travelodge • *Corner of Park St. and Kilda Rd., South Melbourne; tel. 699–4833* • Near Kings Domain and a tram ride to downtown. Restaurant/bar, pool. Doubles A$180.

Chateau Melbourne • *131 Lonsdale St., Melbourne 3000; tel. 663–3161* • Near the Greek-Lebanese restaurant quarter. Restaurant, bar, pool, sauna, mini-bars, parking. Rates start around $A120.

Magnolia Court • *101 Powlett St., East Melbourne 3002; tel. 419–4222.* • Another boutique hotel, not far from Fitzroy Gardens. Rates start around $A95–120 double.

Town House Hotel • *701 Swanston St., Carlton; tel. 347–7811* • Close to the university, green and leafy residential area northwest of the city center; on tram lines. Sauna, pool, barbecue, handicapped facilities. Doubles A$125; suites from A$200.

Astoria City Travel Inn • *288 Spencer St.; tel. 670–6801* • Near the Spencer Street railway station. Restaurant, pool, sauna, barbecue area, limited parking. Doubles A$100.

Melbourne Travelers Inn and Backpackers Center • *2 Enfield St., St. Kilda; tel. 534–8159* • Renovated building in an area close to a beach. Dorms and singles; furnished flats available, courtesy van. Rates from A$18 per person.

YHA Australia • *118 Lonsdale St.; tel. 662–2366* • Single, double or shared rooms. Kitchen, laundry. Discounts for five nights or longer. A$16 for members, A$20 non-members.

RESTAURANTS......................................

Stephanie's • *405 Tooranga Rd. Hawthorn East; tel. 20–8944* • Housed in a National Trust building east of the city center. Changing menu concentrates on fresh Australian foods cooked in a French style. Elegant dining room, good service. Lunch Fridays only; dinner Tuesday–Saturday. *Moderate to expensive.*

Mietta's • *7 Alfred Pl.; tel. 654–2366* • Always one of the city's finest, with the emphasis on French-style fish and native game. Excellent service. Lunch and dinner seven days. *Moderate to expensive.*

Colonial Tram Car Restaurant • *Phone 696–4000* • In a city of tram cards, the best of the lot because it's a restaurant. The tram, built in 1927, is burgundy on the outside, gleaming brass and velvet on the interior. It's white tablecloth, silver setting evening dining, with one-way glass so the slobs can't watch you eat your Seafood en cocotte Matthew Flinders or tenderloin of beef Sherwood. All food is prepared aboard the tram by the chef. Runs seven days a week, but reservations are necessary to book times and days. The whole thing is stabilized so your wine doesn't end up in your lap. *Expensive.*

Tapas Bar • *123 Collins St.; 657–1234* • In the Hyatt. Upstairs from the food court. Grilled prawns, stuffed croquetas, empanadillas, marinated veggies and other assorted Spanish finger food. Spanish and Australian wines and sangria. Flemenco dancing Friday and Saturday nights. Open 5 p.m.–late Monday–Saturday. *Expensive.*

Melbourne Oyster Bar and Seafood Restaurant • *209 King St.; tel. 670–1881* • Award-winner; specializing in lobster, prawn, crabs, fresh fish plus oysters, of course. Latin music nightly. Lunch from noon, Monday–Friday; dinner from 6:30 p.m. seven days. Reservations necessary. *Moderate to expensive.*

River Garden • *Flinders Street Station Concourse; tel. 614–2828* • Chinese specialties. Overlooking the Yarra River, Princes Bridge and the Victorian Arts Centre. Peking and Cantonese style cuisine. Live seafood tanks. Live music Friday and Saturday nights. Lunch noon–3, Sunday–Friday; dinner 5:30–11 p.m. seven days. *Moderate to expensive.*

Sawasdee Restaurant • *139 Little Bourke St.; tel. 663–4300* • Thai cuisine, winner of best ethnic restaurant awards. Some seating in small booths with Thai-style roofs. Music Wednesday–Sunday nights. Chili prawns, noodles, seafood. Thai-style buffet from noon–3 p.m. Sundays. Lunch noon–2:30 Monday–Friday; dinner from 6 p.m.; seven nights. *Budget to moderate.*

Cafe Bombay ● *396 Bay St., Port Melbourne; tel. 645–1933* ● On Port Phillip Bay southwest of town. When you walk in, look for the tandoori oven in a corner, typical Indian style. Naan bread with variety of dips; masala chicken curry; boneless chicken marinated in yogurt or lamb marinated in rum and spcies. BYO and licensed. Lunch noon–2:30 p.m. Tuesday–Friday; dinner 6–11 p.m. Tuesday–Sunday. *Moderate.*

Tsindos ● *197 Lansdowne St.; tel. 663–3194* ● Greek fare, specializing in fresh fish. Live Greek music and plate smashing Friday and Saturday nights. BYO and licensed. Lunch Monday–Friday; dinner from 6 p.m. Monday–Saturday. *Moderate.*

Copperwood ● *318 Lygon St., Carlton; tel. 347–1799* ● Restaurant or bistro style dining. Restaurant is seafood and steaks; bistro Italian and French. Latin music Wednesday–Saturday nights. Lunch and dinner seven days. *Moderate.*

Pancake Parlor ● *Three locations, including Centrepoint basement of the Bourke Street Mall* ● BYO. Family restaurant. Pancakes and crepes, excellent coffee. Open early to late, seven days a week. *Budget.*

Stalactities ● *Corner of Lonsdale and Russell sts.; tel. 663–3316* ● Open 24 hours; specalizes in Greek and Mediterranean food. Takeaways. BYO and licensed. *Budget to moderate.*

BEYOND MELBOURNE......................

The Blue Dandenongs

When Sidneysiders want to get away from it all and breathe some fresh air, they head for the Blue Mountains, which can be seen from the city's skyscrapers on a clear day. When Melbournians have the same urge, they turn to the Dandenong Ranges, a long hop and a short skip from the city center. The low, forested ranges, the highest of which is Mt. Dandenong at around 2000 feet, are only about 30 miles southeast of the city. The area is easily reached by getting onto Toorak Road, which in turn becomes Burwood Road and leads up into the forests.

There are several sections of public lands in the area, including

Ferntree Gully National Park, the **Mt. Dandenong Forest Reserve,** and several state forests. The mountains were a retreat for Melbourne's rich, and many of their old mansions and cottages have been converted into restaurants and guest houses. One of the more popular spots is at the top of Mt. Dandenong, where there is a **restaurant** with splendid nighttime views of the metropolitan area. Another popular attraction is **Puffing Billy,** a restored narrow gauge steam train that runs from Belgrave about eight miles through the thick forest to Emerald. A complete round trip takes about two hours, and costs about A$20. *Information on the train's schedule is available from Melbourne railway offices or by calling 870–8411.*

   Other spots to see in the Dandenongs are the **National Rhododendron Gardens** in Olinda, part of the Olinda State Forest, admission about A$5, and the **Healesville Sanctuary,** which has an excellent collection of Aussie animals including wombats, platypuses, kangaroos, wallabies, and the elusive lyrebird. In 1944, the staff at the reserve was able to breed platypuses in captivity for the first time. If your visit to Australia and Melbourne is brief, make this a definite stop. Open daily 9 a.m.–5 p.m. Admission charge about A$7. *Information: (059) 62–4022.*

The Mornington Peninsula

The beaches around Melbourne cannot really compare to those in Sydney or the coast of Queensland, but they are very popular with city folks. The most popular seaside area is the Mornington Peninsula, which forms the eastern cusp of Port Phillip Bay starting about 25 miles from the city. From Frankston, a series of small resort areas and beaches run along the bay to the tip of the peninsula at Portsea. The beaches are mostly calm water and are very crowded in the summer; at Portsea, there is a surfing beach. Of note on the bay side is Sorrento, where the 1803 expedition settled. There are more beaches, rockier and wilder, on the ocean side of the peninsula along Cape Schanck Coastal Park. The oceanside beaches can be dangerous—it was at Cheviot Beach, on the tip of the peninsula, where Prime Minister Harold Holt was drowned in 1967. A series of small roads lead from the bay coastal road (the Nepean Highway) to the park. There are also a number of beaches on the northeastern side of the peninsula. It is from Westernport, on the Westernport Bay side of the peninsula, that you catch a ferry to go to Phillip Island.

The Fairy Penguins

Undeniably one of the major tourist attractions in the Melbourne area is the nightly parade of foot-high fairy penguins that live on Phillip Island.

The birds (Eudyptula minor) spend their days fishing in the Bass Strait, then come home nightly to their colony at Summerland Beach on the island's southwest tip. You can watch the penguins struggle out of the surf at dusk from a fenced-off area for about A$5 per person. The penguin parade is included on many bus tours run from Melbourne; an average cost of the trip out from the city is around A$60 per person. *Information available from the Victours office in the city or call (059) 56–8691.* The island also has a large colony of sea lions, and there are koalas snoozing in trees at a sanctuary. The sea lion colony is at a spot called the Nobbies, an area of huge cliffs and enormous swells coming in from the ocean. In fact, the entire island is a hiking paradise and worth more than a penguin visit. Note, however, that it's very popular, with day-trippers by the thousands cramming in on summer weekends. The ferry trip across to the island is about A$5 one way. *Information: (059) 52–1014.* There is an office on the island with maps and information about the penguins and other attractions as you get off the ferry at the Cowes landing. *Information: (059) 56–7447.*

AROUND VICTORIA.........................

The Great Ocean Road

One of the most photogenic stretches of ocean highway in the world—as Northern Californians, this is tough to admit—runs for 180 gorgeous miles along Victoria's southwest coast. Called the Great Ocean Highway, it begins at Torquay, runs southwest to Cape Otway, then northeast to Peterborough. Torquay is near Victoria's second-largest city, Geelong, which sits on the western edge of Port Phillip Bay about 50 miles southwest of Melbourne.

Between Torqay and Cape Otway, the coast is backed by the Otway Ranges and the road passes through miles of Bass Strait surfing beaches. The **Australian Surfing Championships,** for example, are held each year at Bell Beach next to Torquay. There are a number of small resort villages along this stretch, many with old seaside buildings and safe swimming beaches. **Lorne** is the largest of the resort towns, and was a popular watering hole even before the road was completed in 1932. Lorne was almost destroyed in the Ash Wednesday bush fire in 1983. As you come into town from the north, you can still see evidence of the monster fire, which destroyed at least 2000 homes in the area and forced Lorne to be evacuated. Past Lorne, the road starts making its way along steep cliffs and the scenery is poetry-inspiring. At **Kennett River,** there is a turnoff to a trail that takes you on a 1.5-kilometer hike into a gorge with magnificent Victorian blue gums.

The last of the good beaches is at the resort town of **Apollo Bay.** Here the road leaves the sea and goes inland through the lush, fern-ridden forests of **Otway National Park.** The park, filled with ringtail possums, black-tailed wallabies, and satin bowerbirds, is also a treasure house of plant species, including many orchid varieties and huge tree ferns. There is an eight-mile unpaved road that leads to a lighthouse perched on 300-foot cliffs. The lighthouse has been there since 1848 in an attempt (often vain) to keep ships from the hostile shore. The stretch of shore from the lighthouse northwest is known as the **Shipwreck Coast;** more than 1000 vessels have met their doom there. The lighthouse is open Tues. and Thurs. 10 a.m.–noon and 2 p.m.–4 p.m. *Information: (952) 37–9240.* The park has several camping areas, 60 kilometers of towering coastline, and many hiking trails. *Information about the park: National Parks Service, Geelong-Otway District, 28 Murray St., Colac, Victoria 3250; tel. (052) 31–3833. Or ranger in charge, Apollo Bay, tel. (052) 31–3833.*

As the road turns northwest, it comes to some of the most dramatic scenery on the entire continent, a stretch of seastacks and arches and rugged cliffs carved by ocean waves smashing into the limestone formations after roaring unimpeded 15,000 miles from Cape Horn. Australia's second-most famous rock formation (after Ayers Rock) is here: the **12 Apostles,** just one group of sea sculptures among many. The Apostles are contained in **Port Campbell National Park,** a 20-mile strip along the coast that is slowly disappearing as the waves wear away the limestone. In the park is the site of the 1878 wreck of the immigrant ship *Loch Ard,* which sank with the loss of 52 lives. There are a number of turnoffs that take you to the more breathtaking vistas. There is camping in the park. *Information: Port Campbell National Park, Tregea St., Port Campbell 3269; tel. (055) 98–6382.* The road leaves the coast soon after the park. At Warrenambool, about 40 miles from the park, is the **Flagstaff Hill Maritime Museum,** a recreated 19th-century port that has a museum with displays on the dangers of the Shipwreck Coast, including artifacts salvaged from the *Loch Ard.* It's open 9:30 a.m.–4:30 p.m.

Wilson's Promontory National Park

The Prom, as it's known, is as far south as you can go on the Australian mainland, and is the most popular national park in Victoria and one of the top draws in the nation. More than 100,000 people a year come to enjoy the park's bushwalking trails, camping facilities, huge flocks of birds, and good beaches. The park is basically 360 square miles of granite peaks and eucalypt forests, and lies about 150 miles southeast of Melbourne. The park area once was part of the land bridge across the Bass Strait to Tasmania. The park has several tall peaks, the highest being **Mt. Latrobe** at about 2500 feet.

Among the most popular of the park's animals are rainbow lorikeets and the noisy rosellas. Also, you'll find wombats, laughing kookaburras, gray kangaroos, and emus. In parts of the park, trees grow 200 feet tall, but there are also mangroves and ferns. There are a number of hiking trails, but access is limited as rangers try to keep the environmental impact of the annual summer tourist invasion to a minimum. Some parts of the park are off-limits completely and camping is by permit only to prevent overcrowding. The park is so popular that space in the park's rental cabins is decided by a lottery. There are camping fees and a day-use fee of A$2. *Information about the park is available from the ranger in charge at Wilson's Promontory National Park, Tidal River via Foster 3960; tel. (056) 80–8538. Or from the National Parks Service, South Gippsland Office, Main St., Foster 3960; tel. (056) 82–2133.*

Gold Country

Victoria's gold fields, site of the 1851 gold madness, lie northwest of Melbourne, centered between the two boomtowns of Ballarat and Bendigo. The rush saw a flood of prospectors wash into the area, and by 1854, there were 100,000 people looking for gold. It was from this one of the nicknames for Australians arose: diggers. **Ballarat** was also to earn an unending place in Australian political history as well when it became the site of the miner's strike and the famous **Eureka Stockade** incident. (See the History section). After a time, the easy gold was all taken and the mines became large, company-owned operations. The gold fields returned to their pastoral beginnings and Melbourne, which had become a ghost town during the boom, grew back to normal size.

In its wake, just like its 1848 counterpart in California, the 1851 Victoria Gold Rush left the residues of sudden wealth: mansions, ornate public buildings, fine hotels, and large churches. It was the peak of the Victorian age, remember, and when the newly rich diggers built, they modeled their efforts after England's finest. Ballarat is worth a visit if for nothing else than a look (and a jar) at the incredible wooden bar at **Craigs Royal Hotel.** You can also get a room (nothing fancy) for about A$60–80. Information: (053) 31–1377. The whole town is a rich stew of Italianate, Gothic, Romanesque, and French Renaissance touches, all highlighted by intricate wrought iron grilles. Nearby Creswick has a wonderfully ornate **town hall,** and Clunes, a nearby town where the first strike was made, is famous for its **verandahs** and **elegant banks.** Bendigo, where some of the richest lodes of gold in the world were discovered, is noted not only for its Victorian architectural excesses but also its history of racial tension, when thousands of Chinese flocked into the area to look for gold.

Ballarat is the usual destination in the area because of **Sovereign Hill,** a touristy re-creation of a working gold field and boomtown, complete with stagecoach rides, gold panning, costumed residents, and shops and businesses from the era of the Rush, including a small **Chinatown** and more steam-age machinery than you can imagine. Needless to say, it's often packed with people. The Hill is open daily 9 a.m.–5 p.m., admission charge about A$10. *Information: (053) 31–1944.* Nearby is the **Gold Museum,** open 10 a.m.–5 p.m. with displays of Gold Rush and Aboriginal history of the area; admission A$2. Also in Ballarat is the **Eureka Stockade,** which has a memorial to the uprising and an historical display; open 9 a.m.–5 p.m.

One of the main draws in **Bendigo** is the **Central Deborah Mine,** restored to working order and open to daily tours above and below ground, and the **"Talking Trams"** which start at the mine and give a taped commentary as they wind around the town. They run hourly, starting at 9:30 a.m.; the fare is about A$4. Worth a look in town are the tall spire of **Sacred Heart Cathedral,** the impressive **Victorian Post Office** and nearby, **Sandhurst,** a smaller recreated mining community. Northeast of Ballarat on the Western Highway is a **wine-growing region** centered around Great Western, known for its white table wines and sparkling wines.

The Victorian Age

Victoria says it has the largest ski resort in the Southern Hemisphere, **Mt. Buller,** just three hours from Melbourne in that part of the Great Dividing Range known as the Victorian Alps. The mountains are the highest in the state, leading up to the border of New South Wales and **Snowy River National Park.** The entire area is becoming increasingly popular both for downhill and cross-country skiing in the winter and for bushwalkers and trout fishers in the summer. There are a half-dozen major ski resorts in the state, with runs for all skills and ages. In addition, there are several national parks. **Accommodations** at the ski resorts run from motels to fancy lodges. In addition to Mt. Buller, which is served by V/Line buses from Melbourne, other resorts include **Falls Creek,** with 22 lifts and more than 50 runs; **Mt. Buffalo,** with one lift; **Mt. Hotham,** the highest in the state, with three lifts; **Bogong High Plains,** a mecca for cross-country skiers; **Mt. Baw Baw,** the southernmost of the resorts; and **Lake Mountain,** only 1½ hours from Melbourne and popular with novice skiers. *Information about the resorts and accommodations is available from the Victorian Ski Association, P.O. Box 210, South Melbourne, Vic. 3205; tel. 699–3292. Or the Ski*

Touring Association of Victoria, GPO Box 20A, Melbourne 3001; tel. 329–2262.

National parks in the area include **Bogong,** which contains the 10 highest peaks in Victoria, including Mt. Bogong, a popular target for skiers and hikers, trout fishing, camping and climbing. *Information: National Parks and Wildlife Service, North East District Office, P.O. Box 456, Wangaratta 3677, tel. (057) 21–5557.* Also **Mt. Buffalo National Park,** camping, hiking, skiing and 140 kilometers of trails. *Information: Mt. Buffalo National Park, Mt. Buffalo 3745, tel. (057) 55–1466.*

The Mighty Murray

Australia's Mississippi, complete with paddlewheelers, drove early explorers crazy—it was believed that after it started flowing from its source near Mt. Kosciusko in New South Wales, it flowed inland to a great central lake. It doesn't, of course; it goes almost due west and dumps into the ocean in South Australia after a run of about 1200 miles. After it gets serious east of Albury and creates the watery recreation area at **Lake Hume,** the Murray meanders through the dry country of north-central Victoria, now green thanks to irrigation schemes, and along the way passes some old steamboat towns that recall the days when boats came all the way up from Adelaide. Taking a cruise on the Murray is a popular vacation, although most of the fleet operates on the South Australia stretch of the river.

The most famous of the river towns was (and is) **Echuca,** which sits at the confluence of three rivers and still has a wooden pier to mark its days of glory. The old **Star Hotel,** dating from the 1860s, serves as the city's information center. Several paddlewheelers are available for cruises in Echuca, including the *Canberra,* with a one-hour trip going for about A$5. Tickets are available at the **Bond Store;** (054) 82–2141. The Bond Store is an old building where goods were stored until customs duties were paid to all three states on the river, a complicated procedure.

Another famous river town was **Swan Hill,** about 100 miles downstream from Echuca. The spot was named by an irate explorer who was kept up all night by black swans honking on the river. The **Swan Hill Pioneer Settlement** is a reconstruction of a 19th-century river town, along lines of Sovereign Hill in Ballarat. On hand are a blacksmith forge, a Cobb and Co. coach, shops, and the *Gem,* the Murray's largest paddlewheeler, preserved and open to tours. Admission to the village, open from 8:30 a.m.–5 p.m. daily, is about A$10 per person. At night, there's a light and sound show, also about A$10. *Information: (050) 32–1093.*

Mildura, near the three corners where New South Wales, South

Australia, and Victoria meet, is the heart of the state's citrus industry, made possible in this dry and dusty area by Murray irrigation waters. Also in the area are **vineyards** of two of Australia's giant winemakers, Lindeman's and Mildara, as well as other wineries. Mildura also claims to have the largest bar in the world—about 300 feet, housed in the **Workingman's Club.** You can take a 5-day-long excursion aboard the *P.S. Coonawarra,* which goes from Mildura downstream and includes a side trip up the Darling River, and enters the Murray at Wentworth, a few miles away. The cost, including meals, is about A$620 per person for a cabin with private facilities. Book it through Ron's Tourist Centre in Mildura; tel. (050) 21–1166 or 23–6351. Another boat to try is the *P.S. Emmylou,* which departs from Echuca, and depending on river conditions, goes upstream or down about 70 kilometers. A two-day, two-night cruise, including most meals, is A$350 per person. *Information: Emmylou Enterprises in Moama, NSW; tel. (054) 82–3801.*

SOUTH AUSTRALIA

Much of the island continent of Australia is a contrast between the often lush and very livable verges around the coastlines and the dry and often unlivable central deserts. Perhaps nowhere is that contrast as obvious as in South Australia, the driest of the nation's states, yet a state also known for its graceful, almost-English farmlands and rich bounties of wine, fruits and wheat. But it is also the state where you find the town of Coober Pedy, on the southern edge of the Great Red Centre, where temperatures are so beastly, most of the population lives underground. A full two-thirds of the state is either desert or near desert, and because of this, almost 75% of all South Australians live in Adelaide, making it the most urbanized state in Australia. The city itself averages less than 25 inches of rain a year.

South Australia has long had a reputation as one of the most conservative states, a tradition begun when the colony was founded in 1836. It was thought, by the men suggesting the colony be started, that many of the things that gave Australia such a bad image in those days could be avoided with a little fiscal responsibility. Looking at the brash crop of colonists over in New South Wales, especially in Sydney, the founders of South Australia ordained that land in their new colony would be sold for a high price, thus assuring that those who came to settle were neither riff nor raff, but solid citizens. Starting with such a base, it is no surprise that South Australia came to be a tad conservative, but the brush that painted that picture has been a little too broad. South Australia, for example, was the first state to give women the vote and to allow women into universities. More recently, it ruled that homosexuality between consulting adults was legal, a step that is about as volatile as can be taken in a country with Australia's long history of macho male ethic.

South Australia is called the festival state, so-named because of the many ethnic, artistic, and harvest festivals held there, especially the **Festival of the Arts,** Australia's premier gathering of performers and artists, held in even-numbered years. It is also the home of the **Australian Grand Prix,** and its diversified industries produce automobiles, chemicals, and steel, along with a host of other commodities. It has one of the world's largest **copper mines** (a copper boom in the 1840s assured the success of the fledgling colony) and also boasts one of the world's largest **uranium mines.** The country's **rocket and nuclear research station** is located at the top-secret Woomera Prohibited Area off the Stuart Highway in the north. And, of course, South Australia produces some of the best **wines** on the continent. The state has more than 150 wineries, the most famous of which are in the **Barossa Valley** near Adelaide. South Australian vines produce almost 60% of all Australian wine, and most of the tourists who come to the state do so because of wine—and to visit the green velvet tables of the **Adelaide Casino.**

The Essential South Australia

INFORMATION • For information about South Australia in North America, contact **Tourism South Australia,** 2121 Ave. of the Stars, #1210, Los Angeles, Calif. 90067; tel. (213) 552–2821.

GETTING THERE • Adelaide is served by the major national airlines, including **Ansett** and **Australian.** Air fares from Sydney will cost between A$200 and A$280 one way. It's about a 1½-hour flight from Sydney. The airport is about four miles west of the city. Taxi fares into town are about A$8; the airport shuttle bus downtown, with stops at some hotels, is A$3.

Adelaide is a major rail transportation hub. The **Indian Pacific,** which runs from Sydney to Perth, passes through Adelaide, and the **Ghan,** which runs north to Alice Springs, starts here. The trip from Sydney on the Indian Pacific takes about 27 hours and costs about A$250 first class. There is also a daily speedlink service between the two capitals, which takes about 20 hours. There is also Mon.–Sat. service to Melbourne and service to Perth five times a week. *Information is available from the South Australia Travel Centre, 18 King William St.; 212–1505. Hours are weekdays 8:45 a.m.–5 p.m.; Tuesdays 9–5; weekends 9 a.m.–2 p.m.*

TELEPHONES • The area code for Adelaide area is (08).

TIME • South Australia, like the Northern Territory, is on Central Standard, which puts it a half-hour behind Sydney. Daylight savings time is in effect from October–March.

CLIMATE • As noted, it ranges from Mediterranean in and around Adelaide to forbidding desert north and west. Adelaide averages around 85° in the summer and around 60° in the winter. Up north, it can get well above 130° in the summer and freezing during a winter night.

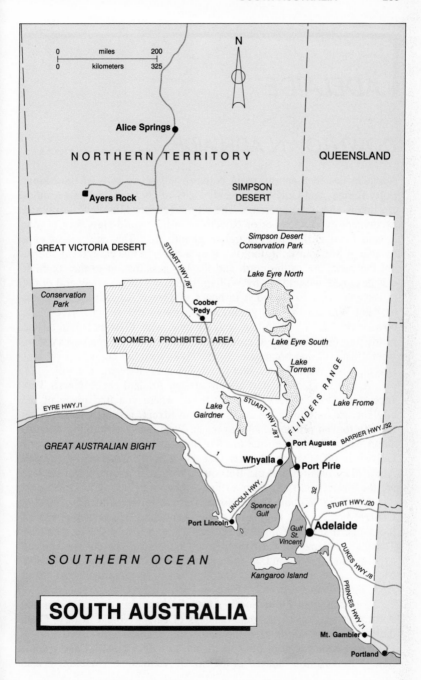

SOUTH AUSTRALIA

ADELAIDE

DOWNTOWN ADELAIDE.....................

Adelaide lies in a coastal plain between the gentle rolls of the Mount Lofty Ranges and Gulf St. Vincent, a city of churches and parks, modern hotels and old Victorians. The city streets are filled with noise and excitement every October or November, when world-class drivers roar around town during the Australian Grand Prix. The city is sort of a reverse of Melbourne: it, too, is cut by a river, in this case, the Torrens, but the parks are to the north and the business district to the south. It was designed and laid out by William Light, the surveyor-general of the infant colony, who named it in honor of Queen Adelaide, the consort of King William IV. His grand, very symmetrical designs have made downtown Adelaide a perfect walking city, with Victoria Square at the heart, four other squares at each corner, and beyond, green parks everywhere. The outside boundaries of the downtown are delineated by four streets, East, West, North, and South Terraces. Population 1 Mil.

A logical place to start a walk around Adelaide is on **North Terrace,** four lanes wide with shady trees, where you find many of the city's major buildings. On **King William Street,** just off the terrace, is the **city tourist office,** which has maps. Within a short walking distance along North Terrace are the **old Parliament building,** the **casino,** the **University of Adelaide,** the **Art Gallery of South Australia,** the **South Australia Museum** and the **Botanic Gardens.** Also on North Terrace are the Ansett and Australian airlines offices.

Up King William from North Terrace is the **Adelaide Festival Centre,** home every two years of the Adelaide Festival of the Arts. It looks like a series of huge tents, and sits in a lovely grassy area near Torrens Lake (part of the river). It has four theaters, a concert hall, an experimental theater and an open-air amphitheater. Tours are available Mon.–Fri. 10 a.m.–4 p.m., and four times on Saturday; cost about A$3. *Information: 216–8713.*

The **Art Gallery of South Australia** has a mixture of Asian and Australian art, including some displays of early colonial history. Open daily, 10 a.m.–5 p.m., free admission. *Information: 223–7200.*

Next door is one of the best displays of Aboriginal art and anthropology in Australia, housed in the **South Australian Museum.** It also

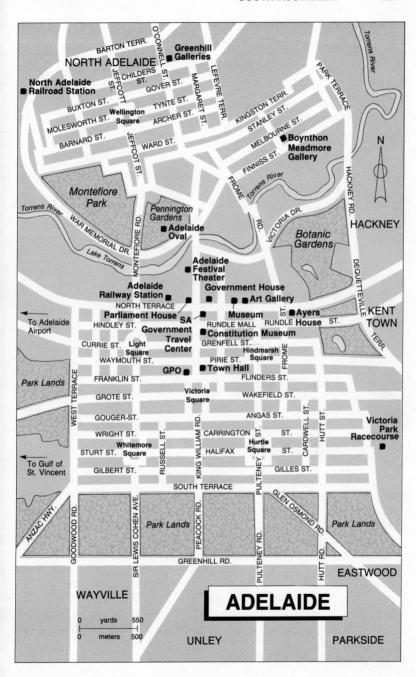

ADELAIDE

boasts one of the world's largest displays of meteorites. Open daily, 10–5; free admission. *Information: 223–8911.*

Royal South Australian Society of the Arts • At the corner of Kintore Avenue and North Terrace, it holds regular exhibitions of art-works, plus has a permanent collection of historic paintings. It's about a block east of the art gallery. Open Monday–Friday 11–5; weekends 2–5 p.m.

Tandanya Aboriginal Culture Center • *253 Grenfell St.; tel. 223–2467* • Between King William and Hindmarsh Square. It's one of the country's major Aboriginal arts centers. There is a performing arts area, museum/gallery and workshops. Good collection of contemporary works. Open 10:30–5 weekdays; noon–5 p.m. weekends.

Adelaide Botanic Gardens, Herbarium and Conservatory • *East end of North Terrace; tel. 228–2311* • Here is displayed one of the largest collections of Australian and Malaysian plants in existence. There are walking paths with wheelchair access; free guided tours at 10:30 a.m. Tuesday and Friday starting from the kiosk. Licensed restaurant/bar. The gardens are free and are open Monday—Friday 7 a.m.–dusk; 9 a.m.–dusk weekends. Restaurant information: 223–3526.

Ayers House, on the South side of the terrace near the Botanic Gardens, is an excellent example of the sort of place the early colonial patriciate hung their hats. Built as the home of Sir Henry Ayers, the premier of South Australia, the building now houses the offices of the National Trust and a pair of restaurants. The house is open Tues.–Fri. 10 a.m.–4 p.m. and weekends 2–4 p.m.; admission A$2. *Information: 223–1196.*

The **Adelaide Casino** is housed in half of the city's old central train station, part of a restoration project that included the Adelaide Convention Centre and the new Hyatt Regency Hotel. The casino is a popular night spot, plush, lively, and visited by more than two million people a year. Here's the spot to try your hand at two-up, the Aussie version of odds and evens. There's a carpeted pit, surrounded by betting stations. The game is played with two coins tossed into the air; the coins are blank on one side, marked with an X on the other. You bet that both coins will either come down blank or with Xs. If they come down one of each they're tossed again. If they come down mixed five times (and they do a lot), the house takes all wagers. As an added lure, they try to entice bettors to come toss the dice. It ain't easy to do, and a couple of bad throws can get the crowd ugly. But it's great fun, not too expensive (depending on your bets, of course) and very contagious. It also has a number of bars, a restaurant and a limited dress code. It's owned by the same company that runs casinos in Burswood in Western

Australia, Malaysia and the Bahamas. Hours are 11 a.m.–4 a.m. Monday–Thursday; weekends it opens at 11 a.m. Friday, closes at 4 a.m. Monday. *Information: 212–2811, toll–free (008) 88–8711.*

OTHER ADELAIDE SIGHTS...................

On the south banks of the Torrens northeast of the Botanic Gardens is the **Adelaide Zoological Gardens,** considered by many to be among the best zoos in the world, particularly well known for being able to breed rare and endangered wild animals in captivity. The collection ranges from polar bears to probably the best display of Australian birds in the country. Open 9:30 a.m.–5 p.m. daily. Free tours by calling ahead. *Information: 267–3255.*

Glenelg, southeast of the city, is a fine beach area offering an ocean escape from the fairly routine style of downtown Adelaide. South Australia began here when the province was proclaimed on Dec. 28, 1836. The actual proclamation site is at the corner of MacFarlane Street on the beach. Glenelg is also a major shopping area, especially along Jetty Road where the side streets and arcades offer more than 400 stores and shops. It also has a raft of restaurants, from fast food to fancy. Glenelg is also the home of the *Buffalo,* a replica of the ship that brought the first colonists to South Australia in 1836. In addition to the various historical displays, the ship (built in 1980) has a restaurant and an aquarium. The ship is open Mon.–Fri. 9 a.m.–5 p.m., weekends 10 a.m.–5 p.m. *Information: 294–7000.* Getting to Glenelg is half the fun— hop the **Bay Tram** near Victoria Square and take the 30-minute ride out to the beach for about A$1.80 one way. The trams run 6 a.m.– 11:30 p.m. Mon.–Sat. and 9 a.m.–10 p.m. Sun. The ride is about a half hour. *Information: 210–1000.*

North Adelaide is where the English nabobs and landed gents settled after the voyage from Portsmouth. How gentry were the gentry? Rumor has it that many of them shipped such indispensible items as high mounds of bulky furniture, crates full of silver and crystal, race horses, and even grand pianos, it being well known that life on the frontier, without the proper equipment, was a true bitch. When the city was laid out, only one suburb was planned, North Adelaide, and here the rich flocked to build some of the finest examples of colonial architecture in Australia. You get to the burb by taking either King William street from Victoria Square or Montefiore Street from Light Square. They did let a few lowly born types in, however, and their houses have been converted into upscale boutiques, proving that if you wait long enough, everybody becomes respectable.

Adelaide's late-night party district is along **Hindley Street,** which runs from King William Street to West Terrace in the northwest corner of the central district. Here you find all manner of fast-food joints, ethnic restaurants, pubs, a few adult book stores, and a stripper or two.

THE ESSENTIAL ADELAIDE

INFORMATION • The **South Australia Government Travel Centre** offers city information as well as information about the entire state. *Information: 21 King William St., tel. 212–1644.* There's a hotline for current goings-on around town: 11–688. Emergency medical services available by calling 223–0230, 45–0222 or 275–9911. For information about handicapped facilities, see the Disability Information and Resources Centre, 195 Giles St.; tel. 223–7522. The Royal Automobile Association of South Australia is at Hindmarsh Square; tel. 223–4555; emergency road service 340–0000. Banking hours are Monday–Thursday 9:30–4, Friday 9:30–5. Note: when cashing travelers checks in South Australia, a stamp duty of 10 cents a check is charged.

GETTING AROUND • The city has free bus service around the downtown area on the **Beeline** and **Loop** buses, which run 8 a.m.–6 p.m. Monday–Thursday, 8 a.m.–9 p.m. Friday, and 8–12:15 p.m. Saturday. *Information about the city and suburban bus services, run by the State Transport Authority, is available from the STA Centre, 79 King William St., tel. 210–1000. It also has suburban train schedules.* All interstate/intrastate trains depart from the Adelaide Rail Passenger Terminal west of town off the West beach/airport road (Burbridge Avenue). For bookings and information: 231–4366 or 217–4455. The State Rail Authority also runs a special bus, the O-Bahn, a sort of cross between a bus and a monorail, that takes you on a high-speed ride from Adelaide out to the northwest suburbs along the Torrends River. A major stop is the Tea Tree Plaza Shopping Centre.

There are four major taxi services in Adelaide, running 24 hours: Amalgamated 223–3333; Diamond 47–3222; Suburban 211–8888 and United 223–3111. Access Cabs has wheelchair taxis, 371–0033. Pedicabs available by calling 232–2914.

The **Adelaide Explorer,** a tourist bus disguised as a tram, runs to many of the important sights around town, with service every 90 minutes or so; tickets are about A$15. You can catch it at the government travel centre on King Wiliam St. *Information: 231–4144.*

SHOPPING • Shopping hours are generally 9 a.m.–5:30 p.m. Mon.–Thurs.; 9 a.m.–9 p.m. Fri., and 9 a.m.–noon Sat.

The major shopping area in Adelaide is the **Rundle Mall,** the first enclosed shopping mall built in Australia, situated on a pedestrian-only stretch of Rundle Street east of King William Street. The mall has the big Aussie department stores—**David Jones, Meyer**—plus scads of smaller stores, flower stalls, street musicians, brick streets, and outdoor cafes.

Another favorite haunt of Adelaide shoppers is the **Central Market,** behind the Hilton Hotel on Grote Street, just west of Victoria Square. This is one of Australia's premier flea/produce markets. It's open Tues. and Fri. from dawn to dusk and on Sat. from 7 a.m.–1 p.m. Melbourne Street in North Adelaide is the city's posh boutique area, with lots of clothing and accessories on view. Hours: 7 a.m.–5:30 p.m. Tuesday; 11 a.m.–5:30 p.m. Thursday; 7 a.m.–9 p.m. Friday, and 7 a.m.–1 p.m. Saturday.

ACCOMMODATIONS........................

Hilton International • *233 Victoria Square; tel. 217–0711* • Home of the Grange, one of the best dining rooms in town, which has a huge wine cellar. Mini-bars, pool, spa, sauna, barbecue, handicapped facilities. Doubles A$235–265; suites A$360–925.

Hyatt Regency • *North Terrace; tel. 231–1234* • Part of the redevelopment of the city's old train station (also houses the casino), the Hyatt has the best downtown location. Several restaurants, nightclub, outdoor pool, spa, sauna, parking. Doubles start at A$250; suites A$400–1450.

Adelaide Parkroyal • *226 South Terrace; tel. 223–4355.* • Some rooms with balconies overlooking the park areas. Pool, restaurant/bar, guests-only bar. Doubles from A$110–190; suites A$250–300.

Hotel Adelaide • *62 Brougham Place, Adelaide 5000; tel. 267–3444* • Near North Adelaide, good views of the city. Recently remodeled, with pool, two restaurants, and bar. Around 150 rooms, with doubles starting around $A140; suites A$185–220.

Grosvenor • *125 North Terrace; tel. 231–2961* • Opposite the Casino, a tad seedy but a good bargain nonetheless, popular with business types. Mini-bars, licensed restaurant, bistro bar, parking. Doubles from A$85; suites $1A85.

Ramada Grand Hotel • *Moseley Square, Glenelg; 376–1222* • Next to the jetty and tram station. Our favorite in the Adelaide area because it's on the beach and not downtown. Airy yellow and wood lobby with fancy streetlamps. Close to a golf course and the racetrack. Two restaurants and two bars. Pool. Doubles from A$110–200; suites from A$150–540.

Barron Townhouse • *Corner Hindley and Morphett sts.; 211–8255* • Close to the casino. Pool, barbecue, sauna, mini-bars, parking. Doubles from A$145; suites from A$155.

Adelaide Travelodge • *208 South Terrace; 223–2744* • Next to the Parkroyal. Pool, parking. Doubles between A$95 and A$130.

Newmarket • *Corner of North and West Terraces; tel 211–8533.* • Long of tooth, but still serviceable. Good restaurant, great old pub. Disco Friday and Saturday nights. Doubles from A$90.

YMCA • *76 Flinders St.; tel 223–1611* • Central location; linens and towels supplied, no kitchen. Facilities for women, men, families and groups. Dorm rooms also available. A$18–30 per person.

Adelaide Youth Hostel • *290 Gillies St.; tel. 223–6007* • Modern facility, large lounge, barbecue, kitchen, laundry. Dorm closed during day. A$14 members; $A20 non-members.

RESTAURANTS.....................................

HMS Buffalo • *Adelphi Terr., Patawalonga Boat Haven, Glenelg; tel. 294–7000* • Seafood restaurant and museum. Full size replica of an 1813 ship. Choice of three dining rooms: The Governor Hindmarsh, seats 100; Captain's Table, seats 35; or the First Mate's Cabin, seats 4–6. Large cellar of South Australian wines. Specialties include hot and spicy Oysters Rio, chicken and Atlantic salmon wrapped in filo, or beef with crayfish. One small caveat: the below-deck area carried a faint odor of stale cigarete smoke, if you care. Lunch Sunday–Friday; dinner seven days. *Moderate to expensive.*

Samurai • *137 Melbourne St.; tel 267–3381* • Adelaide's first Japanese restaurant, dating from 1970. Shoes verboten, but you don't have to sit on the floor. Teppanyaki or a buffet menu. Lunch noon–2 p.m. Friday and Saturday; dinner 5:30–11 p.m. seven days. *Moderate.*

Petaluma's • *Bridgewater Mill, Mt. Barker Rd., Bridgewater; tel. 339–3422* • Australian food with a French flair. Choice of dining inside at the Granery or outside overlooking Cox's Creek. National award winner; also has wine sales. Lunch and dinner seven days. *Moderate to expensive.*

Adelaide Tram Car Restaurant • *Phone 410–0044* • Goes from Victoria Square to Glenelg and back. 1920's refurbished tram decorated in an Orient Express theme. Seven runs a day—breakfast, morning tea, lunch, cocktails only or dinner. Dinner in the A$60-per-person range Friday and Saturday nights. Reservations necessary.

Bacall's • *149 Melbourne St., North Adelaide; tel. 267–2030* • New Orleans atmosphere with Creole and Cajun cuisine. Charcoal and wood-oven cooking. Blackened fish, jambalaya, fresh baked breads. Lunch from noon Wednesday–Friday; dinner from 6:30 Monday–Saturday. *Moderate.*

La Trattoria Restaurant and Pizza Bar • *346 King William St.; tel. 212–3327* • Italian stuff; house specialities are veal scallopini and seafood. Take-aways. Lunch noon–3 p.m. Monday–Friday; dinner 5:30 p.m.– 1 a.m. Monday–Thursday, 5:30 p.m.–3 a.m. Friday and Saturday, 5:30–11 p.m. Sunday. *Moderate.*

Rapp's BYO • *178 Hutt St.; tel. 223–1529* • Casual, decorated with pottery by a Clare Valley artist as well as paintings by local artists. Even the napkins are hand-made. Enclosed courtyard full of plants and a pot-bellied stove. French, Italian, Middle Eastern, curries and vegetarian. Brunch Sunday from 11 a.m.; dinner from 6 p.m. Wednesday–Sunday. *Budget to moderate.*

Jerusalem Sheskabab House • *131B Hinley St.; tel. 212–6185* • BYO. Lebanese tucker. Popular with students—crowded on Fridays and Saturdays. Kebabs, hummus, tabouli—the major food groups of life. Lots of vegetarian dishes. Take-aways. Noon–midnight seven days. *Budget to moderate.*

Cafe C • *Main St. Springton; (085) 68–2220* • Small restaurant; part of a winery 20 kilometers east of town. Two rooms and a shaded courtyard. Specialties are red meat with all local produce: rack of lamb with mint pesto crust or blackened kangaroo with blue gum and chardonnay sauce. Local wines. Lunch Friday–Monday; dinner from 6 p.m. Friday and Saturday. Moderate to expensive.

BEYOND ADELAIDE ....

The **Adelaide Hills,** nestled to the east and southeast of the city center, are a combination of farms and parklands dotted with historic buildings, pubs, restaurants, and high spots to look back toward the gulf and the city below. The best view in the hills is from the top of **Mt. Lofty,** about 2300 feet above sea level. There's a road that winds all the way to the top. Near the summit is the **Mt. Lofty Botanic Gardens.** Also nearby is the **Cleland Conservation Park,** where you can get kissing cousin close to koalas, roos, emus, wombats, and anything else that happens to wander by. It's popular for picnics and is open daily 9:30 a.m.–5 p.m. They feed the herds from 2 to 4 p.m. *Information: 339–2572.* The hills are criss-crossed with roads, each one of which seems to have something to gawk at.

A bit farther out (about 20 miles east of downtown) is the touristy Germanic village of **Hahndorf,** where things are leather-panted and umlauted, and you can nosh on wurst and strudel. There is a beer festival every year, and the **Old Mill Restaurant** there is worth a stop.

Wine Country

The **Barossa Valley,** about 30 miles northeast of the city off the Sturt Highway (not Stuart) near Tanunda and Angaston, is the major **wine area** of the state. It was settled in the 1840s by German immigrants and the area is full of Lutheran Churches and wineries with Germanic names. More than 50 wineries are scattered on vineyards in the area, ranging in size from Mom-and-Pop outfits to huge producers such as **Penfolds/ Kaiser Stuhl,** the largest in Australia. **Tanunda,** founded by German immigrants in the early 1840s, is the site of the biennial **Barossa Valley Vintage Festival** held every April in odd-numbered years.

The festival started in 1947 as a celebration to mark the crush, but over the years has evolved into a huge week-long fair with heavy emphasis of Germanic and other European influences. The parade held as part of the festivities draws nearly 100,000 people along the seven-kilometer route, and the three sit-down dinners held each festival are three course, four-hour along affairs that are often booked two years in advance.

If you want to take a tour of the Barossa Valley—or its increasingly popular neighbor, the Clare Valley—contact the South Australian tourism office in Los Angeles. One tour available, for real wine lovers, is a two-week trek through the Hunter Valley north of Sydney, then the wine areas of South Australia. This tour runs about $4200 per person, including round trip air fare from North America, accommodations, wine tastings, gourmet meals and sightseeing. Cheaper, if you're in the area, are tours offered by Festival Mini-Tours. A one-day tour of some Barossa Valley wineries and other sights, including lunch at a winery, is about A$50 per person; other tours available hit the Murray River or the Clare Valley. Information from the South Australian Government Tourism Office in Adelaide; tel. 212–1505. Also note that if you're around Adelaide in August, the vintners of the valley hold a gourmet weekend sometime during the month with tastings and food from local restaurants. The Clare Valley equivalent is held in May. Tastings at many of the wineries are free. You can get to the valley on a tour from Adelaide, or take special buses every day that run between Adelaide and the valley towns. The buses cost about A$5 one-way. *Information from the information centre on King William St.*

Among wineries worth a visit are **Seppeltsfield,** another biggy, *information (085) 62–8028;* the very fashionable and increasingly popular **Wolf Blass,** *information (085) 62–1955;* and **Yalumba,** *information (085) 64–24233.* If you've never taken a winery tour, check the one at **Orlando Winery,** which will take you around and show you how to make wine Aussie style for about A$2. *Information: Orlando, Barossa Valley Highway, Roland Flat 5352; tel. (085) 24–4500.*

There are a number of *motel-type places* in the area, as well as some upscale guest houses. Check the **Lawley Farm** near Tanunga, with doubles starting about A$75. *Information, (085) 63–2141.* Another popular inn is **The Hermitage** in Marananga, with a well-received dining room and its own vines. Doubles are around A$80. *Information: (085) 62–2722.*

One of the most recommended restaurants in the area is the **Pheasant Farm** in Nuriootpa, which specializes in fancy game dishes and country cooking. *Information: (085) 62–1286.* Also popular is the **Barossa Junction** in Tanunda, which has rooms as well as fine food. The rooms range from about A$60 to A$200 double. *Information: (085) 63–3400.*

General information about the Valley: Barosa Tourist Office, 66 Murray St., Nurrioota; phone (085) 62–1866.

Kangaroo Island

The Aussies have been trying to keep Kangaroo Island a secret. It's a wildlife paradise, a hiker's treasure, a wooded getaway with steep cliffs and great beaches. It is also home to about 4000 people, many of whom work small island farms or run charter fishing outfits. The island was discovered in 1803 by the indefatigable explorer Matthew Flinders, who chose to name it after the roos he and his men chowed on while they were there. It was first settled by convicts from Tasmania and served as a whaling base for Yankee skippers. It developed a nasty reputation as a hangout for low-life types who scrounged a living in the sealing trade and by helping at the whaling station. Today, most of the population lives in three settlements: **Kingscote, American River,** and **Penneshaw.**

The island is basically limestone, which has been eroded into bluffs and has also formed large underground caves, one of which, **Kelly Hill Caves,** is open to the public. Among the large group of animals you'll run into are the Western gray kangaroo, a very large critter indeed. Also hanging around are Australian sea lions, almost hunted to extinction and now found at several spots on the island. The seals, although under the protection of the government, are permitted to have visitors. There is also a colony of New Zealand fur seals, also hunted to near extinction. Other furry things include wallabies, possums, and bandicoots. Feathered inhabitants include fairy penguins and emus.

At the western tip of the island is **Flinders Chase National Park,** an area of dense forests and a perfect place to camp. A favorite spot for photographs is at a rock formation called **Remarkable Rocks,** where a pair of giant boulders are balanced on the edge of a cliff. There are at least 60 species of orchids said to be growing in the park. Permits are required for camping. *Information is available from the National Parks and Wildlife Service, 55 Grenfell St., Adelaide 5000; tel. 216–7777. Or ranger in charge, Flinders Chase National Park, PMB 246, Kingscote 5223; tel. (0848) 37–235.*

There are several lodges and motels in Kingscote. One place to check for meals is **Muggleton's General Store,** a BYO in Penneshaw not far from the ferry dock. It's possible to do the island on a day trip with **Lloyd Aviation,** which runs a tour four times a week that includes lunch and a trip to the caves. The flight takes about a half hour from the Adelaide airport and costs about A$150 per person. *Information: Lloyd Aviation, 38 Currie St., Adelaide; tel. 212–5722.* It's also possible to get to the island with your car by taking the weekday boat from Port Adelaide. There is also a ferry from Cape Jervis, at the tip of the Fleurieu Peninsula south of the city. The ferry, the *Philanderer,* is offered with bus service on the island for A$25. *Information from the State Transit Authority in Adelaide or from Philanderer Ferries, P.O. Box 570 Penneshaw 5222; tel. (0848) 31–122.*

If you want to do the island in a big way **Bill King's Australian Experience** has several nummy trips, including four-wheel drive treks and—shades of Alice Springs—a pair of week-long camel safaris. The motorized trip costs about A$620 per person plus airfare. The camel trips run between A$535 and A$780. The company also has treks in the Flinders Ranges. *Information: ATS/Sprint, 1101 East Broadway, Glendale, California 91205; tel. (800) 232–2121 California, (800) 423–2880 USA.*

True Blue Tours has a variety of tours to the island, including air/air trips from Adelaide, or trips from Cape Jervis, the seaport on the

Fleurieu Peninsula south of the city where you catch the ferry to Kangaroo Island. Tours can include accommodation and all meals and go up to a 6-day excursion. The one-day flight trips are about A$160 per person; the six-day around A$600 per person including accommodations and breakfasts. *Information: True Blue Tours, 646 Brighton Rd., Seacliff Park, S.A.; tel. (08) 296–0938.*

Or guided tours are also available from Kangaroo Island Complete Travel Service. A three-day tour, including ferry fares, accommodations, breakfast and dinner and attractions, is about A$325 per person; round-trip air add about A$100. Information: the travel service at 27 Gresham St, in Adelaide; tel. 212–4550. Also check with IR Kangaroo Island, the commuter airline serving the island; information 231–4882.

The Outback

Going north from Adelaide, you have two choices of highways, neither of which will serve city dwellers who hate wide open spaces. The Sturt Highway runs northeast across the Murray River basin to Muldara in Victoria, and the Stuart Highway starts its long, long journey to Darwin. Going south, the South Eastern Freeway runs through the Mt. Lofty Ranges, where it splits to go south or east into Victoria. To go west, you run north to Port Augusta, then hang a left to catch the Eyre Highway, which heads toward the vast nothingness of Western Australia.

The farther north you go, the hotter and drier it becomes as the highways run through empty desert with no towns for what seems like years. Unless you have a lot of time or just love driving, you probably have no reason to go out in that stuff unless you're heading for the **Flinders Ranges,** one of the country's most beautiful—but barren—mountain ranges. The ranges, an extension of the Lofty Ranges near Adelaide, are sedimentary formations with some harder materials that have been buckled and twisted into jagged peaks, a real photographer's treat. One of the most popular spots is a large natural amphitheater, about ten miles by four miles called **Wilpena Pound.** The cup-shaped depression is surrounded by mountains and is home to big red kangaroos, their seldom-seen cousins, the yellow-footed rock wallaby, and numerous parrots and galahs. It's also a scientist's mecca because of pre-Cambrian fossil beds. The floor of the pound is an undulating plain with a few water courses and stands of pine. There are five marked trails in the area, including a 14-mile jaunt that takes you on a circuit to **Cooinda Camp** and back via 3800-foot-high **St. Mary's Peak.** There are also some much easier hikes.

There is only one **camping area** inside the pound, at Cooinda, about 11 kilometers from the park ranger quarters at the entrance. There is a commercial campground and motel at Wilpena, the **Wilpena Pound Holiday Resort,** with a pool, doubles about A$70. *Information: (086)*

48–0004. There are also accommodations available at Hawker, where the road to the national park turns off.

There is regular bus service between Wilpena and Adelaide on **Stateliner buses,** which make the run in about seven hours and charge around A$30 one way. *For schedules and information, call 212–1777.* A number of companies in Adelaide offer tours of variable length in the Flinders Ranges. **Bill King's Australian Experience** also has a variety of treks, from camel safaris to hiking trips. The camels will set you back around A$600 for a week; the hiking trips start around A$500. Information, ATS/Sprint. For information about the Flinders Ranges, contact the ranger in charge, Flinders Ranges National Park, PMB, 10, Hawker 5434; tel. (086) 48–0017. For information about the nearby Gammon Ranges National Park (the same formation, more remote) contact the National Parks and Wildlife Service, Far North District Office, P.O. Box 34, Leigh Creek 5731; tel. (086) 75–2499. Or the ranger in charge, Gammon Ranges National Park, Balcanoona, via Copley 5732

If you drive beyond the two national parks up around **Copley,** the road mostly disappears and the next thing you know, you're on the **Birdsville Track,** the famous cattle drive route that heads up into the Northern Territory. If you go far enough—and only somebody with a desert fetish wants to try—you end up at Birdsville, site of the world's most out of the way pub.

WESTERN AUSTRALIA

Not a whole lot of Americans had ever heard of Perth or Fremantle, or even Western Australia for that matter, until January and February of 1987, when the city hosted the America's Cup competitions. It was the Aussies, you will recall, who did what nobody else had ever been able to do—in 1983, they took the cup away from the United States for the first time in the 132 years the world's premier yachting contest had been in existence.

Hordes of curious yachting fans and tourists descended on the Perth area to see if the uppity Australians could hang on to the silver trophy (they didn't—the U.S. got it back), but in the process, a lot of visitors discovered what many people in Australia already knew. Perth is a friendly city, and Western Australia is, indeed, a land of Western hospitality.

You need a lot of time and a lot of interest to come to the Asian edge of Australia, because it's a long, long way from the nerve centers of the country in Melbourne and Sydney. The nearest state capital to Perth—Adelaide—is 1700 miles away. It's a huge place. Almost one-third the whole continent of Australia. Four times the size of Texas. A coastline almost 8000 miles in length. Vast mineral deposits, mountains of iron, tons of gold, huge fields of diamonds, silver, nickel, lead, and zinc. And, for most of its bulk, vast empty desert.

And, in all that area, only 1.4 million people, most of them concentrated in the area around Perth, the capital. The coastal climate ranges from easy-going Mediterranean around the Swan River and Perth to mushy tropical in the north, where the state meets the Timor Sea. Along the long, long coast, there are small towns whose residents fish for lobster or work in the ports that ship Western Australia's ores to the world.

If you go to Perth expecting excitement, you'll be disappointed. It is nothing more than it has ever wanted to be: an easygoing, fairly laid-back city of a million plus, with life centered along the Swan River and its growing prosperity rooted in the minerals that lie beneath the state. Only a few miles in from the coast, you begin running into the beginning of huge deserts where paved roads are few and far between and people are about as common as rain.

In 1868, Western Australia was the last colony to abandon convict labor (the first settlers needed convicts because nobody was willing to go there to work), and the first years after its founding in the late 1820s were grim. When Australia was claimed by the English in 1788, they left out Western Australia, ending their interest at 129 degrees east, which just happened to be the meridian agreed to at the Treaty of Tordesillas in the 15th century when the pope split the world into two halves belonging to Spain and Portugal.

But the things that discouraged early settlers—the sheer vastness of the state, and its often-amazing topography—are beginning to attract more and more people interested in experiencing what remains the most unspoiled part of Australia.

This is the land of the **Hemersley Range gorges,** hundreds of feet deep with pools in their depths. It is the land of the **Kimberleys,** often cited as Australia's last frontier, where saltwater crocodiles lurk in the shallows, and waterfalls tempt photographers. It is the land of the **Bungle Bungle,** a strange Salvador Dali landscape filled with rock formations out of a nightmare. It is a land becoming increasingly important as a wine-growing area, and is a land that is becoming a water sports mecca, particularly along the Great Southern Ocean coast in the extreme south, where fishing is more a matter of how many you have the strength to throw back, not what you might catch.

The Essential Western Australia

INFORMATION • For information in North America, contact the **Western Australian Tourism Commission** office at 2121 Ave. of the Stars, Suite 1210, Century City, Calif. 90067; tel. (213) 557–1987.

GETTING THERE • It's a long haul from the eastern cities to Perth (several Asian capitals are a lot closer), about like flying from Miami to San Francisco. **Ansett** and **Australian Airlines** fly into the new terminal. Fares from Sydney are between A$400 and A$500 one way.

If you have the time, you can go from Sydney to Perth on the **Indian-Pacific,** one of the longest train trips in the world. It takes three days and goes across some of the most vacant real estate you'll ever see—Siberia without snow, one traveler described it. There is a stretch of 300 miles without a single curve, one of the longest straight stretches in railroad history. It's a popular excursion, so book well in advance. The cheapest fare without a pass is around A$300; sleepers go for around A$950 per person one way. Reservations during holidays are often needed a year ahead; in the high season, Sept.–March, at least a month in advance. *Information: Rail Travel Centre, State Rail of New South Wales, 11–31 York St., Sydney 2000; tel. (02) 217–8812. In Perth, contact the*

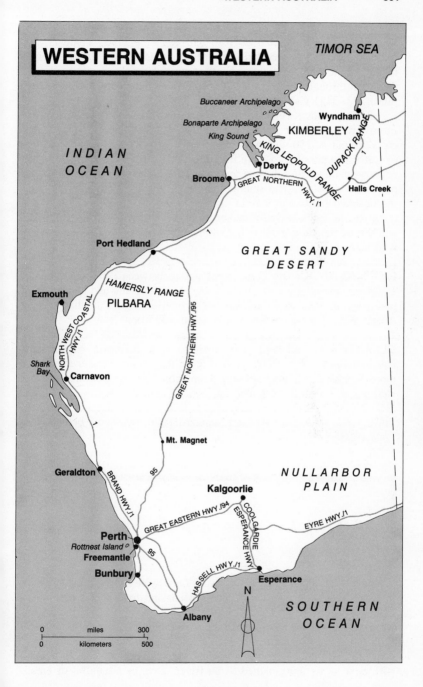

WESTERN AUSTRALIA

TIMOR SEA

INDIAN
OCEAN

Buccaneer Archipelago
Bonaparte Archipelago
King Sound

KIMBERLEY

Wyndham

DURACK RANGE

KING LEOPOLD RANGE

Derby

Broome

GREAT NORTHERN HWY./1

Halls Creek

Port Hedland

1

GREAT SANDY
DESERT

HAMERSLY RANGE

PILBARA

Exmouth

NORTH WEST COASTAL HWY./1

GREAT NORTHERN HWY./95

Shark
Bay

Carnavon

1

Mt. Magnet

NULLARBOR
PLAIN

Geraldton

BRAND HWY./1

95

Kalgoorlie

COOLGARDIE ESPERANCE HWY.

GREAT EASTERN HWY./94

EYRE HWY./1

Perth
Rottnest Island
Freemantle

95

Bunbury

1

HASSELL HWY./1

Esperance

N

Albany

SOUTHERN
OCEAN

0   miles   300
0   kilometers   500

Interstate Booking Office, Westrail Travel Centre, City Rail Station, Wellington Street, Perth; tel. (09) 326–2159 or 2195. There is also frequent service between Perth and the mining town of Kalgoorlie, eight hours, about A$50 one way. North American booking information is available through ATS, 1101 East Broadway, Glendale, Calif. 91205; (800) 232–2121 California, (800) 423–2880 USA.

There is bus service from Adelaide and Darwin, both long hauls. From Adelaide, over the Eyre Highway, it takes about 35 hours and costs around A$150 without a pass.

It's also possible to drive from the Northern Territory, either across country or down to Adelaide and over. From Darwin, it's 2700 miles, paved but desolate. The southern route, on the Eyre Highway through the desolate Nullarbor, has its own perils—it's subject to strange encounters. In 1988, a flying saucer swept over a family on the highway and turned the car's paint into dust. The Nullarbor area, by the way, is well named: Null-arbor; no trees.

GETTING AROUND • There is bus service between Perth and Broome, a popular coastal city 1400 miles away, about 22 hours and about A$150 one way, as well as to inland cities. Interior flights are handled by Ansett WA,; the fare to Broome is about A$350 one way.

CLIMATE • Around Perth, the sunniest city in Australia, expect summer highs in the upper 80s, around 65 in the winter. Farther north, it's more humid and hotter. Interior temperatures in the summer can get well above 100 in the summer and freezing at night.

TIME • The state is on Western Standard Time, two hours behind New South Wales.

PERTH

We have been attacked by black swans only twice in life, once at a park in Queensland, once in Perth. The Queensland fowl was a nesting female, very territorial. The Perth attacks took place because the friends we were staying with were Australians, and being Australians, were full of mischief and wanted to see what would happen when the Yanks were suddenly surrounded by a near-riot of swans. They took us to a small park next to the aplty-named Swan River, gave us a handful of bread,

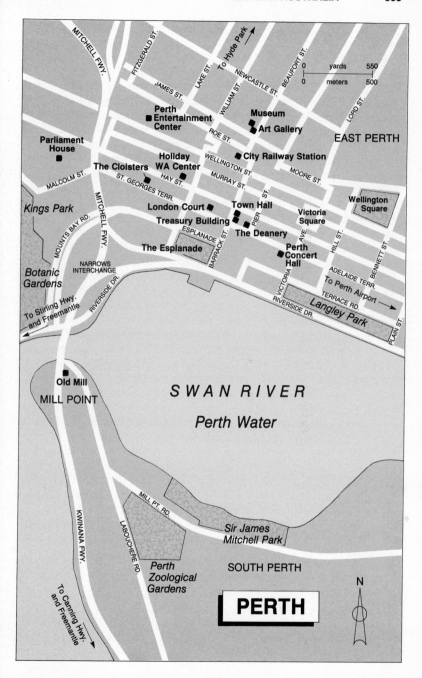

MITCHELL FWY.

FITZGERALD ST.

To Hyde Park

LAKE ST.

WILLIAM ST.

NEWCASTLE ST.

BEAUFORT ST.

LORD ST.

JAMES ST.

yards   0   550
meters   0   500

Perth Entertainment Center

ROE ST.

Museum

Art Gallery

EAST PERTH

Parliament House

Holiday WA Center

WELLINGTON ST.

City Railway Station

MOORE ST.

The Cloisters

MALCOLM ST.

ST. GEORGES TERR.

HAY ST.

MURRAY ST.

London Court

Town Hall

PIER ST.

Victoria Square

Wellington Square

Treasury Building

The Deanery

ESPLANADE

BARRACK ST.

AVE.

HILL ST.

BENNETT ST.

Kings Park

MITCHELL FWY.

MOUNTS BAY RD.

The Esplanade

NARROWS INTERCHANGE

Perth Concert Hall

VICTORIA

ADELAIDE TERR.

To Perth Airport

Botanic Gardens

RIVERSIDE DR.

Langley Park

TERRACE RD.

PLAIN ST.

To Stirling Hwy. and Freemantle

RIVERSIDE DR.

Old Mill

MILL POINT

S W A N   R I V E R

Perth Water

KWINANA FWY.

LABOUCHERE RD.

MILL PT. RD.

Sir James Mitchell Park

To Canning Hwy. and Freemantle

Perth Zoological Gardens

SOUTH PERTH

N

PERTH

and shoved us toward the water. In a nonce, friends, we were awash in swans—a sea of beaks, and ocean of necks and wings, the Mormon Tabernacle Choir of honks. It was wonderful and we always remember Perth that way, up to our armpits in ravenous black swans.

It is truly a shame that Perth is so far from the normal tourist haunts of Australia, because it is probably the most congenial of Aussie cities, the right size, the right weather, the right attitude toward life. It is very California in its approach to the world, both it climate and attitude. This is either good or bad, depending on how you view California. It is sunny, friendly and a lot more relaxed than most of the country. If Sydney and Melbourne are power dressed, Perth and Fremantle are loafers and Levi's.

Perth is not on the coast, but 12 miles up the Swan River from Fremantle, the seaport. The broad and lake-like Swan, unlike many urban Australia rivers, is blue. It was named by Dutch explorers who first sighted the black swans that nest on its banks. The city dads have managed to keep the river mostly pollution free, with industry being situated at Kwinana, on the coast south of the city. It is said that the city has the biggest concentration of tycoons in Australia, mostly mining moguls, whose houses can be seen along the river's north shore. The Indian Ocean beaches on the coast are among the finest in the country, and the city, modern and easy to explore, is comfortable and friendly.

The heart of the city is the **Hay Street Mall,** which runs between William and Barrack streets. Shopping arcades, including the quaint **London Court,** branch off from the sides. The **business district,** whose skyline has a fair number of towers, sits back from the river banks, which are mostly gracious parks. In all, the city and environs claim to have 400 square miles of greenlands. In addition to the Swan, there is also the Canning River, which feeds into the Swan a bit south of town and adds a little watery luster to the southeast suburbs. Paralleling Hay Street is St. George's Terrace (which becomes Adelaide Terrace moving east), with such historic relics as **Government House** (1859), **St. George's Cathedral** (1880) and the **Supreme Court Gardens** (1829). At the western edge of St. George's Terrace is **Barracks Archway,** a small brick arch that is all that remains of a pensioners' barracks built on the spot in 1860. The arch was almost torn down for a development, but local furor won out and saved it.

PERTH SIGHTS ································

The **Old Perth Boys' School,** on the south side of St. George's Terrace, was built by convicts in 1854, a Gothic heap that makes you glad you never studied Greek and logic in its halls. Today, it's the headquarters of the western Australia branch of the National Trust. It's open 9–5 Monday–Friday. *Information: 321–2754.* Another old school is **The Cloisters,** started in 1858 as a boys' secondary school and saved at the last tick from the wrecker's ball. Like many buildings in modern Australia, it now lives cheek by jowl with high-rise office buildings.

Government House, the official residence of the governor of Western Australia, looks like it was transplanted brick by brick from London. It stands next to St. George's Cathedral on St. George's Terrace, surrounded by some very nice gardens. When it was completed in 1864, riots were forecast—the A$30,000 cost was double the original estimate. *Information: 325–3222.*

On the Swan side of the residence is the **Old Court House,** one of the city's oldest surviving colonial structures, built in 1836. It now houses a collection of historical legal artifacts. *Information: 325–4787.*

East of Government House is the **Perth Concert Hall,** where opera and other muscial performances are mounted. It's open weekdays, and there is a licensed restaurant and several bars. *Information: 325–9944.*

To the northeast of the city center is the **Western Australian Museum,** whose centerpiece is an old jail built in 1856. Along with the impressive collection of early Western Australian historical artifacts is a fine display on the life and times of the Aborginals who lived in the area. Another popular item is the Mundrabilla meteorite, one of the largest in the world. Western Australia seems to collect fallen space objects—it was in the state, remember, that the last remnants of the doomed American Skylab fell to earth in 1980. And it was the people of Perth who turned on every light they could find one night in 1962 when John Glenn made his historic orbital trip. The museum is open Mon.–Fri. 10:30 a.m.–5 p.m. and weekends 1–5 p.m. Free admission. *Information: 328–4411.*

The biggest park close to the city center is **Kings Park,** which is largely a chunk of bushland preserved for modern times. The park, almost 1000 acres in area, contains the Botanic Gardens, with displays of Western Australia wildflowers—a reminder that for all its desolation, the state has more types of wildflowers than any other place in Australia, by some estimates, as many as 7000 species. There are excellent views of the city and the Swan from a lookout tower, and if you hunger, there's a small restaurant and a fast-food kiosk. The park is up a hill east of St. George's Terrace, a fair walk. *Information: 321–4801.*

Perth, as least it is claimed, has the third largest casino in the world, the Burswood, located east of the city center in Rivervale. It's part of a multi-million dollar resort complex that includes a hotel, restaurant, night club, and an 18-hole golf course. There are 140 tables of one form or another where you can lose your shirt or break the bank. It's usually crowded. Open 24 hours. *Information: 362–7777.*

Finally, there is the **"Fremantle Doctor."** The doctor in this case—as all those hardy sailors discovered during the America's Cup—is a strong wind that often rises a little after noon and can rip your mizzen and tear your jib and generally make life at sea a trial. It does help cool off hot days in Perth, however.

FREMANTLE.....................................

The folks in Fremantle bet on the come. They were hoping, oh how they were hoping, that the America's Cup would stay put. When the hordes starting arriving in this small port town of 12,000, storefronts were painted, the glasses were polished, the cat was combed and, all in all, things got all gussied up. The Cup, of course, went away, but the benefits of its presence gave the town a shot of confidence that seems to be hanging on, despite the greatly reduced number of tourists who come down for a look. Because Fremantle is a port city, parts of it are Jersey-shore squalid, but the old, preserved parts of it are still enticing. Outdoor life is the way to go in Fremantle, with cafes along the old streets, pubs that brew their own beer, and boardwalks waiting for a stroll.

Amid the many historic buildings that have managed to survive developers' attacks is the **Round House,** the oldest building in Western Australia. It was built in 1831 as a place to house juvenile offenders and sits atop a hill overlooking the ocean and the port. Its displays are essentially penal in nature, including some preserved cells. The building, a 12-sided limestone hulk, is open for tours 10–5 daily. *Information: 335–6422.*

One of the most impressive old buildings in Fremantle is the two-story **Western Australian Maritime Museum,** which houses some of the oldest historical artifacts in the country. The building was constructed in 1850 as a naval stores depot. Including in the displays is a reconstructed section of the Dutch merchantman *Batavia,* which sank off the coast in 1629. One of the real treasures is **Dirk Hartog's Plate,** a pewter plate left as a marker by a Dutch East India captain when he chanced by the Western Australian coast in 1616. The museum is open 10:30–5 Mon.–Thur., 1–5 p.m. Fri.–Sun. *Information 335–8211.*

For shopping maniacs, there are the **Fremantle Markets** at the corner of Henderson Street and South Terrace, where if you want it, you can probably find it among the 150 or so stalls. The markets are open Fri. 9 a.m.–9 p.m.; 9–5 Sat., 11 a.m.–5 p.m. Sun.

Pub crawling in Fremantle is especially rewarding, particularly if you stop in at the **Sail and Anchor** on South Terrace and hoist a pint of the pub's own beer. The Sail and Anchor is housed in a building dating from the turn of the century. The house killer is a little brew called the Dog Bolter, supposedly so strong one will keel you over. It didn't. But they also serve a little number called Redback, named after the spider. Good Suds. Also worth a call is the **Federal Hotel** across from the Town Hall, dating from the late 1880s. Or try the **Esplanade Plaza Hotel,** famous for gin slings and a good place to stay in its own right, probably the best in Fremantle. It's on Marine Terrace, with doubles starting around A$150. *Information 430–4000.*

If you're curious, the **Fishing Boat Harbour,** opposite the Maritime Museum, is where the boats involved in the cup battle were docked. Today, it's just a place for fish and chips and a beer, nothing left of the excitement but memories. The harbor does have one of the largest marinas in Australia, however.

In a huge building on the harbor, craftsmen are working on a fullsize replica of the Endeavor, the ship Capt. James Cook used to explore New Zealand and Australia in 1769–70. The project is sponsored by Alan Bond, the mogul who was largely responsible for the successful Cup challenge. Bondy, as he's known, has fallen on grim days, going from billionaire to millionaire or something, and his vast empire was, at last report, crumbling. So the Endeavor project is on hold, sort of. If it's open, go in and take a look and marvel at the chutzpa it took to sail around the world in such a beamy old tub. There's a small admission charge.

There is regular bus and suburban train service to Fremantle from Perth; by road it's about 12 miles on either the Stirling or Canning highways.

The Essential Perth

INFORMATION ● For the Perth metropolitan area, as well as Western Australia in general, contact the Western Australian Tourist Centre, Forrest Place (corner of Wellington Street); tel. 483–1111.

GETTING AROUND ● Free transportation around the city center is provided on Clipper buses that run every 10 minutes Monday–Friday 7:30 a.m.–5:30 p.m.; Saturday 9–11:30 a.m. The city and suburbs are also served by bus, train and ferry systems. The main bus terminal is located on Wellington Street near Beaufort St. Buses run daily 6 a.m.– 11 p.m. with reduced service on the weekends. Trains run to Fremantle and other suburban locations daily from 5:40 a.m.–11:30 p.m., reduced service on weekends. Suburban trains leave from the City Station on Wellington; interstate trains and some buses run from the East Perth Railway Terminal. Ferries run daily between the Barracks Street jetty and the Mends Street jetty near the zoo in South Perth, 6:45 a.m.–7:15

p.m. The city also operates a bus from the domestic air terminal to downtown. The No. 338 buses run about every 40–50 minutes seven days, reduced service after 6 p.m. There is also a private bus that runs from both international and domestic terminals (they are five kilometers apart) and meets all flights. The fare is about $5; serves most hotels. For information about all city transportation services, contact Transperth, offices in the Wellington Street Central Bus Station; tel. 221–1211.

A taxi ride in from the international terminal is about $A15; from the domestic terminal, about $A10. Major taxis are Swan, 322–0111 and Black and White, 328–8288.

The Royal Automobile Club of Western Australia is at 228 Adelaide terr.; tel. 421–4444. Emergency road service is available by calling 325–0333.

Freemantle has trams to take you on a guided tour of the city. They start every hour from the Freemantle Town Hall daily between 10 a.m. and 4 p.m. and depending on the tour, take between 45 minutes and an hour and a half. Prices range from $A6 to $A10. Information: 339–8719.

TELEPHONE • The area code for the Perth area is (09). The main post office is at Forrest Place near Wellington St. across from the Perth Railway Station. *Information: 326–5211.*

SHOPPING • Normal shopping hours are 9 a.m.–5:30 p.m. weekdays, 9 p.m. Thurs., and 9 a.m.–noon Sat.

Not surprisingly, given its economics, Perth is a major centre for diamonds and opals. Western Australia's Argyle mine is the largest in the world, producing millions of carats a year, mostly industrial diamonds, but also jewel-quality. Australian diamonds are noted for their interesting colors, champagne and cognac among them. There are several major stores around town where you can ogle the baubles, including Quilpie Opals, 68 St. George's Terr., tel. 321–8687; the Opal Centre, St. Martin's Arcade off London Court, tel. 325–7931, and Swan Diamonds, London Court, tel. 325–8166.

As noted, the main shopping drag in town is the **Hay Street Mall,** but wandering through the arcades that you find scattered around is a treat, as well. **London Court,** built in 1937, is especially interesting. You decide: is the mock-Tudor decor quaint or just ticky-tacky? Perth has a fair share of jewelry stores where you can buy Western Australian diamonds, opals, or stuff made from iron. For authentic Aboriginal art, check the **Aboriginal Art Gallery** at 242 St. George's Terrace, a government-licensed store with controlled prices and a fair display of art works. The city's large department stores are found along Hay Street.

ACCOMMODATIONS........................

Parmelia Hilton • *14 Mill St.; tel. 322–3622* • Downtown within walking distance of the Hay Street Mall. Three restaurants, three bars, pool, sauna, shops and lots of marble. Rooms with either river or city views. Doubles from $A210; suites from $A300–820.

Observation City Resort • *The Esplanade, Scarborough; tel.; 245–1000* • Alan Bond built this complex on one of the best beaches in the Perth Area, about 10 miles outside town. Rooms are done in coral and turquoise, have balconies and ocean views. Four restaurants, six bars, two levels of shops, tennis court, pool, sauna, health center, bottle shop. Upper room levels are reserved for the Observation Club, with personal valets. Doubles from $A150–235; suites with spa and two or three bedrooms, $A485. Observation Club level rooms from $A255. Some weekend specials.

Burswood Casino • *Great Eastern Highway, Rivervale; tel. 362–7777* • Multi-story pyramid on the shores of the Swan, probably the best views of the city around the area. The lobby atrium is almost big enough to have clouds. Three restaurants, two bars, pool, health facilities, tennis, bike hire. Next to golf course. Doubles from $A210–275; suites from $A475.

Sheraton • *207 Adelaide Terr.; tel. 325–0501* • Large entrance with nice color themes, facing the Swan River. Three restaurants, four bars, disco, pool, sauna, handicapped facilities. Doubles from $A180–280; suites from $A360.

Hyatt Regency • *99 Adelaide Terr.; tel. 323–0121* • Corner of Plain Street, formerly the Merlin, now an Asian-influence with huge atrium, shops, rooftop pool, sauna, tennis and squash courts, executive library, three restaurants. Doubles from $A190–220; suites $A390–875.

Freemantle Esplanade • *Corner of Marine Terr. and Essex sts.; tel. 430–4000* • Refurbished and redecorated in 1989. On the beach. Pool, sauna, spa, parking, atrium garden restaurant, two bars and disco on the weekends. Doubles from $A140–200; suites with harbor view and spa, $A280.

Perth Parkroyal • *54 Terrace Rd., Perth 6000; tel. 325–3811* • All 100 rooms overlook the Swan. Pool, spa, licensed restaurant, and two bars. Doubles start around A$155.

Transit Inn • *37 Pier St.; tel. 325–7655* • Ruby's Restaurant, pool, parking, breakfast available. Doubles from $A140; suites from $A160.

Chateau Commodore • *417 Hay St., Perth 6000; tel. 325–0461* • Close to the mall, baronial motif. Pool, bar, and licensed restaurant. Doubles start around A$75.

Tradewinds • *59 Canning Highway; tel. 339–8188* • Units with cooking facilities. Restaurant/bar, pool, spa, parking. Doubles $A55–64; suites $A100.

Regatta • *560 Hay St.; tel. 325–5155.* • B&B. About half the rooms are air conditioned. Steak restaurant; three bars; live entertainment. Cooked brekkie. Doubles $A65.

Perth Youth Hostel • *62 Newcastle St.; tel. 328–1135* • Former guesthouse built in 1899. Fifteen minute walk to the city; open all day. Bike rentals. Four- six- and eight-bed rooms. $A12 per person.

YMCA • *119 Murray St.; tel. 325–2744* • Downtown. TV lounge, no kitchen. Shared rooms $A15 per person; doubles $A35.

Sorrento Beach Caravan Park • *West Coast Dr., 20 kilometers from town; tel. 448–1072* • Laundry, kitchen, barbecue, store, rental TVs, on the beach. On-site caravans $A45 double shared, $A55 private.

YHA Freemantle • *98 Hampton Rd.; tel 335–3467* • Short walk from railway station. Large rooms, mostly with four beds. Kitchen, laundry, lounge and recreation room. Bike rentals. $A12 members; $A15 non-members.

RESTAURANTS.................................

Oyster Beds • *26 Riverside Rd., East Freemantle; tel. 339–1611.* What Doyle's is to Sydney, this is to the Perth area. Established in 1932, it sits on the Swan. Wide seleciton of seafood. Reservations necessary. Lunch and dinner seven days. *Moderate to expensive.*

The Hind Quarter • *101 Canning Hwy.; tel. 367–4308* • The oldest steakhouse in town (20 years). Char-grilled, grain-fed beef. Reservations essential. Dinner from 6:30 seven nights. *Moderate.*

Verde's Brasserie on the Terrace ● *46 Marine Terr.; 430–4000*
● Esplanade Hotel. Delightful brasserie style food such as mushroom
soup with crayfish served cappuccino style; linguini tossed with aba-
lone, mushrooms and cream. Fresh olive bread. Tasty, very tasty. Lunch
and dinner seven days. *Moderate.*

Han Palace ● *73–75 Bennett, East Perth; 325–8883* ● Cantonese
cuisine. Nice decor with hand-painted murals, hand-crafted furniture,
indoor garden. Private rooms available. Parking. Lunch and dinner seven
days. *Moderate.*

Chunagon ● *46 Mews Rd., Fremantle; tel. 336–1000.* Japanese steak
and seafood. Teppanyaki room or ala carte. Lunch and dinner Tuesday–
Sunday, closed Saturday; dinner from 6 p.m. Saturday. *Moderate to
expensive.*

Horsefeather ● *Corner of William and Murray sts.; tel. 481–1000.*
Family restaurant, serving large juicy burgers, pasta, steaks, potato skins
and full breakfasts. Open 7 a.m.–10:30 p.m. seven days. Owned by the
same folks who own the place next door, the Moon and Sixpence, a
traditional Brit pub. Pub grub, English ales on draft, entertainment most
nights. Open 11 a.m.–midnight Monday–Saturday; noon–9 p.m. Sunday. *Budget to moderate.*

BEYOND PERTH ●●●●●●●●●●●●●●●●●●●●●●●●●●

Rottnest

It's good that Willem de Vlamingh spoke Dutch and not English. Otherwise one of the Perth area's favorite attractions would be called the
Rat's Nest. But he did speak Dutch, so the island 10 miles offshore
from Fremantle is called **Rottnest,** which doesn't sound quite as bad.
De Vlamingh was given cause to name the island what he did because
when he landed in 1696, he came across herds of little furry critters he
just assumed were big rats. And at first blush, that's just what a quokka
looks like, a very large rat.

Well, what quokkas really are are some of Australia's friendliest
marsupials—tame, spoiled rotten, and generally delightful—which draw
thousands of visitors to the island every year. If you want to get tech-
nical, quokkas (the Aboriginal name) are also called short-tailed wallabies, Setonix brachyurus. They are endangered species that also exist
along some parts of the mainland coast.

But the island is much more than quokkas. There are good beaches, great hiking, and even hotels, motels, campgrounds, and bars. It's where many Western Australians come to spend a week's vacation lazing around and feeding the quokkas, and it's often booked well in advance, especially on weekends.

The island is not very large, about seven miles long, three miles wide, and closed to automobile traffic. The only way to get around is by foot or rental bicycle or one of the buses that take visitors on tours of the island—get there early, on busy weekends, all the bikes are snapped up. The rental place is a short walk up from the island jetty, just behind the Hotel Rottnest; bikes go for about A$10 a day. Phone 292–5043. The island scenery is mixed, with cliffs, stunning white beaches, groves of pine and cypress, and crystal clear water. It was the site of the first settlement in Western Australia, in 1830, and later served as a prison for Aboriginals until after the turn of the century. Many of the early colonial and prison buildings have been restored. In addition, as a treat for snorkelers and divers, there are at least a dozen shipwrecks scattered around the island. It's criss-crossed with trails and there are a number of salt-water lakes in the interior suitable for swimming. There is also a nine-hole golf course, horses for rent and boat rentals.

In addition to the quokkas, other animals you can look for on the island are several species of ducks, pheasant, peacocks, rock parrots, rainbow bee eaters, and osprey. Coral reefs near the island are home to many tropical fish as well as shrimp and crabs. Also around Rottnest you find huge spiny sea lobster (they're called crayfish), the largest in Western Australia. There is a glass-bottomed boat for reef and shipwreck views. It leaves from the island jetty and costs about A$13. *The island's information office is in a kiosk at the jetty.*

A popular place to stay or hoist a beer is the **Rottnest Hotel,** which dates from 1864 and was built as the summer residence for the governors of Western Australia. Rates at the hotel, often called the **Quokka Arms,** are around A$90 double, weekly rates available. *Information (09) 292–5011.* The upscale **Rottnest Resort Lodge,** now owned by the once-very rich Alan Bond, has been remodeled and upgraded. It has a pool, and rooms range around A$210 to A$260 double. *Information, 292–5161.* For information about kitchenette units and tenting, contact the Rottnest Island Authority, Rottnest Island 6161; tel. 372–9727. *Information and bookings are also available through the Western Australian tourist offices in Perth.*

The cheapest way to get to the island is to take the two-hour **ferry** from the Barrack Street Jetty in Perth (stops in Fremantle), which costs about A$45 for a round trip fare. *Information: Boat Torque Cruise Ferries, 325–6033 Perth or 335–7181 in Fremantle.* Air service to the island is available through Rottnest Airlines, for about A$40 round trip. *Information: 478–1322 Perth or 292–5027 Rottnest.*

Wine Country

The wines of Western Australia, while not produced in the quantities of the nation's other areas, have an excellent reputation. Perth is lucky because most of the state's major wineries are only a short drive outside of town in an area called the **Swan Valley.** The vineyards are nestled around the towns of **Guildford** and **Midland,** and range in production from big operators such as Houghton's down to Mom-and-Pop shops.

Houghton's is set up for crowds, with picnic areas and tastings of its very popular white burgundy. It's open 10 a.m.–5 p.m. Mon.–Sat.; noon–5 p.m. Sun. *Information, Houghton's, Dale Road, Middle Swan 6056; tel. 274–5100.*

Other wineries to check are **Sandalford,** riesling a speciality, open 10 a.m.–5 p.m. Mon.–Sat.; noon–3 p.m. Sun; *information, Sandalford, West Swan Rd., Caversham 6055, tel. 274–5922.* Or **Evans & Tate,** noted for its reds and a few whites, open 10 a.m.–5 p.m. Mon.–Sat.; noon–3 p.m. Sun. *Information, Evans & Tate Swan St., Henley Brook 6055, tel. 296–4329.* Wine is also produced in the southwestern region of the state around Margaret River.

One nice way to get to the Swan River wineries is by boat. Among the boats that ply the river are the *Miss Sandalford* and the *Lady Houghton,* which go to the wineries they're named after. Both boats cost about A\$45 for a full-day cruise, including lunch. *Information: Boat Torque Cruises, Barrack St. Jetty; tel. 325–6033 or 444–4686.*

AROUND WESTERN AUSTRALIA·····································

The **Pinnacles,** about 150 miles north of Perth on the Indian Ocean coast, are a weird collection of limestone fossils standing around like the remnants of some huge Druidic metropolis. The thousands of stone monuments sit in sand dunes and are found from pencil-lead thickness to huge pillars 15 feet high and seven feet wide. They are definitely worth the four-wheel-drive trip it takes to see them. The Pinnacles are the remains of ancient roots that were fossilized by rainwater leeching through mineral-laden topsoils. The formations are part of **Nambung National Park,** which is reached from the coastal highway. Camping is allowed; see the ranger on duty. The park, which also has a big supply of seabirds, is noted for its wildflowers blooms in September and November. *Information: Nambung National Park, P.O. Box 62, Cervantes 6511; tel. (096) 52–7047.*

The southwestern tip of the state, where the Indian Ocean meets the Southern Ocean, is the most fertile area of Western Australia, with cattle farms, orchards, and the vineyards of the Margaret River area. The **Rainbow Coast,** basically the Southern Ocean side of the area, is noted for sports fishing. At the extreme southwest edge, about 165 miles from Perth, is **Leeuwin-Naturaliste National Park,** which is famous for its forest of huge kauri trees, which grow 200 feet high. The park also has a number of limestone caves, four of which are open for guided tours; there are others set aside for experienced cavers. The park sits on top of a granite ridge that runs for about 60 miles; the ridge can be hiked its entire length. Camping is permitted; check with rangers. *Information: Leeuwin-Naturaliste National Park, Post Office, Augusta 6290; tel. (097) 58–5182.*

The main settlement in the southwest is Albany, one of the oldest towns in Western Australia, which doubles its 20,000 population during the tourist season. It has air service from Perth, and has a large fleet of sport fishing boats. *Information: Albany Tourist Bureau, Peels Place, Albany 6330; tel. (098) 41–1088.*

Not far north of Albany is **Stirling Range National Park,** which is the wildflower capital of Australia. The area has been a public preserve since the early part of this century, and its 290,000 acres are home to at least 500 plant species, 100 of which grow nowhere else in the world. The best time to go is September and October. It's also home to quokkas, western gray kangaroos, emus and 100 species of birds. Camping permits are required; sites about A$3 for two people. *Information: Stirling Range National Park, Post Office, Amelup via Borden 6338; tel. (098) 27–9230.*

Farther north, about 175 miles east of Perth, is one of the country's most photographed natural formations, **Wave Rock.** The rock formation, about 300 feet long and 50 feet high, looks like an ocean wave suddenly frozen in stone, and is the result of 2.7 million years of molding and coloring. It's near the wheat-country town of Hyden. *Information: Hyden Tourist Information Centre, Lynch St., Hyden 6359; tel. (098) 80–5182.*

About 500 miles north of Perth on the coast is **Shark Bay,** where Dirk Hartog came ashore and left his plate behind. It also where you find the famous Monkey Mia bottlenose dolphins, wild but so used to humans that children can pet them standing in the surf. The dolphins are protected, and there are rangers around to help you shake flippers. Also in the Shark Bay area is the beginning of **Shell Beach,** a 60-mile stretch of coast composed of seashell deposits that are 30 feet deep. *Information: the Shark Bay Visitor and Travel Centre, Knight Terrace, Denham 6537; tel. (099) 48–1253.*

Boomtowns

The Western Australia Gold Rush of 1892 started at **Coolgardie,** and within four years, the town was the third largest in the state with a population of around 15,000. There were almost 20 hotels on the main street, seven newspapers, and scads of expensive and impressive public buildings. Today, the town only has about 1000 population, one hotel, and scads of impressive buildings—now used as museums. Worth a stop is the **Goldfields Museum,** where there are displays of area history and gold field technology. *Information: Coolgardie Tourist Bureau, Bayley Street; tel. (090) 266–090.*

Kalgoorlie, not far away, is the site of the biggest strike of the whole rush. In 1893, an Irish prospector named Paddy Hannan hit gold on what was to become known as the **Golden Mile,** a square mile of land that has produced gold to the present day—70% of all the gold mined in Australia comes from here. Farther north is the tiny town of **Menzies,** once a boomtown and site of a mine managed in 1897 by a young American named Herbert Hoover.

The Pilbara

The richness of Western Australia's mineral deposits is starkly revealed in the Pilbara, a desolate swath of gorges and peaks that runs across the center of the state. Here you find mountains almost literally made of iron, part of geological formations that are among the oldest on earth. In the heart of the Pilbara is **Hammersley Ranges National Park,** almost 1000 miles north and east of Perth. The hardy visitors who travel to the park come because of its gorges, considered by many to be the most spectacular in Australia. The park has several camping areas, and there is a hotel, motel and caravan park at Wittenoom, just to the north of the park. *Information: Wittenoom Souvenirs and Tourist Shop, Sixth Ave., P.O. Box 24, Wittenoom 6752; tel. (091) 89–7011.*

There are at least a dozen major gorges in the system, many with cool pools of water at their bottoms, oases in a very harsh land. One of the most beautiful of the gorges, most of which can be reached on dirt roads in ordinary cars, is **Dales Gorge.** The gorge, 200 feet deep and 200 feet wide, runs for about 30 miles, but just under a kilometer is accessible. At the bottom, near a campsite, is a large pool, and nearby, a waterfall. Nearby **Hammersley Gorge** has a swimming hole, nestled among towering cliffs, and everywhere you find water, you find gum trees and wildlife. The park has many hiking trails, from easy to tough. There is an information display about 15 miles west of Wittenoom at the turnoff to Yampire Gorge, which takes you to Dales Gorge. *Information: Hammersley Range National Park, (091) 89–8157, or the De-*

partment of Conservation and Management, P.O. Box 835, Karratha 6714; (091) 86–8288.

Less primitive camping conditions and popular swimming areas are located at another Pilbara recreational area, **Millstream-Chichester National Park** about 90 miles in from the coast road near Roebourne. The park has water, toilets, swimming, barbecues, and a large collection of flying foxes. *Information: (091) 84–5125. Lodging is available in Roebourne. Information: Roebourne Tourist Bureau, 173 Roe St., Roebourne 6718; tel. (091) 82–1060.*

The Kimberleys

This is cattle country, gorge country, the land of the Fitzroy River, and the place you find the dramatic knobs and hummocks of the Bungle Bungle Range. It's a harsh land, where a short rainstorm can make travel impossible for days, and where the summer temperatures rise well into the 100s. Its northern location makes it subject to cyclones, and its tidal basins, estuaries, and mangrove swamps are home to saltwater crocodiles.

The main settlement in the area is the coastal city of **Broome,** which at the turn of the century was the largest pearl diving center in the world with more than 300 boats involved in the trade. The industry has shrunk considerably, and the boom-town years of the early 1900s are gone. But pearls remain big business in the port's many commercial beds of cultured pearls. It's history has been much influenced by Asia, as can be seen in its mixed race population and ethnic buildings. The town was bombed by the Japanese in 1942 and almost 100 people were killed, many of them refugees fleeing the Dutch East Indies. Broome's small population (about 6000) swells at least double in August or September every year during the **Shinju Matsuri,** or Festival of the Pearl. *Information about the town is available from the Broome Tourist Bureau, corner of Bagot Rd. and the Great Northern Highway, Broome 6725; tel. (091) 92–2222.*

A major chunk of the Kimberley is composed of a huge, deep limestone formation, the remains of a gigantic coral reef. In places, where the river systems have cut through the old reef, there are immense gorges where flash floods five stories high can roar through after a rainstorm. About 220 miles northeast of Broome is **Windjana Gorge,** whose major feature is a 3.5-kilometer-long gorge cut through the Devonian limestone in some places to a depth of 300 feet. The gorge's permanent pools are home to freshwater crocodiles, and there are many examples of old Aboriginal art. The park is reached on a good dry-weather gravel road. Camping is available, and from April through October, rangers are stationed at the park.

The most popular of the gorge parks, however, is **Geikie Gorge National Park,** near the small village of Fitzroy Crossing. The nine-mile-long gorge averages about 100 feet in depth and its bottom is almost always wet with pools and river flows and supports a variety of wildlife including freshwater crocodiles. In parts, there is enough water for ranger-guided boat tours, usually available only after April when the annual Fitzroy floods have subsided. Camping is available at the park, and bushcamping is allowed with permits. *Information: Ranger in charge, Geikie Gorge National Park, C/O Post Office, Fitzroy Crossing 6765; (091) 91–5121.* There are two caravan parks, a lodge and a motel in Fitzroy Crossing. *Information: Derby Tourist Bureau, 1 Clarendon St., Derby 6728; tel. (091) 91–1426.*

The newest national park in Western Australia is the **Bungle Bungle,** established in 1987 and already becoming popular because of its strange rock formations. The park has one of the most sensitive ecosystems in the country. The sandstone pillars are criss-crossed with thin growths of lichen, which protect the delicate sandstone from being dissolved by monsoon storms. The most-photographed spot, where the rock formations and vertical cliffs faces are nothing less than spectacular, is at **Piccanninny Creek** at the southern edge of the park. One special plant found in the park is the huge fan palm.

Access to the park is being kept primitive because of its ecology, and the only way in is by four-wheel drive. Camping is allowed at designated campsites only, and the park is closed from January through March. *Information: Bungle Bungle National Park, Department of Conservation and Land Management, P.O. Box 242, Kununurra 6743; tel. (091) 68–0200.* **Accommodations** are available at Hall's Creek, about 100 miles south of the park, or at Wyndham or Kununurra, about the same distance north. *Information: Hall's Creek Tourism and Commercial Association, P.O. Box 21, Hall's Creek 6770, or from the Kununurra Visitors Centre, Lot 75, Coolibah Dr., Kununurra 6743; tel. (091) 68–1177, or Wyndham Tourist Information Centre, O'Donnell St., Wyndham Port 6741; tel. (091) 61–1054.*

Excursions to all the major national parks and attractions in Western Australia can be arranged through Western Australia tourism offices. Feature Tours has a one-day wildflower trip in Tuesday, Friday and Sunday between August and October for about A$70, including lunch; information 479–4131 at the Perth domestic airport. Or Westrail Travel Centre has a series of wildflower tours from three to six days. The three-day tour, including meals, accommodations, narration and wildflower guides, is about A$400; the six-day is about A$750. Information: Westrail Travel Centre, City Rail Station (Wellington street); tel. 326–2159. A one-day tour to the Pinnacles with Safari Treks, including lunch and afternoon tea, is about A$80; information: 322–2188.

In addition, **Bill King's Australian Experience** has a number of four-wheel-drive camping and hiking trips, ranging from overnights to two-week treks. They can be booked through ATS/Sprint, 1101 East Broadway, Glendale, Calif. 91205; tel. (800) 232–2121 California, (800) 423–2880 USA.

TASMANIA

How can you not love a place that has produced two famous movie stars, one handsome, one ugly? Well, that's Tasmania, birthplace of Errol Flynn and the Tasmanian Devil. Flynn became famous playing Robin Hood and the field. The Devil became famous in Warner Bros. cartoons trying to make goulash out of Bugs Bunny.

These days, Tassie, as it's called, is a peaceful, pastoral place, with splendid mountains and gorgeous rivers, magnificent rain forests, and preserved colonial villages. But once, this state was used as a name to frighten bad little children into being good. Back then, it was called Van Dieman's Land, and its world-wide reputation as a terrible penal colony was often warranted. Tasmania got many of the hard cases, the convicts who came to Australia because of a crime or mistake in England and then did something wrong when they got to Australia, earning them double trouble. It is the prison past of Tasmania, especially the ruins of the Port Arthur prison area in the southeast corner of the state, that attracts most tourists to this small island south of the mainland across the Bass Strait.

In Tasmania, you find that same sort of quiet resignation you observe in Hawaii now and then. Sure, Hawaii's part of the United States, but it's so far away, if you're Hawaiian, you get the feeling that nobody back in the continental U.S. knows you're alive. They feel the same way in Tasmania, sometimes bitter at what they see as disinterest or mockery on the part of all those clods up in Sydney and Canberra. But Tasmanians fight back as well as they can, referring to the mainland of Australia as "the northern island," and printing maps that show Tasmania as huge and the mainland just a dot. The island, at 25,000 square miles, roughly the size of Ireland, has a population of only around 450,000. It is the most decentralized state in Australia, with less than half the people living in Hobart, the capital. Other major population centers are Launceston, Devonport, and Burnie. Most of the people live in coastal areas. Almost the entire west coast area, because of the mountains and thick forests, is uninhabited. The state actually is a group of islands; others include King and Flinders islands in the Bass Strait.

Tasmania's wonderful forests and mountains have been a continuing battleground between the mining and lumber industries and environmentalists for years, and the often angry, sometimes violent confrontations show no sign of receding. In the southwest corner are ugly examples of some of the worst environmental damage in the whole country—whole mountains have disappeared to get at the minerals they contained.

If you spend a lot of time in Australia, your later memories of it are usually brown, mostly because of the huge interior deserts and the dusty roads. But if you go to Tassie, your memories are always green. Colonial Australians thought it was just like Mother England, and built their farms and homes just like they had back home. Well, it's not that sort of green, English green. It's Tasmanian green, which is a special color all its own, giant ferns and hardwoods and rare pines and bush so dense nobody can hack through it—some areas are unexplored to this day. If the loggers are kept under control, it might just stay that way.

The Essential Tasmania

INFORMATION • For information about Tasmania in North America, contact **Tourism Tasmania,** 2121 Ave. of the Stars, suite 1280, Los Angeles, Calif. 90067; tel. (213) 552–3010.

GETTING THERE • There are five airports in Tasmania: at Launceston, Hobart, Wynyard, Devonport and Flinders Island. Service is provided by **Ansett, Australian** and **East-West** airlines. The flying time from the mainland is around an hour either from Sydney or Melbourne, and high-season, one-way fares are around A$245 Sydney–Hobart or around A$180 Melbourne–Hobart.

A very popular way to make the trip is on the *Abel Tasman,* a 843-passenger car ferry that makes overnight trips from Melbourne to Devonport and back. The ferry leaves Melbourne at 6 p.m. Mon., Wed., and Fri., arriving in Devonport at 8:30 the next morning. The return trip follows the same schedule on Tues., Thurs., and Sun. The ship has a dining room, cafeteria, pool and sauna, disco, and several bar areas. The ferry can carry up to 235 vehicles. In the main tourist season, Dec.–March, one-way rooms range from doubles with private bathrooms for around A$200 per person to four-berth economy cabins for A$90. **Note:** there are no single cabins; doubles reserved for one person are charged at an adult and a half rate. Also note that as big as the *Abel Tasman* is (480 feet long, 19,200 gross tons) the Bass Strait can get so stormy that it can be very unpleasant even with the ship's stabilizers. If you want to take a vehicle over, rates start at around A$110 for a car to around A$400 for a very large camper. Bicycles are charged about A$15. The ship can be booked at Tasbureau offices in major Australian cities. In North America, contact TT-Line, (213) 393–8262 Los Angeles, (800) 445–0190 California, (800) 551–2012 USA.

Faster service is now offered on the SeaCat Tasmania, a big catamaran car ferry that makes the crossing from the Mainland to Tasmania

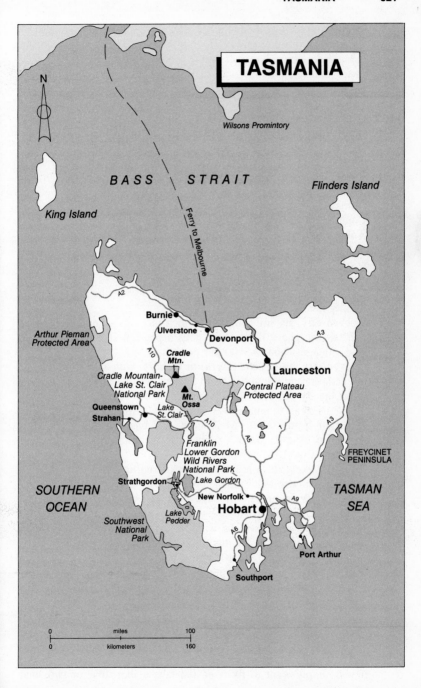

N

TASMANIA

Wilsons Promintory

BASS STRAIT

Flinders Island

King Island

Ferry to Melbourne

Arthur Pieman Protected Area

A2

Burnie
Ulverstone
Devonport

A10

Cradle Mtn.

A3

1

Launceston

Cradle Mountain-Lake St. Clair National Park

▲ *Mt. Ossa*

Central Plateau Protected Area

Queenstown
Strahan

Lake St. Clair

A10

Franklin Lower Gordon Wild Rivers National Park

A5

1

A3

FREYCINET PENINSULA

Strathgordon

Lake Gordon

New Norfolk

Hobart

TASMAN SEA

SOUTHERN OCEAN

Lake Pedder

Southwest National Park

A6

A9

Port Arthur

Southport

| 0 | miles | 100 |
| 0 | kilometers | 160 |

in about 4½ hours. If you have a car, you drive 200 kilometers east of Melbourne on Princes Highway to Port Welshpool, directly opposite Launceston and George Town. If you're afoot, you can take the RoadCat bus service that goes all the way to Hobart. Fares, including bus and ferry are Melbourne to Georgetown, about A$120; to Launceston, A$130 and to Hobart, A$150. The schedule is such that you leave Melbourne at 9:30 a.m., arrive at Hobart at 10:30 p.m.; coming back, you leave at 4:30 a.m., arrive in Melbourne at 5:15 p.m.

Passenger fares on the SeaCat are about A$100 one way. Cars go for about A$150; big campers A$75 a meter. Information: in Melbourne, tel. (03) 826–6599; in George Town, (003) 82–3000; or toll free (008) 03–0131.

Tasmania is very aware that it gets a lot of money from tourism, and is one of the best states in Australia at providing options for visitors. **Tabureaus,** working with the various airlines and the shipline, offer a bunch of fly-drive or sail-drive packages leaving from either Sydney or Melbourne. There are so many plans available, in fact, there's no space here to list them all. But a few for-instances, based on high season (January–April) rates; other times of the year, the prices can be substantially less:

A seven-day, fly-sail package, which includes going one way on the *Abel Tasman* and a flight back, plus a pop-top Hertz camper with unlimited mileage, about A$600 per person.

A seven-day stay at the Sheraton Hobart, with a small rental car (or small camper) and round-trip air to Sydney, about A$1000 per person.

A 12-day fly-sail trip, which includes a trip on the *Abel Tasman,* bus excursions to all the major destinations in Tasmania including tours of Port Arthur, return air to Melbourne, and bus transport from Melbourne to your original starting point, and accommodations and some meals, is around A$1500 per person.

Tasmania likely has the largest fleet of **rental campers** per capita in Australia, and caravaning is by far the most popular way of visiting the island. Fly-drive or fly-sail-drive trips can be booked in advance through travel agents or in Australia at any Tasbureau office. **Note:** on all rental vehicles, there will be a A$50 security deposit. To drive in Tasmania, you must have an international driver's license. The highways are all excellent, if a tad narrow here and there, and there are dozens of RV parks and campgrounds. The packages can be booked for a wide range of accommodations, from five-star down to B&Bs, and a wide range of vehicles is available by paying higher rates. In addition, there are car rental agencies in Tasmania not affiliated with Tasbureau or the airlines. *Information about RV parks is available from the Caravan and Holiday Parks Association of Tasmania, Launceston (003) 43–1313.*

If you simply want to fly over and take a short tour or two, that also is possible. There is no passenger train service in Tasmania, but there is regular **bus service** as well as tour buses. A full-day bus tour from Hobart to Port Arthur, for example, costs about A$80 per person. **Redline Coaches** has a one-week, unlimited bus pass for about A$60 per person. *Information: Redline Coaches, 9 Edward St., Devonport, (004) 24–2585; Harrington St., Hobart, (002) 34–4577, and 112 George St., Launceston, (003) 31–9177.* **Air tours** from Hobart around the east coast and to the West Coast wilderness areas will run around A$300 per person, depending on destination. Check with a Tasbureau office or with **Tasair,** Cambridge Aerodome, Box 451 E, Hobart 7001; tel. (002) 48–5088.

CLIMATE • Tasmania has four distinct seasons, from summer heat to winter cold, but it never gets as hot as the mainland. In fact, it's probably the most temperate of all Australia's states. Nights, even in the summer, can be cool, and the highlands are subject to rain—or snow—all year.

TIME • Tasmania is on Eastern Standard Time, the same as Sydney and Melbourne.

HOBART

Of all Australia's capital cities, Hobart has probably kept the look and feel of its colonial past the best. It sits in a wonderful location on the Derwent River, so wide at this point it creates a natural harbor as it meets the Tasman Sea on the island's southeast coast. Hobart was the second city founded in Australia, after Sydney. The British, agitated because of French interest in the area, decided in 1803 to stake out a claim to Van Dieman's Land and attempted settlements on the north coast and explored the Derwent estuary. In February 1804, a colony was begun in a cove on the Derwent and named Hobart Town after the English secretary of state for colonies. Behind the city is 4100-foot-high **Mt. Wellington,** often cloud-covered, sometimes snowy. It is the combination of colonial buildings, the preserved waterfront with its seafaring spirit, and the agreeable climate that makes Hobart seem much more like a European coastal city than the other Australian cities.

The **National Trust,** responsible for preserving historic buildings in Australia, has a full bag in Tasmania. Just in Hobart, there are several days' worth of touring involved to see everything—more than 90 buildings. The Trust's headquarters are at 39 Paterson St., Launceston; tel. (003) 31–9077. There is an office in Hobart (see below.)

The most interesting sections of downtown are Salamanca Place and Battery Point. **Salamanca Place** is a cobbled street lined with Georgian sandstone warehouses and storerooms left over from the 1830s and 1840s when Hobart was one of the major whaling ports in the world. Today, the buildings are full of small shops, restaurants, pubs, and galleries. Included among the older buildings are **Sullivan's Cove,** a fashion shop housed in the street's oldest building (1833); **Stoppy's Waterfront Inn,** a favorite watering hole set in a block of three buildings dating from 1840; and the **Salamanca Arts Centre,** a nest of small arts and crafts shops, in a building erected in 1844. At 33 Salamanca Place are the offices of the National Trust, which has a small gift store and information about the city's old buildings. It's open 9:30 a.m.–5 p.m. Mon.–Fri. and 9:30 a.m.–1 p.m. Sat. *Information: 23–7371.* Every Saturday morning, Salamanca Place turns into a large open-air **flea market** with food stalls.

Battery Point, which lies on a hill above Salamanca Place, is named after a battery of guns set up to guard the port entrance in 1818. This is a wonderful old neighborhood, with 150-year-old houses, small restaurants and pubs, narrow streets and a village green. One of Battery Point's landmarks is **St. George's Church,** the so-called mariner's church, begun in 1836.

Not to be missed at Battery Point is the **Maritime Museum of Australia** on Secheron Road, which has materials relating to Tasmania's history dating back to the voyages of Abel Tasman. The museum is open 1 p.m.–4:30 p.m. Mon.–Fri.; 10 a.m.–4:30 p.m. Sat., and 1 p.m.–4:30 p.m. Sun. *Information: 23–5082.*

The major landmark in the city, much boasted of, is the **Wrest Point Casino and Hotel,** a tall white tower sitting on the shore at Sandy Bay south of Battery Point. Small by most gaming standards, it was the first casino in Australia and is still a popular spot.

Anglesea Barracks, on Davey Street back of the downtown area, is the headquarters of Australia's armed forces in Tasmania, and is the oldest military establishment in the country still in use. Its Georgian buildings have been restored. The area, but not the buildings, is open for free tours 8 a.m.–10 p.m. Mon.–Fri. *Information: 21–2205.*

One of the oldest buildings in Hobart is **Parliament House,** which started life as a customs house in 1840. There is a visitors gallery for viewing when the house is in session. Next to it is a very nice garden area that leads into Salamanca Place.

A good display of Aboriginal history is available at the **Tasmanian Museum and Art Gallery,** housed in new quarters at 5 Argyle St. that include remnants of the city's oldest building, the **Commissariat Store,**

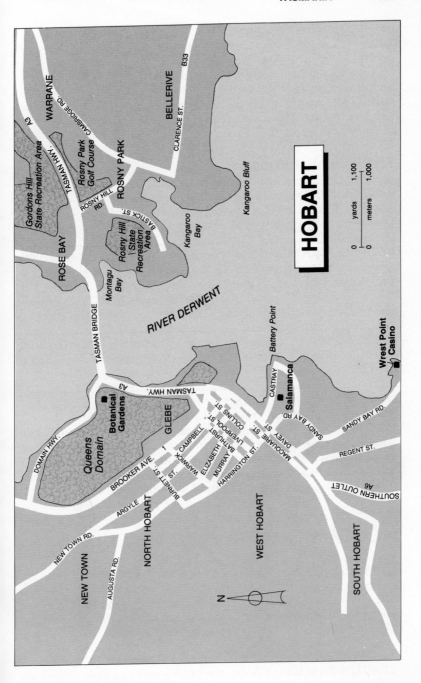

HOBART

yards 0 1,100
meters 0 1,000

WARRANE

B33

BELLERIVE

CAMBRIDGE RD.

CLARENCE ST.

A3

TASMAN HWY.

Rosny Park
Golf Course

ROSNY HILL
RD.

ROSNY PARK

Gordons Hill
State Recreation Area

BASTICK ST.

Rosny Hill
State
Recreation
Area

Kangaroo Bluff

ROSE BAY

Montagu
Bay

Kangaroo
Bay

TASMAN BRIDGE

RIVER DERWENT

Battery Point

DOMAIN HWY.

A3

TASMAN HWY.

Botanical
Gardens

GLEBE

CASTRAY

Salamanca

Wrest Point
Casino

Queens
Domain

BROOKER AVE.

1

WARWICK
ST.

CAMPBELL
ST.

ELIZABETH
ST.

MURRAY
ST.

BATHURST
ST.

LIVERPOOL
ST.

COLLINS ST.

MACQUARIE ST.

DAVEY ST.

HARRINGTON ST.

SANDY BAY RD.

REGENT ST.

BURNETT ST.

ARGYLE

NORTH HOBART

WEST HOBART

SANDY BAY RD.

SOUTHERN OUTLET

A6

NEW TOWN RD.

AUGUSTA RD.

NEW TOWN

SOUTH HOBART

N

built in 1808. The museum has a stuffed Tasmanian wolf and artworks dating back to the 18th century. It's open daily 10 a.m.–5 p.m. *Information: 23–1422.*

The **Royal Tasmanian Botanical Gardens** are small but mighty, with some really excellent displays of cacti, tropical plants, and an herb garden. The gardens sit on the Derwent north of downtown, and are well worth a look. Hours are from 8 a.m. to dusk. *Information: 34–6299.*

The Essential Hobart

INFORMATION • The **Hobart Tasbureau office** is located at 80 Elizabeth St., Hobart 7000; tel. 30–0211. Hours are 8:45 a.m.–5:30 p.m. Mon.–Fri., 8:45 a.m.–11 a.m. weekends and holidays.

GETTING AROUND • There is regular service around Hobart and the suburbs on **Metropolitan Transit Trust buses.** *Information, 71–3232.* The Hobart airport is about 10 miles outside of town. There is bus service into town for about A$5; taxi fare about A$15. The **Redline bus** from the *Abel Tasman* dock in Devonport to Hobart is about A$30.

TELEPHONES • The area code for the Hobart area is (002). The main post office is at the corner of Macquarie and Elizabeth sts. *Information 20–7351.*

SHOPPING • Normal shopping hours in Hobart are 9 a.m.–6 p.m. Mon.–Fri.; some stores open until 9 p.m. Fri.

The heart of downtown Hobart shopping is the **Cat and Fiddle Arcade** between Elizabeth and Murray sts., which has a number of shops. It leads into the **Hobart Mall,** another area of small shops. Look for shops offering items made from the island's rare wood, huon pine. You'll also find stores along Liverpool and Collins sts.

ACCOMMODATIONS.......................

Sheraton Hobart • *1 Davey St.; tel. 35–4535* • Located at the city harbor, opened in 1987. Probably the best in town, with two bars, a cafe, and licensed restaurant. There is a health club and an indoor pool and sauna. Rooms come with a view of the harbor or Mt. Wellington. Doubles start around A$175–240; suites from $A300.

Wrest Point Federal Hotel and Casino • *410 Sandy Bay Rd.; tel. 25–0112* • Three bars, a disco, the gaming tables, a night club, a revolving restaurant, and an Asian restaurant: in short, a rocking place to hang out. The views are great, although it's a bit out of town. It has a pool, sauna, gym, and tennis facilities. The casino is open every day but Good Friday and Christmas. Doubles start around A$190; suites A$285–340. Motel -style rooms are also available from $A100 for doubles.

Inkeepers Lenna of Hobart • *20 Runnymede St.; tel. 23–2911* • Ideally located for exploring Battery Point. The main building is a restored 1880s mansion; other units attached. Excellent seafood restaurant. Doubles start around A$140; suites A$160.

Four Seasons Downtowner • *96 Bathurst St.; tel. 34–6333* • Located to the west of downtown. Licensed restaurant. Doubles start around A$100.

Westside • *156 Bathurst St.; tel. 34–6255* • Same area as the Downtowner. Licensed restaurant. Doubles start around A$135.

Inkeepers St. Ives • *67 St. George Terrace; tel. 30–1801* • Another Battery Point lodging. Restaurant/bar, laundry, handicapped access. Doubles $A95–125.

Hobart Pacific Motor Inn • *Kirby Court, West Hobart; tel. 34–6733* • Cooking facilities, restaurant/bar, great views; from August–May, it has a theater restaurant. Free laundry. About two kilometers from the city center. Doubles start around A$95–120.

Bellerive YHA • *52 King St., Bellerive 7018; tel. 44–2552* • Singles about A$7.

Hobart Youth Hostel • *7 Woodlands Ave., New Town; tel. 28–6720* • Singles about A$10.

RESTAURANTS......................................

Mure's Fish House • *5 Knopwood St., Battery Point; tel. 23–6917* • Cited all over the country as one of the best seafood restaurants in Australia. The licensed restaurant is in an 1840s Georgian house, and booking ahead is mandatory. No lunch service on weekends. *Moderate to expensive.*

Mure's Fish Centre • *On Constitution dock near the Sheraton; tel. 31–1999* • Same owners, much more modern, still great seafood. Licensed, closed Sun. *Moderate.*

Dear Friends • *8 Brooke St.; tel. 23–2646* • Housed in yet another old port building, antique surroundings. Licensed, French/seafood. Moderate to *expensive.*

Silver-Skillet • *Four Seasons Westside; tel. 34–6255.* • Licensed. International. No Sunday lunch. *Moderate.*

Alexander's • *Inkeepers Lenna; tel. 23–2911* • Arches, glitter, and great seafood. *Expensive.*

Dirty Dick's Steak House • *22 Francis St.; tel. 23–3103* • In the heart of Battery Point. Licensed. Small, intimate, steaks and seafood. *Moderate to expensive.*

BEYOND HOBART......................

Port Arthur

The location of Australia's most famous prison is no accident. It was placed on the Tasman Peninsula, about 60 miles southeast of Hobart, because the peninsula is attached to the mainland by a tiny neck of land, making escape a very chancy and difficult endeavor. Enough time has passed since Port Arthur was abandoned—1877—that the old prison and its grounds have taken on the look of an ancient and crumbling Irish castle estate. The wide lawns and moss-covered bricks have gentled and softened what once was the most feared penal colony in the British Empire, although during its entire 50-year history, only 12,000 convicts passed through its gates, including 90 Americans. After it was closed, many of the buildings were damaged or removed because it reminded Victorian Australians of their sometimes shady roots. But over the years, preservationists finally won out and the old prison and the area around it are one of the most popular tourist destinations in Australia—for Australians; most international visitors never make it to Tasmania, let alone Port Arthur.

The prison was begun in 1830 as a sawing station to provide lumber, and was set aside for the penal system's worst prisoners. In the mid 1830s, a prison for juvenile male offenders was built, and not far away was a coal mine which had the worst working conditions in the whole prison colony. Port Arthur had a peak prison population of around

1200 convicts at one time, plus a military and civilian support force of around 1000. Between 1840 and 1853, most of the convicts sent from England went to Tasmania, requiring a larger and more permanent prison facility to be built. Its most infamous period was when it housed a "model prison," based on the quaint Victorian thought that isolation was better than physical abuse. Prisoners were not allowed to speak, never saw one another, and spent their time in jail in one-man isolated cells. (During exercise periods, they all wore masks.) Many prisoners went insane because of the isolation. After transportation to Tasmania was outlawed in 1853, the prison gradually became a sort of old folk's home for elderly prisoners and a mental asylum. Many of the buildings left standing after the prison was closed in 1877 were badly damaged in bushfires in 1895 and 1897. What was left was finally saved for good in 1979 when Tasmania and the federal government set up a joint preservation project to excavate and restore the old prison. The result, of course, is why Port Arthur is such a big tourist attraction.

The first stop at Port Arthur should be at the **visitors center and museum,** where guided tours can be booked, information is available and there is an audio-visual program on the prison's history. Admission to the Port Arthur site is $7 per person. The most popular building in the complex is the **penitentiary/grain mill** built to supply flour to the prison in 1844. The grist mill was powered by 24 convicts on a treadmill. It was enlarged into its present size in 1853, and held about 600 prisoners.

The other always-photographed building is the **old church,** first started in 1836, and able to hold 1000 convicts and 200 officials. Nothing remains now but the shell; the church was the victim of the late-century bush fires, as was the grain mill.

Other structures on the site are an ornate, round **guard tower** dating from 1836; the **commandant's house,** a timber and brick edifice with very nice gardens, 1833; the **model prison,** 1848, with its attached asylum, 1867; the **hospital,** 1842, and the **pauper's mess,** used to feed the elderly former prisoners, 1864. In addition to the buildings in the main complex, there are excursions to the **Isle of the Dead,** a small island not far from the prison, which served as the settlement's graveyard. There are about 2000 graves on the island, mostly prisoners. The trip, on the M.V. Bundeena, operates daily and costs about A$5 and can be booked at the visitor's center.

You can either take a leisurely drive to Port Arthur from Hobart (the A3 to Sorell, the A9 to Port Arthur), or join one of the many tours operating from Hobart. If you want more than a day trip, there are a hotel, youth hostel, craft shop, and cafe on the site. The craft shop has a nightly showing of the film based on Marcus Clarke's classic, *For the Term of His Natural Life,* a silent epic shot on the site in 1926. The cost is A$5, including tea. *Information: 50–2242.*

The Port Arthur Motor Inn on the Tasman Highway has doubles starting around A$90, with some great views of the settlement. *Information: (002) 50–2101.* Another good place to stay is the **Fox and Hounds Resort,** a mock Tudor hotel/motel with bar and restaurant located about two miles from Port Arthur on the main highway. Doubles start around A$95. *Information: (002) 50–2217.* A third choice are the modern log cabins of the **New Plymouth Holiday Village,** not far from the prison. The village has a decent restaurant, the Lady Franklin. *Information: 50–2262.*

If you're in a camper, try for the **Garden Point Caravan Park,** about a mile from the prison, which has very nice sites and facilities. When you check in, ask whoever's in charge if the wombats are around. They're tame and cuddly and very wombattish, and probably the only time you'll get that close to a really tame one. *Information: 50–2340.*

For information about the prison, contact the Port Arthur Historic Site Management Authority, Farm Overseer's Cottage, Port Arthur 7182; tel. (002) 50–2363.

As long as you're in the area, you might as well take advantage of your one sure chance to see a Tasmanian devil up close and—yes, it's true—even touch one without losing your arm up to the shoulder. About ten kilometers south of Eaglehawk Neck at the top of the Tasman Peninsula (or 10 kilometers north of the prison) is the **Tasmanian Devil Park** in all its touristy glory. It's basically a roadside zoo sort of attraction with wallabies and such, but the stars of the show are two female devils, Paradise and Angel, and they make the A$6 per person fee worth it. Also available at the park is a short movie taken of the last known Tasmanian wolf left alive in Australia, which died in captivity in the 1930s. *Information: (002) 50–3230.*

The east coast of the Tasman Peninsula is sedimentary rock, mostly Permian sandstone, and the constant wave action has created high cliffs and some spectacular blowhole-like formations. Two of the more notable are the **Tasman Arch** and **Devil's Kitchen,** huge collapsed caves drilled through the rocks by wave surges. Another popular spot is **Remarkable Cave,** a tube cut into the rocks that is dry at low tide and can be reached by a set of stairs. It's south of the prison. The other formations are reached by taking a turnoff at **Eaglehawk Neck.** The neck is so narrow that it is was once guarded by a single line of dogs to stop convicts from escaping across it.

Richmond

The **oldest bridge** in Australia still in use is found at Richmond, a restored colonial village about 15 miles northwest of Hobart. The bridge was built in 1823 with convict labor. In the village itself are a number of historic buildings, including **St. John's,** the oldest Catholic church in Australia (1836), and the **Richmond Gaol,** which dates from 1825, but which saw most of its use for convicts in the 1840s. The gaol has cells and articles of punishment on view; A\$2 admission. One of the prisoners reportedly housed there was Izzy Solomons, a London brothel-keeper and fence who supposedly was the inspiration for Fagin in Dickens' *Oliver Twist.*

Launceston

Tasmania's second city, Launceston (pronounced LAWN-cess-tun) is also one of the oldest settlements in Australia. The city, which sits 40 miles from the ocean at the confluence of the north and south forks of the Esk River (which then becomes the Tamar River), was founded in 1805. It is named after a town in Cornwall. The city, population around 65,000, is the main settlement in the northern part of the island, which is largely rolling hills filled with sheep, cattle, and crops, and vistas that gave rise to the English-like image of the state. The Launceston area code is (003).

In addition to being a major starting point for Tasmania tours, the city has a few attractions in its own right, including a bunch of **colonial buildings,** notably along St. John and George sts. In the countryside around the city are some of the finest preserved **colonial homesteads** in Australia, all under the care of the National Trust. One major attraction, a tad tacky and sometimes silly, is **Penny Royal World,** a recreation of a 19th-century industrial park, with a cannon factory, cornmill, and several ships. It also has a restaurant, tavern, and gift shop. The site is open 9 a.m.–4:30 p.m. daily, admission about A\$10. *Information: 39–1106.*

Not far outside of town is **Cataract Gorge,** which has been a playground for the good people of the area almost since the city was founded. The South Esk River has cut a very sharp, deep gorge through the rocks, and a couple of natural dams have created large lakes where swimming and boating are popular. There is a suspension bridge at the first dam, and a number of hiking trails in the area. The most popular attraction at the gorge is a high, very high, **chairlift** that goes across the depths. The chairlift, they claim, has the longest single span of any lift in the world: 1010 feet. The lift costs about A\$5 per person. *Information, 31–5915.* In the park is the licensed **Gorge Restaurant** with seafood and game specialities, surrounded by a very nice park and gardens. *Information: 31–3330.*

The Launceston area is a major wool milling area, and the best tour is in one of the oldest, the **Waverly Woollen Mills** just outside of town off the A3 (Tasman Highway.) The mill, which has a wide array of weavings, including jackets and skirts and some very nice rugs, was built in 1874 and has been producing goods ever since. One thing to look for is the collection of **tartans,** including the earth-toned Australian tartan. Tours of the mill are offered every day 9 a.m.–4 p.m., and the showroom is open to 5 p.m. Tours are A$2 per person. There is a small **coffee shop** that serves Devonshire teas. Adjacent is the **National Automobile Museum of Tasmania,** where you can see some choice old cars. Waverly also has an outlet at 81 Salamanca Place in Hobart. *Information on the mill: 39–1106.*

The local tourist bureau is located at the corner of St. John and Paterson Streets; tel. 32–2411.

Accommodations

Federal Hotel Casino • *Country Club Ave.; tel. 44–8855* • About four miles outside of the city, with casino, pool, licensed restaurant, and sports facilities. Doubles start around A$170; suites from A$300.

Penny Royal Motel • *145 Paterson St.; tel. 31–6699* • There are actually three motels on the theme park site, with doubles starting around A$110.

Colonial Motor Inn • *corner George and Elizabeth sts.; tel. 31–6588* • Licensed restaurant. Doubles start around A$120.

Great Northern Hotel • *3 Earl St.; tel. 31–9999* • Licensed restaurant. Doubles start around A$100.

Launceston House Hostel YHA • *36 Thistle St.; tel. 44–9779* • Singles about A$10.

Restuarants

Shrimps • *72 George St.; tel. 34–0584* • Seafood, licensed. In a National Trust building. Seven days, no lunches on weekends.

Burgundy's • *124 George St., 31–5422* • Local specialties. Licensed. Seven days, no weekend lunches.

The Superb Folly • *In the Old Bakery Inn, corner of York and Margaret sts.; tel. 31–7900* • Licensed. Seafood, local specialities. Seven days, no lunches weekends.

Minnas in the Mall • *Brisbane St. on the Mall, tel. 31–8110* • Licensed. Danish/Australian. Sat. night smorgasbord. Closed Sun.

The East Coast

One of the most popular destinations in Tasmania is the east coast, which has some very fine white beaches and several small resort communities. In many cases, visitors driving around the island plan out a circle trip starting either from Hobart or the Devonport/Launceston area, hitting Port Arthur, the western wilderness or the central mountains and the west coast. It can be done in a few days if you're in a hurry, but a week is better, particularly when you remember most fly/drive or sea/drive packages are priced for a week.

The two main resorts are **St. Helens** and **St. Mary's,** which are on the way to the **Freycinet Peninsula,** which has a popular national park. In addition to beaches and sports fishing, both towns are major fishing and lobstering centers. You'll find motel **accommodations** in both towns. Try the **Bayside Inn** at 2 Cecilia St, in St. Helens, which has a seafood restaurant and pool. Doubles A$75. *Information: (003) 76–1466.*

Freycinet National Park, on a peninsula off the Tasman Highway northeast of Hobart, has some of the best scenery in Australia. The name is French, pronounced FRAY-sin-ay, so-named by French explorers who passed by in 1802 and caused the English so much anxiety they decided to start the first colonies in Tasmania. The main features of the park are its red granite cliffs, including a range called **The Hazards,** and many beaches, hiking trails, and wildlife. It's not unusual at all to run into very friendly Bennett's wallabies on a hike, and there are some major bird breeding grounds in the area, including those of the black swan and fairy penguins. The park is also home to wombats, devils, echidnas, and possums.

One of the best hikes is a 2½ hour, fairly easy trek up over the spine of the mountains to Wineglass Bay, which is simply stunning. The trail is a self-guided nature tour. It's also possible to hike to the top of the Hazards. There is a good **RV site** at the park, as well as campgrounds and the **Chateau,** a B&B motel at Coles Bay north of the park entrance. *Information, The Chateau, tel. (002) 57–0101. Doubles are A$75. Information on the park is available from the ranger in charge, Freycinet National Park, via Coles Bay 7215; tel. 57–0107.*

The West

The true glories of Tasmania, at least to us, are the rain forests and dense vegetation of the western half of the island. From Hobart, take the A10 to the Queenstown-Strahan area, which is the heart of the Gordon River headwaters country. There are several magnificent national parks in the area, the **Cradle Mountain-Lake St. Clair Park** and the **Franklin and Lower Gordon Wild Rivers National Park.** These parks are for the outdoor-minded, with whitewater sports, excellent brown trout fishing, mountain climbing, and hiking.

Cradle Mountain itself rises to about 5000 feet and is a favorite target for hikers and climbers. **Lake St. Clair** proves that once upon a time, Tasmania had glaciers. The whole region is alpine and semi-alpine, and subject to sudden and dramatic changes in weather. The wildlife is unavoidable, especially the ever-present Bennett's wallabies, who apparently were born to mooch food. Please don't give them bread, only fresh fruits and vegetables. There is something in bread that will make them ill.

One of the most popular hiking trails in Australia is here, the 52-mile-long **Overland Track,** which has huts along the way. It passes along some simply delicious scenery and costs $10 per hiker. It's normally done in about a week, and all hikers must register with the rangers. For those who like their pleasures a bit more civilized, there is the **Cradle Mountain Lodge,** a famous and cozy inn on the north edge of the park. It's rustic, with rooms in the main lodge or in cabins, and has a licensed restaurant, a pub and a food kiosk. It's a P&O lodge, owned by the same organization that operates Heron Island on the Great Barrier Reef. Doubles in the lodge start around A$160–200, but book early. Information: (004) 92–1303. Reservation information: P&O Resorts, 520 Monterey Dr., Rio Del Mar, Calif. 95003; tel. (408) 685–8903. In Tasmania, contact the lodge at (004) 92–1303 or (003) 63–5164. Bus service to the park is available from Devonport on **Cradle Mountain Coaches,** (004) 92–3167 or from Launceston on **Mountain Stage Lines,** (003) 34–0442. *Information about the park is available from the ranger in charge, Cradle Mountain National Park 7306; tel. (003) 63–5187.*

The Gordon River

Once past the Cradle Lake area, the highway passes through some forests, dark and wide, and passes **Queenstown,** where, if you are of the conservationist bent, you'll want to scream. The whole area has been mined to death and the town, which sits next to a working mine, has all the lure of a dead carp. Underneath all those forests are mountains rich in minerals, and virtually unregulated mining has created a shameful moonscape. It's worth a trip here just as a reminder of what the world would be like if nobody cared.

Past Elizabeth town is **Strahan** (pronounced strawn), the gateway to the **Gordon River** and **Macquarie Harbour.** Both the river and the harbour are examples of all that was bad in Australian history.

After Hobart was established in the early 1800s, it became obvious that civilized society was no place for really hard-rock bad guys, so the colonial officials looked around for a place to stash them. The first place they tried, before Port Arthur, was Macquarie Harbour, the huge estuary of the Gordon River on the extreme west coast of Tasmania. There was a capitalistic rationale behind all this, as well, because the area was rich in huon pine and coal. The pine, now very rare, was an exceptionally fine ship-building material. It's very dense, easy to work and was highly valued by shipwrights supplying colonial and Royal Navy vessels.

Convicts were brought to mine the coal and fell the pines, and were forced to live at one of the worst prison facilities in Australia, **Sarah Island,** which sits near the mouth of the Gordon. The island has no natural water, so supplies were brought in every day, and the living conditions were often ghastly. The island was eventually abandoned in 1834, and the convicts sent to Port Arthur. Some parts of the buildings from the prison still stand and can be seen on a Gordon River cruise.

The river itself is the site of one of Australia's most famous environmental battles. The Tasmanian government decided to dam the Franklin River, which feeds into the Gordon, for hydroelectric power to provide jobs for the West Coast. Many people, feeling the dam would destroy some of the best whitewater in the state, as well as lead to destruction of the west's primitive beauties, started an eight-year campaign that not only stopped the project, but toppled the state government in the process. At one point, the Gordon, not far from where the Franklin flows in, was blockaded by protestors in rubber boats who stopped heavy machinery from being moved to a construction site. In the end, the conservationists won out, and the site of the blockade is a favorite stop for tour boats.

At Strahan, you can catch a half-day or full-day cruise that will take you up the Gordon and out to the headlands where Macquarie Harbour begins with a stop at Sarah Island. The company, **Gordon River Cruises,** operates three boats, which are licensed, have guides, and offer soft drinks and snacks. Advance bookings are necessary. Half-day tours are about A$40 per person; full-day about A$50. *Information: Gordon River Cruises, P.O. Box 40, Strahan 7468; tel. (004) 71–7187.* The tours can also be booked through Tasbureau offices.

Your best bet for whitewater rafting, or camping treks in the central mountains, is with **Bill King's Australian Experience,** which offers a wide variety of Tasmania trips including week-long Franklin River excursions, Cradle Mountain bushwalking, kayaking, and four-wheel-drive expeditions. *For information and bookings, contact ATS, 1101 E. Broadway, Glendale, Calif. 91205; tel. (800) 232–2121 California and (800) 423–2880 USA.*

INDEX